The Christian Jew and the Unmarked Jewess

THE MIDDLE AGES SERIES

Ruth Mazo Karras, Series Editor
Edward Peters, Founding Editor

A complete list of books in the series
is available from the publisher.

THE CHRISTIAN JEW AND THE UNMARKED JEWESS

The Polemics of Sameness in
Medieval English Anti-Judaism

Adrienne Williams Boyarin

PENN

UNIVERSITY OF PENNSYLVANIA PRESS

PHILADELPHIA

Published by
University of Pennsylvania Press
Philadelphia, Pennsylvania 19104-4112
www.upenn.edu/pennpress

Printed in the United States of America on acid-free paper
10 9 8 7 6 5 4 3 2 1

A Cataloging-in-Publication record is available from the
Library of Congress
ISBN 978-0-8122-5259-0

For my mother, Suzanne Neta ל"ז, and my daughter, Eleni Neta

CONTENTS

ABBREVIATIONS

AND	*Anglo-Norman Dictionary*. Edited by Stewart Gregory, William Rothwell, David Otter, Michael Beddow, et al. 2nd ed. Publications of the Modern Humanities Research Association 17. London: Maney, 2005–. https:/www.anglo-norman.net.
BL	London, British Library
Bod.	Oxford, Bodleian Library
CCR 1231–34	*Close Rolls of the Reign of Henry III, 1231–1234*. London: Mackie and Co. Ltd. for HMSO, 1905.
CCR 1237–42	*Close Rolls of the Reign of Henry III, 1237–1242*. London: The Hereford Times Ltd. for HMSO, 1911.
CCR 1247–51	*Close Rolls of the Reign of Henry III, 1277–1251*. London: HMSO, 1922.
CCR 1272–79	*Close Rolls of the Reign of Edward I, 1272–1279*. London: Eyre and Spottiswoode for HMSO, 1900.
CCR 1330–33	*Close Rolls of the Reign of Edward III, 1330–1333*. London: Eyre and Spottiswoode for HMSO, 1898.
CFR [+ year]	*Calendar of the Fine Rolls of the Reign of Henry III* [*1216–1242*], available both on the *Henry III Fine Rolls Project* website (https://finerollshenry3.org.uk) and within *Calendar of the Fine Rolls of the Reign of Henry III*, ed. P. Dryburgh and B. Hartland, technical ed. A. Ciula and J. M. Vieira. 3 vols. Woodbridge: Boydell and Brewer, 2007–9.
CJB	*The Chronicle of Jocelin of Brakelond Concerning the Acts of Samson, Abbot of the Monastery of St Edmund*. Edited and translated by H. E. Butler. Medieval Classics. New York: Oxford University Press, 1949.
CRR 1233–37	*Curia Regis Rolls of the Reign of Henry III, 1233–1237*. With introduction by C. A. F. Meekings. Vol. 15. London: HMSO, 1972.
CT	*The Canterbury Tales*. In *The Riverside Chaucer*. Edited by Larry D. Benson. 3rd ed. Boston: Houghton Mifflin, 1987.
CUL	Cambridge, Cambridge University Library
DMAJH	*The Palgrave Dictionary of Medieval Anglo-Jewish History*. Edited by Joe Hillaby and Caroline Hillaby. Houndmills, Basingstoke: Palgrave Macmillan, 2013.
DMLBS	*Dictionary of Medieval Latin from British Sources*. Edited by Richard Ashdowne, David Howlett, and Ronald Latham. 3 vols. Oxford: Oxford University Press for the British Academy, 2018.

DOE	*Dictionary of Old English: A–I Online*. Edited by Angus Cameron, Ashley Crandell Amos, Antonette diPaolo, et al. Toronto: Dictionary of Old English Project, 2018. https://www.doe.utoronto.ca.
EETS	Early English Text Society [o.s. for Original Series, e.s. for Extra Series]
HMSO	Her/His Majesty's Stationery Office
JEGP	*Journal of English and Germanic Philology*
JHSE	Jewish Historical Society of England
MED	*Middle English Dictionary*. Edited by Robert E. Lewis et al. Ann Arbor: University of Michigan Press, 1952–2001. Online edition in *Middle English Compendium*. Edited by Frances McSparran et al. Ann Arbor: University of Michigan, 2018. https://quod.lib.umich.edu/m/middle-english-dictionary /dictionary.
MLN	*Modern Language Notes*
ODNB	*The Oxford Dictionary of National Biography*. Oxford: Oxford University Press, 2004–16. https://www-oxforddnb-com/.
OED	*Oxford English Dictionary*. Oxford: Oxford University Press, 2019. https:// www-oed-com/.
PIMS	Pontifical Institute of Mediaeval Studies, University of Toronto
PMLA	*Publications of the Modern Language Association*
PREJ (1–6)	*Plea Rolls of the Exchequer of the Jews*. Vol. 1, *Calendar of the Plea Rolls of the Exchequer of the Jews*, edited by J. M. Rigg (London: Macmillan for JHSE, 1905); vol. 2, *Calendar of the Plea Rolls of the Exchequer of the Jews*, edited and translated by Hilary Jenkinson (Edinburgh: Ballantyne for JHSE, 1910); vol. 3, *Calendar of the Plea Rolls of the Exchequer of the Jews*, edited and translated by Hilary Jenkinson (Colchester: Spottiswoode, Ballyntyne and Co. Ltd. for JHSE, 1929); vol. 4, *Calendar of the Plea Rolls of the Jews Preserved in the Public Record Office*, edited and translated by H. G. Richardson (Colchester: Spottiswoode for JHSE, 1972); vol. 5, *Plea Rolls of the Exchequer of the Jews Preserved in the Public Record Office*, edited by Sarah Cohen and Paul Brand (London: JHSE, 1992); vol. 6, *Plea Rolls of the Exchequer of the Jews*, edited by Paul Brand (London: JHSE, 2005).
Rolls	Rolls Series: Chronicles and Memorials of Great Britain and Ireland During the Middle Ages (Rerum Britannicarum medii ævi scriptores)
Select Pleas	*Select Pleas, Starrs, and Other Records from the Rolls of the Exchequer of the Jews, A.D. 1220–1284*. Edited and translated by J. M. Rigg. Seldon Society Publications 15. London: Bernard Quaritch, 1902.
SELIM	*Sociedad Española de Lengua y Literatura Inglesa Medieval / Journal of the Spanish Society for Medieval English Language and Literature*
TEAMS	Teaching Association for Medieval Studies
TNA	The National Archives of the UK

A NOTE ON THE TEXT

Quotations and translations of the Bible follow the *Biblia sacra iuxta Vulgatam versionem* (Stuttgart: Deutsche Bibelgesellschaft, 1994) and the *Douay-Rheims Holy Bible* (Fitzwilliam, NH: Loreto, 2000). Unless noted, all other translations are the author's.

INTRODUCTION

Saming the Jew

For in every town, at least in most parts, Jews act just like Christians.
—Judah HeHasid (d. 1217), *Sefer Hasidim*

Confusion has developed to such a degree that no difference is discernible.

—Lateran IV, Canon 68 (1215)

Many studies of medieval anti-Jewish texts and images in recent decades have discussed difference.[1] This book is concerned, instead, with realities and fantasies of sameness. Examining texts produced before and in the wake of the 1290 Expulsion of Jews from England, and in application to representations of both the Jew and the Jewess, it focuses on the means by which medieval Christians could identify with Jews and even think of themselves as Jewish.[2] While this is fundamentally a book about anti-Judaism, then, it seeks to elucidate an essential and underexplored part of the rhetoric employed in anti-Jewish materials, what I call "polemics of sameness." Polemics of sameness argue for the indistinguishablity of Jew and Christian—to erase, assimilate, or embody Jewishness—and they function most effectively in concert with political and historical modes of oppression and alongside the possibility of real or performed visible similarity. Medieval Christian writers and artists frequently sought to reveal, manipulate, and cope with the problematic sameness of Christians and Jews.

Further, where studies of anti-Judaism in medieval England have focused mainly on the post-Expulsion absence of Jews or on explication of overtly negative representations within that always-looming absence, this book argues for full attention to Jewish presence, both real presence (in texts that engage or represent medieval Anglo-Jews) and presence signaled by textual moments where the historical, representational, and exemplary overlap so thoroughly that contrast and absence are insufficient frames of analysis. Medieval Anglo-Jewish history shows a consistent tension between presence and absence—what some have called "absent presence"[3]—and between otherness and sameness. As Tamsin Barber has argued about modern urban diasporas, such tensions function "according to nationally specific historical power relations that render 'difference' more or less visible."[4] As I will argue here, the care that medieval English writers take to emphasize the likeness of a Jewish character to a Christian, or their own inability to know the difference, works similarly: difference can be rendered less visible as both a tactic and a concession, such that Jewishness and Jewish history are occupied and redefined in the place where actual Jewish people and history continue. Even when merely notional or communicated between Christian audiences, sameness thus functions, as Gilles Deleuze might put it, "in conformity with what the state wants."[5]

In Canon 68 of the Fourth Lateran Council, Pope Innocent III connected control of Jewish and Muslim dress, for instance, to Holy Week ostentation on the part of Jews. The presumption was that ritual practice, speech, and affect would distinguish Christian and Jews where appearance alone might not, or when appearance could not be sufficiently legislated. Jews were forbidden to "appear in public" on the three days before Easter "because some of them, as we understand, on those days are not ashamed to show themselves more ornately attired and do not fear to amuse themselves at the expense of the Christians, who in memory of the sacred passion go about attired in robes of mourning."[6] The problem is not essential but performative: it allows for scenarios in which Jews and Christians could be mistaken for one another. What if a *Christian* appeared better dressed than others? What if a *Jew* wore robes of mourning? In England, the response to Canon 68 meant frequent reissuing, and progressively increased specification, of the English version of a Jewish identifying badge,[7] and nervousness about distinguishing Jews from Christians continued to trouble royal and ecclesiastical authorities even as the Jewish population of England dwindled in the second half of the thirteenth century.

The significant corpus of medieval Anglo-Christian texts about Jews evinces a polemical investment in sameness ("they are like us," "we should be like them," or, more insidiously, "we *are* them"). Erasure of distinctions between Jews and Christians in English literature—expressed here by a mix of legal, historical, devotional, visual, and literary narrative—is as potent as the creation of contrast and conflict. The Jewish character or compatriot can be understood as

Christian, used for the express purpose of Christian self-identification, or turn out to be Christian through conversion or reinterpretation. Distinct from Anthony Bale's arguments about why we find some non-Jews in devotional illustrative traditions marked as Jewish, the texts and illustrations I discuss here do not feature "contradistinction between Christian and post-incarnation Jewish bodies" but rather similarity.[8] In Bale's important study *Feeling Persecuted*, "meaning is made through antithesis"; the Jew's role in Christian narrative and devotion is to be "halting and shocking and difficult."[9] For the cases I will discuss (which run alongside, not as challenge to, Bale's), the interpretive struggle is for synthesis and assimilation, sometimes to the point of semantic collapse, such that the alikeness of Christian and Jew is itself the difficulty.

Sameness, thus, is not easily mapped onto previous scholarly conceptions of the medieval Jew in Christian books as "mutable," "hermeneutical," "virtual," "protean," or "spectral."[10] All of these terms grapple with the ambivalence underlying Christian notions of Jewish difference, especially as managed through typology and theology, but the representations with which I am concerned highlight, instead, Christian-Jewish *simul*taneity. They regard the present (the Jewish neighbor) and the past (the priority of Jewish scripture and types) simultaneously, and so take a different route to dealing with difference and ambivalence, by imagining the Jew or Jewess as the ever-present alternative to self. Where typology embraces doubling, mirroring, and supersession as imperative to the development of Christianity—the Jew and Jewishness are necessarily fundamental to any Christian-Jewish polemic—arguments for Christian-Jewish sameness take typological modes for granted and extend their logic. On the one hand, as Kathleen Biddick has argued, "suppersessionary notions . . . have rigidly bound the contexts in which Christians have encountered Jews"—"typology never lets go."[11] On the other hand, as Sylvia Tomasch has noted, positive (typological) and negative portrayals of the Jew are "not merely conjoined, but, as with Mary and Eve, they are the same."[12] Can we pause on "the same"? There is a dialectic of difference *and* sameness in typology, but in the moments of conjoining we will find that supersession gives way to embodiment and uncertainty. To return to Biddick: "At the core of figural thinking is the fact that it is impossible to move from the [historical] event to its [typological] fulfilment without passing through doubleness. . . . Without the fantasy of supersession the figure of the Christian is always possibly the truth of the Jew."[13] Otherness and sameness are always contending with one another. Engagement with sameness is crucial to a full understanding of the nature of medieval anti-Judaism.

The 1290 Expulsion of Jews from England is a key event around which to situate such analysis. This is not because the Expulsion signals the presence or absence of Jews, but because it changes the conditions and circumstances of interpretation. Denise Despres has communicated one side of this effectively: "Fourteenth-century English audiences could witness [anti-Jewish representations of Jews] from a historically unusual perspective, for, having expelled the Jews, they could interpret these signs from a position of wholeness."[14] But English audiences before the Expulsion could *not* interpret from a position of (imagined) wholeness. The many twelfth- and thirteenth-century texts I will discuss here are *not* functioning on solely theological or ideological levels but have implications for interactions with, and quotidian attitudes toward, Anglo-Jews. Those written within fifty to eighty years of the 1290 Expulsion (about as far as we are now from World War II) continue to engage a national memory of Jewish presence. I do not believe that attitudes toward, and representation of, Jews in England changed significantly after the Expulsion, though some have argued for it,[15] but I do think that the development of such attitudes in the context of living Anglo-Jewish communities and English programs of conversion and expulsion is worth examining in terms of Christian conceptualizations of *both* likeness and difference. Because of its medieval bureaucracy, and particularly the output of the Exchequer of the Jews, England has left us rich records of Jewish-Christian interaction and negotiation in this period. The opportunity, then, is to think through these records in relationship to the literary, pastoral, devotional, and historiographical productions of the same era.

We know also that historical and fantasy versions of Jewish/Christian doubling participate in the longer story of England to a striking degree. Some time ago, Nicholas Howe's influential reading of the Old English *Exodus* argued persuasively that pre-Conquest Englishmen saw their own island isolation and conversion aligned with the migration history of the biblical Israelites, an "identification between Israelites and Anglo-Saxons" that could "possess both religious truth and imaginative life."[16] Janet Adelman established that English interest in the sameness of the Jewess certainly persisted into Shakespeare's time, when his "*Merchant* [*of Venice*] worries the problem of visible difference between Jew and Christian."[17] As Lisa Lampert-Weissig has cogently observed, Shakespeare's Jessica "embodies the threat of indeterminate identity" and effectively critiques notions of the "hermeneutical Woman and the hermeneutical Jew" because they have "relied on oppositions" too heavily.[18] Even for what appears to be the earliest English caricature of living Anglo-Jews—in 1233, of Mosse Mokke (Moses son of Abraham of Norwich) and a woman called Avegaye, or Abigail (see Figure 3)—Sara Lipton has recently concluded that the artist provides not contrasts but a visual commentary on the financial and political bonds between Christians and Jews: "The implicit message is that, far from being utterly different from and universally hated by Christians, at least some Jews were all too similar to, perhaps even admired or desired by, Christians."[19] The complex similarities of Christian and Jew in such remnants work against good/bad or past/present dichotomies.

The sameness of Christians and Jews in medieval England is thus a critical topic. When and how Jews are made to be the same as Christians should be as important a question as when and how Jews are made grotesquely distinct. Polemics of sameness, however, and to be absolutely clear, are never philosemitic or neutral; they are not more humane than readily recognizable medieval Christian depictions of male Jewish physicality or violence. Rather, as an English discourse that begins with living Anglo-Jewish communities and continues throughout the medieval period and beyond, sameness can function (and be analyzed) apart from difference and antithesis. I do not think, as Miriamne Ara Krummel has argued, that Thomas Hoccleve, for instance, resists anti-Jewishness with his apparent self-debasing "connection to Jewishness" or his positioning of himself as "socially Jewish" when he self-identifies as a coin clipper and murderer in his *Dialogue with a Friend*.[20] Hoccleve may eschew one type of polemic for another, and so mark his outsider status with insider discourse, but this is not evidence of "a slow process . . . toward a more tolerant view."[21] Hoccleve, instead, continues the rhetoric of Christian identification with Jewishness (and consequent erasure of Jewishness) that was long established in England. Recognition of his rhetoric as polemical allows a more thoroughgoing understanding of English anti-Judaism.

It should not be surprising that a simultaneous struggle to identify and disidentify an "other" might develop in England's circumstances. Andrew Jacobs has nicely summarized Jacques Lacan's thinking on such matters, not coincidentally in a book about the circumcision of Christ: "The 'other' is not only an object of *distinction* and *difference* by which I know myself (the 'not-I') but also an object of desire and identification for myself (the 'ideal-I')."[22] This kind of desire has implications for notions of racial and regional identity: "The politics of race and nationhood become more pliable and open to critique when we begin to see that the very attempt to bound and define constitutes a hidden act of dissolution and blurring."[23] And there is no sense in which Anglo-Jewish life in England was not bound up with national and religious paradigms of self and community. The extraordinary bureaucracy around medieval Anglo-Jews, along with the oft-noticed preoccupation with Jewish or Judaized characters in Anglo-Christian medieval literature, makes England and its Expulsion a unique point of reference for study of the mechanics of difference and sameness in medieval Christian-Jewish polemics, for the line between polemic and history is difficult to draw when the apparatus that creates the archive is legislating and enforcing difference and absence but also dwelling on cases of sameness and uncertainty. We arrive at a cultural imaginary: in this, it is not possible cleanly to separate government record keeping, the political or personal decisions of individuals, the written remains of legal interpretation, or other kinds of literature.

Indeed, the many types of English texts that ask readers to reconsider the boundaries between Christian and Jew also ask the reader to redefine the meaning of "Christian" and "Jew," to play or voice the Jew, or to be productively and didactically uncertain about the relative merits of Jewishness. In what follows, I may describe such moments—when artists or writers, through various methods, create connections between Christians and Jews that highlight similarities, or that purposefully construct "Jewish" Christians or Christian "Jews"—as moments of "(a)likeness," "resemblance," "similarity," "mimicry," "doubling," or "indistinguishability." All of these should be understood under the umbrella of "sameness," which I use as a key term not only to denote the modern usage one can find in the *OED*—"the quality of being the same," of an object or person "having the same attributes with another or with itself at another time"[24]—but also with the Middle English sense of *samnen* (to same)—that is, "to gather together, meet, assemble," "to collect," "to unite," "to join" in order to make new meaning—a verb often used in the Middle Ages to describe the uniting or harmonizing of disparate people or contradictory texts.[25] This kind of sameness, or the processes of sam*ing* (as opposed to, and alongside, processes of othering), has consequence: in the meeting, overlap, and gathering together, it changes meaning through connections and contradictions. Its polemics seek to explicate the point of similarity and *to same* the Christian and the Jew by uniting or harmonizing them for positive or negative didactic effect, or by mimicking the "other" with the "self." This is why Audre Lorde called the "myth of sameness" a destructive force; it distorts difference and can be misapplied or disruptive.[26] It keeps things hidden, blows things up, quietly erases the real.

My attention to what polemics of sameness have hidden, most consequentially, uncovers a new corpus of, and articulates a new framework for understanding, representations of the Jewish woman in medieval English books, national records, and historiography. In this book, I am ultimately dedicated to opening the door on a world of gendered caricatures of "the Jewess," previously hidden in critical blind spots. Lipton, for instance, in her book *Dark Mirror* and an earlier essay, asks, "Where are the Jewish women?" but finds little evidence of stereotypes or remarkable attitudes toward the Jewess until the end of the Middle Ages; Jewish and Christian women, she argues, are frequently indistinguishable in Christian art because "in the Christian imagination, for better or worse, the Jewess's femaleness trumped her Jewishness"[27]—that is, her gender already othered her and left little room for further distinction. Lipton's conclusion is in line with Lampert-Weissig's more literary argument that "women and Jews . . . are not simply the Other for the Christian exegetical tradition; they also represent sources of origin" that allow for the becoming of the (human and Christian) self.[28] These influential positions, however, focus on an invisibility and malleability that subordinates study of the Jewess to study of the Jew and contributes to a wider sense that Jewish women function, in the myriad medieval texts in which they are present, not as themselves but, mostly, as Christians. The Jewess, in this light, is femininely "pliant and impressionable," "particularly susceptible to Christianity's 'truth,'" or a Christianized foil for "the real villain [who] is the Jewish male."[29] By contrast, when we look for authors' and artists' deliberate play with sameness, mimicry, and invisibility, the Jewess is revealed as a consistently characterized figure in English letters, one who sits in a doubled and ambiguous space *designed* to engage notions of Christian Jewishness.

In my readings of the Jewess, the categories Woman and Jew converge: the feminine malleability or pliancy noticed by others is not her primary attribute, nor is Jewishness per se. Rather, Christians *same* the Jewess, both in the dominant modern sense (making her similar, showing how she is like something else) and in the medieval sense of gathering together or harmonizing. "Jew" and "Christian" are simultaneously recognizable in the figure of the Jewess, who, in turn, represents specific and contemporary historical understandings of the Anglo-Jewish woman and speaks to regionally specific religious and political anxieties. Sander Gilman's explication of the doubled Jewess in nineteenth-century German culture is helpful here: when the "fixed relationships of the empowered male to the stereotype of the woman . . . become strained," as I will show they do with medieval Anglo-Jewish women, "the problem of the construction and externalization of stereotypes in culture becomes a means to measure the limits of th[e] 'double vision' which constructs the image of the Jewish woman."[30] If malleability occurs, it functions purposefully and polemically. It creates fantasies of sameness, prompts interaction with Christian viewers and readers, and invites moments of uncanny recognition. The figure of the Jewess in England becomes powerfully useful and flexible not only because women are origin points or lack the phallus (and so the Jewish mark of circumcision) but also because Jewish women's interactions with the Anglo-Christian state strained (male) expectations of both women and Jews. In the Jewess, therefore, sameness works beyond, or separately from, ideas of projection (of rejected aspects of the self onto the other) and toward notions of embodied interchangeability. Indeed, the presence of an unmarked Jewess who can manipulate her near Christianness, or be manipulated because of it, goes to the heart of Anglo-Christian thinking about Jews. As I will show, a Christian desire to be the correct(ed) Jew—not just to supersede but to absorb or become the Jew—finds its focus in the figure of the Jewess.

What follows is structured in two parts: Part I ("The Potential of Sameness") establishes the terms and range of polemics of sameness, and Part II ("The Unmarked Jewess") reveals the strongly gendered dynamics of such polemics, through examination of the figure of the Jewess in medieval English texts and images. The two parts make their arguments not only conventionally (through analysis of texts, images, and contexts), but also structurally (through storytelling, thematic organization, and the movement of individual texts through multiple chapters). Continued recontextualization of the objects of analysis, as the book progresses, allows a discourse around sameness to develop in and between genres and time frames. In the final chapters, this method also helps to establish the corpus of books and texts that portray the Anglo-Jewish woman (and her represented form as "the Jewess") because it allows that corpus to speak in relationship to many genres, authors, and syllabuses.

Part I makes the case for polemics of sameness, and it shows how they work in a range of English texts, from cases recorded in the Plea Rolls of the Exchequer of the Jews and Curia Regis Rolls to the twelfth-century homily collection known as the *Orrmulum* and the *Chronicle of Jocelin of Brakelond* to the thirteenth-century Judas Ballad and devotional poetry in the mid-fourteenth-century BL MS Harley 2253 (The Harley Manuscript). In this part, I examine what sameness is and how it operates in a variety of contexts, particularly those that exploit typological and physical resemblances, Christian-Jewish identifications in positive and negative senses, and medieval and biblical ideas about Christian Jewishness. To do so, I reintroduce texts that have never been studied for their narratives and polemics or have not been thought to hold notable anti-Jewish content. My scholarly gaze in this part stays fixed, too, on male Jews and (Christian) male thought-worlds: royal or ecclesiastical bureaucracies and monastic or theological acts of interpretation and storytelling.[31] Sameness is at work in such literature, and, in order to establish it as a broadly applicable polemical mode in medieval England—one with significant interpretive potential—Part I shows how sameness behaves in texts that typically engage supersessionist epistemologies.

Part II turns to the Jewish women of medieval England. Its subject is both the careers of Anglo-Jewish women before and after the 1290 Expulsion and representations of Jewish women in English historiographical, devotional, and literary records (from about 1200 to 1400). Part II contends that Anglo-Christian treatment of Jewish women marks the epitome of polemical uses of sameness, and it focuses on how rhetorical strategies that blur the line between saming and othering uncover distinct representations of Jewish women. If the Jewess has seemed absent from or undetectable in medieval illustration, or if she has seemed present in literary roles only to the extent that she is pliant or seducing, this is not because she reflects only misogynistic stereotypes of femininity (as opposed to stereotypes of Jewishness). Rather, like more readily identifiable tropes of Jewish male grotesqueness, her similarity to Christian women is a matter of caricature. Both before and after the periods in which art historians note a consistent visual repertoire of villainy and difference around Jewish men,[32] English authors point out and exploit Jewish women's indistinguishability from Christians, so that the Jewess becomes either a dangerous but unseeable enemy or a sign of the always-convertible self. Anglo-Christian legal and historical records, moreover, show that such rhetoric surrounded actual Anglo-Jewish women, so that history and polemic mingle. Part II makes its case through letters of women converts; a variety of legal texts (especially, again, the Plea Rolls of the Exchequer of the Jews); miracle stories and pseudohistoriographical libels; and illustrations of Jewish women in devotional books. It includes significant new readings of the *Passion of Adam of Bristol*, the *Life of Christina of Markyate*, and the Anglo-Norman "Hugo de Lincolnia," stretching also to Bod. MS Eng. poet. a. 1 (The Vernon Manuscript), the alliterative *Siege of Jerusalem*, and *Titus and Vespasian* (all ca. 1370–90), which embrace long-standing English stereotypes about the sameness of the Jewess.

Both Parts I and II begin with *historiae*, a helpfully fuzzy term in medieval Latin usage that denotes histories, stories and tales, descriptions of the past, and narrative illustrations. All denotations are applicable to the stories that introduce each side of this book's diptych, and each *historia* speaks to and becomes a reference point for the chapters that follow it. Part I's *historiae* concern a Jewish man who dressed up as a friar in 1277 (Sampson son of Samuel of Northampton) and a Jewish/Christian boy (Jurnepin/Odard of Norwich) found near a river in 1230. Both survive to us through national records, the Exchequer of the Jews and the King's Bench, respectively. Both also show the potential for a confusion of Jewish and Christian identities, for the ability of the Christian or Jewish body to be seen as the other, and for English theologians and authorities to struggle with sameness even as they attempt to reinscribe difference. Part II's *historiae* tell of an Anglo-Jewish woman who converted to Christianity before 1272 (Alice of Worcester) and a smart but villainous (fictional) Jewess of Bristol who was featured in a ritual murder story written around 1290 (the unnamed Jewish sister of the *Passion of Adam of Bristol*). Alice survives through an extraordinary set of letters, two written by her, and the Jewess of Bristol speaks through a unique manuscript copy of a tale that has sometimes been cited among historical cases of libelous murder accusations.[33] Together, these women reveal the extremes of Anglo-Christian hopes for and fears of Jewish women. Both extremes, as their stories will make clear, depend on the Jewish woman's ability to be understood as Christian.

Finally, the four appendices that conclude this book present new editions and translations of several featured texts. These allow ready access to stories not previously widely known or available.

As a whole, *The Christian Jew and the Unmarked Jewess* establishes a new framework and set of questions for reading medieval Anglo-Christian literature about Jews. It widens the scope of what texts about English Jews look like, and it argues that a focus on sameness yields significant conclusions in application to characterizations of Jewish women. Just as Canon 68 of Lateran IV legislated the problem of distinguishing Jews and Muslims from Christians—not only because of holiday ostentations (as noted above) but also because Christians might "through error . . . mingle with the women of Jews or Saracens, and, on the other hand, Jews and Saracens mingle with [the women] of the Christians" (complicating identity categories through miscegenation and reproduction)[34]—English texts of the era evince vexed interests in the possible indistinguishability of Jews and Christians, and especially Jewish and Christian women. Narrative fantasies of accidental or nefarious passing expose and exploit these social anxieties, much as medieval legislation around clothing or the sharing of food and medicine.[35] Such regulations, and the narratives that reveal and undermine them, tell us that interaction and sameness were an expected norm. They will also show us that the sameness of Christian and Jew could be fetishized and aspired to, just as it could be feared and regulated.

I will note finally that *The Christian Jew and the Unmarked Jewess* is primarily a study of the postbiblical Jew and Jewess—mainly of Christian ideas

about contemporary Jews—even though I do discuss authors' treatment of
New Testament Jews or use of typological pairings that require some discussion
of Old Testament "Jews," like Samson, King David, or the matriarch Rachel. In
Part I in particular, explication of how polemics of sameness develop from and
with medieval typological methods and supersessionist rhetoric is necessary to
show how monastic and ecclesiastical authorities approached Jewish/Christian
relational identities and to establish the terms of my larger arguments. It is not
my purpose, however, to conflate the polemical discourse I identify with typological exegesis. As I have already noted, they may interact, but they are not
identical. Ultimately, I am most interested in—and see polemics of sameness
most obviously consequential within—sources that describe or imagine Jews as
medieval people, communities, and neighbors. I am interested in the associated
desires to harmonize Christian and Jew and, conversely, in the unease that
arises from assimilation of the Jew into the Christian or the Christian community, and vice versa. If supersession and typology are at the root of these desires
and discomforts, they also give them life beyond the confines of exegesis and
biblical pasts. The works I analyze here always make clear that supersessionist
rhetoric is reaching out to the contemporary English landscape, struggling not
to supplant but to inhabit the Jew.

It is not uncommon to read in studies that examine processes of othering
and prejudice that "like" and "unlike" require each other, that "us" and "them"
coexist of necessity and would not need to be distinguished if they were not so
much the same, that repulsion mirrors attraction, that opposition entails resemblance. I agree. If past studies have accepted these propositions as self-evident,
however, this book makes them central by looking seriously at the "like" side of
the equation. *The Christian Jew and the Unmarked Jewess* explores the likeness,
attraction, resemblance, and sameness of Christian and Jew in the context of
medieval English writing, and it shows what a paradigm shift that centers sameness instead of difference can produce. Most importantly, it uncovers, for the
first time, the unmistakable presence of Jewish women in medieval English
literature.

PART I

THE POTENTIAL OF SAMENESS

Mimicry is at once resemblance and menace.

— Homi K. Bhabha, "Of Mimicry and Man"

The Friar and the Foundling

If one's the type, all that's needed is a little nerve.

—Nella Larsen, *Passing*

The Friar

For a long time I have been thinking about a Jewish man in medieval Northampton. His name was Sampson son of Samuel, and he was arrested, thirteen years before King Edward I's expulsion of all Jews from England, for impersonating a Franciscan friar and preaching false Christianity. His case, recorded among the Memoranda for Trinity Term 1277 in the Plea Rolls of the Exchequer of the Jews, was set down in Latin by a Christian scribe. Little is known of the circumstances of the offense, nothing of the reasons for it. Sampson and his extraordinary con exist only in the legalistic narrative of an Anglo-Christian, state-sponsored economic apparatus. And what can this expose about a Jew? A man with the nerve to test the fragile boundaries of Jewish-Christian identity and speech, was Sampson a hero? An activist? A joker?

A unique penalty, emphatically supported by the king, was devised by the archbishop of Canterbury, at that time the Dominican Robert Kilwardby. Sampson was to walk naked through city streets with a flayed calf around his neck and the calf's entrails in his hands. It is unlikely that this punishment was ever carried out—Sampson seems to have escaped, perhaps with the help of the Northampton sheriff—but the sentence is horrifying and inventive. It betrays a dialogue between medieval English Christians and Jews and permits us an astonishing view of Christian-Jewish identifications, assimilations, and anxieties over likeness. Sampson's inhabiting of Christian clothing and speech was a transgression, and the prescribed punishment imagines correction for both Jewish and Christian observers. It does so not by reinstating a Jew/Christian dichotomy, but by reinterpreting *the ability of the Jewish body to be seen and understood as Christian.*

Here is part of Sampson's case:[1]

> A certain Jew, Sampson son of Samuel, was seized and detained in prison at Northampton by the sheriff of Northampton. . . . And the sheriff sent word that he had seized Sampson son of Samuel because he assumed the habit of a Friar Minor, preaching certain things in contempt of the Christian faith and the aforesaid Order, of which he was recently convicted before the Archbishop of Canterbury, whereby it was adjudged as sentence that he should go naked for three days through the middle of five cities—namely London, Canterbury, Oxford, Lincoln, and Northampton—carrying in his hands the entrails of a certain calf and the calf flayed around his neck, which he [the sheriff], holding the same Jew in the castle until the king command something different on the matter, would not allow to be done without special order of the king, concerning which the archbishop wrote to the king.
>
> And since this Sampson did not appear . . . nor was anything done after that, and also the presiding justices were made aware that the lord king through his writ under the Great Seal had ordered this sheriff that the aforementioned Jew should in the first place be made to undergo the previously noted punishment enjoined on him by the Archbishop of Canterbury, the sheriff was commanded to enforce the pending judgement in this matter according to the tenor of that order, such that the aforementioned Sampson should suffer the aforesaid punishment. In addition, because the same justices were made aware that the aforementioned Sampson was released from prison, even though the same sheriff previously indicated that he would not release him without special order of the king, likewise he was commanded that if this Jew should be absent he should attach the . . . Jews Samuel and Isaac, who had previously mainperned the same Jew . . . so as to have their bodies present . . . on the morrow of St James to stand to right and do for that Jew the penance enjoined on him.[2]

The contours of the event are clear enough from this summary of the case, but we can know nothing of the precise nature of what Sampson did beyond what the Exchequer scribe records. It is hard to tell if what he preached "in contemptum fidei christiane" (in contempt of the Christian faith) was satirical or blasphemous, or whether he actually made it difficult to distinguish Jew from Christian. Did Sampson go mendicant through city streets, costumed and undetected for some time? If his preaching had been openly blasphemous, the imposition of what is a relatively nonviolent punishment is hard to imagine. Around the same time, Northampton Jews were executed on coin-clipping charges and had been accused of the attempted murder of a Christian child; two years later, in 1279, the king would issue a proclamation warning Jews against blasphemy "under peril of life and limb," and a Norwich Jew was burned at the stake for blasphemy.[3] The punishment enjoined on Sampson is not of this sort. It is, rather, a grotesque performance of Jewish identity within Christian space. It expects a viewing audience, and it suggests that Sampson's ruse was successful.

The punishment makes more sense if Sampson made a convincing friar. The requirement that he go naked, revealing his genitals and thus his circumcision, would have practical purpose in proving that he was Jewish, and it is tempting, then, to reason that the five cities named in the memorandum of his case correspond to cities in which he preached, where bodily demonstration of his Jewishness might matter most. The content of Jewish and Christian preaching may not be radically, or at all, different, and we need not imagine Sampson parading about cursing Christianity and Franciscans to conclude that he was speaking "in contemptum." We might even consider Sampson's religious cross-dressing as a complement to a moment in Judah HeHasid's early thirteenth-century *Sefer Hasidim*, where the author advises that Jewish women disguise themselves as nuns to protect themselves while traveling.[4] As Ivan Marcus notes, "The assumptions behind this prescription for 'cross-dressing' illuminate many aspects of intergroup relations"; it is evidence of "inward acculturation," whereby "Jews who did not convert or flirt with converting retained a strong collective Jewish identity and sometimes expressed it by internalizing or transforming . . . Christian culture in polemical, parodic, or neutralized manners."[5] Sampson's actions might be perceived as a challenge to the dominant culture in general and to mendicant orders and their attempts to convert Anglo-Jewish communities in particular—perhaps even one aimed at the archbishop of Canterbury himself.

Many have attributed a generalized increase in anti-Jewish sentiment in the second half of the thirteenth century to the rise of the mendicant orders

and especially to Dominican and Franciscan preaching.[6] By 1280, in line with
Pope Nicholas III's 1278 bull *Vineam sorec*, Edward I had charged his sheriffs
and bailiffs with ensuring attendance of Jews at Dominican sermons, with the
express purpose of converting them.[7] This was probably not a new idea, and
Kilwardby, once provincial prior of the Dominicans in England, would have
been sympathetic to it. A Paris-educated grammarian and theologian,
Kilwardby "favoured the conversion of Jews by theological argument and
preaching."[8] On the one hand, he was apparently friendly with the prominent
London rabbi Elijah Menahem, whom he found to be "of better disposition
than any of the other Jews" (quem inter caeteros Judaeos melioris inveni volun-
tatis), and for whom he had interceded when secular officials denied the rabbi's
right to excommunicate a London Jew in 1275.[9] On the other hand, Kilwardby
worked closely with Robert Burnell, bishop of Bath and Wells and chancellor of
England, a man involved in several cases of Jewish-Christian conversion in
these decades,[10] and the king had given him control of a case oddly similar to
Sampson's in 1275, when a Dominican friar and Hebraist called Robert of Reading had converted to Judaism and begun preaching "contra legem Christianam"
(against Christian law).[11] With this context, we can surmise that Kilwardby
was not a man prone to remarkably violent action but that he was, by predisposition or under the king's orders, interested in such cases, and he may have found
Sampson's demonstration of the vulnerabilities of fraternal preaching particularly galling.

It is significant then that the Exchequer scribe describes the sentence
against Sampson as a "penance enjoined on him" (penitenciam sibi iniunctam).
The word *penitencia*, which in the full record is deployed twice to describe
Kilwardby's imposed punishment, suggests that the judgment could be understood as a performance of religious repentance and reconciliation, and there are
several plausible religious allegorical readings of the naked Jew and the slain calf
that might be applied to support such an understanding. For Christians, the
most familiar scriptural description of a slain calf comes in the parable of
the prodigal son, wherein the unworthy and absent son is welcomed home with
the slain fatted calf ("vitulum saginatum"). The calf is mentioned three times
in the parable, and the father, as is well known, insists that the calf is for the son
who "was lost and is found" (Luke 15:24). The other easily recognizable biblical
calf ("vitulum" in the *Vulgate*, as in the description of Sampson's punishment) is
the Golden Calf of Exodus 32. The *vitulum* in this instance is the sign of Israel's
inconstancy, and, mirroring Kilwardby's punishment, Israel goes naked as evidence of its sin. In the Vulgate, the Hebrew *paru'a* (untamed, wild) is rendered

nudatus (naked), and thus Moses's imposition of violent punishment on Israel is preceded by his awareness that Israel is naked: "Moses saw that the people were naked [nudatus] . . . [Aaron] had set them naked among their enemies [inter hostes nudum constituerat]" (Exod. 32:25). The nudity here is both the proof and the shame of apostasy, the calf the material evidence of it. When Kilwardby decided he wanted to send Sampson of Northampton "inter hostes nudum," carrying a calf, the connection cannot have been far from the theologian's mind.

In light of the parable of the prodigal son and Kilwardby's Dominican allegiances, however, display of a slain calf must also call up the eschatological hope—so near and dear to thirteenth-century mendicants' hearts—that Jewish conversion was imminent. The "finding" of Sampson, the son turned from God, symbolic of Israel turned from God, allows the archbishop to display his Jewish body as both sinful and prodigal, and to enforce his return. The flayed and disemboweled calf, from this perspective, can also be linked to the vision of the new Temple in Ezekiel 43, wherein the shame of Israel is expiated first by a "calf that is offered for sin" (vitulum qui oblatus fuerit pro peccato), and perhaps more generally to the descriptions of animal offerings and their entrails in Leviticus 1–7. The flayed calf thus sets on Sampson's shoulders both the old bloody sacrifice and the hope of atonement for Israel's sins, among which are profanation and disbelief (Ezek. 43:8).[12] This is an extraordinary burden to place on the stripped body of one man among few in the then-dwindling Jewish community of Northampton, but it found support among most of the relevant officials and the king himself. Sheriffs were bound to protect "the king's Jews" and ensure separation of ecclesiastical and civil authority—as it seems the Northampton sheriff attempted to do—but demonstration of Sampson's *penitencia* evidently had utility to both church and state.[13] Sampson transgressed in a way that achieved restricted power (the power to preach, to travel unmolested, to demand Christian hospitality), and the urgency was not to kill him but forcefully to resituate him within the majority Christian understanding.

At issue in Kilwardby's imposition of a Jewish *penitencia* is the attempt to correct a problematic Jewish-Christian identification by creating a kind of Christian identification with the Jew that was acceptable. While the punishment would shame Sampson before other Jews and confirm his Jewishness for Christians through viewing of his circumcision, it also seeks to make of him a biblical Israelite and the always potentially Christian Jew of the New Testament. Sampson's attempt to pass as Christian—whatever its tone—had troublingly reinforced mechanisms of assimilation and fear, and the punishment for it was not only about Sampson. As the Exchequer of the Jews memorandum makes clear, it could make its theological point and accomplish its civil goals even if forced on other Jewish men: if Sampson could not be found, the penance was to be performed by his two mainpernors.

It appears that all three men escaped. Gilbert de Kirkeby, the Northampton sheriff at that time, was amerced for lying about Sampson's whereabouts and ultimately admitted that the Jewish friar and his mainpernors "non fuerunt inuenti in balliua sua" (were not found in his bailiwick) any longer.[14] Gilbert had a history of protecting Jews from punishment and imprisonment, beyond the scope of his responsibility, either by conveniently losing or freeing those he was supposed to have imprisoned or by employing delay and confusion tactics like those he exhibits in Sampson's case (in the full record, he gives the justices multiple conflicting statements). In the year prior, he had been accused of "despising the king's order, maliciously obtaining delay for certain Jews," fined for "depart[ing] in contempt of the Court" and, separately, because he "answered to the Justices and others face to face that he would not do in pursuance" of an order to bring Northampton Jews to answer for coin clipping.[15] This behavior was not uniformly his habit, however. When a year earlier he delivered our same Sampson son of Samuel to London to answer for a tallage owing on debts, he did so without noted objection.[16] It is in the cross-dressing case that Gilbert is at his most diversionary. Not all officials, it seems, and not one who may have called Sampson neighbor, were willing to enforce such a humiliating punishment. In the end, however, those who wielded the most power agreed that it was appropriate and necessary for some Jewish body to answer publicly and penitentially for testing the boundaries between Jew and Christian—if only to make Sampson's Christian likeness useful to the story of Christian identity.

The Foundling

Half a century before Sampson of Northampton preached as a Franciscan, a strange case of Jewish-Christian similarity unfolded in Norwich around a five-year-old boy who was found distraught, bleeding, and claiming to be Jewish near the River Wensum. The Curia Regis Roll for 18 Henry III (1234),[17] which includes the fullest account of the event, tells of two communities that struggled to interpret the foundling. The child, discovered in 1230, said he was a Jew, and Jews tried to claim him, but by the time his case was recorded he was judged to be the Christian victim of a forced circumcision, and six of thirteen accused Jewish men had been outlawed or imprisoned for the offense. Jeffrey J. Cohen

has framed the case as one of "intractable hybridity," a story that shows medieval Jewish and Christian "bodies caught in a difficult middle";[18] more recently,
he has linked it to premodern racialized concepts of consanguinity, a case that,
through circumcision and lawfare, "illustrates the complicated connections between identity and blood in the Middle Ages."[19] I want to reframe it, or also
frame it, as a story about the alikeness of Jews and Christians. At the very crux
of this case is the ability of the Christian or Jewish body to inhabit the other, to
appear *like* the other, even where bodily distinction should make the boundary
less fragile.

    In this instance, the possibility of sameness challenges certainty even where
bodily evidence of difference is available, and the textual remnants of the case
reflect and contribute to the evidence of medieval Anglo-Christian negotiations of the boundary between Jew and Christian. The surviving records cannot communicate beyond their own structural prejudices and motivations, and
our ability to know anything beyond the texts suffers further under the distance of time, defunct systems of archival oppression, mixed genres, and the
current state of the most significant survival. The 1234 curial roll that provides
the only extended narrative of the case is extremely damaged, while multiple
short documents dated between 1231 and 1249 provide only a fragmented view
of the several Jewish men who lingered in prison, were condemned, and had
their property divided between heirs and accusers. One fictionalized summary
by Matthew Paris in his *Chronica majora* (assigned to 1240 but written in the
years after) tells us that four Jewish men were executed for the crime.[20] The
foundling's case was drawn out over at least ten years: the 1234 account was
written when the boy was nine, and the corroborating documents suggest that
the case was not closed until he was at least fifteen (1240/41). The struggle to
make the "Jewish" child Christian was not easy, nor was it disconnected from
historiographical and hagiographical influence.

    The long 1234 account—called in the roll a "recordum loquele," a formal
record of testimony and proceedings related to an inquest—tells of a five-year-
old who had appeared four years earlier "sedens iuxta ripam Norwici" (sitting
near the Norwich river). A Christian woman named Matilda and her daughter,
the scribe writes, found him "plorantem et vlulantem et dicentem quod erat Iudeus" (crying and wailing and saying that he was a Jew).[21] They quickly discovered that the boy had been recently circumcised, and there was considerable
debate over whether he was a Jew or a Christian. Resolution was still forthcom-
ing six years later, when the king first authorized and then reneged on a request from the imprisoned Jews for further deliberation before a mixed jury of

Christians and Jews: on 18 January 1240, the king ordered the mixed jury; on 21 February 1240, he rescinded the January order and urged local authorities to bring the case to an expedient close.[22] In 1234, nonetheless, it was already clear that there would be severe consequences, and at least one Jewish man had been punished by 1231.[23] The circumcision was understood, according to the curial scribe, "in despectu crucifixi et christianitatis" (as an insult to the Cross and Christianity). The Benedictine monk Matthew Paris later went so far as to describe the crime as an attempted crucifixion and reported that the four executed Jews were dragged behind horses and hanged—a mode of execution that suggests a charge of treason, also described for Jews in historiographical and literary accounts of the purported ritual murder of Hugh of Lincoln in 1255 and in Chaucer's "Prioress's Tale."[24] One of these unfortunate men was Mosse Mokke, named in the 1234 account, enrolled in 1235 among those who paid the king 300 marks for a trial and 50 marks for bail, named in the 1240 writs among those requesting a mixed jury, and finally named again in documents from 1241 and 1242 as convicted and hanged.[25] Mosse Mokke (Moses son of Abraham of Norwich) is perhaps now better known as one of the subjects of a Christian scribe's satirical illustration at the head of a 1233 Norfolk tallage roll (see Figure 3),[26] but the last decade of his life was bound to a child's circumcision.

What really happened to the Norwich boy is not clear. The 1234 "loquele" record contradictory testimony that already suggests hagiographic influence, either on the part of the scribe or the witnesses, and particularly on the part of the boy and his father. They testified together that the child had been playing ("iuit ludendo") in town when he was taken ("cepit eundem") and carried to a Jewish home, a claim that echoes (though inverts) the beginnings of the then-popular Marian miracle story known as "The Jewish Boy," in which a Jewish child plays in town with Christian friends before he is led to a church to take communion.[27] The scribe also tells us that the hue and cry of neighbors ("clamorem vicinorum") led to the discovery of the child at the Jewish home, a claim similar both to "The Jewish Boy" and the "Child Slain by Jews" Marian miracle types, which feature parents, neighbors, and civil officers noisily searching for and discovering harmed boys in Jewish homes.[28] The boy testified that he was held down and blindfolded while circumcised ("unus illorum tenuit eum et cooperuit oculos suos"), opening the door to fantasies of crucifixion-like scenes similar to the one described in Thomas of Monmouth's *Life and Passion of William of Norwich*, a hagiographic account of a boy killed by Jews in the same city almost a century earlier.[29] This idea clearly caught Matthew Paris's imagination, and the initial testimony of the boy's father, that he found his son in the home and hands of a Jew called Jacob ("inuenit in manibus ipsius Iacobi"), supports this fantasy. Other witnesses, however, testified that the boy had left or "escaped Jewish hands" (euasit de manibus Iudeorum) and was alone at the river when Matilda found him and "took him" (cepit eundem) to her home. The boy first said he was a Jew but later, after his father appeared, answered to a Christian name. The dispute that followed was focused on how, if he was a Christian, he came to be circumcised.

It is clear from the record that the boy had indeed been recently circumcised or at least suffered circumcision-like wounds, that both Jews and Christians involved in the case between 1230 and 1234 sincerely thought he was one of their own, and that the boy himself, at least for the day or two after he was found, was a bit uncertain. At the age of nine, he confidently appeared before the court and said he was abducted and forcibly circumcised by a group of Jews. Matilda and her daughter, however, said that when he was five, he recognized the Jews who came to retrieve him and answered to the Jewish name Jurnepin ("little Jornet," a nickname for Joseph, which the boy later says was given to him because it was also the name of the man who first found his foreskin in a strange postcircumcision game of hide-and-seek).[30] The Jews who arrived to claim him certainly believed him to be Jewish: when gathered Christians refused to hand him over, the Jews advised them not to let the child eat pork, "quia dixerunt ipsum esse Iudeum" (because, they said, he was a Jew), and then sought help from the constable of Norwich Castle and two local bailiffs. When his physician father Benedict ("Magister Benedictus fisicus") was called, after one of Matilda's neighbors said she recognized the child, the boy first maintained that he was "a Jew called Jurnepin" (Iudeus uocabatur Iurnepin) but then answered to the Christian name Odard and acknowledged Benedict as his father. Four years later, witnesses said that he first answered to Jurnepin only out of fear, but the Norwich constable confirmed that "venerunt Iudei ad eum et questi fuerunt quod Christiani voluerunt auferre eis Iudeum suum" (the Jews came to him when he was at Norwich Castle and made complaint that the Christians wanted to steal their Jew from them). When the constable arrived at Matilda's home that day, he "inuenit ibi congregationem magnam Christianorum et Iudeorum" (found a great crowd of Christians and Jews there), all arguing over little Jurnepin/Odard's identity.

Cohen is right to emphasize "the complicated connections between communal identity and body" in this case, and to highlight how it begs questions about the meanings of blood, sacraments, and identity, but it is also true that Jurnepin/Odard's body does not answer any questions about the nature of the sacraments and rituals to which it may or may not have been subjected. Even in the medieval attempts to find answers this was true. It appears that there was always disagreement over the nature of the crime. Both the king and the church wanted jurisdiction: the 1234 account tells of a huge deliberative gathering—with a decision taken "coram domino Rege et domino Cant' et maiori parte Episcoporum Comitum et Baronum Anglie" (before the Lord King and Lord of Canterbury and a great part of the Bishops, Earls, and Barons of England)—that resulted in reverting the matter to ecclesiastical courts. The king, nonetheless, must have continued to see it as a criminal case, or at least one of economic interest to him. Henry III likely reneged on his 1240 order to convene a mixed jury (necessary by English civil law pertaining to Jews) only because he had finally reached some compromise with church officials that would allow a resolution.

In the midst of such basic disagreements, the poor boy was repeatedly, to the point of absurdity, physically examined. Ecclesiastical, civil, and Jewish authorities all testified that they had viewed his genitals. When he was found in 1230, the Norwich archdeacon's official and Norwich coroners examined him, and "uiderunt predictum puerum circumcisum et qui habuit membrum suum grossum et ualde inflatum" (they saw the aforesaid boy circumcised and with a large and very swollen penis). In 1234, the archdeacon's official appeared "cum magna secta sacerdotum" (with a large group of priests) and testified that they had *all* examined him: "viderunt predictum puerum recenter circumcisum habentem membrum suum grossum et ualde inflatum et sanguinolentum" (they saw the aforesaid boy when he was recently circumcised, with his penis large and very swollen and bloody). A further group of "county coroners, coroners of the city of Norwich, and thirty-six sworn jurors from Norwich" (Coronatores de Comitatu et Coronatores de Ciuitate Norwici et xxxvj homines de villata de Norwici iurati) likewise verified before the king's justices "quod predictus puer ita circumcisus fuit" (that the aforesaid boy was thus circumcised). The constable of Norwich Castle also testified that had examined him in 1230, "habentem membrum suum abscisum sanguinolentum et grossum inflatum" (with his penis cut, bleeding, and swollen big). During the 1234 proceedings, again, the king's justices took the opportunity to see for themselves: "Et puer visus est coram Iusticiariis et liquidum est quod circumcisus erat" (and the boy was seen in the presence of the justices, and it is clear that he had been circumcised). Examination by the justices was conducted at a proceeding attended by the Benedictine prior of Norwich Cathedral, a group of Franciscans and Dominicans, and many other clergy and laity. Finally in 1234, despite initial insistence that

Jurnepin/Odard was Jewish, the Jewish community paid a gold mark (a huge sum) to have the boy independently examined:

> Super hoc uenerunt omnes Iudei in communi et optulerunt domino Rege vnam marcam auri per sic quod puer uideatur coram ipsis Iudeis si circumcisus fuit vel non. . . . Et visus est puer et menbrum eius uisum est pelle coopertum ante in capite.

> Furthermore, all the Jews came as a group and proffered one mark's worth of gold to the Lord King so that, through this, the boy might be viewed before these Jews as to whether he was circumcised or not. . . . And the boy was seen, and his penis was seen covered with skin [only] before the head.

This excessive and repetitive examination of the boy's genitals signals the weakness of the visual identifying markers of Christianness or Jewishness. Bodily proof of the male Jewish or Judaized body could constitute evidence of Jewish belonging (he must therefore be a Jew) or emphatically Christian identity (he must therefore have suffered at the hands of Jews). As with Sampson son of Samuel of Northampton, sentenced to parade naked through city streets to prove that he was a Jew, bodily display stands as the determining evidence when such contradiction arises. In Jurnepin/Odard's case, however, even circumcision is misleading. Rather than a solution, it produces ongoing anxiety over its meaning; it can be misplaced, misunderstood, or misrecognized; it must be viewed and interpreted again and again from multiple perspectives and at different times. From Matthew Paris's point of view, the boy's genitals were evidence of a botched ritual murder attempt—"Reservabant . . . illum ad crucifgendum in contumeliam Jesu Christi crucifixi" (They kept . . . him to be crucified as an insult to Jesus Christ crucified).[31] The physical evidence of a Judaized body, for Matthew, was equally evidence of the ideal Christian body. In his bodily similarity to a Jew, this child was most Christian.

In his still masterful and important achievement, *The Jews of Medieval Norwich*, Vivian Lipman outlined Walter Rye's 1877 assessment of the Christian claim to Jurnepin/Odard and the Norwich Jewish community's response to the case:

> Rye . . . suggested that [the father] Benedict was a converted Jew—his name and the fact that he was a physician confirm this hypothesis;

and that the Jews were reclaiming his son for the Jewish faith. Otherwise, it is difficult to understand why they acted so openly and indeed complained to the sheriff and bailiffs. One puzzling feature is why a gold mark was paid for an examination of the boy to see if he had been circumcised. If the Jews had acted in order to bring the boy back to Judaism, they would have known that examination would only confirm the case against them. Rye suggests that only a few Jews were concerned and that those who were arrested, or at any rate those who paid the fine of a gold mark for an examination, did not know the real story and thought the accusation completely baseless.[32]

Lipman leaves the story here and continues to other matters of the same decade, apparently accepting Rye's solution as well as the implication that the accusation was not completely baseless—but the Victorian hypothesis is not an end point. Rye's supposition does not make it clear why the five-year-old Jurnepin/Odard would have been so recently circumcised as to be swollen and bleeding at the time he was found, nor why the Norwich Jews who claimed him were so willing to confront the gathered Christians and seek protection of the law, apparently without providing any further explanation of the situation. There is nothing in any of the surviving records that mentions a conversion, even though disputes over conversion are a regular topic in Anglo-Jewish legal history.[33]

Without doubt, however, there was confusion and miscommunication over the boy's identity at the local level, between king and church, and among both Jews and Christians. This is itself noteworthy. The available devices of resolution for both parties—recourse to the Crown, repetitive close physical examination, a mixed jury, ecclesiastical jurisdiction, the eventual determination that the act must be an affront to the whole Christian body, and the prolonged term of litigation as the boy grew older—are likewise remarkable. They are indications of uncertainty and difficulty in determining what had happened and what to do. In Matthew Paris's *Chronica majora* account, we also see the point at which an actually complex and eventually tragic event slipped into hagiographic libel. Matthew's fictionalization wants to deflect the fact that Christian-Jewish difference was ever so hard to determine: ten years from his own claim that he was a Jew, and both communities' fight over acceptance of that claim, Jurnepin/Odard becomes a Christ figure precisely because he had a Jewish body. Around this child's body, too young to wear an identifying badge or items of clothing distinct to Jewish men,[34] the partially integrated Norwich community of Christians and Jews had come together to betray the fragility of what divided them and the dangerous potential of sameness. The child himself, once claiming to be a Jew, stands for real possibilities of indistinguishability—just as, more deliberately, Sampson son of Samuel of Northampton in his Franciscan drag.

Jurnepin/Odard's growing and eventually decisively Christian body remains Judaized. His archived genitals, repeatedly examined and written about over the course of a decade and more, make this clear. Odard must always be the little "Jewish Boy" of his story, even as the national machines of king and church work at, and succeed in, making him Christian. His story and its Christian outcome depend on the ability of his body to signal both Jewishness and Christianness. The strange resonances between legal record, fictionalized historiography, and hagiography are not incidental. As Andrew Jacobs says of libelous narratives, the "body stolen away into illicit Jewish space was *already* imaginable as a circumcised, and therefore Judaized, male body."[35] The ideal Christian body was always a Jewish body, and Christians throughout the Middle Ages were increasingly expected to meditate on and imitate it. All stories of Jewish boys who turn out to be Christian are stories of the birth of Christianity.

CHAPTER I

The Same, but Not Quite

What does "Jew" mean? Who can say "I am Jewish," without a
shudder of the tongue and mind? Oh! This sentence and this verb to
be in the present, always in the present, they demand reflection.
—Hélène Cixous, *Portrait of Jacques Derrida*

"Jew" means to us (be assured this is true): the man who repents
inwardly in his heart before God and openly acknowledges his sins
before man.
—Orrm, *Orrmulum*

What Is a Jew? Contradictions and English Definitions

Speaking at the Modern Language Association Convention in Vancouver in
2015, Barbara Newman, while addressing her work on the parodic anti-Jewish
commemorative poem "The Passion of the Jews of Prague," wondered aloud:
"How can the Jews stand for the suffering Christ *and* the stereotypical Jew?
Did any medieval person notice the contradiction?"[1] My answer to the latter
question is an emphatic yes. The conflation of Jewish suffering with Christian
suffering—and the conflation of Jewishness with the ideal of Christ—could
work affectively and intellectually precisely because of the contradiction. Not
only did medieval Christian writers notice the contradiction between the stereotyped postbiblical Jew and the well-understood Jewish identity of Christ,
but they exploited it. They used their identitarian connection with Christ *and* a
theological opposition between Christ and living Jews to create emotional re-

sponses to Jews and Jewish characters. The Jewishness of Christ could be as much a matter of *imitatio* as humility or poverty, as much a topic for anguished cross-temporal connection as the sight of baby boys in the street, in whom Margery Kempe famously saw Jesus.[2] The model Jews of Christ's life and the early church, too, provided not only a way to identify with Jews and claim a Jewish self for Christians, but also a way to reject living Jews or postbiblical Jewish characters as perversions of self. My question is how awareness of the contradiction, and its implicit demand for an *imitatio Judaei*, might inform Christian definitions of "Jew" and "Jewish."

Stories like those of Jurnepin/Odard of Norwich or the Marian miracle tale known as the "The Jewish Boy," wherein a Christian boy becomes Christlike by first being Jewish, can be seen as inversions of libelous stories like those told around William of Norwich, Hugh of Lincoln, or the little chorister of Chaucer's "Prioress's Tale," wherein a Christian boy becomes Christ-like by first suffering martyrdom at Jewish hands. These story types offer two approaches to the same problem—it is not accidental that Matthew Paris collapsed them when he fictionalized the Jurnepin/Odard case—and the apparent contradiction of Christian-Jewish likeness is central to both. As with other stories of Christian/Jewish boys in medieval England, Jurnepin/Odard is a fraught site of interpretation because he highlights rather than deflects the prominence of likeness. He becomes a focus of community definition because of his initial likeness to Jews and his consequent ambiguity. As many scholars have pointed out, young or adolescent boys are sites of potential, and polemics around them frequently engage communal concepts of identity formation and reproductive futurity;[3] not fully actualized, and privileged by their gender, boys are opportunities for negotiation and becoming.[4] Denise Despres has argued, for instance, that little William of Norwich's age at death spoke to twelfth-century understandings of spiritual formation and maturity, especially in the monastic context. When Thomas of Monmouth, the Benedictine author of the *Life and Passion of William of Norwich*, says that little William was twelve when Jews killed him in 1144, he engages twelfth-century ecclesiastical authorities who claimed twelve as the age when personhood and personality were formed.[5] William's age is also a deliberate *imitatio Christi* in Despres's view, evoking the twelve-year-old Jesus when he was found in the Temple disputing the rabbis (Luke 2:41–52).[6] William could be a martyr like Christ because he had reached the pivotal age where such (Jewish) spiritual discretion was possible.

In Jurnepin/Odard's case, eighty-seven years later in the same city, the age of five likely had special significance to the Jewish community's understanding of spiritual formation. In thirteenth-century Ashkenazi Jewish tradition, five was the age of school initiation, when a boy was ritually transferred from the care of women to the care of male teachers to learn Hebrew and Torah. This included (suggestively in Jurnepin/Odard's case but perhaps only coincidentally) a ceremony in which the boy was wrapped in a prayer shawl and carried to his teacher, then led to a riverbank to see the rushing flow of the river as the flow of a lifetime of learning Torah.[7] To claim a boy at this age, from a thirteenth-century Jewish perspective, would either allow him to begin a Jewish life or keep him from it.

For both Jews and Christians, in other words, the male child was the seed of distinct identity and learning, a person in the act of becoming, and therefore a vehicle through which one could, at least for a time, identify with the other. In medieval Christian legends, libels, and associated legal cases—as becomes true for Jurnepin/Odard—the boy also resonates with the Christ-child, especially in the potential of the Jewish male to become or reflect the idealized Jewish/Christian body of Christ. If, as Carolyn Dinshaw and Steven Kruger have noted, medieval anxieties about bodily similarity and segregation "were based on some conviction that Jewish and Saracen bodies were different from Christian bodies,"[8] then Jurnepin/Odard's circumcision case answers, by contrast, how little difference was perceived between Jews and Christians, even in the face of marked bodily difference. Indeed, the balancing conviction that Jewish and Christian bodies could be the same is vital to the case's polemical retellings and violent conclusions. For such a body to be Christ-like, as Matthew Paris makes it, it must also remain a Jewish body. The Jewish-Christian doubling that we usually understand to be, by definition, the stuff of typology thus reveals itself also in legal record and historiography around living Jews and in the literary manipulation of postbiblical Jewish characters. If we explore the large range of what "Jew" and "Jewish" can mean to English writers and thinkers in this light, we find that the theological pressure of twinned religious identities plays with power dynamics in ways that make the usual understandings of exclusion and antithesis less tenable.

Sampson son of Samuel of Northampton makes a good case study in this regard: the Jew dressed as a Christian preacher who must be stripped down to his marked, bodily Jewishness yet made to mean Christianly, paraded through English cities on the eve of the Expulsion like a relic of the prodigal son, a fantastical staging of Christian and state domination, and linked indelibly to English institutions and record making. His story matters from both a figural and a historical perspective. It is literally and emotionally visceral, connected to real bodies (human and animal) and to aggressive acts of Christian interpretation. In studying the dynamics of Christian-Jewish representation in the medieval past, Sampson reminds us that the figural can be imposed on the historical and the Christian on the Jew. The *figura*, the figure or type taken up in typology, as Erich Auerbach defined it, vacillates between historical event and its fulfillment in interpretation; it "attaches truth . . . to historical, earthly events," and any "figural structure preserves the historical event while interpreting it as revelation; and must preserve it in order to interpret it."[9] While it may be unusual to read a legal record for a figural structure, it does seem that Archbishop Kilwardby tried to place the *figura*, as a spiritual act of interpretation, atop Sampson son of Samuel, and that he did so because Sampson's Jewish body and its resistance could not be left to their literal meaning: Sampson looked and spoke *like a Christian*. This being true, he had to be fulfilled interpretively, so that the medieval English Jew, the repentant Israelite, and the prodigal son could make meaning together. Kilwardby's punishment asks Sampson to enter the Christian fold, to return to the moment of Christian-Jewish overlap, when right belief, not just a simulacrum or ersatz representation, was possible.

Sameness has a polemical use in such negotiations that has received insufficient attention. The concept of a polemic focused on sameness is necessary to a case like Sampson's: the Exchequer scribe's account of the Jewish friar and his punishment forces recognition of both Sampson's ability to be seen as a Christian and Kilwardby's struggle to harmonize his similarities and differences with the expectations of Christian viewers. The facts are that Sampson could look and speak like a friar; a sheriff could resist king and archbishop in enforcing a punishment that sought to undo and reinterpret this performance of similarity; one Jewish man could stand in for another; an archbishop and a king could redress a seeming Christian in a different costume and make him a bodily and figuratively meaningful Jew. What Kilwardby and Edward I would have lost had they sentenced Sampson to execution was the opportunity to make him Jewish, and the devised punishment would be unnecessary without the fact and possibility of Jewish-Christian sameness.

A figural structure—a reading of signs and resistance to signs, the laying of costumes (Jewish and Christian) and temporalities (Old and New Testament times, thirteenth-century England) on top of one another—adheres to the Jewish Exchequer's account of Sampson's crime. How otherwise do we reconcile his Christian likeness with the need to display him as a (Christianized) Jew? I see the punishment Kilwardby tried to impose, within its particular historical moment, as typological in its yearnings if not its textual framework—and I freely admit that my reading helps me to think of Sampson as an activist responding to the polemical positions of men exactly like Kilwardby. I imagine Sampson was a man who knew he risked his life to critique the chimera of friars' attempts to convert Jews. I imagine his costume and speech were designed to show how small and illusory the boundaries between Christian and Jew were, how one could easily fake religious identity, how similarity is so close to difference, even as the Northampton Jews were being mercilessly taxed, rounded up on coin-clipping charges, and escorted from their homes because the Northampton *archa* had been closed in the wake of the 1275 Statute of the Jewry; Sampson lived in the midst of what Joe and Caroline Hillaby have labeled "the community in crisis."[10] I imagine that he was irreverent and angry, and that Sheriff Gilbert de Kirkeby helped his Jewish countrymen evade punishment in this and other cases, as indeed the Jewish Exchequer rolls suggest. One wants to see noncon-formity and resistance in deplorable histories.

The most remarkable outcome of my figural reading of Sampson son of Samuel, nevertheless, is that neither his mode of resistance (dressing and speak-ing like a Christian) nor the prescribed punishment (Kilwardby's insistence on particular biblical types for Sampson) are about Christian/Jewish dichotomy. The figural identities imposed on Sampson return him not to the stereotypical negative and grotesque representations of Jewishness evident in many medieval Christian representations of Jewish men, but to moments of choice and further potential likeness. Sampson does not fit, neither in his crime nor in his assigned penance, into dichotomous roles. He is neither the good Jew nor the bad Jew, that is, neither the Old Testament righteous subsumed into a Christian salvific order nor the post-Crucifixion deicide doomed to repeat acts of disbelief and deception in tales and exempla perpetual. In his allusions to the prodigal son and the golden calf, Kilwardby places Sampson, rather, at historical pivot points, crossroads where Israel had the chance to repent or recognize Christ. The parable figure of the prodigal sets him after the incarnation but before the Crucifixion, temporally in the space of Christ's ministry; the golden calf and the naked people of Israel set him in a pre-Christian history, between the break-ing of the first tablets and the new giving of the Law to Moses, and admit an unbroken ancestral line between Jews and Christians. Sampson's action, his would-be punishment, and the nature of its recording combine to display the multitemporal and multitextual struggles of history and representation with which Christian anti-Jewish rhetoric so often contends.

This is not just semantic play—or if it is, it is a play that we may consider self-consciously performed by medieval writers and artists. Thomas of Monmouth, for instance, is as quick to make Jews of Christians as he is to make of little William of Norwich a Christ. Not only does he question whether William's abductor, ostensibly a cook in the Norwich archdeacon's kitchen, is Jewish or Christian—"christianum nescio siue iudeum" (I know not whether a Christian or a Jew)[11]—and therefore very early in his *Life and Passion of William of Norwich* emphasizes Christian/Jewish indistinguishability, but he also Judaizes those who associate with Jews. The Norwich sheriff, for instance, whom Thomas deems an ally and "iudeorum defensorem" (protector of the Jews), dies after "per posteriora eius sanguis guttatim profluere inchoauit" (drops of blood began to flow, drop by drop, from his posterior).[12] This description aligns the sheriff with medieval physiognomical tracts and exempla that claimed Jewish men suffered from hemorrhoidal or menstrual-like bleeding,[13] and, more explicitly for Thomas, it aligns the sheriff with the bloody stain of Jewish guilt for the Crucifixion: "Adeoque diuina circa cum claruit ultio" (And so divine vengeance showed itself upon him), declares Thomas, "ut reuera cum iudeis dicere et ipse possit: *Sanguis innocens super nos et super filios nostros*" (so he himself could truly say with the Jews, "His innocent blood be upon us and our children").[14] Christian readers who doubt his claims are also castigated with terms he uses elsewhere to describe Jews, even as he fashions himself as "alter Dauid ex aduerso concurrens" (a second David . . . rushing ahead from my ranks).[15] Thomas evidences a familiar divide between the Old Testament "Jewish" righteous and post-Crucifixion living Jews, but William's young body, imitating Christ's, becomes the suffering Jewish body between them.

Thomas of Monmouth's facility with blurring the lines of Jewishness—so that Christians can become contemporary Jews by virtue of allegiance, he can become a new King David, a Norwich archdeacon's cook can feasibly be Jewish, and William's body can be Christ's—shows just how aware he is of the contradiction between the suffering Jewish Christ and the stereotyped Jews he fashions. His manipulation of sameness and difference, wherein an unsettling of the two is polemically productive, even uses this contradiction to suggest a national expulsion a hundred years before one actually happens. Thomas imagines that the Norwich Jews, among themselves, must have worked to hide William's body, because otherwise, as he ventriloquizes through his own "Jewish" voice, "profecto improuidentie nostre, culpa non immerito genus nostrum . . . ab Anglie partibus funditus exterminabitur" (due to our lack of foresight, and not undeservedly, our people will . . . be totally eliminated from the realm of England).[16] This seemingly prophetic statement is not a post-Expulsion interpolation; it was written around the year 1200 in the unique surviving manuscript of the *Life and Passion of William of Norwich*.[17] The idea that a crucifixion by Jews will lead to an expulsion is most likely, rather, a plot trope associated with medieval Christian stories of the destruction of the Second Temple, wherein the conquest of Jerusalem is a just consequence of the Crucifixion and results in the exile of Jews from Judea.[18] Thomas's text puts Jewish desire for homeland alongside anxiety over exile, as if these are the predictable outcomes of the crucifixion of a Christ-child. As Miri Rubin has put it, Thomas "remade Christian history in a contemporary English city."[19] In his reimagining of the death of a Christian boy, accordingly, he fantasizes a reenactment of the destruction of a Jewish homeland (England) and the beginning of a new diaspora.

Such fantasies of Jewish infiltration and national expulsion sit on a continuum of historical, legal, and religious polemic. Homi Bhabha's concept of colonial "mimicry" is applicable: "Mimicry is the desire for a reformed, recognizable Other, *as a subject of a difference that is almost the same, but not quite.*"[20] English texts and images in this period, even records of historical events, that simultaneously double the Jew, supersede the Jew, other the Jew, *and* claim ancestral or spiritual continuity with the Jew are working with both the "resemblance and the menace" of mimicry,[21] not unlike what Bhabha sees in later colonial texts. The situation of medieval Anglo-Jews, whose history and scripture is necessary to a functioning Christian theology but, in their time and place, is also grafted onto Jewish bodies contributing to the national economy and protected by the Crown, fits Bhabha's arguments for how mimicry develops as a reflex of and response to state systems, as "a complex strategy of reform, regulation, and discipline, which 'appropriates' the Other as it visualizes power."[22] We might see Sampson of Northampton as someone who mimics his colonizers, but the direction of exchange (as Bhabha allows) ultimately goes both ways: the results are "a disavowal that denies the differences of the other but produces in its stead forms of authority."[23] Anglo-Christian authors writing before and around the 1290 Expulsion show a related elasticity of concept in representation of Jews and Jewishness. The inherent contradictions of sameness and difference, resemblance and distinction, are activated in service of appropriative power, to define and delimit the correct Christian self. It is an aggressive act to argue or imply, or even play with the idea, that Jew and Christian are interchangeable. It makes little space for the actual Jewish bodies that England expels and whose expulsion it must continue to rationalize and justify. There is a narcissistic pathology at the root of this first national expulsion of Jews; when only self-definition matters, all space is occupied by the self.

Indeed, "Jew" and "Jewish" are continually redefined in this era to suggest the possibility of Jewishness to Christians, and the rhetorical acrobatics required to create Christian-Jewish sameness in Christian polemical literature depend on what "Jew" means to those using the term. It does not, of course, mean the same thing at all times. As Cynthia Baker has recently made clear, the key word "Jew" has, for much of its history and in many languages, been a debated term of alterity, always already difficult to define:

> What is it about this particular identity term—*Jew*—such that it can be made to convey so broad a range of often diametrically opposed meanings? *Jew* has served as a cipher for materialism *and* intellectualism, socialism *and* capitalism, worldly cosmopolitanism *and* clannish parochialism, eternal chosenness *and* unending curse—and the list goes on. What is the fascination and phobia of *Jew*, and whence does the word derive such persistent malleability and power throughout history and across continents[?][24]

Medieval use of the terms "Jew" and "Jewish" could also function paradoxically, and then, as now, definitional rhetoric runs amok when political or religious, let alone actual, lives are at stake. Baker offers that Jewish "owning" of the word has been persistently difficult: "For most of two long millennia, the word *Jew* has been predominantly defined as a term of *not-self.* . . . *Jew(s)*—signifier and signified, word and connotations—has become a constant element not only in the historical formation and formulation of Western (Christian and post-Christian) identities but also of the categories by which the contours of identity are articulated."[25] Leonard Cohen's short, sarcastic poem "Not a Jew" answers this problem efficiently: "Anyone who says / I'm not a Jew / is not a Jew / I'm very sorry / but this decision / is final."[26] Cleverly playing with definitional identity through simultaneous yes/no claims, Cohen suggests that *he* owns the term and those who seek to delimit it should be regarded with suspicion or pity. In medieval England, some Christian thinkers who explored the contours of "Jew" through notions of both self *and* not-self might have agreed.

The problem is not new. Biblical scholars know this well. In June 2014, for instance, *Marginalia Review of Books* published an article by Adele Reinhartz in which she expressed concerns over translation of the New Testament Greek *Ioudaios* as "Judean" rather than "Jew," a move that emphasizes ethnogeographic rather than religious identity. She worried that this translation, technically more correct and usually intended to lessen the anti-Jewish tenor of the

Gospels, especially the Gospel of John, nonetheless performs an odd erasure; "Judean" does not cover the nuances of the Greek or allow for a historical presence of religiously identified Jews.[27] The lively debate that ensued prompted *Marginalia* to publish a Forum on the issue, with many important voices in biblical studies weighing in (Reinhartz, Steven Mason, Daniel Schwartz, Annette Yoshiko Reed, Joan Taylor, Malcolm Lowe, Jonathan Klawans, Ruth Sheridan, James Crossley), all arguing responsibly about the weighty intellectual and cultural work of history and translation, especially where marginalized, persecuted, diasporic, and historically evolving identities are involved.[28] Klawans pointed out that the problem may be a particularly English-language one, and that the debate has ideological edges too, more to do with claims to historical continuity with Jews and the Holy Land than with accurate translation: "Ethno-religious-cultural fluidity appears in full force by the Second Temple period," he argues, and "the [English] term 'Jew' has been and will continue to be perfectly adequate to convey this complexity."[29] In the summer of 2017, *Marginalia* published another Forum continuing the debate in light of Baker's study, with contributions from more eminent scholars of religious studies and a response from Baker herself; she concludes the second Forum by quoting from her book's introduction: "One final word on *Jew*: there is, of course, no final word on *Jew*."[30]

As David Nirenberg has pointed out, however, it is clear that the words we use to designate Jews and Jewishness matter in ways that are both historically and linguistically rooted *and* transhistorically unrooted: "We all know that . . . *Jew* is not the same as *Hebrew*, *Israelites* are not Israelis, *Israeli* need not mean Zionist or Jew (or vice versa), and many who have been called "Jew" or "Judaizer" in no way identify with Judaism at all. Yet all of these and numerous other words exist in close proximity . . . and have so often bled together across the long history of thought."[31] In medieval England too, the word "Jew" could bleed. One can find many medieval texts wherein Old Testament Israelites coexist with their stereotyped foil, the deicidal post-Crucifixion Jew who refuses to accept Christ. One can also frequently find, unsurprisingly, historical or literary medieval Jews and Christians set in antagonistic relationship to each other. But more nuanced in the medieval corpus, and not necessarily less frequent, are attempts to trouble distinctions and denotations and make "Jew" and "Jewish" exist as, or in close proximity to, "Christian." It is reasonable, furthermore, to wonder whether claims to the Holy Land and historical identification with Jews, which Klawans rightly flags as important contexts of definition and usage, were functioning in the English language even in the Middle Ages. What kind of fluidities and complexities were already working in the word "Jew" for early English-language writers who produced their work alongside Jewish communities in England and within a crusading Western world?

Wherever the Christian definition of "Jew" is fluid, the issue for Christians is the establishment of a theologically "Jewish" line. At stake is the claim that Christians are the *real* descendants of the chosen Israelites; they are the Jews who made the right choice. This need for ancestral connection is sometimes coupled with a desire for the conversion of Jews, a fantasy of assimilation that can nevertheless be construed as a longed-for unity with those who share scripture and have deep religio-historical connections with Christians. Such discourse can present itself as philosemitic. It is not intellectually far removed from present-day American evangelical support of the State of Israel;[32] "allosemitic" may be a better word to contain this kind of rhetoric or its underlying motivation, because its logic requires "Jew" and "Christian" to shift and merge into one another even as it continues to depend on a narrative of Jewish obstinance, incorrectness, and vulnerability.[33] This is especially true of texts that pause on moments of Christian potential or sameness before turning to more obviously anti-Jewish vitriol, where the polemical point is to showcase the relative ease of right belief and so necessarily to emphasize the likeness of Jews and Christians, the ability of one or the other to change places through internal (invisible) rather than external (visible) signs. A Jew might begin a story as a Jew and end it as a Christian with nothing more than a shift in faith. This is the eschatological hope, and the basic plot of many medieval miracle stories involving Jews.[34]

I have come to think of such narratives as reflections of what one early Middle English writer framed as "Nathaniel's choice." The twelfth-century Augustinian homilist Orrm—whom Michael Clanchy has called the man who "pioneered English verse"[35]—reads the first chapter of the Gospel of John as a story about how the good Jew is also the good Christian: the disciple Nathaniel, a Jewish man of great learning in Orrm's estimation, first questions whether any good can come out of Nazareth but then accepts Jesus. For Orrm, this signals a combination of ideal Jewishness and ideal Christianness, and Nathaniel thereby becomes the occasion to provide the first explicit definition of the word "Jew" in the English language: as the epigraph to this chapter shows, Orrm defines "Jew" as a word that seems to mean "good Christian."

His long metrical sermon collection—called the *Orrmulum* "forrþi þatt Orrm it wrohhte" (because Orrm made it)—was finished by 1180.[36] It is a text best known for its linguistic idiosyncrasies, famously signaled by Orrm's unusual doubling of consonants and precocious insistence on a correct English orthography, but it is also a work that, throughout, is preoccupied with explanation of the relationship of Christians to Jewish scripture and history, and occasionally to living Jews. The *Orrmulum* was a massive undertaking: a verse translation of the lections for the full liturgical year with explanatory sermons accompanying each. Only about two-thirds of a first volume survives, however, or approximately one-eighth of the planned work, in Orrm's own hand, as Bod. MS Junius 1.[37] The sermons in it are organized historically rather than strictly liturgically, beginning with Luke 1 and jumping to other Gospels and eventually into the Acts of the Apostles as the time line demands. Because of this organization, the work is sometimes characterized as an early "Life of Christ,"[38] but it was not intended to be this in any generic sense; if all of the work survived—as Orrm's own "contents list" of pericopes suggests—it would have continued through the Acts of the Apostles, progressing chronologically rather than liturgically or biographically.[39] Orrm's primary organizational concern was the historical continuity of Christianity and the growth of the church, and in this he wanted his readers and listeners to understand themselves and their own religious practice in relationship to what he presents as an essentially Jewish story. As James Morey correctly notes, "The explanations of how the Jews and their traditions fit into Orrm's own time are some of the most interesting features of the collection."[40]

In his opening double homily on Luke 1:5–25, for instance, it is difficult for Orrm to move past the first part of his first gospel verse without describing and explaining the priestly casts and duties outlined in Leviticus. Luke 1:5 begins "Fuit in diebus Herodis, regis Judææ, sacerdos quidam nomine Zacharias de vice Abia" (There was in the days of Herod, the king of Judea, a certain priest named Zachary, of the course of Abia), and this leads Orrm to a long tangent on the clothing and duties of "Jewish" priests, the sacrificial practices of the Second Temple period, and details of each type of burnt offering outlined in the opening chapters of Leviticus, which in turn become the main topic of his first double homily (lines 255–1797) and its Christian lesson. All of this, Orrm urges, is necessary to teach Christians "hu ȝe muȝhenn lakenn Godd / Gastlike i gode þæwess wiþþ all þatt Judewisshe lac / Þatt icc ȝuw habbe shæwedd" (how you can make sacrifice to God, spiritually, through good practices, in accordance with all the Jewish sacrifices I have shown you).[41] That is, from the beginning of his pastoral project, Orrm is interested in persuading the laity to continue Jewish practice and follow Jewish law within the Christian spiritual rubric. He wants, in other words, to communicate how one can be Jewish in a Christian way. This is so much the case through so much of the *Orrmulum* that one modern scholar has argued that Orrm must in fact be a converted Jew preaching to other Jews.[42]

Much as Orrm is concerned to define English as a written language in his text, through a self-devised orthographical system that he insists is correct, his use and definition of the words "Jew" (*Judew* in his early Middle English) and "Jewish" (*Judisskenn* or *Judewisshe*) are where he most explicitly tackles the existential and identitarian question of what it means to be an English Christian. The words are used throughout the *Orrmulum* equally to describe Old Testament Hebrews and Israelites back to Moses, first-century inhabitants of Jerusalem and Judea, Judah (the man and the tribe), and medieval Anglo-Jews. Such fluidity might seem either sloppy or unimportant—evidence of a degree of historical ignorance, or an accident of newly translating the Gospels into English, as Orrm was also doing in the composition of his metrical sermons, since all begin with a passage from the Gospels or Acts—but Orrm invites such fluidity at key points and in service of didactic goals. His imprecision is deployed in redefinition of the words themselves, in order to make an argument that good Christians are good Jews and Jews are potentially good Christians. His destabilization of the meaning of "Jew" is overt. It is necessary to his arguments about how Christian identity works.

The most significant passage in which Orrm clearly applies this method—his reading of the disciple Nathaniel that I mentioned above—is one in which he redefines "Israelite" to mean "Jew," and "Jew" to mean something like "good Christian practice." In his homily on John 1:35–51, where he offers explication of Jesus's meeting with Nathaniel, whom Jesus calls "a true Israelite" ("vere Israhelita" in the Vulgate), Orrm writes:

> Natanaæl wass swiþe depe læredd
> Onn all þatt hallȝe boc þatt wass þurrh Drihhtin sett onn erþe
> Þurrh Moysæsess hande writt.
> ...
> ꝥ Crist sahh þatt he comm ꝥ cwaþþ till þa þatt neh himm
>   wærenn,
> Loc here nehȝeþþ toward me forr me to sen ꝥ herenn,
> An soþ Israelisshe mann þatt niss nan fakenn inne.
> Crist let wel off Natanaæl ꝥ cwaþþ, loc here uss nehȝheþþ
> An soþ Issraelisshe mann: þatt wass alls iff he seȝȝde,
> An duhhtiȝ Judewisshe mann iss þiss þatt here uss nehȝeþþ,
> For þurrh þatt lare þatt he cann he seþ ꝥ underrstanndeþþ

Hu mann birrþ lefenn upponn Godd ⁊ lufenn himm ⁊ þewwtenn
⁊ affterr þatt he seþ he doþ ⁊ gaþ þe rihhte we33e.
Forr Issraæl tacneþþ þatt mann, þatt witt tu wel to soþe,
Þatt seþ wiþþ herrtess e3he Godd ⁊ þewwteþþ þess te bettre.
⁊ swillc wass þiss Natanaæl, þatt we nu mælenn ummbe.
⁊ Judew tacneþþ uss þatt mann, þatt witt tu wel to soþe,[43]
Þatt innwarrdli3 biforrenn Godd birewwseþþ inn hiss herrte
⁊ opennli3 biforenn mann annd3æteþþ hiss missdede. (13562–66,
13602–33)[44]

Nathaniel was very deeply learned in the whole holy book written by
Moses' hand, which was put on earth by the Lord.... And Christ saw
him coming and said to those who were near him, "Look, here comes
toward me, for people to see and hear, a true Israelite in whom there is
no deception." Christ thought well of Nathaniel and said, "Look,
here comes toward us a true Israelite." That was as if he said, "A great
Jewish man comes toward us here, for, through that learning that he
has, he sees and understands how man ought to believe in God and
love and serve him—and according to what he sees, he does, and he
goes the right way." For "Israel" means (be assured this is true): the
man who sees God with the eye of his heart and serves him thus the
better. And such was this Nathaniel of whom we now speak. And
"Jew" means to us (be assured this is true): the man who repents
inwardly in his heart before God and openly acknowledges his sins
before man.

Shortly after giving these inclusive definitions of "Israel" and "Jew," however,
Orrm contrasts Nathaniel to other Jews who might have or should have recognized Christ:

⁊ her mann unnderrstanndenn ma33, 3iff mann itt
   ummbeþenkeþþ,
Hu þatt Judisskenn laþe follc þatt henngde Crist o rode
Wass þurrh þe laþe gastess mahht forbundenn ⁊ forrblendedd,
Þatt sahh ⁊ herrde da33whammli3 hallf ferþe 3er þe Laferrd
A33 spellenn god ⁊ a33 don god onn alle kinne wise
⁊ tohh swa þehh ne keppte himm nohht to lufenn ne to
   trowwenn,

Acc sloȝhenn himm þurrh hete ˥ niþ all gilltelæs o rode.
˥ tiss Natanaæl forrþrihht toc upponn Crist to lefenn,
Forrþrihht i stede son summ he sahh Crist ˥ herrde himm
    mælenn. (13764–87)

And here [in Nathaniel] one can understand, if one thinks about it,
how the evil Jewish people who hung Christ on a cross were bound
and blinded through the power of the evil spirit—they who, daily for
three and a half years, saw and heard the Lord, always preaching good
and always doing good in all kinds of ways, and nevertheless they
considered him nothing to love nor believe in but slew him, totally
innocent, through hate and enmity, on the cross! But this Nathaniel
righteously accepted Christ, righteously, on the spot, as soon as he
saw Christ and heard him speak.

The implication is that any Jew, at least any learned Jew, might have done what
Nathaniel did in quickly acknowledging Christ, but instead, through blinding
and binding by the devil, other Jews became the "laþe folcc þatt henngde Crist"
(evil people who hanged Christ). The contrast developed through this reading
of the Gospel story, however, should not lead us to conclude that antithesis between Nathaniel (the *true* Israelite, the *great Jewish man*) and living Jews is
Orrm's ultimate point. Rather, both categories of Jewishness matter for him,
and he wants both categories to be recognizable and meaningful to his audience. It is fundamental to Orrm's didactic methods that one possible model of
Jewishness looks exactly like Christianness.

Orrm's insistence on using the words "Jew" and "Jewish" across time and
space, and for both of his Jewish types, allows him to maintain and use both
sides of his contrast and give both, paradoxically, an imaginative life in relation to the other. Based on his definitional propositions around the Nathaniel story, we can parse his argument this way: to say someone is an Israelite is
the same as saying he is a Jew; to say someone is a *true* Israelite ("an soþ Issrae-
lisshe mann") is the same as saying he is "a great Jewish man" (an duhhtiȝ Judewisshe mann); and the man who acts "according to what he sees . . . and
goes the right way" is the definition of "a great Jewish man." In the same semantic scope, and audaciously disconnecting the words from their Hebrew
denotations, Orrm claims further that "Israel" means "the man who sees God
with the eye of his heart and serves him thus the better" and that "Jew" on its
own denotes "the man who repents inwardly in his heart before God and

openly answers for his sins before man." Yet, after these positive redefinitions, which together sound very much like working definitions of the ideal Christian, Orrm moves quickly to the problem of "þatt Judisskenn laþe follc þatt henngde Crist o rode" (the evil Jewish people who hung Christ on the cross), as if to invite confusion about the lexical values of his key words and ensure that his audience is *simultaneously* thinking of an admirable "great Jewish man" and stereotypes of evil contemporary Jews—either to underscore, or to create slippage and possibility between, past and present, even future, categories of Christian Jewishness.

Indeed elsewhere, in his homily on the wedding at Cana (John 2:1–11), Orrm reiterates that the definitional issue is a matter of parsing Jewish and Christian understanding, exegesis, and practice across time *and* a matter of glossing the word "Jew" in a specifically English, presentist context. In considering why the evangelist might point out that the water pots at the wedding in Cana were there for ritual washing "secundum purificatione Judaeorum" (according to the manner of the purifying of the Jews) (John 2:6), he reasons that since nothing in the Gospels is extraneous, we must, hearing this, think seriously about how Jewish practice signifies. He gives a reading, then, that attempts to account for both Jewish and Christian understanding of the ritual but ultimately serves as a further gloss on "Jew":

> ⁊ witt tu wel þatt nollde nohht þe Goddspellwrihhte mælenn
> Off þatt te Judewisshe follc hemm wesshenn swa wiþþutenn
> Off swillke fetless ȝiff þatt he ne wisste whatt it shollde
> Bitacnenn eȝȝþerr hemm ⁊ uss to sen ⁊ tunnderrstanndenn.
> Itt tacneþþ till Judisskenn follc þatt all þatt witeȝhungge
> Þatt hallȝe witess writenn hemm inn alle þeȝȝre timess
> Wass hemm bitahht þurrh Godd, forr hemm to clennsenn ⁊ to
>   bæwenn
> Off all þatt teȝȝ missdidenn þa, wiþþ bodiȝ ⁊ wiþþ sawle.
> ⁊ uss it tacneþþ þatt uss maȝȝ full wel inn ure time
> All Goddess lare off eȝȝþerr boc, off þalde ⁊ off þe newe,
> Clennsenn off all þatt ifell iss, ȝiff þatt wet willenn follȝhenn,
> ⁊ innwarrdlike ⁊ illke daȝȝ anndgætenn ure sinness,
> ⁊ lofenn Godd ⁊ wurrþenn Godd ⁊ lufenn Godd ⁊ þewwtenn,
> Forr baþe tacneþþ uss Judew, þatt word on Ennglissh spæche,
> Þatt uss birrþ lofenn Godd ⁊ rihht anndgætenn ure sinness.
> (15140–69)

And understand well that the gospel writer would not speak of the fact that the Jewish people thus cleanse their bodies from such vessels if he did not know what it should mean—either for them or for us to see and understand. It signifies to Jewish people that all the prophecy that holy prophets wrote for them in their times was given to them by God: that they should be purified and made clean of all they did wrong then, in body and in soul. And for us it signifies that we can very well, in our time, purify all God's teaching, from either book, from the old or from the new, of all that is wicked, if we will follow it and inwardly, and each day, acknowledge our sins, and praise God, and honor God, and love and serve God. For both signify for us "Jew," that word in the English tongue: that we ought to praise God and rightly acknowledge our sins.

This glossing of "Jew" clearly evokes Orrm's previous definition, but it also refines and connects "Jew" to an explicitly vernacular understanding. Though the syntax is difficult here—as if Orrm himself has lost track of his words—he shows that he is thinking about Jewish and Christian temporality ("in their times" and "then" versus "in our time"), the necessity of supersessionist exegesis ("the prophets" who wrote "in their times" versus the Christian ability now to read "either book, from the old or from the new"), and about interlingual understanding. Orrm introduces the Hebraic meaning of "Jew," etymologically linked to "Judah" (*yehudah*), meaning "praise," but hooks this to his prior denotation as well: "Jew" is, also or still, the person who acknowledges sin and pays attention to an inner spiritual life. When he finally declares that "baþe tacneþþ uss Judew" (both signify for us "Jew"), it is difficult to be certain of the referent for "baþe"—both Jewish and Christian significations? both the Old and the New Testaments? both us and them?—but the slippage itself is significant. *Both* signify: for Orrm, there is a doubleness to the definition of "Jew" and to his notion of Christian scriptural and practical identity. Correct Christian understanding and practice will make Jew and Christian almost indistinguishable. His Englishing project is thus bound up in his aim to "purify" the Hebrew word and the Testaments of "wicked" (read: singularly Jewish or literal) interpretation, even as it teaches that Jewishness is actually Christianness. Correct *English* translation will gloss "Jew" as a Christian inhabitation of Jewishness, and only with false translation and interpretation, which leads to wicked choices and limited understanding, does the English word "Jew" become a category of negative difference.

Orrm implies, with these definitions and rationales, not only that contemporary Anglo-Jews do not know what "Jew" really means, but also that Christians can be like the disciple Nathaniel; Christians can be great Jews. In this implicit equation, it is important that Orrm is not unaware of or unthinking about living, practicing Jews. He is able, at other places in his work, to offer more standard vitriol against the living Jews who are his countrymen. In this comment, for instance, which comes after a list of miracles Christ performed during his ministry on earth, Orrm writes in a *contra Judaeos* mode familiar in Western theological writing by the late twelfth century:

> All þuss ꝺ tuss he [i.e., Christ] did god amang Judisskenn lede,
> Amang þatt illke laþe follc þatt he was borenn offe.
> ꝺ tohh swa þeȝȝ tokenn himm wiþþutenn hise gillte
> ꝺ cwaldenn himm o rodetre þurrh þeȝȝre depe sinne.
> ꝺ itt comm hefiȝlike onn hemm þurrh Godess rihhte wræche,
> Onn alle þa þatt nohht nass off to betenn ohht tatt sinne.
> ꝺ Godd Allmahhtiȝ ȝife uss swa to betenn ure sinness. (15520–30)

> In all these ways he did good among the Jewish people—among that same evil people from whom he was born—but nevertheless they seized him, with no evidence of his guilt, and killed him on the cross because of their profound sin. And, through God's righteous vengeance, it bears heavily on them, on all those who were not inclined to beat out that sin. And God Almighty allow us to thus strike at our sins.

But even here Orrm is working to maintain a paradox, a contrast that always suggests a likeness. He subtly aligns his Christian audience with "that same evil people from whom [Christ] was born" even as he harshly criticizes them. Though Modern English translation has difficulty with Orrm's repetitions and consequent verbal echoes, the repetition of "betenn" in the final lines of this passage (some Jews did not "betenn ohht" their sins and recognize Christ, and Christians should pray to "betenn" their sins in this way) suggests simultaneously that some Jews can repent and choose to be Christians and that some Christians may turn out to be like present-day Jews, if they do not beat away their sins.

It is perhaps this kind of qualification, or the identifications with Jewishness evidenced in his Nathaniel and Cana readings, that has made David Lawton describe Orrm as an author whose "handling of the relationship between Judaism and Christianity is unusually free from vindictive superiority,"[45] but the case is just the opposite. The identification with Jewishness, and even the ability to claim it, depend absolutely on the assumption of Christian superiority. Orrm's anti-Jewish rhetoric is too often tinged with vindictiveness to divorce it from his contrasting positions on what constitutes positive Jewishness or Christian Jewishness. Even when he organizes his first homily around teaching Christians "Jewish sacrifices," as noted above, he is clear about the temporal and definitional games that must be played to maintain Christian continuity with Jews and indeed to maintain his own English definition of "Jew." In an attempt to clarify why he will explain Temple sacrifices or discuss "Jewish" practice at all, for instance, Orrm writes:

> ⁊ *nu* icc wile shæwenn ȝuw summ del, wiþþ Godess hellpe,
> Off þatt Judisskenn follkess lac þatt Drihhtin *wass* full cweme
> ⁊ mikell hellpe to þe follc, to læredd ⁊ to læwedd,
> *Biforrenn* þatt te Laferrd Crist wass borenn her to manne.
> Acc *nu* ne geȝȝneþþ itt hemm nohht to winnenn *eche* blisse
> Þohh þatt teȝȝ stanndenn daȝȝ ⁊ nihht to þeowwtenn Godd ⁊
>   lakenn,
> For all itt iss onnȝæness Godd, þohh þatt teȝȝ swa ne wenenn,
> Forrþi þatt teȝȝ ne kepenn nohht noff Crist noff Cristess
>   moderr. (962–77)

And *now* I will show you some part, with God's help, of the Jewish people's sacrifice, which *was* fully pleasing to the Lord and a great help to the people, to learned and to unlearned, *before* Christ the Lord was born here as a man. But *now* it profits them nothing as far as earning *eternal* joy—even if they stand day and night to serve and sacrifice to God—for all of it is against God, though they do not think so, because they do not care at all about Christ nor about Christ's mother. (emphasis mine)

Splitting familiar supersessionist hairs, Orrm claims the superiority of Christianity in spite of the priority of Judaism. Before he teaches how Christians can continue to act "wiþþ all þatt Judewisshe lac" (in accordance with all the Jewish sacrifices) (1120–21), he must clarify that Jewish practice can only be understood historically, and only in relation to Christianity. It *was* good and pleasing to God in the past, *before* Christ came, but the Jews *now*, in the same *now* in which he preaches, are damned *eternally* regardless of their own quotidian continuity of practice. In the same work in which he counsels Christians to understand and continue Jewish practice and repetitively redefines the word "Jew" to signify good Christian practice, that is, Orrm also consigns living Jews to a practice cyclically out of time and devoid of understanding.

It is worth taking a moment to emphasize—as Orrm carefully delineates before-time, now-time, and eternal-time, and redefines the basic meanings of "Israel" and "Jew" for his congregants—that he preached to congregations in Lincolnshire, perhaps in Bourne near Stamford, which had an established Jewish community by the time he was composing and still revising his work,[46] and that Stamford's community was significant enough to be one of seventeen Anglo-Jewish communities formally recognized by Henry III's 1218 Council of Regency.[47] Both documentary and chronicle evidence of Jewish lending and business with religious communities—from the monastic to the parochial—survives from near the time and region associated with Orrm's text. One debt record even suggests Jewish business dealings with Augustinian canons, like Orrm and his brother Walter, to whom he dedicates the *Orrmulum*.[48] This is not an incidental fact when part of his message about the disciple Nathaniel's choice and the slippery temporality of Jewish identity suggests that living Jews, now wasting their time continuing to practice their Judaism in a Jewish way nearby, might yet choose to fulfill the promise of their Jewishness by recognizing Christ and repenting of their sins. And English-speaking Christians, whom Orrm argues *ought* to be great Jews like Nathaniel, might fulfill the promise of their Jewishness by emulating Nathaniel, *or* they might choose to reject Jesus, not beat out their sins, interpret scripture wickedly, and therefore act like the "evil" Jews who now unwittingly serve God day and night.

So where does this extraordinary first definition of "Jew" in the English language get us? In Orrm's view, "Jew" denotes both Jew and Christian, both good and bad practices and beliefs. His definition of "Jew," strongly bonded to "Christian," works in a Möbius-strip structure, so that one word can move across both sides and return to meet its seeming other; neither the sameness nor the antithetical difference can be removed in service of the other, though they sometimes seem to be far apart. Orrm uses his definitions to bind historical and theological boundaries together, and his argument can inspire a kind of nervousness about Jewishness as an identity category that puts pressure both on Christian historical knowledge and on Christian perception of Jewish neighbors. His definitions also strain the interpretive possibilities of the *Orrmulum*'s anti-Jewish passages, almost to the point of semantic collapse: it is impossible to read them without recognizing the contradicting use of the same word and needing, therefore, to accept the possibility of simultaneous contradictory definitions. "Jew" and "Jewish" are, by design, unstable signifiers. The great Jew who knows his Torah is an aspirational category, as is the desire for purification that John 2:6 evokes as "of the Jews." The first English definition of "Jew" makes it difficult to understand how the best Christians are not also the greatest Jews, and it insists that the sameness of Jew and Christian must coexist with the othered Jews of negative difference.

Pontius Pilate and Other English Breakdowns

In early Middle English (ca. 1100–1350), forms of the words for "Jew" and "Jewish" may maintain the Germanic or Latinate root *jud-*, as "judissken" throughout the *Orrmulum*, or the French root *jui-* or *giu-*, as in *Ancrene Wisse*'s "giwene." Occasionally the noun form in an English-language text is "judeus"— as in the *Peterborough Chronicle*'s account of the purported 1144 ritual murder of William of Norwich[49]—so that it is difficult to tell whether the English plural or Latin singular is intended. A Jew is not called a Hebrew in English of this period. Though *Hebreus* is used as an identifying term in Latin literature of this time—that is, to identify Jewish people and not only Old Testament Hebrews or Hebrew as a language—Middle English "Ebreu" does not begin to appear regularly as an identifying term until the Wycliffite Bible. The word "Jewry" to identify either Jewish people collectively or the location of Jews was not in common usage either: the only place it appears before the mid-fourteenth century is in *Ancrene Wisse*'s Christ–Knight allegory (ca. 1225), and once in Robert of Gloucester's *Metrical Chronicle* (ca. 1300),[50] where it is probably Englishing the Anglo-Latin *Judaismus*, which in Latin legal vocabulary denotes a Jewish community or area (often seen as "in Judaismo," i.e., "in the Jewish area").[51] Neither is there any gender-specific rendering of "Jew" in this period: with the exception of one possible surname in a Latin court document of 1299, which may identify the woman as a convert from Judaism, the word "Jewess" does not appear until the 1390s.[52] Within such a limited lexical field, we might say that English as a language encourages semantic slippage between Israelite, Hebrew, Judean, Jew/Jewess, and thus between Jew and Christian in supersessionist rhetoric, where Israelites and Judeans can be models of righteous biblical Jews or Christian types. Or perhaps the language already reflects a cultural conceptualization. As in the *Orrmulum*, many English texts of the pre-Expulsion period and shortly after complicate the semantic range of the term "Jew" purposefully, or play self-consciously with the language's limitations, to suggest the possibility of sameness and interchangeability.

One such case is the description of Pontius Pilate in the so-called Judas Ballad, a unique short poem (thirty-three lines in manuscript), written down in the mid-thirteenth century in Cambridge, Trinity College MS B.14.39 and regarded by Francis Child as the earliest English ballad.[53] The subject is Judas Iscariot and his betrayal of Christ, but Judas himself is not the focus of Christian ire or anti-Jewish stereotyping in this poem. Instead, he is a hapless figure. In a creative elaboration of John 13:29, Jesus has entrusted Judas with thirty coins to buy food for the Passover meal. On his errand, Judas meets his sister, a figure unique to this poem, who coaxes him to fall asleep in her lap and then steals the money.[54] Judas is so distraught at the theft that he pulls out his hair until he is bleeding, and those watching him think he has gone mad. At this point, Pilate approaches and asks if he is willing to sell Jesus, but Judas refuses, unless Pilate can give him back the lost thirty coins so that he can buy the food that Jesus sent him to fetch. Later at the meal (the Last Supper), Jesus declares that he has been bought and sold for the food. When Judas asks if he is the one who has done this, Peter interjects to boast that he would never sell Jesus, but, in the final lines, Jesus informs Peter that he too will forsake him—three times before the cock crows.

Among much else that is inventive here, at the very center of the poem Pontius Pilate is labeled "þe riche ieu":

> þe iewes out of iurselem awenden he [Judas] were wode.
> fforet hym com þe riche ieu þat heiste pilatus.
> wolte sulle þi louerd þat heite iesus? (18–20)[55]

> The Jews from Jerusalem thought he was mad.
> The rich Jew who is called Pilate came forth to him:
>   "Will you sell your lord who is called Jesus?"

The line that oddly labels Pilate a Jew follows immediately on the mention of onlooking Jews in Jerusalem, and these are the only two uses of the word "Jew" here: twelve words apart at the structural and emotional center of the poem, and seemingly set in definitional contradiction *and* relation to each other. How can we understand Pilate as a Jew among the Jews of Jerusalem? How can we take seriously the naming of the Roman prefect as Jew alongside the naming of Jesus (a Jew) as Lord?

No other text so bluntly casts Pilate as a Jew. Jews are ambiguously portrayed in the Judas Ballad as a whole, however, and the poet is clearly working to double characters and terms throughout. If we understand Judas Iscariot as an archetypal, and sometimes etymologically marked, Jew in the medieval Christian tradition, he should always stand in for some negative claim about Jewishness, but he is pathetically portrayed here. He believes in Jesus. He chastises his sister, who curses him for believing in a false prophet: "be stille leue soster þin herte þe tobreke. / wiste min louerd crist ful wel he wolde be wreke" (Be quiet, dear sister, may your heart break. / If my Lord Christ knew, certainly he would be avenged) (11–12). He wants to fulfill Jesus's wishes, and his betrayal is part of a circumstance not of his own making, brought about by his violent desperation to serve, even after he has himself been betrayed. The poet also juxtaposes the betrayals of Judas and Peter, as if to suggest that Peter just as easily could have been a Judas, and that neither Peter nor the poem's audience or readers should consider themselves radically distinct from the betrayer. Pilate, as a Jew, is paired with Judas to effect the betrayal, but Judas is separate from the Jews of Jerusalem.

One wonders if something is lost in translation. The poem's epithet for Pilate—"þe riche ieu"—can mean the wealthy or powerful Jew, the admirable or strong Jew, the best Jew of his kind; all of these denotations of "riche" are possible at this date,[56] though certainly the subject matter of the poem pulls the meaning toward "wealthy." Anthony Bale reads this Pilate "become Jewish" as an early example of "the move, common in late medieval religious media, towards a violent adversarial relationship between Christ and the Jews,"[57] but he does not comment further on the conflation of Pilate with Jewishness nor on Pilate's wealth. Irina Dumitrescu, reading the poem as a commentary on usury, suggests rather that "this Pilate is intended to evoke stereotypes of Jewish moneylenders that thirteenth-century English would have had readily to mind," but she rejects the idea that the poet sees Pilate in the same category as the Jewish high priests of the Gospels and notes that the poem's anti-Jewish rhetoric is complicated by the fact that "there is no move to designate [Judas] as Jewish in this poem"; on the contrary, as I noted just above, "we are invited to think of him as distanced from the Jewish community of Jerusalem."[58] Any medieval English reader or listener would have known that Pilate was not in fact a Jew, if what we mean by "Jew" is a religiously or ethnically identified Jew. The Gospels are never unclear about this, and there are many medieval legends and dramas about Pilate and Judas, along with stories in the "Vengeance of Our Lord" tradition, that do not cast Pilate as a Jew.

It is clear from other Middle English texts of the same period and earlier, meanwhile, that Pilate could be pulled into the orbit of Jewishness, especially in its most negative connotations. In the late twelfth-century Bodley Homilies (Bod. MS Bodley 343), for example, Jews and Pilate are part of the same diabolical body:

Soðlice þe Iudeus wæren alle deofles limen, þe ðe ure Hælend to deaþe demdon. Pilatus wæs eac deofles lim, þe ðe ure Drihten lichamlice ahon hæt.[59]

Truly, the Jews, those who condemned our Lord to death, were all limbs of the Devil. Pilate, he who commanded our bodily Lord hung, was likewise a limb of the Devil.

While Pilate and the Jews are not exactly the same in this formulation, they work together in opposition to the Christ-body, and this alignment of Pilate with Jewish guilt for Jesus's death, especially in association with Judas, is not uncommon. In the anti-*vitae* of Judas and Pilate in the *South English Legendary* (ca. 1260), as in the Judas Ballad, Pilate and Judas have business together and are well acquainted. The Judas *vita*, echoing twelfth- and thirteenth-century Latin legends about Judas, has him employed as a steward to Pilate, noting that "Þe o shrewe wiþ þe oþer mayster was as riȝt was / Vor ech þing loueþ hys ilyk" (The one evil creature was master over the other, as was proper, / For each thing loves its like); and the sentiment is mirrored in the Pilate *vita*, where the author comments almost proverbially that Judas's stewardship to Pilate is natural, "Vor twei schrewen wolleþ beo freond" (For two evil creatures will be friends).[60] Long after the Crucifixion, the Roman emperor Vespasian in this text also scathingly passes judgment on Pilate: "Encentede he to the Gywes whanne he nas noȝt of her lawe" (He assented to the Jews even though he was not of their law).[61] Pilate becomes Jewish, if not a Jew, by virtue of participation in Jewish decisions.

While the Middle English contexts allow for a kind of tandem identity (which certainly, didactically, should impact the way Christians think of their relationships with Jewish neighbors), the elisions of the Judas Ballad also have roots in John 18:28–40, where Jesus's trial before Pilate features the question "Am I a Jew?" ("Numquid ego Judeus sum?" in the Vulgate, John 18:35). That the ballad is an experiment with an affirmative answer to this question, even a parodic one, seems plausible, especially because this poet is already clearly playing with John 13:29: "For some thought that, because Judas had the purse, that Jesus had said to him: 'Buy those things which we have need of for the festival day'" (quidam enim putabant quia loculos habebat Iudas quia dicit ei Iesus eme ea quae opus sunt nobis ad diem festum). This poem as a whole asks: What if that was indeed the case? The designation of Pilate as a Jew treats the "Am I a Jew?" quip similarly.

When the Jesus-before-Pilate scene that includes the question is elsewhere translated into English—an early Middle English example exists in Oxford, Jesus College MS 29 (ca. 1275), in the poem known as the *Passion of Our Lord*—it shows little alteration from the Gospel account:

> Pilates clepede ure louerd and þus hym seyde to:
> Þu ert gywene kyng, þeyh hi þe schome do.
> Vre louerd him onswerede, iblessed mote he beo:
> Hweþer systu hi þi seolf oþer oþre seyde by me.
> Pilates hym onswerede: am ich Gyu þenne.
> Þe byspes þe me bitauhte and mo of þine menne.[62]

> Pilate called our Lord and spoke this way to him: "You are King of the Jews, though they treat you shamefully." Our Lord, blessed may he be, replied, "Do you say this yourself or do others say it about me?" Pilate answered him, "Am I a Jew then? The bishops and others of your people brought you to me."

This text adds Pilate's characterization of Jewish actions—that the "bishops" (i.e., high priests, *pontifices* in the Vulgate) and other Jewish officials act shamefully in turning over Jesus—but the passage otherwise maintains, and adds no comment on, the ambiguity of Pilate's question about his own identity as it stands in the Vulgate. Is Jewishness implied by the idea that Pilate has been discussing the matter with Jews? By the idea that he might recognize that Jesus is king of the Jews? Should the "numquid" of the Vulgate signal indignation? Sarcasm? Genuine disbelief at the possibility? This play with uncertainty and perception, in the English *Passion of Our Lord* poem and in the Judas Ballad, is echoed by juxtaposition to Judas's question about his own culpability (Matt. 26:25): "Mayster am ich þilke þat þe wile so dyhte" (Master, am I he who will condemn you thus?) in the *Passion of Our Lord*,[63] and "Lord am i þat" (Lord, am

I he?) in the Judas Ballad (29). In these juxtapositions, what Judas and Pilate most clearly share is a lack of self-awareness about their own identities and guilt. The ballad, in response, takes Pilate's Gospel question "Am I a Jew?" seriously, and it quietly answers yes.

Pilate, historically neither Christian nor Jew, can be "the rich Jew" not because he was Jewish but because he is a Jewish character. This is not unlike how the *Orrmulum*'s Nathaniel, despite Orrm's emphatic positioning of him in historical association with Jews and Jewish learning, becomes an ideal Christian.[64] Nor, since it produces its complexities in negative notions of sameness, is this conjoining unlike Theresa Tinkle's reading of Herod as "a stereotypical Jew" alongside other Jews who conversely "represent monastic hermeneutics and monastic virtue" in the thirteenth-century Fleury Playbook's Latin *Herod*.[65] The flexibility that such possibilities require in the Jew-Christian matrix, however, seems to be embraced in early Middle English literature in particular, where issues of translation and lay devotion were very often primary, and when Anglo-Jewish communities were present or easily remembered. These novel uses of "Jew" in the developing English language widen the range of potential denotations and connotations and place them before a wide range of readers as well. Whether positive or negative in tone, they invite meditation on how a non-Jew can be or become Jewish.

BL MS Harley 2253 (compiled ca. 1340 but with individual pieces composed much earlier) contains another good example of a distinctively English use of the word that invites Christian inhabitation of the Jew (Figure 1). In a penitential English lyric called, for its first line, "God þat al this myhtes may" (God who wields all this power) occurs the only English-language use of the word "Jew" in Harley 2253. The poem begins the manuscript's sixth booklet (on fol. 106r); it is a fifty-six-line prayer-poem, written in twenty-eight lines on the page (i.e., two verses per line), and at its core is the line "Ich holde me vilore þen a gyw / ꝺ y myself wolde bue knowe" (I consider myself viler than a Jew, and I want myself to be known).[66] The material contexts and evidence of readership have some relevance to this case: in the manuscript, the word "gyw" falls exactly at the center of this poem. That is, the word "Jew" is central not only in terms of its content but also visually: there are thirteen lines above it and fourteen below, and, on the page, it sits precisely in the middle of the poem and of the verse, just where a *punctus elevatus* separates the two parts of the written line. As it happens, some later reader, in a sixteenth-century hand that appears nowhere else in the book, added the interlinear gloss "Jew," so that a Modern English spelling of the word appears exactly between the top and bottom fourteen written lines,

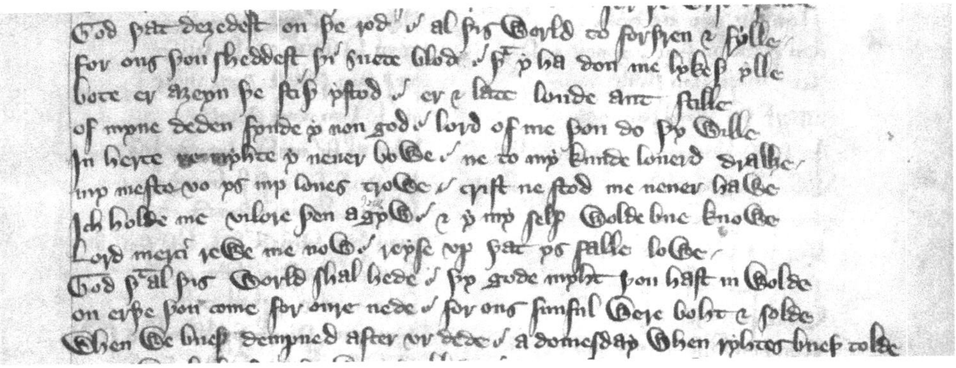

Figure 1. Central lines of the lyric "God þat al þis myhtes may"
with interlinear gloss ("Jew"). ©British Library Board.
BL MS Harley 2253, fol. 106r.

doubles the poem's content, and marks for us where one reader either stumbled over or wanted to emphasize the word.

But the word "Jew"/"Gyw" should not have surprised any reader of this manuscript, despite its unique appearance there in English. Jews come up with some frequency in Harley 2253, especially in the French material at the beginning of the book, which includes an earlier scribe's copy of Hermann de Valenciennes's *La Passioun Nostre Seignour*, a Gospel of Nicodemus, two pseudoletters of Pontius Pilate, and, as the book's penultimate item, a French prose piece on the Passion.[67] Notably, another French prose text that directly precedes the penitential lyric, at the end of booklet 5—a paraphrase of Genesis, Exodus, and Numbers—has a unique passage against Jews (*judeux* or *gyus*): "judeux" are now "cheytyves entre nous" (captives among us), it says, and the "synagoge, que fust temple as gyus, ore est ordyné eglise a chretienz pur fere sacrifice chretiene" (synagogue, which was a temple for the Jews, now it is ordained a church for Christians to make their Christian sacrifice).[68] This is supersessionist ideology not far removed from, though less concerned with doubling and continuity than, the *Orrmulum*'s teaching on Jewish Temple sacrifices, but it nevertheless efficiently expresses the Christian ability to inhabit Jews and Jewish space while simultaneously oppressing Jews. It is also linguistically interesting in its relationship to the English lyric that follows closely upon it, and by comparison with the English-language texts I have discussed so far, for it marks the only time that the French biblical paraphrase uses the vernacular words for "Jew"; everywhere else the designation is "Hebreu" or "Hebreus."[69] In the French, in other words, the lexical division between Old Testament righteous (Hebrews) and contemporary Jews is linguistically maintained, and this is exactly what we *do not* see in early Middle English texts.

But if a historical distinction is carefully maintained in the nearby text, and the French and English words used (*gyu/gyw*) are so closely related, why does "gyw" need a gloss in the English lyric, particularly if a reader is attuned to the nearby content—or, why might it be worth highlighting? That is perhaps the better question. The central line I quoted above—"Ich holde me vilore þen a gyw"—at first glance suggests a Christian speaker who is distinct from the "Jew" through negative comparison. In the lines around it, however, the implication of the claim is more complex than any rigid positive/negative dichotomy allows, for the lyric's Christian speaker, before and after this line, is fashioned as a disbelieving Jew who may yet choose to accept Christ. "Ich holde me vilore þen a gyw," on second glance, then appears to function in an aspirational sense. Jewishness, as in the Nathaniel model that Orrm created, is what the repentant Christian speaker *can get to*, even if he or she is now lamenting a lower spiritual state.

Stereotypical anti-Jewish characteristics, especially as connected to culpability for Jesus's death and obstinate denial of truth, identify the penitent speaker in most other lines of the poem. The speaker is God's "foo" (foe) and "to wyte" (to blame) for their own spiritual state, even though they "wiste my lay" (knew my Law) (4–5). When addressing Jesus, the speaker laments, "er agayn the stith Y stod" (I always stood firmly against you) (21) and later confesses that "Crist ne stod me never hawe" (Christ was never worth a thing to me) (28). The penitent's best deeds are "bittrore then the galle" (bitterer than the gall) (12), evoking the vinegar and gall fed to Jesus as he suffered on the cross (Matt. 27:34), traditionally associated with Jewish mocking of Christ in medieval iconography.[70] Finally the speaker admits, "Unbold Ich am to bidde the bote" (I lack courage to call you savior), even though "Fals Y wes in crop ant rote / When Y seyde thy lore was lees" (I was false, in growth and root, / When I said your teaching was lies) (41, 45–46). The poem, too, repeatedly claims that Christ died and bled specifically for the penitent who has so aggressively denied him (9, 17–19, 35–36), as if to make a general case for the speaker's stubborn resistance to Christian belief.

The line "Fals Y wes in crop ant rote" (45) is particularly striking. The Middle English phrase "in crop ant rote" can idiomatically mean "from head to toe" or "in every way," as Susanna Fein has translated it,[71] but the imagery here, in the context of consistent self-comparison to the Christ-denying Jew, also adverts to the genealogical tree of Jesus, in Middle English most often called the

"Jesse rote" or the "Dauid rote."[72] The falseness in the root and branches of the tree suggests not only a thorough denial, then, but also historical denial and the corruption of a shared genealogical line. In this poem, however, the stubborn Jew, the one who knew his Law and nevertheless denied Christ and his teaching and corrupted the tree at the root, is the Christian. The Christian voices the Jew and takes on a vicious Christian conception of Jewishness in order to be more profoundly, authentically, and appropriately Christian. The claim that the penitent is "vilore þen a gyw" ultimately comes in an attempt to redefine the fantasy of the contrite and submissive Jew as a feature of Christian identity: the speaker is "vilore" only than a Jew who will not regret his denial—the comparative identity can still be Jewish—but quintessentially Jewish in the Christian fantasy of self.

Caroline Walker Bynum's arguments for how symbolic reversal works when monks imagine themselves as women while maintaining women's inferiority can be relocated here to support the idea that a Christian can imagine himself as a Jew in order to be an ideal Christian:[73] in such reversals, and precisely through their contradictions and conjoinings, individuals move closer to God by means of debasement, that is, by acknowledging their own weakness and worthlessness. Just as Orrm defines the "Jew" as one who humbles himself before God and man—who "repents inwardly in his heart before God and openly acknowledges his sins before man"—the Harley 2253 lyric seeks simultaneously to reject and redefine "Jew" through both degradation and aspiration to God. The Christian penitent, by virtue of his contrition and humility, can both reject and be the same as the Jew. Once again, the best Christians and the best Jews should be, in their ideal forms, indistinguishable.

This kind of polemical position is along the lines of what Nirenberg has allowed that Karl Marx knew well, and manipulated, about "Jew" as a semantic (rather than historical or religious) category:

> He understood that some of these basic tools [of the economy] . . . were thought of in Christian culture as "Jewish," and that these tools therefore could potentially produce the "Jewishness" of those who used them, whether those users were Jewish or not. "Judaism" then is not only the religion of specific people with specific beliefs, but also a category, a set of ideas and attributes with which non-Jews can make sense of and criticize their world. Nor is "anti-Judaism" simply an attitude toward Jews and their religion, but a way of critically engaging the world.[74]

In the medieval context, similar thinking about Judaizing was prevalent by the eleventh century,[75] and Bale has shown that the affective function of the Jew in visual and narrative devotional modes could work this way too. That a character can be Jewish when not Jewish is part of the conclusion of Bale's sensitive reading of illustrated persecutors in the Salvin Hours (BL MS Additional 48985, a book produced ca. 1275): one of the artists "depicts the persecutors of the saints if not as 'Jews' then in the 'Jewish' visual register. . . . Those responsible for post-biblical martyrdoms are depicted 'as Jews'" whether they are Jewish or not.[76] Meaning is slippery under such conditions. Likeness is easy. The Christian assumption of idealized or fetishized Jewish attributes is made insidiously possible by both the priority and the presence of the Jewish twin, the object of Christian nostalgia and eschatology.

When the Christian can become the Jew or must accept that Christians can be Jews and vice versa—for instance, when an archbishop needs to force a Jewish friar into a typological performance of himself, or when a court scribe must report on a Christian child who first seemed to be Jewish, or when a preacher urges us to understand the word "Jew" as "Christian," or when Pilate can become Jewish by association with Jews, or when a penitent can fantasize herself voicing a Jew in order to become a better Christian—we are encountering sameness as a real problem and as a functional polemic. The definitional arguments that present or explicate sameness urge an unbroken line between the Israelites and the English; they want not moments of violence and antithesis but *moments of choice*, the times when, as Orrm emphasizes, one can make Nathaniel's choice—the desire to make Nathaniel's choice continually, and the fear of making Pilate's. The word "Jew" could exploit a Christian reader's uncertainty about its meaning in relationship to Christian identity across time, and it could create contradictions, but the uncertainty and paradoxes are productive. Arguments that allow the positive or negative sameness of Christian and Jew work with the historical and scriptural connections between the two, but they also prompt reflection and contrition. They signal the fragility of Christian identity and potential, and the reiterative and didactic value that that fragility holds.

CHAPTER 2

English "Jews"

The Jew came with letters.
—Jocelin of Brakelond, *Chronicle of Jocelin of Brakelond*

"Jew" Written Right

More must be said about Orrm, the twelfth-century Augustinian homilist who "pioneered Middle English verse,"[1] and whose unique homiliary first defined "Jew" in the English language. Later in this chapter, I will also discuss Orrm's contemporary and fellow vernacular preacher Abbot Samson of Bury St Edmunds (d. ca. 1211), but first let us consider whether Orrm was a Jew. Though he was an Augustinian canon from Lincolnshire with a biological brother named Walter and a name (Orrm or Orrmin, from Old Norse *ormr*) that suggests Scandinavian ancestry, and though he wrote in English using a remarkable number of Norse loanwords and was clearly fluent in Latin if not French,[2] one modern scholar has argued that Orrm was likely a converted Jew preaching to English Jews. Guzmán Mancho, judging that "most of Orrmin's discourse . . . is aimed at Jewish-conversion purposes," contends "that the former Jew Orrmin, aware of the difficult situation of his former co-religionaries in the area, took up the task to compose *Orrmulum* for a group of learnt Jewish catechumens to help with this spiritual task."[3] Based on analysis of Orrm's exegetical approach to Hebrew scripture and consideration of the situation of Anglo-Jewry at the end of the twelfth century, including massacres of Jews in the wake of the coronation of Richard I in 1190, Mancho suggests that "the converted-Orrmin could consider himself as the most adequate person to preach and convert English

Jewry as they all had an original common faith," and that perhaps he even did this "to save lives."[4] While this conclusion is clearly false—not least because Orrm does not seem to have much facility with Hebrew beyond what can be found in glossaries of Hebrew names, was almost certainly finished writing the *Orrmulum* by 1180, and the vernacular of twelfth-century English Jews was French[5]—Mancho's thesis is provocative, and it is based on legitimate observations of Orrm's text.

As James Morey has more judiciously observed, "Orm regards the Jews as his principal rivals in biblical interpretation," and his "explanations of how the Jews and their traditions fit into Orm's own time are some of the most interesting features of the collection, not least since the *Ormulum* predates Edward the First's expulsion of the Jews from England in 1290."[6] It is certainly true that anyone who reads the *Orrmulum* as a whole will be struck by its consistent and direct engagement with "Jewish" practices and biblical histories, as I discussed in the previous chapter. Morey's summary that Jews are "rivals" here is not hyperbole, and Mancho's conclusion that Orrm must then be a kind of vernacular Petrus Alfonsi is perhaps a productive thought experiment. Orrm is formally, exegetically, and aesthetically interested in the people and scripture that he understands to be his personal and textual exemplars. Indeed, his definitional, formal, and orthographic commitments look less eccentric if we consider them as expressions of particular kinds of typological and supersessionist views. The *Orrmulum*, in this light, is not only a mirror of its author's vision of sacred history and practice but also a reflection of the *contra Judaeos* tradition that appeared with renewed scholarly vigor in the twelfth century.[7]

To understand how this can be true of a work still mostly known for its orthography and the messiness of its material survival, we need to think in greater detail about Orrm's approach to the composition and recording of his opus. As a rule, the homilies of the *Orrmulum* proceed by paraphrasing one or two pericopes and then explicating the biblical text(s) by way of an interwoven fourfold exegesis not uncommon in medieval sermons and also observed by the earlier English-language homilist Ælfric,[8] that is, through literal (or historical), allegorical, tropological, and anagogical interpretations. Orrm writes in unrhymed fifteen-syllable lines that are based on Latin septenaries but, especially with their strong caesurae and rhythmic quality, are also suggestive of English alliterative long lines.[9] He clearly conceived of his work as a continuous composition that would stay together and be used together: he gave it a self-referential title, provided a dedicatory preface and "contents list" of lections, and imagined that the whole would be copied. In the partial draft that survives, Orrm wrote mostly in double columns, on whole sheets of parchment cut from the herse but otherwise untreated and sometimes on scrap parchment he used for changes and additions, and he revised and edited his work over a long period of time.[10]

Orrm describes his project in this way:

> Icc hafe sammnedd o þiss boc þa Goddspelless neh alle
> Þatt sinndenn o þe messeboc in all þe ȝer att messe,
> ˥ aȝȝ affterr þe Goddspell stannt þatt tatt te Goddspell meneþþ
> Þatt mann birþþ spellenn to þe follc off þeȝȝre sawle nede.
> (D 29–36)[11]

> I have united [samed] in this book nearly all of the gospels that are in the Mass Book in the whole year at Mass, and always after the gospel stands that which the gospel signifies, which it befits one to preach to the people for their soul's sake.

His description seems straightforward, but, as I noted in the previous chapter, the *Orrmulum* is not in fact written in strictly liturgical order; rather, Orrm harmonizes the Gospels so as to move chronologically from the advent of Christ to Christ's early ministry and through to the establishment of the early church, and he is as preoccupied with "saming" Hebrew scripture with the Gospels as he is with saming the four Gospels with each other. What survives of the *Orrmulum* seems to be about two-thirds of a first volume, that is, about 10,000 long lines, or most of twenty-three homilies explicating 31 of his nearly 250 planned pericopes.[12] All is in Orrm's crabby and overinked handwriting; the extensive revisions are mostly by Orrm too, though minor contributions from a second hand are visible.[13] According to Malcolm Parkes, all of what survives was finished by 1180, but Orrm must have been working on the *Orrmulum* for many years.[14]

Medievalists and linguists know Orrm for his peculiar orthography, as "the first individual whose name we know to attempt English spelling reform."[15] His self-devised system aims both to create a stable phonetic guide to oral delivery, likely for speakers of French,[16] and to ensure correct copying of his text, though we do not know if any part of it was ever copied. He consistently doubles consonants following short vowels and wherever consonants end a word, and he uses, less consistently, a series of diacritical marks to syllabify, mark short or long vowels, and distinguish two words that might otherwise be confused in pronunciation. The doubling of letters, however—strikingly visible at a glance and the most space-consuming—is the element of Orrm's writing system that he cared about most. It is the only element that he wrote, as a mandate to future copyists, into the content of the *Orrmulum*:

> ⁊ whase wilenn shall þiss boc efft oþerr siþe writenn,
> Himm bidde icc þatt he't write rihht, swa sum þiss boc himm
>   tæcheþþ,
> All þwert ut affterr þatt itt iss uppo þiss firrste bisne,
> Wiþþ all swillc rime alls her iss sett, wiþþ all se fele wordess—
> ⁊ tatt he loke wel þatt he an bocstaff write twiȝȝes
> Eȝȝwhær þær itt uppo þiss boc iss writenn o þatt wise.
> Loke he well þatt he write swa, forr he ne maȝȝ nohht elless
> Onn Ennglissh writtenn rihht te word. Þatt wite he wel to soþe.
> (D 95–110)

And whoever might wish to write this book another time, I ask him that he write it right, just as this book instructs him, precisely according to how it is in this first exemplar, with all the verse as it is set here, with all the many words—and that he take care that he write one letter twice everywhere where it is written that way in this book. May he take care to write it thus, for he cannot otherwise write words right in English. He should rest assured that is true.

As Christopher Cannon has shown, Orrm's precocious concern with the "rightness" of English writing, this imagined "rightness" of doubled letters within the process of doubling the text (via copying and transmission), is related to but also transcends linguistic inquiry. Repetition of letters is only the start: Orrm repeats phrases, lines and half lines, sometimes full passages. Cannon introduces Orrm's text, for these reasons and because of the state of its material survival, as "almost impossible to read";[17] Katharine Breen has characterized its central conceit as "a path that is simultaneously winding and 'anwherrfeddleȝȝc' [unvarying]";[18] J. A. W. Bennett calls *repetitio* Orrm's "one rhetorical device."[19] Orrm's methods, however, can also be understood, at least in the attempt, as sophisticated: a circular or interweaving style that perhaps evokes the meaning of the author's name ("worm" or "snake"); formal structure capable of creating a "centrifugal" effect; or, as Morey adds, *repetitio* is "not so much the rule as variation by means of rhetorical *expolitio*,"[20] that is, by series of parallelisms and doubles that subtly expand upon and shift meaning as they accrue. Still, Cannon has argued that Orrm's repetitions are "evidence that the prior use of the same words failed" and that the "sameness" of his words "winds itself up into a self-consuming spiral" until tautological "nonsense" results.[21] Like Breen, who appreciates Orrm's remarkable "experiment in vernacular grammar" but concedes that "by all practical measures, the *Orrmulum* was a failure,"[22] Cannon ultimately allows the *Orrmulum* aesthetic value only in its "forms of signifying failure."[23]

My own assessment is similar to Cannon's in some ways but quite different in others. In Cannon's view, repetition "is not simply a mode Orm employs . . . but a direct consequence of a definition of spelling [from Middle English *spellen*, both to spell words and to preach or interpret] that makes repetition *signify*"; for Orrm, repetition is not simply formal, then, but "crucial and poetically constitutive."[24] I grant this but go further, and I do not concede that Orrm's repetitions have their end point in "not the redoubling, but the cancellation of meaning"[25]—though certainly they make meaning difficult. Rather, the lengthy process by which definitions and signification erode can be didactically and polemically useful, and exegetically constitutive, for Orrm's repetitions are visual and oral cues to think typologically. If his repetition makes reading difficult, it is not because Orrm has failed. It is, rather, a symptom of his view of Christian history and word-making (which of course includes and repeats Jewish history and Jewish word-making) that necessitates doubling ad infinitum: repetition is the historical, scriptural, liturgical, and textual site of experience in the *Orrmulum*. It is evident at the word level (through doubled letters) but also in Orrm's structural and figural doublings, which signal his way of looking at words, yes, but also at scripture, time, and self. Doubling and saming are his orthographic *and* exegetical principles. One of the great successes of the *Orrmulum* is that these principles function at both superficial and profound levels.

Orrm's self-naming and self-titling provide a small but useful initial step in substantiating my arguments: "Þiss boc is nemmnedd Orrmulum," he says in a single long line, "forrþi þatt Orrm it wrohhte" (This is book is named *Orrmulum* because Orrm made it) (P 1–2). It has been suggested that Orrm is evoking, in the form of his title, the Latin meaning of the word *speculum* (mirror), if not speculum genres (e.g., mirrors of the church, for princes, and the like), even though the use of "speculum" in titles does not appear very commonly until the thirteenth century; further, as Meg Worley has pointed out, the Latin word *Orrmulum* most obviously means "little Orm."[26] Not only is Orrm's repetition in this line visible on the visual and sonic levels, then—the syllable "Orrm" repeats in both half lines, and consonants are doubled as usual—but the line also describes the text as a repetition of its author, either (or both) by imagining that the work is a mirror of Orrm, a reflection of the authorial self, or that it is a miniature Orrm, a metaphorical clone of its author. Even in this somewhat trivial instance, Orrm's conceptualization of self and text in relation to one another is a matter of repeating and recreating the self through doubles and reproduction.

One of the central questions of the *Orrmulum*, in my view, is, What exactly constitutes meaningful Christian repetition of the Jew? Form and content meet in Orrm's considerations of the answer. While it is not surprising, as Morey has summarized, that "Orm reads Jewish practices typologically in the superior light of Christian revelation"[27]—and Orrm's typological doublings do come in predictable forms (e.g., Moses is Jesus, David is Jesus, Elijah and John the Baptist and Jesus are all each other, Passover is communion, circumcision is baptism, etc.)—it *is* notable that explicit naming of "Jewish" models and scripture is so consistently central to his exegesis. It is partly the starkness of this aspect of the *Orrmulum* that led Mancho to suggest that Orrm must be a converted Jew speaking to Jews. Orrm is interested in reproducing a correct or corrected Jew (Jews like the disciple Nathaniel), and his rhetoric often suggests that he is more invested in finding ways to double or harmonize Christian and Jewish practice than to erase, suppress, or denigrate Jews. In the Auerbachian sense, his figural methods move so quickly back and forth between "historical, earthly events" and their "fulfillment in interpretation" that it is difficult to keep track of where Orrm himself is in relation.[28]

His concern with the rightness of his writing as it repeats itself through time (via scripture) and through transmission (via translation and scribal copying) is crucial in this. Orrm initially presents this concern as care for the "firrste bisne," that is, the first good manuscript exemplar. As I noted above, he writes into his dedicatory material that he wants any future copyist of the *Orrmulum* to "write he't rihht, swa sum þiss boc himm tæcheþþ, / All þwert ut affterr þatt itt iss uppo þiss firrste bisne" (write it right, just as this book instructs him, precisely according to how it is in this first exemplar) (D 97–100). In this passage, the word *bisne* clearly means "exemplar," though with Orrm's other very frequent uses of the noun,[29] scholars typically understand *bisne* more generally to indicate a positive "model" or "example," as in the line "Þatt dide he forr he wollde swa uss alle ʒifenn bisne" (He did that because he wanted, in this way, to give us all an example) (9068), where Orrm uses *bisne* to explain why Jesus was obedient to his earthly father and mother. If, however, we think of *bisne* more consistently with the denotation that Orrm first gives it, that is, as a word that applies to a textual exemplar to be diligently copied by a good scribe, we can see how the Modern English distinction between "exemplar" and "example" might be too strong. The verbal echoes created by Orrm's textual and typological uses of *bisne*, rather, can be read metaphorically: history and scripture are a matter of correct copying, and Orrm's Jews and their "Judisskenn wise," too, constitute exemplars that can be copied, *so long as they are copied correctly.*

Allowing the textual usage of the word *bisne* to compete with other possible translations in Orrm's habitual use of the word helps to reveal his commitment to arguments for the sameness of Jews and Christians and Jewish and Christian practices, whether through individual figures like the disciple Nathaniel or through general discussion of the Old and New Testaments. A commitment to following the *bisne* fits his larger exegetical mode. When Orrm discusses the Testaments, for instance, he similarly focuses on the existence of past physical books and the nature of their transmission:

> Þatt Goddess enngell [i.e., Gabriel at the Annunciation] . . .
> Droh ut off Ysayȝess boc witness off Cristess come:
> Þatt dide he forr he wollde uss swa full wel don tunnderrstandenn
> Þatt baþe droȝhenn all till an [book] of Jesu Cristess come,
> Þe Judewisshe folkess boc ⁊ Goddspellbokess lare. (3062–71)

> The angel of God . . . adduced evidence of Christ's coming from the
> book of Isaiah. He did that because he wanted us to understand very
> well that both together add up to one about the coming of Jesus
> Christ: the Jewish people's book and the teaching of the gospel book.

Orrm describes Gabriel's use of Hebrew scripture as similar to his own. For both Gabriel and Orrm, the conjoining of the Testaments is more persuasive than the overwriting of the Old. Jesus, as Orrm says elsewhere, "ne was nohht wurrþenn mann bitwenenn menn onn erþe / Forr to forrwerrþenn aniȝ lott off Moysæsess lare" (did not become man among men on earth to discard any part of Moses's teaching) (15184–87). The lesson is not only about supersession, but about preservation and curation. Two books become one in the copying, but the prior book remains and must be preserved. This simultaneity of scripture matters to Orrm: doubled writing (copying) and doubled understanding (translating, harmonizing) is explicitly *not* expunging or forgetting or replacing. As with the sound of a consonant in relation to its written form, or with a copy produced from an exemplar, the Testaments must be both one and two at the same time.

Orrm's punning explication of the Levitical sacrifice of male goats in the Temple provides another, more playful example of this proposition. Concerning the scapegoating ritual prescribed in Leviticus 16, he writes:

> Þe Judewisshe folkess boc hemm seȝȝde þatt hemm birrde
> Twa bukkess samenn to þe preost att kirrkdure brinngenn;
> ⁊ teȝȝ þa didenn bliþeliȝ swa sum þe boc hemm tahhte
> ⁊ brohhtenn tweȝȝenn bukkess . . .
> Þe tweȝȝenn bukkess tacnenn uss an Godd off twinne kinde.
> (1324–30, 1352–53)

> The Jewish people's book told them that they ought to bring two bucks together to the priest at the church door, and so they happily did just as the book taught them and brought two bucks. . . . The two bucks mean to us one God from twin natures.

Here, Orrm is working with two books (the "Jewish book" that he is explicating through the Christian book), two bucks (male goats), a doubling of the Temple and Church (historically and typologically), and the two natures of Christ (i.e., divine and human). Into this he weaves word-group repetition (*twa, tweȝȝenn, twinne*), repetition of sounds (through the pun on *boc* and *buk*), and of course his usual doubled consonants. The pun on *tweȝȝenn bukkess* is primary: sensically and sonically, the topic of this passage is really the *tweȝȝenn bokess*, the Old and the New Testaments. Implicit is the idea that the Jews, in following their one book and bringing two bucks to the high priest at the Temple door, in fact bring two books to the church door. That the English pun is embedded in Orrm's reading of the scapegoat means both that the scapegoat's typological relationship to Jesus is present (as Orrm explicitly acknowledges) and also that the necessity of the two books to the Christian-as-double is cleverly interposed.

The continued relevance of priestly prescriptions in Leviticus and Exodus for Orrm is not only a matter of reproduction through figural interpretation but also, more unusually, a matter of reproduction through cause and effect, and even sound, over time. The connections he crafts between Christians and Jews are more direct than mere typology. When he explicates the Temple high priest's ephod and robe as it is described in Exodus 28, for example, he links

Jewish and Christian priests by focusing on the bells that lined the robe and
were to ring as the high priest approached the holy of holies:

> Þe belledræm bitacneþþ ȝuw þatt dræm that ȝuw herenn,
> Whannse þe preost ȝuw telleþþ spell biforenn Godess allterr;
> ⁊ ȝiff he nohht ne spelleþþ ȝuw þe Goddspellbokess lare,
> He falleþþ wissliȝ forr þatt gillt i Goddess wraþþe ⁊ wræche,
> All swa summ þatt Judisskenn preost þurhh Drihhtin shollde
>   swelltenn,
> ȝiff þatt he wære reckelæs to ringenn hise belles.
> Nu loke ȝure preost tatt he ȝuw bliþlike spelle,
> Þatt he ȝuw illke Sunenndaȝȝ att allre læste lære,
> Off all hu ȝuw birrþ ledenn ȝuw ⁊ lefenn uppo Criste
> ⁊ lufenn Godd ⁊ lufenn mann ⁊ Godess laȝhess haldenn;
> ⁊ ȝuw birrþ swiþe bliþeliȝ ȝuw turrnenn till hiss lare,
> ⁊ haldenn itt ⁊ follȝhenn itt aȝȝ affterr ȝure mihhte.
> Nu ȝiff þatt ȝure preost ⁊ ȝe þuss farenn ȝuw bitwenenn,
> Þa maȝȝ ben god till ȝure preost ⁊ till ȝuw sellfenn baþe,
> Þatt tatt Judisskenn preost wass swa bihenggedd all wiþþ belless,
> ⁊ tatt himm wass swa mikell ned þatt Godd hemm herrde
>   ringenn. (918–53)

The bell sound should signify to you the sound that you ought to hear
when the priest preaches to you from God's altar. And if he does not
preach the teachings of the gospel book to you, he stumbles for that
sin, justifiably, into God's wrath and vengeance, just as the Jewish
priest could be killed by God if he were careless about ringing his
bells. Now take care that your priest preach to you happily, that he
teach you every Sunday, at least, about all that pertains to how you
should conduct yourself and live up to Christ and love God and love
man and keep God's laws. And you ought to turn very happily toward
his teaching, and hold to it and follow it always, with all your might.
Now, if you and your priest have such a relationship, it becomes good
for both your priest and for you that the Jewish priest was so burdened by bells, and that it was so urgent that God hear them ring.

This passage is occasioned by Orrm's exegesis of Luke 1:5, specifically the phrase
"sacerdos quidam nomine Zaccharias" (a certain priest named Zachary); Orrm

has interrupted his reading of the Gospel pericope to explain what it means that Zachary was a priest and to explain Zachary's place in the line of those who continued "Jewish" priestly duties after Aaron. But Orrm, as the preacher, becomes here both the figural doubling and the outcome of the Jewish high priests, of Aaron and of Zachary. The Christian preacher at the church, with the sound of bells behind him, mirrors the high priest at the Temple in procreative and causal senses: if that Jewish priest had not been burdened by bells, and if God had not wanted to hear his bells ring, Orrm's congregants could not be where they are nor understand how to seek a good priestly relationship: to understand the lesson, they must see and hear the Jewish priest and his Jewish bells through time—and continue to see and hear them in their church and in Orrm himself.

In this sense, Orrm's readings of Jewish law move beyond supersessionist lessons and typology to urge actual repetition. As he claims in justification of his long discussion of the Levitical burnt offerings, "icc wille shæwenn ʒuw ... hu ʒe muʒhenn lakenn ... / Wiþþ all þatt Judewisshe lac" (I will show you ... how you may sacrifice to God ... with all the Jewish sacrifices) (1115–22). Finding a way to do this matters to him because the "Judewisshe lac" (Jewish sacrifice/s), as written in the Jewish book, "ʒifeþþ bisne" (provide an exemplar) (e.g., 1230, 1239, 1291, and passim). Orrm's conviction that anyone who copies his work adhere to his *bisne*, both his textual exemplar and his scriptural models of behavior and morality, in other words, aligns and converges with his conviction that Old Testament Jews and Jewish law constitute an exemplar that can be copied correctly, both in good deeds and through textual transmission and interpretation.

Even at the rhetorical and poetic height of his reading of Temple sacrifices, Orrm's moving account of how a Christian can sacrifice sheep is expressed through a metaphor that imagines an oppressively exact and continuing set of repetitions. Christians now sacrifice a sheep, says Orrm, by listening for God meekly and quietly amid, paradoxically, a cacophonous landscape where the same sound emits from a thousand creatures that look confusingly similar:

> Forr lamb is softte ⁊ stille deor ⁊ meoc ⁊ milde ⁊ liþe,
> ⁊ it cann cnawenn swiþe wel hiss moderr þær ʒho blæteþþ
> Bitwenenn an þusennde shep þohh þatt teʒʒ blætenn alle.
> ⁊ swa birrþ þe cnawenn wel þin Godd ⁊ all hiss lare,
> ⁊ all forrwerrpenn hæþenndom ⁊ oþre goddess alle,
> Swa summ þe lamb fleþ oþre shep ⁊ follʒheþþ aʒʒ hiss moderr.
> (1312–23)

For a lamb is a soft and quiet creature, and meek and mild and gentle,
and it can know very well its mother where she bleats between a
thousand sheep, even though they are all bleating. And it befits you
thus to know your God well, and all his teaching, and reject heathendom and all other gods, just as the lamb flees other sheep and always
follows its mother.

Amid Orrm's repetition of sounds and letters and words, amid a thousand
sheep loudly bleating the same sound, a Christian (the lamb) must learn to recognize the *right* sound—the one that is the same, but not quite. Then, says
Orrm, "þu cnawesst rihht tin Godd" (you know your God correctly) (1300),
and then you continue the "Jewish" sacrifice correctly too, not by bare replica-
tion or cloning but as a good scribe, copying and doubling as directed.

In the same register, Orrm routinely describes Jewish understanding as
"stafflike." The word means "literal," but Orrm does not mean "literal" in the
modern or even the exegetical sense when he uses it: "letter-like," in line with the
Latinate *litteralis* (concerned with letters or writing), is a better translation for
his usage.[30] The word is the adverbial and adjectival form of the singular "staff"
(a letter, an alphabetic character) in the *Orrmulum*, and it is importantly distinct
from the doubled "bocstaff" (written letter, consonant) that Orrm insists must
be copied from his textual exemplar. Orrm is the only Middle English author to
use the word *stafflike*,[31] and he uses it only to apply to Jewish understanding of
Hebrew scripture, as in the following examples (with my emphases):

> Þa bokess þatt te Laferrd Crist ȝaff gastliȝ tunnderrstanndenn,
> Þeȝȝ wærenn Moysæsess boc ⁊ Sallmsang ⁊ Profetess,
> Þatt wærenn aȝȝ till Cristess daȝȝ . . .
> unnderr stafflike lare. (14288–95)

The books to which the Lord Christ granted spiritual understanding,
they were Moses' book and Psalms and Prophets, which were always,
until Christ's time, . . . governed by *letter-like* teaching.

> ⁊ ȝet ta stod stafflike witt amang Judisskenn þede
> Off Moysæsess laȝheboc ⁊ off hallȝhe profetess. (18190–91)

At that time a *letter-like* knowledge of Moses' law-book and of the
holy prophets held place among the Jewish people.

⁊ ȝiff þu þiss thurrh Haliȝ Gast deplikerr unnderrstanndesst,
Þatt Moysæs iss Jesu Crist þatt ledde þurhh himm sellfenn
Mannkinn ut off Egippte land, off sinness þessterrnesse . . .
⁊ tatt te Laferrd Jesu Crist oppnede thurrh hiss come
Off all þe Judewisshe boc þe depe diȝhellnesse . . .
Þa takesst tu gastlike witt off staffliȝ witeȝhungge. (14840–65)

And if you, through the Holy Spirit, more profoundly understand
this—that Moses is Jesus Christ who led mankind out of Egypt, out
of the darkness of sin, . . . and that the Lord Jesus Christ revealed the
profound secret of the whole Jewish book, . . . then you accept
spiritual knowledge from *letter-like* prophecy.

The singular, letter-like understanding that Orrm marks as Jewish is reinforced
in this last example by a series of doubles: individual letters are doubled, knowedge
is doubled by revelation, Moses is doubled by Jesus, the exodus is doubled by the
forgiveness of sins, and the Jewish book is doubled by Jesus's opening and trans-
mitting of it. Letters must be seen and used, and they may look or sound alike—
think of any one of Orrm's individual words, or the bleats of a thousand mother
sheep—but they are insufficient to Christians unless doubled.

In most ways, the typology that informs the Jewish-Christian relationship
in the *Orrmulum* is orthodox, but Orrm's execution and methods are
surprising—and sometimes virtuoso. To echo Cannon's arguments, though I
am applying the point differently here, Orrm's formal commitments are also
the metaphorical vehicles for his message. Orrm sees the Jew and the Jewish
book as the exemplars for the Christian and the Christian book, and the fas-
tidiousness of his orthography and notions of correct transmission are uncannily in line with the repetition of Jewishness and Jewish practice that he
preaches. For Orrm, Christians are Jews written right: Jews are the "firrste
bisne" (first exemplar), and those who copy them must take care to avoid merely
"stafflike" (letter-like) labor and instead "an bocstaff write twiȝȝes" (write one
letter twice). If Orrm is not the converted Jew that Mancho sees, there is every
reason to believe that he wanted himself and those in his congregation to be the
"duhhtiȝ Judewisshe mann" (great Jewish man) that he saw in the disciple Nathaniel. And if Nathaniel is the exemplar to copy faithfully (the good Jew, the
Christian Jew), negligent scribes may still end up copying "þatt Judisskenn
laþe follc þatt henngde Crist" (the evil Jewish people who hanged Christ, i.e., the
Jews who continue to copy a letter-like Judaism and practice their faith to no

eternal purpose). Such Christians might transmit the Jewish book and the Jewish self badly.

The wordplay that marks such arguments, like Mancho's experiment with Orrm's Jewish identity and Orrm's own commitment to correct transmission of the *Orrmulum*, is bound up in English history and the English language. As Orrm insists, one "ma33 nohht elless / Onn Ennglissh writtenn rihht te word" (cannot otherwise write the words right in English). Indeed, the content of the *Orrmulum* and its authorial voice have long been treated as evidence of continuity in English literary history, as linguistically, or even natively, English—a category that for medievalists normally (with the exception of Mancho) presumes the exclusion of Jewishness. In scholarly assessments since the nineteenth century, Orrm has been a man with "Anglo-Saxon" literary roots: the first editor of the *Orrmulum* emphatically placed him in the long "History of Anglo-Saxon Literature."[32] David Lawton has emphasized that we should "take Orrm seriously" primarily "as a sign of continuity of Englishing from Ælfric,"[33] to whom he is often compared as a late if lesser extension.[34] The scholarly history of medieval English sermons, as Bella Millett outlines, shows a general tendency to focus on "features which link the early Middle English sermon with the pre-Conquest preaching tradition,"[35] and, though Millett works skillfully to disrupt this tendency, she nevertheless sets the *Orrmulum* in "a no man's land . . . between the older and new preaching traditions."[36] Even when Orrm is granted such status as a transitional figure, though, his relationship to later Middle English literature is characterized as pioneering or foundational, so that he still stands out in the scholarly imagination as an Englishman in some fundamental way.[37] Part of my point, however, is that Orrm communicates his Englishness in more substantial and complex ways than his connections to Old or Middle English literary canons can do. If instead of casting him as a late and lesser Ælfrician—"near ridiculous" or "beleaguered" or "tedious"[38]—we make use of his preoccupation with Jewishness to align him with other twelfth-century religious men writing in Latin, we get a very different kind of authorial portrait.

In Orrm's lifetime, many biblical scholars thought of Jews as their principal rivals. In light of his Latin sources, indeed, Orrm looks something closer to a representative of the twelfth century described in Elizabeth Salter's *English and International* than a man nostalgic for pre-Conquest Englishness. For Salter, Orrm's century is marked by the presence of "'international exchange'—an exchange which concerns the relationships between England and the continent, and, no less, between England, the continent and Scandinavia"—that must eclipse "theories of 'hidden continuity'" between the Old and Middle English periods, because such theories "become a useful way of disguising what appear to be empty spaces" and tend to create "a false impression of the literary contexts of apparently isolated English works."[39] The literary contexts of the *Orrmulum* are not isolated. Since the 1980s, much has been published on Orrm's sources (notably by Stephen Morrison and Nils-Lennart Johannesson),[40] and what emerges from this research is layered use of contemporary continental works.

Orrm is not the writer and preacher that Robert White and Robert Holt thought him to be in the Victorian era—that is, mostly long-winded, attached to an "Anglo-Saxon" canon, and borrowing "copiously from the writings of St. Augustine and Ælfric"[41]—though this is a characterization that has been unfortunately persistent. Rather, in addition to the originality of versification and the exegetical methods outlined above, he creatively mixes sources, translates loosely, makes independent and unique connections between disparate texts, and writes much original content. Whether one finds the *Orrmulum* tedious or unreadable, Orrm is an author as sophisticated as many to whom we give more credit: he is working with scholars of his own century, and he is versifying and combining them with older authorties; he is multilingual, and he is mixing new modes of continental exegesis with pre-Conquest models admired but already antiquated in his day.[42] To the extent that Orrm continues pre-Conquest traditions, as Morrison has shown, he does so with "the recollection of phraseology traditionally favoured in late Old English homilies ... by one who understood its [Old English's] authoritativeness and appreciated its affectiveness."[43] Orrm's engagement with Old English homiletics, however, is not primary in the intellectual and exegetical content of his work. The *Orrmulum* is, instead, the product of an author immersed in contemporary hermeneutics.

Among Orrm's Latin sources are several associated with the school of Laon, the conservative but influential school of Anselm of Laon and his disciples.[44] Orrm makes substantial use, as has long been maintained, of the *Glossa ordinaria* (compiled at Laon beginning in the early twelfth century),[45] but also of the *Ennarrationes in Mattaei Evangelium* (composed in the mid-twelfth century but associated with Anselm of Laon), Bede's *In Lucae Evanglium* (probably as filtered through the *Glossa* at Laon), and the ninth-century Irish monk Johannes Scotus Eriugena's *Commentarius in Evangelium Johannis* as it appeared in the holograph manuscript used by Anselm of Laon (now Laon, Bibliothèque municipale MS 81) in the late eleventh century, that is, in the copy Anselm used as he worked on the earliest iterations of the *Glossa*.[46] Johannesson has argued persuasively, given these links, that the dedicatory preface to the *Or-*

rmulum, which follows a format typical of prefaces to twelfth-century biblical commentaries, is informed by the model of Anselm and Ralph of Laon (d. 1117 and 1136, respectively), the brothers who were the early compilers of the *Glossa* and leaders of the Laon cathedral school. Orrm's opening lines dedicating his work to Walter—his brother "affterr þe flæsches kinde . . . i Crisstenndom . . . [ɿ] þurrh þatt witt hafenn takenn ba an reȝhellboc to follȝhenn / unnderr kanunnkess had" (biologically, . . . in Christendom, . . . and in that we have both decided to follow a Rule under a canon's hood) (2–9)—seem to allude to Anselm and Ralph's similar "threefold brotherhood": "like Walter and Orm, Anselm and Ralph were brothers in the flesh, brothers in the faith and also Canons Regular."[47] Orrm may have seen the Laon brothers, Johannesson surmises, "as predecessors of Walter and himself"[48]—men at the forefront of the new modes of biblical exegesis and pedagogy, albeit in the vernacular. The association of his library with the school of Laon, furthermore, makes sense if Orrm was indeed a canon at Bourne Abbey (founded in 1138), as Parkes first suggested.[49] Bourne was under the direct authority of Arrouaise, and some of the early members of the Arrouaisian order were from the Laon school, a group "finely tuned . . . to the problems and principles that are earmarks of early twelfth-century theology."[50]

Among Orrm's other now-established twelfth-century sources are sermons of Bruno Astensis (abbot of Montecassino, d. 1123) and Peter Cellensis (abbot of St Remy and bishop of Chartres, b. ca. 1115), the *Expositio in Cantica Canticorum* and *Speculum ecclesiae* of Honorius Augustodunensis (d. 1154 in Regensberg), and works by Godefridus Admontensis (abbot of Admont Abbey, d. 1165).[51] Orrm was, as Johannesson has painstakingly documented, consistently "combining material from different source texts" even within single homilies,[52] and his use of such sources shows that he had many works laid out before him and "was not slavishly dependent on his principal [older] authorities."[53] Michael Clanchy was right (perhaps more right than he could have known when he wrote it) that Orrm was not only a pioneer of Middle English verse but also representative of "the schoolmen and clergy, the masters of Latin" of his time.[54] Orrm merges, I think, an Augustinian sense of Jews—as necessarily preservable and transmittable figures of the letter[55]—and engagement with a broad range of sources. Not limited by Augustinian sensibilities, that is, the *Orrmulum* shows influences of Benedictine approaches and contemporary supersessionist commentaries and dialogues.

In its treatment of Jews, Orrm's work echoes the sentiments and arguments of the many *contra Judaeos* tracts that began to appear in the late eleventh and early twelfth centuries, from both English and continental theologians such as Gilbert Crispin, Guibert of Nogent, Petrus Alfonsi, Peter the Venerable, and Peter Abelard (who famously argued with his onetime teacher, Anselm of Laon). In thinking and writing seriously *adversus Judaeos*, these and others re-established an early Christian genre and anti-Jewish vocabulary. In the late eleventh and twelfth centuries, the genre became an obsession of monastic and academic circles, who were slowly revising milder Augustinian approaches to Jewish presence. As Jeremy Cohen has explained, the period gave rise to a "new 'discourse of otherness'" as "the Jew and his tradition nourished the newly reinvigorated Christian study of the Old Testament," even as "increased cultural contacts . . . intensified Christian sensitivity to contemporary Jews and Judaism"; the twelfth century "produced more extant works of Christian anti-Jewish polemic than all previous centuries combined."[56] Among them was the *Liber de haeresibus* of Honorius Augustudensis, whose *Speculum ecclesiae* Orrm used in crafting his homily on John 2:1–11, that is, the homily that occasioned his English definition of the word "Jew" around the disciple Nathaniel.[57]

Of course the *Orrmulum* is not a piece of disputational anti-Jewish polemic like Gilbert Crispin's *Disputatio Judaei et Christiani* (ca. 1095), Petrus Alfonsi's *Dialogus contra Judaeos* (ca. 1109), or Peter the Venerable's *Adversus Judaeorum inveteratam duritiem* (ca. 1140); much of my argument here is that unlike, and perhaps in response to, such texts, Orrm seeks to copy the Jew correctly and thus incorporate the Jew into the Christian—but the *Orrmulum* does evoke the *contra Judaeos* tradition and evidence vernacular participation in it. Cohen notes, for instance, the peculiarly twelfth-century penchant in *contra Judaeos* texts for "indiscriminate use of the word 'heresy' to characterize Judaism—and 'heretic' when referring to Jews"—and he uses Honorius Augustudensis's *Liber de haeresibus* as a key example.[58] Since we know that Orrm had access to works by this author, we might, as an exercise, compare his vocabulary to Orrm's: the only term that Orrm employs in opposition to Christians other than "Jew" or "Jewish" is "hæþene." Might this function similarly to Honorius's use of the word *haereticus*? Orrm uses "hæþene" similarly imprecisely, sometimes to refer to pre-Christian or non-Jewish nations (gentiles), sometimes to first-century Romans, and sometimes to Muslims or their Arab predecessors. So he may use the word in contrast to Jews, but, at the same time, his usage is ambiguous. The passage about mother sheep quoted above, where Orrm shows how Christians can make a "Jewish" sacrifice to God in a Christian way by listening for God's maternal bleating and rejecting "hæþenndom ⁊ oþre goddess," is a good example. The mandate to reject heathendom and other gods, in the context of that homily, apparently urges rejection of the bloody literal ("Jewish") sacrifices under discussion; nothing else in the long, double homily from which it is excerpted points to a concern for any other religion or people.

A similarly odd use of "hæþene" comes in Orrm's reading of the Annunciation, where he relates how the angel Gabriel told Mary that her son would sit on the throne that "Davidd his faderr held amang Judisskenn þede" (David his father held among the Jewish people), hold his kingdom eternally "bitwenenn þatt Judisskenn þeod þatt Jacob wass bilenge" (among the Jewish people who belonged to Jacob), and "newenn turrnenn Judisskenn follc till Crisstenndom" (for the first time convert Jewish people to Christianity) (2225–38). Orrm then adds his commentary on what this means for Christians and includes yet another definition of the English word "Jew":

> Acc witt tu wel þatt alle þa þatt lefenn uppo Criste
> Off baþe, off þatt Judisskenn þed ꞇ off hæþene þede,
> Þatt witt tu wel þatt alle þa ȝuw sinndenn her bitacnedd,
> ȝa þurrh Jacob ȝa þurrh Judew, affterr gastlike lare.[59]
> Forr Jacob tacneþþ all þa þatt tredenn dun ꞇ cwennkenn
> All þatt tatt iss onnȝæness Godd inn alle kinne sinne,
> ꞇ Judew tacneþ alle þa þatt lofenn Godd ꞇ wurrþenn
> ꞇ innwarrdlike anndgætenn aȝȝ wiþþ muþ ꞇ ec wiþþ trowwþe
> Þatt niss nan Godd wiþþutenn himm þatt alle shaffte wrohhte,
> ꞇ innwarrdlike anndgætenn aȝȝ alle þeȝȝre sake ꞇ sinne
> ꞇ stanndenn inn to cwemenn Godd onn alle kinne wise.
> ꞇ swillke sinndenn Cristess follc ꞇ Christess kineriche.
> (2239–60)

But be assured that all those who believe in Christ—from both, from the Jewish people and from heathen people—be assured that all those are signified to you here, either through "Jacob" or through "Jew," according to spiritual teaching. For "Jacob" means: all those who trample and extinguish all that is against God in all kinds of sin. And "Jew" means: all those who love and praise God and always inwardly acknowledge, with mouth and also with faith, that there is no God but he who made all creation, and who always inwardly acknowledge all their guilt and sin and continue to please God in all kinds of ways. And such are Christ's people and Christ's kingdom.

It is not clear why Orrm includes "hæþene þede" in this passage. "Heathens" are mentioned briefly elsewhere in this homily, about three hundred half lines earlier, to cite Jewish laws against gentile mates (1945–60), but this usage adds little sense to Orrm's spiritual and definitional point: that all Christians are denoted through the words "Jacob" and "Jew." For "Jacob" he gives a definition related to its Hebrew meaning (from *ekev*, "heel"), and for "Jew" he gives both a Hebrew definition (linked to *yehudah*, "praise") and a lengthier gloss that echoes definitions elsewhere in the *Orrmulum* and, once again, makes "Jew" mean something like "good Christian." If anything, verbal echoes between this and the homily's earlier passage make inclusion of "hæþene þede" even stranger: "all follc wass hæþene þa ⁊ all it wass unnclene," Orrm had explained earlier, "Wiþþutenn þatt Judisskenn follc þatt ta wass Gode cweme" (all people were heathen then, and all were impure, except the Jewish people who then were pleasing to God) (1949–52). In the later passage, quoted just above, Orrm echoes the same phrase—"cweme to Gode" (pleasing to God)—now to define Jews in their Christian state: they "stanndenn inn to cwemenn Godd," that is, they *continue* to please God. There is no sense of "hæþen," however, that continues into this later passage, despite the echo—*unless* Orrm has been influenced by the free application of *haereticus* (heretic) to the Jew and Judaism in twelfth-century Latin *contra Judaeos* texts and thus allows his terms to bleed. *Haereticus*, in this view, perhaps lies alongside *paganus* (heathen, pagan) and *gentilis* (gentile, non-Christian) in Orrm's efforts to create a Middle English vocabulary from both Latin and Old English readings: in Old English, *hæþen* could equally well refer to Jews, Danes, Muslims, gentiles, or pagans.[60]

In Orrm's definitions, doublings, and repetitions, then, "Jew" loses its particularity in the service of establishing Christian ancestral and spiritual identities. This is compatible with Cohen's and R. I. Moore's observations that terms like "leper, heretic, and Jew became virtually interchangeable designations in twelfth-century Christian taxonomies."[61] It is Orrm's unique approach within a field of English and continental scholars, however, that makes "Jew" become virtually interchangeable with "Christian." In the *Orrmulum*, he applies himself to a formal and linguistic execution that embraces sameness as an approach to scripture, sources, exemplars, and Jews. Where Cannon's Derridean reading of Orrm's repetitions and resulting recursions assigns negative value to sameness—because repetitive use of the same words "can actually exhaust their capacity to mean"[62]—I see polemical value. Both the extended exegetical procedure by which Orrm defines and undermines "Jew" and the resulting semantic uncertainty that arises mean that Jews, an actually distinct people, are little more than preacher's rhetoric within a Christianity that seeks, precisely, to "undermine [their] signification"; Cannon's more optimistic allowance for a resulting "heightened awareness," "the recognition that, even after they are pressed together as if one . . . two terms are *still* different," is, in my view, the point.[63] It is what Orrm knows when he preaches the sameness of Christian and Jew and instructs his parishioners in Christian Jewishness.

We can now return to that thought experiment that began this chapter: could Orrm from Lincolnshire be an English Jew who converted to Christianity, became an Augustinian canon, and wrote English vernacular sermons in an attempt to convert other English Jews, perhaps those in nearby Stamford? No. It is an interesting question to ponder, but an affirmative answer is possible only in a monolingual environment and without acknowledging Orrm's polemics or scholarly contexts. Neither Orrm nor England was monolingual or isolated. The fact that Orrm so thoroughly engages the "newly reinvigorated Christian study of the Old Testament" makes him not a converted English Jew but a learned English Christian of his time—one of the "Latin masters," as Clanchy has it—writing with knowledge of contemporary anti-Jewish genres and exegesis.[64] His unique contribution is his elaborate formal, exegetical, and pastoral commitment to the transmission of sacred, textual, and oral knowledge of Jewishness. He effects this through doubles, corrections, and repetitions, and through imagined copies of his text, Jewish texts, the Christian self, and the "Jew." Orrm's English copy of the Jew, as it turns out, had at least one modern critic fooled.

The Jew at Bury St Edmunds

Around the time that Orrm was finishing the *Orrmulum*, another vernacular preacher was confronting Jewish presence and Jewish practices at the Abbey of Bury St Edmunds. Samson of Tottington (d. 1211) was a monk at Bury by the 1160s and abbot by 1182, when he was forty-seven years old. His biographer Jocelin of Brakelond describes him as a man who "erat eloquens, Gallici et Latini" (was eloquent both in French and Latin), and who "scripturam Anglice scriptam legere nouit elegantissime, et Anglice sermocinare solebat populo, set secundum linguam Norfolchie, ubi natus et nutritus erat" (read English perfectly, and used to preach in English to the people, but in the speech of Norfolk, where he was born and bred).[65] To support his English preaching, Jocelin says, Abbot Samson "pulpitam iussit fieri in ecclesia . . . ad utilitatem audiencium" (ordered

a pulpit to be set up in the church ... for the benefit of his hearers) (40). He was
a poet too, like Orrm: he wrote "uersus elegiacos" (elegaic verse) for a choir
screen he commissioned (9). Like Orrm, Samson would have had access to Old
English biblical translations and homilies in his abbey's library,[66] and he sought
to make vernacular preaching a feature of his institution.[67] While we do
not know as much about the life and ambitions of Orrm, Samson and Orrm
were similar creatures, and their similarity extends to the fact that they can be
characterized, in different ways, as men who incorporated "Jewish" features
into their views of the correct Christian self. Samson's biographer Jocelin of
Brakelond, at least, with his detailed accounts of institutional bureaucracy
and careful use of typological doublings, wrote Samson as another Christian
Jew.

The *Chronicle of Jocelin of Brakelond* opens, in the years before the election
of Abbot Samson, with Bury St Edmunds indebted to Jewish moneylenders.
Jocelin juxtaposes this indebtedness to a certain intimacy with the local Jewish
community. He complains that the Jews before Samson's abbacy

> liberum ingressum et egressum habebant, et passim ibant per
> monasterium, uagantes per altaria et circa feretrum, dum missarum
> celebrantur sollemnia; et denarii eorum in thesauro nostro sub
> custodia sacriste reponebantur, et, quod absurdius est, uxores eorum
> cum pueris suis in pitanceria nostra tempore werre hospitabantur.
> (10)

> had free entrance and exit, and went everywhere through the
> monastery, wandering by the altars and about the feretory while
> masses were being sung, and their money was kept in our treasury
> under the Sacrist's custody—and more unseemly still, in the days of
> the war their wives and children were put up in our pittencery.

This description, early in a text that is primarily interested in the abbacy and
character of Samson, is an arresting one. Jocelin's Jews are wandering Jews ("va-
gantes," he calls them), and they will eventually have no home in Bury. Their
presence means a juxtaposition of Jewish bodies with the sacred places of the
monastery (the altars), sacred ritual (the Mass), and sacred bodies (the eucharistic body present in the Mass but also the contents of the feretory where relics are
kept, in this case the body of Saint Edmund). In addition to his complaints
about debt and proximity, Jocelin claims to have written an account of the

death in 1181 of little Robert of Bury, reputedly killed by Jews: "Eodem tempore fuit sanctus puer Robertus martirizatus, et in ecclesia nostra sepultus, et fiebant prodigia et signa multa in plebe, sicut alibi scripsimus" (At this same time the holy boy Robert suffered martyrdom and was buried in our church, and many signs and wonders were performed among the common folk, as I have set down elsewhere) (16). Whatever Jocelin wrote about Robert is lost, but we know from other sources that the case was indeed one of those early English anti-Jewish ritual murder libels and that this child had a shrine at Bury, likely a rival to that of William of Norwich.[68] Given what we know of the decorative features of the Bury church at this time, it is likely that Samson promoted the cult.[69]

Seemingly as a climax to the purported problems created by the Bury Jews in its early folios, about a third of the way through his *Chronicle*, Jocelin gives an account of Samson's 1190 expulsion of Jews from Bury St Edmunds "arma manu conducti" (under armed escort) (46), an act connected to the massacres at Bury and other cities that took place after Richard I's coronation.[70] This expulsion of Jews is just one indication, says Jocelin, of Samson's "magne probitatis" (excellence) in the first decade of his abbacy (45). We should note, however, that despite Samson's consequent threat of excommunication for anyone who might let a Jew back into the liberty of St Edmund, Jocelin takes care to detail how Richard I's men at home in some ways undid Samson's historically precocious act:

> Quod tamen postea dispensatum est per iusticiarios regis, scilicit, ut si iudei uenerint ad magna placita abbatis ad exigendum debita sua a debitoribus suis, sub hac occasione poterunt duobus diebus et ii. noctibus hospitari in uilla, tercio autem die libere discedent. (46)

> Nevertheless, afterwards the King's justices ordained that, if Jews came to the Abbot's great pleas to exact the money owed them from their debtors, they should under those circumstances have leave to be lodged in the town for two nights and two days, and on the third day should depart in freedom.

In other words, though they are not mentioned again after this passage, Jews and their documents continue to surround Samson. The figure of the Jewish moneylender and debt collector remains, and Jewish bodies, we should understand, are thus ever, silently and potentially, present. Indeed, the presence of Jews is fundamental to the whole of Jocelin's *Chronicle*. His descriptions of Jews' association with the monastery, his mention of the death of little Robert, his praise of Samson's explusion, and his note that Jews still entered the liberty are introductory to the text, set as polemical framing devices, and structurally crucial to his understanding of the abbot's character.[71] But what purpose do they serve for Jocelin's ultimate valorization of Samson?

Jocelin is sometimes praised for his historical accuracy and realism, especially in terms of his reliable recording of dates and figures, and because of his lively and occasionally moving descriptions of people and places.[72] Antonia Gransden used him as an example of the tail end of a tradition of "realistic observation in twelfth-century" English historical writing, one of the later but classic examples of a tradition that valued, among other things, description of "people's physical appearance, character and behaviour both individually and corporately as social beings."[73] While Gransden praises the "immediacy and humanity" of Jocelin's text, however, she reminds us too that "realism" does not mean "real": this kind of descriptive writing, rather, "often had commemorative intention" that might cause a writer to imbue a "person or object with holy association," or be motivated by "Christian piety" or "the study of classics," especially of Suetonius and Sallust, who shared an interest in the physical appearance of great men and the ways in which "the trivialities of everyday life" might be indications of moral character.[74] Neither should we forget the profound influence of the hagiographic tradition on monk historians, like Jocelin, who were bound to a range of hagiographic genre conventions when they approached biographical topics. Jocelin's formation of Samson in relationship to Bury Jews, in this light, has an important narrative function. In a nationalistic Anglo-Christian historiographical text that is interested in both expelling Jews and developing the character of a man who did, the biographer's knowledge and use of hagiographic, exegetical, and devotional modes, that is, should not be forgotten.

With some anatomizing of the early parts of Jocelin's *Chronicle*, indeed, it becomes clear that Jocelin exploits Christianized Jewish symbols and types to introduce Samson as heroic, as others have similarly posited.[75] More counterintuitively, though, Jocelin constructs a Christianized Jewish identity for Samson in this process. That is, Jocelin writes Samson as a man who—in the tradition of typology and symbolic reversal—not only opposes but also *resembles and incorporates* the people he seeks to expel and supersede. To show how this works, I will focus here on three ways that Jocelin characterizes Samson in relation to Jews: first, through the presence and use of documents; second, through allusions to the Israelite Samson of the book of Judges; and third, through his physical description of Abbot Samson.

First the documents. Both the presence of documents in Jocelin's *Chronicle* and observation of who carries and controls them are significant. As Daniel Gerrard has highlighted, Jocelin's text is "awash with documents."[76] Not only does the *Chronicle* begin with the compounding of documents associated with Jewish moneylending—as Jocelin puts it in his opening sentences, "semper renovabantur carte" (bonds were continually renewed) (1–2)—but Jocelin is also at pains throughout the early parts of his text to show that "documents were . . . central to Samson's approach to governing" and often employed with "theatricality" to emphasize their "important symbolic roles."[77] This theatricality (or, we might say, performativity) is key: documents function in the *Chronicle* not only as real objects but also as character attributes, as props. And there are only two sets of hands controlling the documentary transactions that involve these props: the hands of Jews and the hands of Samson.

If we then focus on how documents *change* hands in this text, Jocelin's description of wandering Jews in the abbey, with their money and bodies brushing uncomfortably against Christian sacred space and ritual, becomes a climactic one. His note of the presence of Jews near the altars and feretory is not just annoyed commentary but also punctuates a fast series of encounters with Jewish men carrying documents. As Jewish debt and people proliferate, so too do the "cartae" (charters or bonds), "literae" (documents, letters), and "sigilla" (seals) that Jocelin associates with them and their conspirators. The figure of the Jew carrying or holding documents appears nine times in the *Chronicle*'s first two manuscript folios (six printed pages in *CJB*):

1. "Uidi et aliam cartam fieri Isaac filio Raby Ioce" (I saw another bond given to Isaac the son of Rabbi Joce) (2)

2. "et terciam cartam fieri Benedicto iudeo de Norwico" (and yet a third [bond] to Benedict the Jew of Norwich) (2)

3. "sacrista . . . appruntauit a Benedicto iudeo xl. marcas ad usuram, et ei fecit cartam signatam quodam sigillo quod solebat pendere ad feretrum" (the sacrist . . . borrowed forty marks at interest from Benedict the Jew and gave him a bond sealed with a seal that used to hang from the feretory) (2)

4. "uenit iudeus portans literas domini regis" (the Jew came with letters from our lord the King) (2)

5. "aliquis . . . ita circumuenit abbatem, quod passus est cartam fieri Benedicto iudeo . . . et facta est carta sigillo conuentus signata" (someone . . . so deluded the Abbot [Hugh] that he allowed a bond to

be given to Benedict the Jew . . . and a bond was given sealed with the Convent's seal) (3)

6. "et facta est nova carta" (and a new bond was made [for Benedict the Jew]) (3)

7. "Habuit et idem iudeus plures alias cartas" (The same Jew also held a number of other bonds) (3)

8. "celerarius . . . appruntauit denarios a Iurneto iudeo . . . super cartam supradicto sigillo signatum" (the Cellerar . . . borrowed money from Jurnet the Jew . . . on a bond sealed with the aforementioned seal) (5)

9. "carta iudei usque hodie remansit apud iudeum" (the Jew's bond has to this day remained in the possession of the Jew) (6)

These passages and bonds do not represent nine individual Jews—the same Jews (notably brothers Benedict and Jurnet of Norwich[78]) appear several times—but their documents multiply, and the cumulative effect is *figuratively* powerful: the repetition results in an obscuring of the historical situation, such that a near tableau-like, and theologically meaning-laden, image of the law-bearing Jew remains. The figure of the Jew carrying letters and bonds—the "Judeus portans literas"—appears in the opening moments of the *Chronicle* almost to the point of caricature.

We can see how Jocelin aligns Samson with this caricature right away, as a parallel motif, and with a considerable number of verbal echoes. When we first see Samson in action, he is someone who, along with a Master R. Ruffus, has "impetraverunt literas" (secured letters) from the king (8). Not much later, he is singled out as the abbey's law-bearer: en route to the king's court to elect a new abbot, Samson, like the Jew "portans literas" (carrying letters), travels as the abbey's "provisor expensarum" (manager of expenses), and "circa collum scrinium portans, quo litere conuentus continebantur" (hung about his neck he carried a lettercase containing the letters of the convent) (19). Elsewhere, as he takes up his abbacy, he collects and displays documents and seals to great effect, forbidding others to have control over seals and debt bonds (30, 38), at one point dragging into chapter "sacculum plenum cartis cancellatis" (a bag full of cancelled bonds) and crying "Ecce . . . Ecce tot carte" (Behold . . . Behold all these bonds!) (30), to illustrate with what efficiency he has resolved debts to Jews within his first year as abbot.

A list of passages that feature Samson with documents and seals—offered below somewhat repetitively for ease of consideration in relation to the previous list—begins shortly after Jocelin's litany of Jewish debt bonds:

1. "Magister Sampson et Magister R. Ruffus . . . impetrauerunt literas"
   (Master Samson and Master R. Ruff . . . secured letters) (8)

2. "Postremus omnium fuit Samson prouisor expensarum. . . . circa
   collum scrinium portans quo litere conuentus continebantur" (Last
   of them all was Samson, who had charge of their expenses. . . . Hung
   about his neck he carried a case containing the letters of the convent)
   (19)

3. "Dixit nouum sigillum esse faciendum. . . . sigillo autem prioris nostri
   hucusque usus fuerat, singulis literis in fine subscribens, quod
   proprium sigillum non habuit, unde et sigillo prioris oportuit uti ad
   tempus" (He said that a new seal must be made. . . . Up to this time he
   used the Prior's seal, adding at the end of each letter that he had no
   seal of his own, wherefore he had to use the Prior's for the time being)
   (26)

4. "confirmauit nobis nouo sigillo suo xl. solidos. . . . Et proposuit
   edictum ut nullus de cetero ornamenta ecclesie inuadiaret . . . nec
   aliqua carta sigillaretur sigillo conuentus nisi in capitulo coram
   conuentu" (he confirmed to us sixty shillings with his new seal. . . .
   And he issued an edict that henceforth no man should pledge any
   ornaments of the church . . . and that no charter should be sealed with
   the seal of the Convent save in Chapter in the presence of the
   Convent) (29–30)

5. "intrauit capitulum . . . extrahens sacculum plenum cartis cancellatis
   adhuc sigillis pendentibus . . . de quibus omnibus pacem faceret infra
   annum post eleccionem suam. . . . 'Ecce,' inquit . . . 'Ecce tot carte'"
   (he entered the Chapter . . . drawing forth a bag full of cancelled
   bonds, with their seals still hanging from them. . . . For all these
   bonds he had come to terms within a year of his election. . . . "Behold," he said . . . "Behold all these bonds") (30)

6. "iussit in capitulo, ut quiccumque sigillum proprium haberet, ei red-
   deret . . . et inuenta sunt triginta tria sigilla" (he gave orders in Chapter
   that anyone who possessed a seal of his own should deliver it up to
   him . . . and thirty-three seals were found) (38)

Through this early emphasis on Samson's carrying and accumulating of documents and seals, Jocelin aligns the abbot with his earlier-established figure of
the Jew carrying and accumulating documents. As he takes up his abbacy, Samson has literally canceled Jewish law and transferred its symbolic object to him-

self. In a distinct mirroring of the economic concerns of the Jewish lenders at the start of the *Chronicle*, Jocelin even pointedly comments amid these descriptions that "cum peruentum erat ad denarios capiendos raro remittebat quod iuste accipe potuit" (when it was a matter of getting money, he [Samson] rarely remitted what he might justly receive) (34–35). Samson overtakes and supersedes Jewish documents and Jewish legal processes, yes, but his character, or caricature, is visually, affectively, and performatively like the figure he has superseded.

Alongside Jocelin's use of documents, his use of biblical typology in his characterization of Samson becomes more notable than it might otherwise be. At the same time that he creates his mirrored figures of Bury Jews and Abbot Samson carrying documents, Jocelin explicitly evokes Samson's biblical namesake. In fact, he first does so very shortly after introducing the future abbot, so that we must always read two Samsons in this text: Samson the abbot of Bury and Samson the righteous Old Testament Israelite, who is the narrative and exegetical counterbalance to the living *Iudeus portans literas* that Abbot Samson both opposes and reflects. Jocelin's first extended characterization of Samson includes this typological double, and it surrounds the above-quoted complaint about Bury Jews wandering near the abbey's altars and feretory.

When Samson was subsacrist, we are told, he busied himself repairing and beautifying abbey structures—sometimes, as I have already mentioned, with his own poetry. "In diebus illis," says Jocelin, "chorus noster fuit erectus, Samsone procurante, historias picture ordinante, et uersus elegiacos dictante" (In those days our choir-screen was built under the direction of Samson, who arranged the painted stories and composed elegiac verses for each) (9), using money of uncertain origin to do so. Jocelin's account of the associated suspicions of William the Sacrist—a rival to Samson, whom Jocelin calls the "pater et patronus" (father and patron) of the Jews (10)—occasions his comment about the wandering Jews at Bury, and it also causes him to recount how William, to stop the future abbot from continuing to use money for such things, plotted "qualiter irruerent in Samsonem inimici uel aduersarii eius" (how his enemies or adversaries might fall upon Samson) (10). Since William succeeds in stopping Samson for a time, Jocelin declares: "Et sic illusus est Samson, et recessit ab eo fortitudo eius" (And thus Samson was outwitted, and his strength went from him) (11). In this, Jocelin quotes the biblical phrase that appears at Judges 16:17 and 16:19, when Delilah cuts off Samson's hair. When, later, two king's custodians are removed from oversight of the abbey—they had been put in place during the abbatial vacancy before Samson's election—Jocelin adds that Samson "resumptis uiribus suis, et subuersis duobus columpnis" (recovered his strength, and those two pillars were removed) (11), thus also alluding to the two pillars of the Philistine temple that the Israelite Samson topples in an act of self-sacrifice in Judges 16:29–30.

Elsewhere in the *Chronicle* Jocelin explicitly uses the Israelite Samson to describe Abbot Samson's troubles with rents and tax collection. In 1197, says Jocelin, Samson had settled a series of rent disputes "et quasi in pace dormisset" (and as it were, slept in peace), until, "ecce iterum" (behold once more), a complaint arose from London herring merchants who felt they had been wrongly taxed by Bury reeves; or, as Jocelin somewhat melodramatically expresses it, "Philistiim super te, Sampson" (The Philistines be upon thee, Samson!) (76). This is of course an echo of Delilah's dissembling words as she tries to discover the secret of the biblical Samson's strength, repeated four times in Judges 16 to rouse the Israelite strongman from sleep after each attempt to weaken him.

Other echoes of the biblical characteristics of Samson can be gleaned throughout the *Chronicle* in this light. Samson's constant barely contained rage might be compared to the rage of the biblical hero after he loses his first Philistine wife in Judges 15, as might Jocelin's commentary on how the monks of Bury feared Samson.[79] Jocelin notes how Samson boasted in response to challenges, "Ego numquam flectar" (Nothing shall move me) (98), and that he was always the "fortiorem" (braver) and "potentiorem" (stronger) in any fight (120). There are several anecdotes in the *Chronicle* in which Samson threatens to destroy buildings,[80] and he is sometimes described as figuratively blind—"tanquam non uidens erat" (as one who saw not) (40), once threateningly pressing his fingers against his eyes, in response to threats to the abbey's hereditary rights, and shouting "perdam oculos istos" (may I lose these eyes!) (58)—which we can connect to the biblical Samson's blinding by the Philistines in Judges 16:21. Abbot Samson, Jocelin says further, prefers to eat "mel et consimilia dulcia libencius quam ceteros cibos comedebat" (honey and the like more than any other food) (40), recalling the biblical Samson's eating of honey from the lion's mouth at Judges 14:8–9. But we need not explore all of these allusions in great detail. What is clear is that the biblical story is activated in the *Chronicle*: the more elements of the Samson story Jocelin alludes to (explicitly or implicitly), the more the story becomes present in the narrative, and the greater the encouragement to readers to reflect on its range of meanings.[81]

The standard patristic sources available in twelfth-century England for this purpose, including those cited in the *Glossa ordinaria*, emphasize first that the biblical Samson is "at the literal level . . . a mighty defender of his people and a tragic victim of treachery and deceit; [and] allegorically, he is Christ"; he is a hero of Hebrew scripture whose birth, temptation, suffering, destruction, and victory all prefigure Christ.[82] And the Christ allegory is certainly not at odds with Jocelin's depiction of Samson: for example, Jocelin describes him entering the abbey after his election in 1182 as a figure of Christ entering Jerusalem. Samson arrives on Palm Sunday, barefoot, riding a horse and "multitudine hominum constipatus" (surrounded by a multitude of men) (24). The liturgy and liturgical props for this day would have made Samson's entrance almost a dramatic performance of Christ's entrance into Jerusalem.

More interesting for my purposes, however, are corresponding associations of the Samson story with the oppression of Jews. This can express itself through the figure of Delilah, who, as a type, was frequently associated with the Synagogue, and "for that reason, she is a symbol of the Jews,"[83] but the most compelling contemporary instance of Samson as an oppressor of Jews appears in the *Pictor in carmine*, a popular large compilation of versified biblical types and antitypes compiled in England in the late twelfth century. The *Pictor* was used for church decoration and *tituli*, that is, for captions or verses that might accompany paintings or illustrations; it was probably a West Midlands monastic production, and it survives in at least twenty manuscripts.[84] The work expresses its typological reading of Samson's victories in a series of "*tituli*-couplets" that succinctly triangulate Samson, Christ, and Jews:

(1) Vi quatiens postes Samson ruit et necat hostes.
Sic tua, Christe, reos mors in cruce uicit Hebreos.
(2) Gens datur erumpne duplicis sub mole columpne.
Que perit est frendens plebs, qui quatit est cruce pendens.
(3) Fit mors Samsonis Gaze pressura colonis.
Sic genus in laqueum crux Christi ducit Hebreum.

(1) Breaking the doorposts Samson falls and kills his enemies.
Your death on the cross, Christ, conquered the guilty Jews.
(2) People are subjected to suffering under the heap of the two columns.
He dies who is lamenting; he breaks the columns who hangs on the cross.
(3) Samson's death becomes an affliction for the dwellers in Gaza.
Thus Christ's cross puts the Jewish people in fetters.[85]

The *Pictor* shows that the association of Samson with power over Jews—via Samson's typological association with Christ—was not unusual in Jocelin's time and place. It was standard enough to be part of this popular artist's handbook of correct types and antitypes to use in church design, compiled by an author or authors interested in instructing illiterate and lay audiences in the basics of the figural and spiritual meanings of Christian scripture.

To conceive of the range of typological possibilities that Jocelin embedded in his text, however, requires some associative leaps. At a figural level, the *Chronicle* allows that we simultaneously read Abbot Samson as (the Jew) Christ, the Israelite hero Samson, and the document-carrying twelfth-century Jew (or the superseded, corrected document-carrying Jew); but we also have the Philistines as Jews (just as the *Pictor in carmine* couplets express it, via connection to Christ's "conquering" of Jews through self-sacrifice), and we have the Philistines as the merchants and royal officials around Bury St Edmunds ("The Philistines be upon thee, Samson!"); and finally, of course, everyone is also plainly themselves, both within the history that Jocelin narrates on a literal level and also in the *Chronicle*'s Anglo-Christian centric history, through a presumed-shared sense of Jewish past and Christian future. The historical and the typological depend on one another, in other words, and this complex figural structure thus extends even to those parts of Jocelin's *Chronicle* that appear to be most representative of the realistic and accurate historical observations that Antonia Gransden recognized in his work.

It is also the nature of typology that a type resembles what it opposes. Jocelin surely plays on Samson's Hebrew name to create a connective contrast between the good, old Hebrew and the bad, current Jews,[86] but let us emphasize that creating this contrast requires making Samson recognizably *like* the "real" Bury Jews. If Jocelin's typology turns Abbot Samson into the self-sacrificing Israelite hero who is also a type of Christ conquering the old Jewish law, at the same time and of necessity, it must turn him into an image of the expelled Bury Jews who wandered about the abbey's altars and feretory. I have already shown how this happens through Jocelin's repetitive parallel imaging of both the Jews and Samson as letter carriers who hoard money-related documents and seals, but a final element of Jocelin's characterization will push the productive tension between opposition and resemblance further. For Jocelin's famous, seemingly realistic, physical description of Abbot Samson can be read as a costuming of Samson that creates a moment oddly suggestive of Jocelin's and other medieval Christian caricatures of living Jews.

Jocelin tells us, in his long passage on Samson's appearance, that the abbot had "naso eminente, labiis grossis" (a prominent nose, thick lips) and that though he was nearly bald and gone gray in his later years, he had a "rufa barba" (red beard) and "capillos nigros, et aliquantulum crispos" (black hair and rather curly) (39).[87] Large noses, thick lips, beards, and red or dark curly hair are not necessarily always associated with medieval stereotypes and caricatures of Jews, especially at this early date in the history of such caricatures, and we should be careful not to read such descriptors in a modern or even late medieval racialized register. It is almost needless to point out, for instance, that Christ is usually depicted in this period with a beard, that red hair could be understood as a physiognomic indicator in other registers,[88] or indeed that the face of Saint Edmund himself is later described by Jocelin as possessing "nasum ualde grossum et ualde eminentem" (a nose which was very large and prominent) (114), so that Samson also physically resembles Saint Edmund.[89] Such physical markers could, too, be associated with the heroic Israelite Samson.[90] Still, the particular combination of attributes noted in Jocelin's text is striking, and Jocelin's overall description of Samson's physical and emotional personality fits well with recent scholarly assessments of medieval visual and physiognomic stereotypes of Jews in the twelfth and thirteenth centuries. These include a large nose, deformities of the face or lips, and a predisposition to passion, fear, or anxiety.

Though visual caricatures before the thirteenth century are relatively rare, both Anthony Bale and Irven Resnick have summarized the typical physical stereotypes in descriptive caricatures of Jews from the twelfth century, especially in university physiognomy texts: "hallmarks of the medieval Jewish stereotype" were set by the late twelfth century and included "'curve of the nose,' 'deformity' [of the mouth], . . . 'passion' and 'fear'," says Bale, quoting the twelfth-century Italian scholar Boncampagno da Signa.[91] Or, according to Resnick, "we do have some evidence from the twelfth and thirteenth centuries that suggests that Jews *were* seen" as physically different, despite likely indistinguishablity from Christians that elsewhere caused anxieties over passing; male "Jews increasingly will be depicted [in Christian books of this period] with dark skin tones, bulbous eyes [and] hooked noses," with the large "'Jewish nose'" being "one of the most important physiological markers used to designate ethnicity."[92] More specifically worth consideration is Samson's red beard, as red hair and red beards could be associated with Jews throughout the Middle Ages, and particularly with Judas Iscariot.[93]

Bale calls the stylization of Judas as "the red-haired traitor" "one of the most common, and misunderstood, medieval images," so old and fundamental that through it red hair and red beards are still found to be idiomatically associated with Judas in much of Western Europe.[94] Ruth Mellinkoff describes "red hair, red beard, ruddy skin (or all three)" as the typical visual markers for Judas, and by extension Jews, well into the Renaissance period.[95] Denise Despres reminds us, too, that "other unmistakable Old Testament characters link Jews with red hair, including Cain and David," but that red hair or beards are "largely indicative in medieval art with [sic] scurrilous Jews," and English manuscripts provide some of the earliest examples.[96] Examples of the trend exist in well-known English manuscripts earlier than and roughly contemporary with Jocelin's *Chronicle*: BL MS Cotton Nero C IV (The Winchester Psalter), a mid-twelfth-century English manuscript, shows red-haired arresters and torturers of Christ in its illustrations of the Betrayal and the Flagellation (fol. 21r), where Judas and the arresters in particular are shown with red and/or curly hair that is notably distinct from Christ's; in Hildesheim, Dombibliothek Hildesheim, St. God. 1 (The St Albans Psalter), another mid-twelfth-century English monastic production, a full-page illustration of the Mocking of Christ shows Jesus with several caricatured red-haired tormentors (fol. 43r); and BL MS Arundel 157 (The Munich Psalter), produced in England in the first quarter of the thirteenth century, features the red hair and beard of Judas at the Betrayal, again as distinct from those around him (fol. 9v).

But if Jocelin associated Samson with the Jews mainly through typological and symbolic reversals—most explicitly through allusions to his heroic Israelite namesake, but also through his parallel holding, hoarding, and canceling of documents—why might he also allow such a potentially negative caricature of Samson to creep in? The answer, I think, lies in consideration of the meaning of redness in association with Judas Iscariot. Bale has argued convincingly that Judas's red hair or beard in medieval illustrations is a more ambiguous sign than it might seem: it is "a bloody marker, not an 'ethnic' fact"; it functions in accordance with "Christian physiognomic theory [that] red hair . . . indicated 'rashness, / lack of providence and discretion [and] biting wrathfulness.'"[97] This sounds much like Jocelin's less flattering descriptions of Samson, wherein fellow monks took to "discrecionem abbatis feritatem lupi appellantes" (styling the Abbot's prudence as the ravening of a wolf) (89). As Bale points out, red hair "as a performed 'sign'" could be Judas-like or Jew-like not as a mark of actual Jewish identity but merely inasmuch as it associated Judas with "spilt blood and violent martyrdom," especially Christ's, and thus, like the association of blood-red symbols with other martyrs, had the potential to turn "the stain of bloody violence into a valorized image of baptism."[98] Bale's argument is compelling in this context, especially because Jocelin straightforwardly associates Samson with Judas's betrayal of Christ *at his very first mention of Samson*. He puts in Samson's mouth, at that moment, a line from Luke 22: of the abbey's indebtedness to Jews, Samson says, "Hec est hora tenebrarum" (This is the hour of darkness) (4–5; cf. Luke 22:53). Jocelin thus has Samson's first words in the *Chronicle* echo Jesus's words to his disciples in the chapter of Luke that narrates Judas's betrayal. This red mark (red hair or red beard) can thus be read as evidence *both* of some connection with Jews *and* a further typological connection with Christ. It is similar in this way to how the biblical Samson functions as a Christ type, and to how Jocelin uses the legal document as a transferable symbol between Jews and Christians. All of these indications of sameness are simultaneously signs of Jewish rejection of Christianity and Christian incorporation of Jewishness.

What I am arguing about the complexity of Jocelin's anti-Jewish polemic and related characterization of Abbot Samson could upset the notion that what we have in Jocelin's *Chronicle* is a historiographical tradition of "realistic observation," but none of what I say here requires mutual exclusivity with the "real," and certainly not with "realism." The links in the associative chain I am describing around Jocelin's introduction and description of Samson—Jews, money, altars and relics, documents, Samson and Delilah as Christ and the Synagogue, physical caricatures related to Jewish types, red hair as a meaningful mark connected both to Jews and to Christian martyrs—all occur together in the first third of the *Chronicle* and create a triangulation between the biblical Samson, Abbot Samson, and Jews. All are part of the introduction of Samson into the *Chronicle*'s narrative, and all have some connection to Jocelin's later developments of his character: Samson as heroic and raging, as an expeller of Jews, as a controller of documents and money and buildings, indeed as someone who begged Henry II to take the cross to recover Jerusalem (*CJB* 53–54). It is even possible, if we imagine the possible content of Samson's English sermons in light of Orrm's homilies, composed in the same historical period and not too far away, that Jocelin's implicit arguments for the sameness of Old Testament, New Testament, and twelfth-century English "Jews" reflect Abbot Samson's own ways of teaching and preaching.

Jocelin's connection of Abbot Samson to Christ, even as he characterizes him as the Israelite Samson *and* the expelled Bury Jews, is a symptom of slippage between difference and sameness. Kathleen Biddick's comment that figural methods cannot "move from the event to its fulfillment without passing through doubleness" should come to mind again now: since "figure and letter are both real and possible," they "therefore are always doubled and consequently

can be *self-reversing*."⁹⁹ Once we notice that Jocelin explicitly evokes the Israelite Samson, a full range of associated interpretive possibilities are available, and
Samson may "pass through doubleness" in this process. Blurring of the contrasts and oppositions creates interpretive and affective difficulties; Jocelin very
often suggests sameness even as he (with Samson) rejects the people who are
apparently the same. The struggle through such difficulties, however, is also the
point: Jocelin and other thinkers of this period are in the process of considering
how to incorporate, assimilate, and be "the Jew" while still rejecting the living
Jews around them. The act of drawing attention to sameness then becomes polemical in itself. As a polemical mode, sameness is intellectually and devotion-
ally stimulating: it urges, and exists in service of, continual and challenging
inquiry into Christian identity.

Another way to read Jocelin's use of Christianized Jewish types and symbols is to say bluntly that Samson becomes the Bury Jew whom he expels, but
that it is only possible for him to become the Jew because he has already expelled the Jews. The assumption of idealized or fetishized Jewish attributes,
Jewish features, and Jewish heroics is made insidiously possible by both the priority and the erasure of the Jewish twin, both in Christianity generally and in
Bury St Edmunds and Jocelin's text specifically. From this perspective, what
Samson becomes in Jocelin's work, exactly as Orrm preaches in the homilies of
the *Orrmulum*, is the Jew who signifies an unbroken line between Israelite and
(Christian) English history. This too, of course, is a polemical outcome: it is not
realistically or historically true, but narratively and typologically it justifies the
absence of living Jews by creating a new kind of Jewish presence. This expulsion,
accomplished by the figural methods employed in the *Chronicle of Jocelin of
Brakelond*, is as devastating as any other, for it necessitates an embodiment of
the Jew that it must also forget.

Forgetting Sameness

The forgetting that Jocelin of Brakelond does as he aligns Abbot Samson with
both living and biblical Jews must be interrogated on typological, historical,
and national levels. Polemics of sameness distort difference and resist clear definitions of "Jew" and "Christian" for didactic purpose. Distinct from formal ex-
periments with sameness (which have been fruitfully critiqued in the *Orrmulum*
as failures of signification), polemics of sameness *want* signification to fail; they
argue that "Jew" and "Christian" mean both more and less than any notion of

the difference between them allows. In the examples I have discussed thus far, Jewishness and Jewish presence are not facilitating an us/them binary but a powerful (Christian) urge to identification, self-actualization, and mimicry.

Such polemics have profound implications; they are prerequisite to othering, and they are aimed at manipulations of uncertainty and Christian potential. In England, even the story of the Wandering Jew was always about a Christian. The earliest known images of this "Jew" appear in the works of the Oxford illuminator William de Brailes (in BL MS Additional 39999, The De Brailes Hours, ca. 1240) and the St Albans monk Matthew Paris (in his *Chronica majora*);[100] Matthew's colleague Roger Wendover provided the first English narrative of the Wandering Jew in the *Flores historiarum* annals for 1228, and Matthew copied the 1228 account and reiterated it in his own *Chronica* annal for 1252.[101] The Wendover/Paris account, however, pointedly omits the Jew's Jewishness,[102] and no medieval iteration of the Wandering Jew is clearly related to the legendary figure or his identifying label—*le Juif errant* or *der ewige Jude*—as he came to be known in anti-Jewish propaganda from the seventeenth century on.[103]

The Wendover/Paris narrative, rather, tells of an Armenian bishop who visited St Albans and told the monks of a man called Joseph Cartaphilus (i.e., the dearly beloved), who was "praetorii ostarius et Pontii Pilati" (a doorman of the hall and Pontius Pilate).[104] Separate from the Jews who brought Jesus before Pilate, Cartaphilus watched the scene and, "trahentibus . . . Judaeis Jesum extra praetorium" (as the Jews were dragging Jesus out of the hall), he challenged Jesus to go faster on his way to death. Jesus turned, so goes the story that the St Albans community learned, and said, "Ego vado, et expectabis donec veniam" (I am going, and you will wait until I come).[105] Cartaphilus was baptized shortly after this encounter by the same man who baptized Saint Paul, and he remains alive "in argumentum fidei Christianae" (as proof of the Christian faith), dwelling among clergy as "homo sanctae conversationis et religionis" (a religious man of holy conversation).[106] Like the disciple Nathaniel—Orrm's "duhhti3 Judewisshe mann" (great Jewish man)—Matthew Paris's wandering "Jew" accepted Jesus after a direct encounter with him and uses his "Jewish" encounter with Christ to live as an idealized Christian. The early English illustrations of this man do suggest Jewish caricature or attributes,[107] but the foundational Anglo-Christian narrative works in tension with the fact. Joseph Cartaphilus is associated with Pilate—a fraught association to be sure, and one proximate to Jewishness, as discussed in the previous chapter—but he was never a Jew.

We miss something essential about the use and flexibility of such figures, and indeed their image-text relationships, if we assign marks of difference that are there only proleptically. We miss a polemical mode where stories of Jewish presence and supersession are predicated on a Jewish-Christian sameness that is concomitant with, and implicated in, Christian depictions and narratives of Jewish difference, carnality, or violence. When Christians identify the Christian with the Jew, whether as an aspirational goal or as a negative limit case—or both at the same time—they engage in an intellectual and imaginative territorialism that is ideologically related to physical expulsion and participates in an eschatology that insists on the ingathering or conversion of Jews to Christianity. Polemics of sameness are not merely about supersession, in other words; the case for sameness entails erasure by embodiment. Where is the space for a living Jewish body if the Christian has already gathered it—samed it, harmonized it—to himself?

The various writings I have discussed in Part I—chronologically, those of Thomas of Monmouth, Orrm, Jocelin of Brakelond, the curial scribe who recorded the Jurnepin/Odard case, the Exchequer scribe who recorded the crime and punishment of Samson son of Samuel of Northampton, and the poets of the Judas Ballad and devotional lyrics in BL MS Harley 2253—show a range of possibilities for the use of sameness before and around the 1290 Expulsion of Jews from England. Jewish similarity to Christians could be troublesome in legal realms, just as it could be in devotional, homiletic, and historiographical realms, where a desire to same Jew and Christian for the purpose of Christian self-assessment could result in simultaneously ameliorative and pejorative conceptions of Jewishness. State powers and English authors, across languages and genres, found themselves "passing through doubleness" on the way to establishing difference, typology, and the Christian incorporation of Jewish pasts and futures, and they sometimes used Jewish sameness with intention—sitting in it rather than passing through it—to exploit the conjoining of difference and sameness for pastoral and devotional purposes.

I do not mean to suggest that sameness overtakes difference in medieval English Christian-Jewish polemics, nor do I imply that binary contrasts or simple difference alone mark prior scholarly engagements with the topic (of course not). Rather, I am insisting that taking note of sameness as its own polemical category—and of saming as exegetical processes that can be analyzed like processes of othering—allows us to interrogate evocations of Jewish similarity or ambiguity as they coexist with, and interact with, uses and evocations of contrast and difference. We should not forget sameness because it is (by design) difficult to see, nor because it seems somehow more humane than otherness, lest we unwittingly perpetuate its polemical goals. Wherever mimicry and uncertainty about the line between Christian and Jew exist, that uncertainty itself can be mobilized—legally, didactically, historically, politically—in rhetorical challenge to Jewishness, or in redefinition of both Jewishness and Christianness. Sameness imagines, and can effect and justify, real Jewish absence. The clustering of my evidence before and around the 1290 Explusion of Jews from England, therefore, should be no surprise. The contradiction between the suffering Jewish Christ and the stereotypical Jew, just as the connection between the suffering Jewish Christ and the ideal Christian, is a prompt that encourages reflection on the problem of Jewish-Christian sameness as it also existed (and exists) in the world. Sampson son of Samuel of Northampton, we might say at the end of this part that began with his *historia*, fittingly responded to this rhetorical violence: he inverted legal and clerical attempts to same the Jew by dressing and preaching as a friar, and then he evaded the punishment that sought to reintegrate him into Christian (figural) Jewishness.

In Part II, "The Unmarked Jewess," we will see that a forgetting of sameness, accompanied by scholarly preoccupations with difference, has hitherto obscured understanding of Anglo-Christian polemics around Jewish women in particular, for the Jewish woman (as told and depicted by Christians) epitomizes polemical uses of sameness. It will become clear, also, that the precocious development of a gendered anti-Jewish polemic fits England's historical situation unfortunately well. Pre-Expulsion legal records show that Anglo-Jewish women were more immersed in majority life and literacy than their continental counterparts, and thus that "the Jewess" held a distinct presence in the medieval English imagination. Postbiblical Jewish women appear consistently in the early literature of England, and women of ambiguous religious identity—that is, women who are aligned with Jews but purposefully made unidentifiable—play key roles in several English boy-martyr tales. If we add to these the many who appear in minor roles (for instance in the *Life of Christina of Markyate* or, indeed, the *Chronicle of Jocelin of Brakelond* and other historiographical records), and further add the many surviving records of Jewish businesswomen and female converts from Judaism, the amount of literature from medieval England that is explicitly concerned with postbiblical and contemporary Jewish women becomes a substantial corpus. What might this legion tell us? Is there a hermeneutical Jewess?[108] Is there a stereotypical Anglo-Jewess? In the pages ahead, I will argue in the affirmative and discuss the corpus of texts and images that provide the evidence. Anglo-Jewish women and their stereotypes have been hard to see only because of the subtle polemical devices employed by those who depict them.

PART II

THE UNMARKED JEWESS

More than, and less than, "woman," the Jewess is also both more and less than "Jew."

—Amy-Jill Levine, "A Jewess, More or Less"

The Convert and the Cleaner

> You want to know if I am English? . . . Yes, I will tell you. I am
> English-born. But I am a Jewess.
>
> —George Eliot, *Daniel Deronda*

The Convert

A woman named Alice of Worcester converted to Christianity from Judaism
sometime before 1272. She wrote two letters that survive, one in Latin and
one in French, because she found herself, after her conversion and the accession of King Edward I to the throne, in need of aid for herself and her son
John, who had apparently converted with her.[1] It is difficult to say who Alice
was before her conversion—she took a Christian name upon baptism—but
there is no reason to believe that she was not "of Worcester," and in various
ways her letters suggest that she was likely a prominent woman in the
Worcester Jewish community.[2] The neighboring Worcester and Gloucester
communities were small and intermarried in her time; they shared both ritual and financial resources, and they boasted leading national financiers of
both genders throughout the thirteenth century.[3] Of course, certainty about
Alice's preconversion life—let alone her postconversion life—is unattain-
able. As Monica Green has called for, however, we can expand the "concep-
tual frameworks" around lives like Alice's by "delineating the possible social
and physical spaces in which medieval women may have interacted" and, further, by closely examining "sources that might be creatively employed to illuminate what transpired in those spaces."[4] What can we, in this spirit, glean

about the life and character of Alice of Worcester through her letters? We know that she was a Jewish woman and mother, then a convert, then a person in transition between institutions, with dwindling patience and resources.

We know that Alice was literate and persistent. She petitioned the king directly, and she sent her son to the royal court in Gascony as her courier. In 1274, she wrote to Edward I in French, demonstrating that she had received support from Worcester Cathedral Priory in the past, by order of Henry III, and requesting confirmation of the newly crowned king's support:

> Alice the Convert of Worcester shows how she had charity in the
> Priory of Worcester by the grant of King Henry who was your father
> (may God have mercy on his soul), and then by your grant that you
> gave her in Gascony, where she sent her son when you were in those
> regions and where you granted him a letter that she ought to receive
> the charity until your coming into England. . . . Wherefore, since you
> have arrived in England (thanks be to our Lord), she begs you for the
> sake of God and holy charity, if it please you, that you grant her your
> letter to the Prior and Convent of Worcester that she might have and
> receive the charity as she received it formerly.[5]

Shortly after this message, nonetheless, Alice was destitute, apparently unable to secure help or lodging at Worcester. She thus turned to Robert Burnell, bishop of Bath and Wells, lord chancellor of England, and regent during Edward I's absence on crusade and in Gascony early in his reign. Burnell had apparently assigned her to a Coventry house sometime in or after 1275, but she had not been welcomed there either. Alice calls herself Burnell's "captiva" (his captive, or prisoner) and pleads emotionally for his help:

> I fly to you as to my refuge, praying tearfully, that you might give me
> relief in the matter of these desired things [i.e., sustenance and
> money]. Know that I am staying at Chester for as long as I cannot
> manage travelling, lacking means, until it pleases you to send some
> worthy benefice to me. . . . Would that you act on these things, lest in
> my weakness I am driven to beg and, if necessary, go on feet and
> hands. . . . Have mercy on me, a captive, according to the great mercy
> with which Lord Jesus Christ showed mercy to the blessed Mary
> Magdalene.[6]

A fifteenth-century copy of a third related letter, from Edward I to Worcester Cathedral Priory, takes up Alice's case and shows that the king did eventually advocate for her and her son. He had, it seems, already confirmed his father's grant of charity for Alice and her son after all, but Worcester was disobedient. To the prior and convent he writes,

> Because we do not wish to do injustice to . . . Alice and John, so we command you in this matter, as we have commanded before, that you are to effect such support of the same Alice and John from your aforesaid house as you did for them in the time of our said father, and so deal in this matter that they need not inquire at us for this reason again because of your failure, or show us cause why you have not previously performed our direct order to you.[7]

These letters by and about Alice fall into a period of about eight years at most, between August 1274 and March 1282. The chronology is implicit in the events mentioned: in her French letter to Edward I, Henry III is dead and Edward has recently returned to England from Gascony, probably for his August 1274 coronation; Robert Burnell was consecrated bishop of Bath and Wells in April 1275, and Alice uses that title for him. The first letter, then, likely dates between August 1274 and April 1275, and the second must be after April 1275. The regnal year on Edward's later letter to Worcester Priory is partially obscured by water damage—only the ascender of the single roman numeral is visible—but it appears to be the tenth, that is, 1282,[8] and was given in March of that year at Westminster. Clearly Alice's situation had changed dramatically between the time of Edward's return from Gascony—when she simply asked for renewed confirmation of royal support because, she says, "le Priour e les bone gent de la mesun [i.e., Worcester] le volunt ben" (the prior and the good people of the house truly desire it)—and Edward's later letter admonishing Worcester for disobeying his direct order by withholding that support. In between, though Burnell had sent her to Coventry (probably St. Mary's Priory), she reports that Coventry refused his order, leaving her stranded in Chester without funds. Before her wanderings ended, she also spent time at the Domus Conversorum in London, the house for converted Jews that was founded by Henry III in 1234. Post-Expulsion records list Alice among residents of the Domus in 1280 (apparently without her son), but her whereabouts were unknown by 1308, when Edward II ordered officials to assess the house and its residents.[9]

The two letters from Alice are not preserved in the same hand, and both mention that her son is carrying letters for her. It is likely that she employed scribes, though this fact does not, of course, exclude her authorship. It would not have been difficult to find serviceable scribes for such purposes in monastic houses, nor in city centers. Indeed, Alice's determination to advocate for herself in writing, to do so according to professional conventions, and to appeal to the highest levels of authority in more than one language is related to the kind of literacy we might expect for Anglo-Jewish women of her time, and especially among those involved in the business workings of the wealthiest Jewish families (as I will discuss thoroughly in the next chapter). These letters place her in environments of religious learning too, and her use of Latin for the more personal communication—both a letter and a lament, in the first person—is particularly striking.

The content of Alice's appeal to Robert Burnell and the dates of her letters do allow some educated speculation about how Alice viewed her circumstances and what transpired around and after her conversion. Her circle of acquaintances in the Worcester area likely included those associated with Burnell, including the Giffard family, who were influential in Worcester and nearby Hereford and involved with the Jewish communities of both towns in the same period. Alice may have found sponsorship for her conversion in the Giffards. Godfrey Giffard was bishop of Worcestor 1268–1302, and Walter Giffard may have been bishop of Bath and Wells at the time of Alice's conversion: he was elected in May 1264 and held the office until October 1266, when he was transferred to York, and we know from Alice's letter to Edward I that she converted and received royal orders for monastic support sometime during the reign of Henry III—certainly after 1255, when Henry ordered provision for Jewish converts at monasteries across England.[10] Both Giffard brothers were "notorious traffickers in Jewish debts,"[11] specifically those of the Worcester community, and both would have had to work with Robert Burnell in local and national business; both, like Burnell, also served as lord chancellor (briefly but in quick succession 1265–68). Property that came to the Giffard brothers from purchased Jewish bonds was gifted to their sister Alice Giffard after 1264, and Walter's son and heir to the Worcester bishopric was called John.[12] If our convert Alice was a Worcester financier, she would certainly have known and had dealings with this family, with Burnell, and with their associated institutions, and converts often took their sponsors' names upon baptism. One thirteenth-century convert, for instance, was known as Robert Grosseteste the Convert, because the bishop himself had been instrumental in his conversion.[13]

One might conjecture, also, that the 1275 expulsion of Jews from Worcester had something to do with Alice's travels and changing locations over the course of her letters and lifetime. Jews were expelled from the dower towns of Edward's mother, Queen Eleanor, in that year—Worcester among them—and those expulsions were complete by the end of 1275.[14] In the context of expulsion, it is possible that Worcester Cathedral Priory viewed their resident Jewish converts as Jews despite their conversion. Converts had little luck shedding their Jewish identity, apostasy was possible and sometimes just suspected, and conversions were occasionally disputed.[15] The religious houses to which Henry III had assigned converts resented the burden, and such arrangements were not always welcome or financially sustainable.[16] It is possible, too, that Alice had lingering ties to her former community and family. As Robert Stacey has argued, "In many cases their [i.e., converts'] connections with their former coreligionists appear to have remained closer than were their relationships to the Christian community they had now ostensibly joined."[17] Such connections could cause tension, but, to maintain them, it is conceivable that Alice may have *wanted* to move houses when the Worcester Jewish community was forced out of the area by expulsion.

Very little has been written about Alice's letters. Michael Adler knew of one in the 1930s, and Joan Greatrex briefly mentioned all three in her 1992 essay on monastic care of Jewish converts. Until 2020, only one of the three letters had been published, and Greatrex incorrectly summarized the content of the Latin letter to Burnell in her essay, taking the passive verb form "agar" (I shall be driven, compelled) as a reference to the biblical Hagar—an allusion that is not, in fact, anywhere in the letter.[18] Ruth Nisse, following Greatrex in her recent book *Jacob's Shipwreck*, repeats the agar/[H]agar misreading to interpret Alice's words as a "typological identification of Hagar with Mary Magdalene" that was not unknown in English exegesis of the time.[19] In this inherited misconstrual, Alice "personifies the enslaved Jerusalem" in a medieval exegetical tradition that sees Hagar as a type of exile.[20] Nisse's reading of what such an identification might express for a female convert is part of her wider discussion of conversion and apostasy in English historical, exegetical, and literary traditions, and it is extremely rich, if unfortunately not applicable to Alice's letter. Alice quite firmly aligns herself with Mary Magdalene alone. We must search elsewhere for how she aligns herself with the captive Jerusalem in her letter to Burnell, as indeed she does—and perhaps more subversively than the Hagar/Magdalene doubling can.

Though she does not employ typology, Alice used her biblical allusions confidently and persuasively. The final sentence of her letter to Burnell shows her skill: "Miserere mei, captiue," she writes, "pro maxima misericordia quam dominus iesus christus misertus fuit super beatam mariam magdalen" (Have mercy on me, a captive, according to the great mercy with which Lord Jesus Christ showed mercy to the blessed Mary Magdalene). Elsewhere in this letter, as noted above, she tells him that she is "praying tearfully" to him (lacrimabiliter exorando), and she worries that "in [her] weakness" (in infirmitate mea) she will be forced to beg and crawl as she wanders without the ability to sustain herself. By combining her tears and "infirmitate" with her final evocation of Mary Magdalene, Alice makes efficient and full use of the medieval figure of the Magdalene, a composite of several women, including the woman in the city at Luke 7:37–38, who washes Christ's feet with her tears, and Saint Mary of Egypt, who while alone in the desert was fed by manna from heaven when she prayed. Alice's phrase "in infirmitate mea" explicitly echoes the New Testament Magdalene: the word "infirmitate" (weakness or infirmity) is connected to Luke 8:2, the single passage where the Magdalene is described by name during Jesus's ministry, among "certain women who had been healed of evil spirits and infirmities," that is, in the Vulgate, "et infirmatibus." These allusions and the fact that Alice has experienced a conversion and wanders in need of support are an effective link to the medieval Mary of Egypt-Mary Magdalene conflation that is evident, for instance, in Jacobus de Voragine's thirteenth-century *Legenda aurea*. Alice's self-fashioning as an anxious and wandering "captiva," however, also constitutes an acknowledgment of her continuing connection to a Jewish past.

Alice calls herself "captiv[a]" twice in her letter to Burnell, first in the valediction, as quoted above, but also in the salutation, where she labels herself "sua captiva" (his [Burnell's] captive). The repetition is notable as much for its pathos as for its evocation of a biblical vocabulary specific to Jewish femininity. The word is a biting allusion to Isaiah 49 and 52, wherein Zion worries that she is "transmigrata et captiva" (led away and captive) (Isa. 49:21), and where the "captiva filia Sion" (captive daughter of Zion) is urged to "solve vincula colli tui" (loose the bonds from off [her] neck) and rejoice because she has been freed from her former exile and bondage (Isa. 52:1–2). Echoing Isaiah, Alice uses "captiva" here to marshal—powerfully so because from a female author—commonplace gendered metonyms for Jerusalem (Zion) and for the Jewish people (the daughter of Zion). These may seem stark connections for Alice the Anglo-Jewish convert to make: they suggest that she casts herself, in her post-conversion destitution and wandering, as a figure of Jerusalem before its salvation, as a Jewish captive in foreign (Christian) bonds. But there are only six instances of the word *captiva* in the Vulgate, and only in Isaiah is the *captiva* a woman worried about her children (as Alice with her son), "transmigrata et captiva . . . destituta et sola" (led away and captive . . . destitute and alone) (Isa. 49:21). Alice's choice of the word to frame her letter to Burnell, furthermore, suggests that it is as essential to her identity as his official titles are to his. In this letter, thus, she both takes on the character of a Christian feminine ideal (and convert) through Mary Magdalene *and* straddles Jewish and Christian ideas of the redemption of Jerusalem and the Jewish people by insisting nonetheless on her continued captivity. Alice shows an awareness of her own liminality, in other words—just as Nisse also sees her as "representative of the solitude of unbelief or of . . . liminality" in her captivity[21]—but she does so by making herself the captive daughter of Zion, not Hagar. She crafts herself as a figure of the Jewish people itself, working within a Christian vocabulary of urgency and spiritual need.

Still, these are just a few letters by and about one Anglo-Jewish woman convert writing early in the reign of Edward I. What can we take from them into the next chapters? First, let us remember that this formerly Jewish woman was literate to some degree and at least bilingual. More importantly, these small traces of Alice's life demonstrate the usefulness of looking to in-between spaces—liminal spaces, spaces between Christianity and Judaism, spaces that seem to offer only financial or institutional record—to glean information about Jewish women's lives and how they might be fashioned or perceived. Even if we cannot know who Alice was before her conversion, or what became of her in the end, the back-and-forth of her Christianized representation of herself, along with Edward I's representation of her need and persistence, is valuable for the interchange it reveals. Because of her conversion, Alice might not be considered a Jew, and clearly she understood herself as separate from her former people, but plausibly her Jewishness was part of her textual agency. Likely it influenced how king, bishop, and monks perceived her. *Certainly* it was part of her forced wandering and destitution.

Her willingness and ability to go directly to the highest authority in her own voice, to place her son as a courier to the king's court, and to write in the king's vernacular all correspond with what we know of Anglo-Jewish women's positions in business, legal, and family life in the thirteenth century—as the next chapter will detail. While Alice may be understood (or misunderstood) somewhere between religions, houses and communities, biblical types, and even names, then, it is precisely her place at the interface of religions, languages, and scholarly disciplines that activates her story for us. Voices like hers, and representations of women like her, are difficult to pin down and require creative use of sources from a range of institutions and disciplinary trajectories, but they betray what happens at the juncture points of Christianity and Judaism. They have historical and interpretive potential. They always did.

The Cleaner

Composed during Alice of Worcester's lifetime, and set in the same borderland territories, the grisly story of the ritual murder of Adam of Bristol hinges on the presence of a Jewish woman who appears to be Christian and is expected, by both her brother and a pilgrim priest, to convert to Christianity. Called by modern scholars the *Passion* (or *Legend*) *of Adam of Bristol*, by its thirteenth-century scribe a "pulchrum miraculum" (beautiful miracle), by the nineteenth-century cataloguer of the manuscript that holds it a "fabula ineptissima" (really absurd tale), and by many historians evidence of a historical accusation against Bristol Jews,[22] this *historia* might seem to create what Harvey J. Hames has called "a clear impermeable boundary" between Christians and Jews.[23] But it does not. A hidden Jewess controls both its plot and its outcome, and *Adam of Bristol* should be understood as a complex example of gendered polemics of sameness.

The *Passion of Adam of Bristol* tells the story of a widowed Jewess who pretends to be Christian so she can clean up the crimes of her brother Samuel, who has murdered four Christian boys (including, most recently, little Adam of Bristol) and now also his own wife and son, because they threatened to convert to Christianity. It begins with a divine voice that calls upon all listeners with an allusion to Isaiah 49:1: "Audite insule et attendite populi de longe. Hec dicit dominus deus" (Give ear, islands, and hearken, people from afar—so says the Lord God).[24] Citing the same chapter of Isaiah from which Alice of Worcester knew the "transmigrata et captiva" Zion, this voice thus specifically addresses Englishmen: first, it uses a term for England that was common to both Christians and Jews of the time—medieval Jews referred to England in Hebrew with the biblical phrase 'iyey hayam, "islands of the sea"[25]—and, with a play on *Juda/Judei*, it goes on to demand that "viri Juda" (men of Judah) listen to "quid fecerint michi judei in Anglia" (what Jews have done to me in England). With this regional lens in place, the divine narrator then introduces us to a Bristol Jew who had "unicam sororem et hec vidua erat" (one sister, and she was a widow). This Jew went to his sister to speak to her "in secreto" (privately, in secret), and so the woman took him to "locum secretum" (a secret location), and, once hidden, her brother cried out, "O soror mea dilecta, volo tecum colloqui de mirabili eventu" (Oh, my beloved sister, I flee to you to tell about an incredible event). From this point until about halfway through the narrative, the story is in Samuel's voice: he tells his sister how he has just committed three gruesome murders—first of a Christian boy called Adam, and then, impulsively, of his own wife and son. The latter two, persuaded by miracles occurring around Adam's body, were in the midst of turning to Christ. He has tried to bury Adam's body in his privy, but an angel guards the scene and bars him from entering. He has fled to his sister for help.

Like other ritual murder libels, *Adam of Bristol* fantasizes that Jews reenact the torture of Christ on a young Christian boy around the time of an important Christian festival, in this case the Assumption of the Virgin Mary. Unlike other ritual murder tales, however, it features a Jewish serial killer (Adam is Samuel's fourth victim); it is a Jewish family drama (between Samuel, his wife and son, and his sister); it does not conform to the gender conventions that analogous tales might lead us to expect (Samuel's wife and child are active participants in Adam's murder before miracles cause them to question their actions); and, though the text is complete, there is no conclusion in Jewish conversion or punishment (Samuel's wife and son say they will convert, but Samuel kills them before they can leave the home—and both Samuel and his sister avoid legal consequences and never acquiesce to conversion). The horror and polemics of this story are thus found as much in the ability of villainous Jews to go unnoticed and unpunished among a Christian majority as in the murders themselves.

The unique narrative survives in a gathering of BL MS Harley 957, a miscellany probably compiled into its current form in late fourteenth-century Norwich. The text of *Adam of Bristol* was written down in the late thirteenth century, however, and certainly composed earlier.[26] Its author claims that the events of the story occurred "in diebus Henrici regis patris alterius Henrici" (in the time of King Henry, father of the other Henry) (Cluse 305), and this likely refers to Henry II (r. 1154–89) but may be intentionally ambiguous.[27] The text as it survives is contemporary with repeated royal orders that Anglo-Jews don identification badges,[28] and its author, as Irven Resnick has pointed out, was clearly interested in exploiting Jewish similarity to Christians as a scare tactic.[29] The story is, in general, a fascinating tale of religious, national, and linguistic (porous) identities: it features a port-town location, names the boy Adam's father as William of Wales, sets Jewish homes amid Christian ones, and features characters who speak Latin, Hebrew, Irish, French, and English.[30] After the Jewish sister has heard about the murders and miracles, she enlists the help of an unwitting and sometimes drunk Irish priest who is passing through Bristol on his way to Rome, and the story thus features linguistic jokes and a good number of anti-Irish stereotypes as well.[31] It has yet to receive the thorough literary-historical attention it deserves.

For now, however, I am interested in the sameness of Samuel's sister, that is, her studied lack of Jewish difference. If Jewish sameness is a scare tactic in *Adam of Bristol*, it is in many ways a feminized scare tactic. For the full first half of *Adam of Bristol* (4.5 of its 8.5 folios), Christian readers are put in the position of the Jewish widow, Samuel's sister, harangued by her brother's gruesome account of his own violence and his family's near conversion. We know through Samuel's story that his wife bore witness to Christian miracles and professed her intent to convert, but for half of the text we, listening with her, can only imagine his sister's response. Her delayed characterization, indeed, means we may imagine anything: perhaps the sister will also want to convert, as Samuel's story teaches us a Jewish woman might? Perhaps she is in danger? The horrifying details of the murders allow us to think of the sister as potentially, by comparison with the wife, the ideal (converted) Christian reader:[32] in the face of Samuel's violence and the divine truth signaled through miracles around his victims, his sister *must* be turning Christian, mustn't she? And when the narrative catches up to her, we learn that she is indeed nearly a Christian—but not like her sister-in-law. Once Samuel's tale is finished, rather, his sister becomes his cleaner. Lacking the passions and emotions of her brother, using multiple languages (mostly to gather information and coordinate elaborate deceptions), purposefully appearing to be Christian, she successfully covers up her brother's crimes.

The sister's role in this narrative depends on her simultaneous hiddenness and access to Christians. As noted above, it begins when Samuel seeks her "in secreto" (in secret) at a "locum secretum" (secret place), and the word *secretum* and its derivatives appear seventeen times in the text, sixteen of them connected to the sister and her plans.[33] Her home hides her brother's belongings and wealth,[34] and her ability to conceal her Jewishness facilitates her success. Twice she emphasizes to her brother that passing as Christian is essential: "Pre omnibus caveas ne isti nos percipiant iudeos esse" (Above all, take care that they do not perceive us to be Jews), she tells him; and everything she counsels in the wake of his crimes serves the lie: "Hec et hiis similia fingemus ne percipiant nos judeos esse" (These and similar things we will contrive so that they do not perceive us to be Jews) (Cluse 319). Her ruse also includes lying about why she does not have pork in her house, suggesting that she and her guests go to Mass, paying for four special Masses of the Holy Spirit to be sung in her honor (and they are), and urging her Jewish maidservant (who is also misconstrued as Christian) to have sex with the drunken priest as a sign of Christian hospitality (she does not). She is financially smart—when her brother suggests 40 marks or more for any Christian who will remove Adam's body, she responds coolly, "Samuel frater, minori precio conducam sacerdotem christiane legis" (Samuel, brother, for a smaller price I can hire a priest of the Christian law" (Cluse 317)—and her abilities to negotiate and switch languages are among her related skills. All Jews in this story speak French and Hebrew, which Samuel's wife calls "lingua nostra" (our language) (Cluse 310, 311), and people around them speak English, which they apparently understand.[35] The sister, however, is singled out for her use of her multilingualism. She is knowledgeable about Latin liturgy, and, when she first shows up with the Irish priest and Samuel inquires as to whether the priest "novit ne linguam Anglicanam, vel Romanam" (knows English or French), she replies, "Utramque novit et intelligit" (He knows and understands both) (Cluse 319). Since she has just been chatting with the priest in town to convince him to take up lodgings at her home, the implication is that she knows this because she has approached him in these languages.

When she enters the Latin narrative in a material way, after passively listening and thus at first maintaining a clever alliance with the Christian reader/hearer, the Bristol sister quickly takes control. She begins to question Samuel about practical details: Where exactly are the bodies now? Has he buried his wife and son yet? How did the privy-guarding angel appear? Samuel breaks down in tears, but his sister does not use her gathered information to chastise or comfort. Instead she tells him, "Noli super flere optime. . . . Eamus soli sub silencio ad domum tuam, et ibi videamus invicem quid faciendum sit" (Don't cry so much. . . . Let's go ourselves, in silence, to your house and together consider what should be done there) (Cluse 315). Upon viewing the bodies of Samuel's wife and son, she does weep and scold him, but she also tells him exactly what to do, goes alone into the city to seek a priest, and contrives cover stories for both Christian and Jewish audiences.

For the sake of fellow Jews, she instructs Samuel to bury his wife and son inside his house, with all of their clothing, and claim "quod uxor tua recessit a te cum filio, et nescimus quo abierunt" (that your wife has, with the child, abandoned you, and we don't know where they've gone) (Cluse 315). For Christians, she will offer the priest money to remove the boy's body and bury it outside Bristol, and she will convince the priest to do this secretly by claiming that she and her brother are a Christian couple whose child has been killed by Jews. She prepares her brother and rehearses the plan first:

> Melius est nobis hiis christianis de censu nostro dare, ut deferant corpus pueri extra civitatem et sepeliant ibi in cimiterio vel extra. . . . Dicemus etiam illum mortuum filium nostrum esse et crucifixum et interemptum esse a iudeis in hac urbe, et nolumus ut aliquis in hoc mundo hoc sciat, propter regales ne spoliant nos pecunia nostra. (Cluse 319)

> It is better for us to give these Christians [i.e., the Irish priest she has found and his traveling companions] some of our riches so that they will take the boy's body away, outside the city, and bury it in the cemetery there or elsewhere. . . . Let's also say that the dead one is our son, and is crucified and killed by Jews in this city, and we do not want anyone in this world to know this, lest the king's men deprive us of our money.

She expects that the pilgrim priest will believe (1) that she and her brother are a Christian couple accusing Jews of ritually murdering their son, and (2) that a Christian couple making such an accusation might *not* be believed. The Christian fear she pantomimes is that royal officers will assume Jewish innocence and therefore seize Christian assets as penalty for a false accusation.

She later claims to "confess" (confiteri) exactly this story to the Irish priest, his secrecy compelled by the promise of "excellent silver" (argentei peroptimi) (Cluse 320) for him and each of his companions:

> Domine sacerdos unicum habui filium, et hic abiit pridie ad domum cuiusdam judei pessimi vicini nostri. Et hic judeus iniquus in secreto comprehendit filium meum, et cruci affigens illum, interemit morte crudeli. Et nos invento corpore pueri sepelivimus illum in quadam cloaca, quod si perceperint regales custodes urbis spoilabunt nos omni pecunia imponentes nobis crimen interfectionis pueri. Unde rogamus te sume de pecunia nostra in quam tibi placuerit, et defer caute, corpus filii nostri extra urbem, et sepeli in alico loco secreto, ubi tibi placuerit. (Cluse 320–21)

> Lord priest, I had a son, and he went yesterday to the house of a certain horrible Jew, our neighbour. And this evil Jew attacked my

son in secret, and killed him with a cruel death after tying him to a cross. And after we discovered the child's body, we buried him in a certain privy, because if the city's royal custodians knew, they'd take all our money, putting the crime of murdering the boy on us. So we ask you: take some of our money, however much you please, and carry away the body of our son carefully, outside the city, and bury it in some secret place, wherever you please.

The metanarrative effect of a Jewess-as-Christian, certain of the Christian audience's response, relating a ritual murder story (with all of the markers of the already-established narrative genre) within a ritual murder story is somewhat dizzying—and it works didactically. Who among your neighbors might be feigning Christianity in this complex way? Who among the larger community of Christians is complicit?

Samuel, the violent brother, does not find it so easy to mimic Christian behavior. He cannot contain himself when the priest blesses their shared meal, for instance, and spits on the ground three times at the mention of the Holy Trinity,[36] but his sister continually instructs him—and she is very good at it. Even the priest, described as a "vir simplex et religiosus et timens deum, nisi tamen modo inebrietate" (simple and religious and god-fearing man, unless in any way drunk) (Cluse 320), discovers Jewishness only by divine intervention, when the angel who guards young Adam's corpse informs him of it and orders him to convert the siblings (Cluse 324–25). Nevertheless, the radical strength of the sister's Jewishness is repeatedly affirmed in this story: the divine narrator tells us that she is "ceca fidelis in lege sua" (blindly faithful to her law) (Cluse 315); when Samuel tells her that he hates Jesus "quia dixit *ego sum Christus filius dei vivi*" (because he said *I am Christ, son of the living God*), she responds, "Quid ad nos si dixerit?" (What is it to us if he said that?) (Cluse 316); when he worries that she will want to convert just as his wife did, she proclaims, "visio mille angelorum non subverteret me de lege patrum nostrorum" (the sight of a thousand angels will not turn me from the law of our fathers) (Cluse 316). And when the Irish priest, at the angel's urging, finally insists that she be baptized, she flatly responds, "Non credam in hominem mortalem Ihesum" (I will not believe in the mortal man Jesus); her brother, worried nevertheless, tells her to flee "hinc ne forte verbis sacerdotis decepta credas in Ihesum" (lest perhaps, through the lying words of the priest, you believe in Jesus) (Cluse 325). But she does not leave, nor does she convert. She is a master of seeming Christianity, but she is unrepentantly Jewish. She recedes from the narrative unnoticed, the bodies gone. At the angel's command, the priest takes Adam's corpse home to Ireland and buries it in an undisclosed location, and the text's final words are those of the angel who guards Adam: *"Locus iste ignotus erit tibi et omni humane creature usque in diem prefinita a deo patre"* (This place [i.e., where the boy is buried] will be unknown to you and all human beings, until a day preordained by God the Father) (Cluse 327). The saintly child's body, like the Jewish woman's, remains secret, hidden and unseeable without angelic intervention.

There is no doubt that *Adam of Bristol*, like other such libellous narratives, is a "tale told by Christians, to Christians, to make Christians act and redefine that which made them Christians."[37] This Christian redefinition, however, happens not primarily through the tortured Christ-like boy, nor through the drunken but ultimately good and repentant Irish priest. In the *Passion of Adam of Bristol*, Christianness is interrogated most effectively through the ability of an unnamed Anglo-Jewish woman to appear to be Christian. In contrast to her violent and compulsive brother, the Bristol sister's status as unmarked and versatile—as apparently the same as the Christians—is valuable to the text's polemics. She offers extreme poles of Christian eschatological hopes for, and anxieties about, the Jew: one may expect her to convert, as Jewish women in other Christian miracle tales do, but her feminine malleability also holds the possibility of misapprehended or feigned sameness. Stereotypes of femaleness are *interacting* with stereotypes of Jewishness.

What the *Adam of Bristol* author so deftly communicates—and this is why there is no final destruction of the Jewish presence in the conclusion of the tale—is the potential terror of sameness. The anxiety associated with passing (the ability of the Jew to represent herself as Christian, the inability of the Christian to discern difference) provides the narrative's conflict and its anticlimax, and that passing is, crucially, orchestrated through the knowledge and deceptions of a Jewish woman.[38] Even while the author emphatically marks both Samuel and his sister as Jewish in the most prejudicial ways, he takes care to maintain the fiction of utter misperception of religious identity for Christians around them. The only "actual" Christians in the story—disconnected as they may be from mature, regional, or moral understanding of the situation—cannot discern Jewish-Christian difference publicly or privately, and the ability of the Jews to be the same as Christians then becomes further evidence of Jewish perfidy and dangerous (or disingenuous) acculturation. In this, Samuel's sister is both the framing device and the plot driver. If *Adam of Bristol* provides us with a fictionalization of unchecked religious cross-dressing, even doubts about conversion, it is significant that it does so through the character of a Jewish woman.

We can begin to sketch a new literary type now: the unmarked Jewess who is, by design, difficult to see because she can move through both Jewish and Christian spaces confidently—access that involves financial or linguistic know-how and depends on an appearance that is indistinguishable from Christian women. The Jewess becomes a flashpoint that produces and develops anxieties over Jewish-Christian sameness, but she is also a site where difficulties arise and problems are exposed. We might call this type a quintessential example of al-losemitism, neither about "hatred [n]or love of Jews, but contain[ing] the seeds of both, and assur[ing] that whichever of the two appears is intense and ex-treme," a token of allosemitism's "radically ambivalent attitude,"[39] except that such a label flattens the particulars of Anglo-Christian representations of the Jewess, which—unlike representations of her male counterpart—often create and pivot on her lack of visibly Jewish identity, her missing outward sign of al-legiance and difference. Her sameness is the polemical caricature that emerges. The mark that the Jewess bears in Anglo-Christian literature is, precisely, her *lack* of marking. The Jewess is thus a site of both danger and possibility.

CHAPTER 3

Anglo-Jewish Women

Again and again she comes to the front in a way that proves that she
occupied a position in the life of the Jewry, both within and without
the community, probably unequalled in those days in any other
country.

—Michael Adler, Presidential Address to the JHSE,
19 November 1934

Archived Women

Though their function in anti-Jewish texts has not previously been considered
in any sustained way, Anglo-Jewish women should factor into any discussion of
Christian-Jewish polemics in medieval England. With its nearly-Christian Jewish wife and Christian-seeming widowed sister, the *Passion of Adam of Bristol* is
a good example of the reasons why: its author explicitly focuses anxieties about
Jewish/Christian sameness on women and thus feminizes Jewish passing to
stoke Christian suspicions of Jewish villainy. He imagines, through the tale's
Jewish women, duplicitous passing so thorough that it exploits Jewish indistinguishability by using Christian stereotypes of Jews against Christians. Even so,
Anthony Bale has described *Adam of Bristol* as a story that primarily emphasizes "the grotesque physicality of the adult male Jew";[1] and Irven Resnick,
though he recognizes that "Jews are all the more dangerous" in the tale "because
Jewish identity is easily hidden and concealed," does not note how crucial
women are to this point.[2] We may ask, in response, what if the unmarked Jewess is not merely a foil for the dangerous male Jew but a strategically placed tool

of misdirection, a polemical embodiment of the Christian problem of continuity and identification with Jews? The Bristol sister is one of the many imagined Jewish women who sit in the uncanny valley of medieval Anglo-Christian polemical literature,[3] teetering between the familiar and the monstrous because of their crafted sameness.

The new literary type I propose—the unmarked Jewish woman with access to Jewish and Christian spaces, characterized by financial or linguistic know-how—can be connected to a range of sources from pre-Expulsion records to post-Expulsion vernacular literature, and much in between. The letters of Alice of Worcester give us the voice of one Anglo-Jewish woman, aware of her ability to sit in a problematic middle, identified as both Jewish (always "the convert") and Christian, the *captiva* Zion functioning in the language of the Christian(ized) Bible. But Alice's is only one of the many archived lives of medieval Anglo-Jewish women. National and literary records mutually elucidate each other in examining "the Jewess" type: tropes inherent to literary representations are reflected in the national records, and those records, in turn, help to establish a profile to look for in the literature. Assessment of both the literary and the historical materials shows polemical manipulation of real similarities and ambiguities, and their interplay and mutual influence were always factors in anti-Jewish rhetoric and representation. To understand how a Jewish woman might function in *any* Anglo-Christian text, we must examine in the first place the historical position of medieval Anglo-Jewish women. "Jewess" could have distinct meanings in the English imagination, for the archived as much as for the literary Jewess.

Anglo-Jewish women have accrued an admiring if intermittent scholarly historiography over the last century: they were "probably unequalled in those days in any other country," as the epigraph to this chapter shows Michael Adler put it in 1934; for Barrie Dobson, "the medieval English Jewess was undoubtedly a more influential and even formidable figure than her Christian counterpart"; for Hannah Meyer, "using gender as a primary tool of analysis" of medieval records provides "the inescapable visibility of Jewish uniqueness."[4] We must frankly acknowledge, however, that this picture of the extraordinary and formidable English Jewess—mostly gleaned from legal and financial records— is based on the constraints and discourse of the surviving records and their makers. The historical Anglo-Jewish woman is also a *represented* figure, archived by Christian scribes within a biased state bureaucracy. Polemical tropes and types adhere to the historical as much as to the literary remnants, and thus we must approach what the archives give us, shape for us, and make possible, with caution. If the Anglo-Jewish woman seems extraordinary, to what degree are her attributes part of a cultural imaginary? Keeping the craftedness of the archive ever in mind, can we use national records to deduce what perceptions of Jewish women medieval Anglo-Christians could have had, or as a basis for literary study?

Anglo-Jewish women, I think, have been caught between academic disciplines, between deep scholarly histories that either valorize them or say there is little Jewish material to study from medieval England, or that postbiblical Jewish women simply do not appear much in the medieval sources of the dominant Christian culture. Those who work on English illustration, poetry, or liturgy find few Jewish women there unless they read "Jewish" in relation to Christian conceptions of Old Testament heroines. Jewish studies scholars have relatively little Hebrew to work with from England, much of it financial in nature. Elisheva Baumgarten, in her authoritative studies of Ashkenazi women's ritual and family life, twice notes that English Jews are "not included" in her books, because the evidence they leave behind is "not the same" and "not plentiful enough."[5] Sara Lipton, one of a few scholars to focus on representations of Jewish women in medieval Christian sources, finds little evidence of stereotypes until the late Middle Ages, especially since Jewish and Christian women are frequently indistinguishable in Christian art, where "femaleness trumped . . . Jewishness."[6] There is a general feeling, indeed, that indistinguishability denotes fact: that there is simply no medieval Anglo-Christian, or even European Christian, caricature, stereotype, or notable attitude about the Jewess to study. But a distinctive presence of Jewish women becomes visible, I argue here, when national-historical and literary sources are permitted to elucidate each other mutually and in light of the polemical investments in sameness that I established in Part I.

Elisheva Baumgarten's work has already revealed the "wealth of contact between Jewish women and Christian women" in medieval Ashkenaz broadly. They were, as she has concluded,

> medical colleagues and they met as neighbors. Christian women worked in Jewish homes, and Jewish children were cared for in Christian homes. . . . Jewish women were particularly immersed in the lives of their Christian neighbors, because so many of their daily contacts revolved around home and child care, in which there was employment of, and frequent contact with, Christian women. As such, Jewish and Christian women's interactions can be seen as a channel and a link between Jewish and Christian society.[7]

In England, France, and Spain, these points of contact were augmented by business relationships, small consumption loans between women, and women's participation in moneylending. In England, possibly because of the relatively small size of the Jewish population coupled with periods of violence and legal accusations that consistently affected more men than women, Jewish women's participation in business and lending seems to have been more substantial than on the continent.[8] The facts of material existence in small communities that were, especially in the final decades of medieval Anglo-Jewry, victims of regular county-level expulsions and mass imprisonments, likely made women more crucial to domestic, ritual, and financial stability. Matronymic designations for sons of prominent Jewish women were not uncommon,[9] and the Crown tended to defer to Jewish authorities on questions related to marriage, dowries, and women's inheritance, which augmented women's abilities to maintain comparatively prominent roles in a range of legal and financial interactions.[10]

Barrie Dobson lamented, nonetheless, that "the Jewish woman is nearly always revealed at the most personal, painful, and significant interface between" Christianity and Judaism in medieval England.[11] She survives almost exclusively in texts recorded by Christian scribes, and at some of the most difficult times of her life: deaths of husbands or children, disputes over conversions, disputes over property seizure, fines, imprisonment—and always at an interface, a juncture point where two or more separate systems interact. There are more surviving medieval records of the daily life and interactions of Jewish communities in England than anywhere on the continent—as Cecil Roth quipped, never has it been "possible to assemble so much about so few"[12]—but it is difficult to create anything like a full picture of medieval Anglo-Jewish women. As Judith Olszowy-Schlanger notes in her tomes on medieval Hebrew and Hebrew-Latin documents from England, "Jewish private and community archives from England must have existed, but none have been preserved: *all of the Hebrew documents known to us . . . have passed through the hands of non-Jewish authorities.*"[13] What survives may be an extraordinary or a painful picture, but it is a curated picture.

Still, this picture has power. With it, we can responsibly examine Christian perceptions of what mattered, what was troubling, who stood out, and what was worth recording and preserving. The historical evidence, as prelude to any representational or literary argument about Jews, thus becomes even more essential and more revealing than it might otherwise be: it is part of the story of Christian representation of Jews. If the Anglo-Jewish woman is archived in a context that is primarily Christian, primarily male-authored, primarily produced by or for the (Christian) state—at points of interface, liminality, or trauma—these sources do leave us real traces of her significance to Christians, by which I mean her historical, cultural, troped, and appropriated significance. This chapter, therefore, lays out the archived roles of Anglo-Jewish women: as literate women in (law) courts, as women who interacted with Christian women frequently (in business and domestic settings), as converts to Christianity (often creating debate among Jewish and Christian authorities), as forgers (of documents or seals), and as women accused of violence (especially against other Jewish women).

Women at Court

Medieval Anglo-Jewish women were a significant presence in law courts. There are generations of women who survive in the records of the bureaucracy of thirteenth-century England, most notably in the seventy-two extant rolls of the Exchequer of the Jews for the dates 1219–90,[14] but also in marriage arrangements (*shiddukhin*), close rolls, fine rolls, financial bonds, charters, letters, tallages, and *shetarot* (i.e., starrs: bonds of debt or acquittance written in Hebrew and according to Jewish custom), among other miscellaneous documents. Victoria Hoyle's work on moneylending between Anglo-Jewish and Christian women documents "641 references to 310 distinct and individual Jewish women (all but 23 of whom are named) in the published plea rolls," not counting cases of ambiguity, incomplete records, or unpublished materials;[15] Suzanne Bartlet's study of three Winchester Jewish businesswomen established that they could "head their own family consortia" and maintained "contact with many levels of the social strata, ranging from royalty and the upper echelons of the Church to small farmers, tradesmen and Christian women."[16] Several Anglo-Jewish financiers were women. Licoricia of Winchester, about whom Suzanne Bartlet wrote a posthumously published book,[17] is only the most famous among them. Others include Henna of York, Henna of Oxford, Mirabel of Gloucester, Belia of Bedford, Chera of Winchester, and Abigail of London. These women appeared in court independently, owned their own properties (often through inheritance), and held and sued for bonds in their own names.

The glut of archival material related to these women—"a gigantic lucky dip," as Dobson called it[18]—shows that the majority of financial and related court records do not reflect woman-to-woman interactions. Rather, as Hoyle notes, "the majority of these cases concerning Jewish women involved male

Christian defendants or plaintives [*sic*]."[19] The lack of evidence for a special gendered context for Anglo-Jewish women's transactions, however, demonstrates that they moved through Christian systems more nimbly than similar analyses in French or Spanish contexts have shown, and that they had regular means of contact with those who were in positions to create texts and narratives about them.[20] As Hoyle has summarized,

> Survey work on the plea rolls of the Exchequer of the Jews suggests
> that the court, as it functioned between 1218 and 1280, was excep-
> tional in its treatment of women, both Jewish and Christian and
> whether plaintive or defendant. In common with the equity courts of
> the later fourteenth and fifteenth centuries, the Exchequer of the Jews
> allowed the participation of women independent from their hus-
> bands, fathers or male kin. It further made no effective distinctions
> based on a woman's life cycle status—she might come to court as a
> single woman, a wife or a widow, or in her capacity as a daughter or a
> mother. It accepted pleas from married women concerning their own
> credit interests, and also pleas from women concerned with the credit
> interests of their husbands or sons.[21]

Such treatment extended to issues of criminal damage and marriage rights as well, at least in part because an Anglo-Jewish woman's marriage and inheritances (and thus, often, property, chattels, and bonds) were matters of Jewish rather than Christian law.[22]

Comittissa of Gloucester, for instance, appeared before the justices of the Exchequer of the Jews to accuse other Jews of murdering her husband Solomon Turbe by pushing him out of Gloucester Castle. While she did not win her case, she was nevertheless persistent in her pursual of it: she prosecuted Abraham Gabbay, a beer server called Andrew, and three other men for the murder, and she carried on through a mixed jury trial at which she was evidently present; her case occupies four relatively long entries in the roll for Easter Term 1220.[23] In another instance related to marriage rights, in Easter Term 1267, a widow called Milla brought Samuel of Bolum to court because "Samuel claimed the said Milla to wife by reason of contract and commerce that were between them, which claim Milla resisted, for that no such contract and commerce could lawfully make a marriage"; after the justices of the Jews conferred with a *beit din* (a rabbinical court) on the matter, the case was decided in Milla's favor: she could "do with her chattels however she may be minded."[24] The court's deference to

Jewish authorities on such issues meant that unless state intervention was invited by Jews themselves, Jews had "embedded autonomy" within the Christian legal system, and the Crown did little to legislate Anglo-Jewish women's positions within their own communities.[25]

Court records show us that Anglo-Jewish women were also immersed in documentary and book culture, and that they were multilingually engaged in this. Both Jewish and Christian chroniclers mention the plentiful books of medieval Anglo-Jews: Ephraim of Bonn writes that, in the 1190 massacre at York, not only were Jewish people killed but also "the choicest of books—which they had written many of, more desirable than gold, of which there are [now] none as worthy"—were pillaged and sold on the continent;[26] Bartholomew Cotton, in his *Historia Anglicana*, writes of the 1290 Expulsion that many Jews drowned crossing the Channel, "una cum libris suis" (each one with books).[27] Olszowy-Schlanger has spent the last decades radically reorganizing our sense of medieval Anglo-Hebrew books and records, including most recently the definitive two-volume study of Hebrew and Hebrew-Latin documents known to be extant from the pre-Expulsion period (316 items in total), and she summarizes the linguistic case thus: "People who dealt with documents had to know other languages. The Jews had to know Latin, and some Christians knew Hebrew."[28] Jewish knowledge included Hebrew and Aramaic, and French and English vernaculars as well: "It is more than likely that French-speaking Jews [in England] soon acquired a good grasp of Middle English to which they must have been constantly exposed.... English must have been essential, notably for economic activities involving not only urban but often rural clientele."[29] As Michael Clanchy intuited some time ago from his own survey of the records, this extended to Jewish women: "It was evidently normal for both male and female Jews to be literate in Hebrew. The men, and a notable number of women, who had business dealings with Christians had to understand Latin, French, and English as well."[30]

There is little surviving evidence of Hebrew literacy among, or writing done by, Anglo-Jewish women, but there is some. A list of acknowledgments of *shetarot* (bonds in Hebrew) for Easter Term 1270 in the Jewish Exchequer rolls tells us that a starr of Henna of York, a significant financier after her husband Aaron's death in 1268, was "scriptum littera sua ebraica consignauit" (signed in her Hebrew character) and also personally confirmed by Henna, who appeared before the court to acknowledge the document.[31] In Trinity Term 1267, Belia of Bedford appeared to quitclaim one Alexander of Stokes of all debts to her, in acknowledgment of which "dicta Belya . . . faciet ei starrum de acquietancia"

(the said Belia . . . is to make for him a starr of acquittance).[32] Henna of London, in Trinity Term 1277, similarly promised to make her starr, and "iurauit
predicta Henna super legem moysi quod nec per ipsam nec per preceptum suum
factum starrum de acquietancia" (the aforesaid Henna swore on the Law of
Moses that a starr of acquittance was not previously made, neither by herself
nor by her command),[33] suggesting a distinction between a recognized ability
to write her own Hebrew documents and her (probably usual) practice of having them made by male associates and scribes. Henna was, in court, swearing on
a Torah scroll, as was standard practice for Jews appearing before the justices of
the Jews.[34] A 1219 Norfolk case involving a possibly forged document and a Jewish woman called Damete daughter of Morell suggests that Damete wrote her
own starr,[35] and Dobson, in his work on the York Jewry, also cites a Bellasez of
York, whom the Edward I Close Rolls say was knowledgeable enough about
documentary formulae and practices to forge both documents and seals.[36]

The seal of one Anglo-Jewish woman does survive beautifully intact: Mildegod of Oxford, widow of Copin, leased her inherited property on Aldates
(now the site of Magdalen College) to the Hospital of St John in 1253, and her
seal—an oblong in green wax featuring a bird catching a worm (or possibly
feeding baby birds) with the legend S. MILDEGODE IVD' (i.e., Seal of Mildegod the Jewess)—is appended to the half of the Latin chirograph still held at the
site (Figure 2). The document confirms that Mildegod, whose name is likely an
Englishing of the Hebrew name Johanna (i.e., God is gracious), received into
her keeping the other part of the chirograph, which would have been sealed by
the friars of the hospital.[37]

In considering what degrees of literacy Anglo-Jewish women might have
had, it is worth remembering too that "use of Hebrew was not only a linguistic necessity" in the world of Anglo-Jewish business but "an additional means
of authenticating documents and avoiding frauds."[38] The well-attested Latin
formula "litera mea ebraica" (in my Hebrew script)—present in many surviving Hebrew-Latin documents and used, as noted above, by Henna of York—
indicated not just the presence of witnesses but also their "autograph
confirmation" of the transaction. As Olszowy-Schlanger has established on
the basis of Jewish Exchequer protocols and the requirements of Jewish law,
Hebrew thus "plays a special role in Hebrew documents from England"; the
Exchequer of the Jews repeatedly questioned the authenticity of documents
"on the grounds that they were not written in person by the Jews involved in
the transactions."[39] As Henna of York proves, women too could use the formula indicative of autograph confirmation, and, as Mildegod of Oxford

Figure 2. Seal of Mildegod of Oxford, 1253. Oxford, Magdalen
College Muniments Room, St Aldates 34. Reproduced by permission
of the President and Fellows of Magdalen College Oxford.

shows, they might seal their own transactions in accordance with Christian legal customs as well.

One of the most well-known documents in Hebrew that survives from thirteenth-century England is the 1271 premarital agreement (*shidduch*) between Belaset daughter of Berakhyah of Lincoln and Benjamin son of Joseph, parents of their betrothed children, Judith and Aaron, respectively. In it, Belaset makes arrangements for the marriage and confirms a deposit on Judith's dowry that includes 20 marks and a Bible. Four years in advance of the planned wedding, Belaset transfers possession of this Bible to Benjamin (Aaron's father) for her future son-in-law: "twenty four books in one volume, properly corrected, with vocalization and Masora, on calf parchment with six columns on each sheet and, separately, the Targum for the Pentateuch and Haphtarot, with all written in it."[40] This volume is presented as the property of the mother, passing from her hands and by her arrangement alone and designated by her "for the sake of the [betrothed] children" (both of them). The contract stipulates further that should the marriage not happen, "Benjamin [Aaron's father] has to return to the aforementioned Mistress Belaset the aforementioned book that she handed over to him [for the children] or he will pay her six marks for the book,"[41] thus clarifying that the Bible was her particular concern.

Other enrolled agreements and cases before the justices of the Jews show women's concern with inheritance and trade of books. In one, recorded in the Plea Rolls of the Exchequer of the Jews for Hilary Term 1276, a Belaset of London seeks control over her inheritance after her husband's death, including her household's books, explicitly "que vnquam fuerit ... auunculi sui" (whichever were ... her uncle's) and "excepta libri qui ei acciderint coram Aron ... et Josc'" (with the exception of the books that happened to come to her in the presence of [a certain] Aaron ... and Josce).[42] This is specific enough to indicate that particular books were especially dear to this Belaset, and perhaps that the others were received through trade or as surety on debts. In an earlier and similar suit for books, Floria, the daughter of Abraham of Berkhamsted—a man later made infamous by Matthew Paris's account of him defecating on an icon of the Virgin Mary and murdering his wife[43]—appeared in court to claim the library of her deceased husband Leo, a scholar who had inherited his books from his father, Hamo of Hereford, and then, in turn, left his books and chattels to his mother and brother Ursell. In 1236, Floria remarried and unsuccessfully sued to have Leo's library for herself. In 1240, her father, Abraham, again tried to claim the books, this time on behalf of his granddaughter Contessa (i.e., Leo and Floria's daughter) "according to the laws of the Jews."[44] Whether Contessa (through Abraham) succeeded in the second suit is unclear, but the women in the family, through inheritance law, were understood to have the strongest claim.

Anglo-Jewish women were also dealing in the trade and sale of Christian and Latin books, no doubt those acquired as surety for debts, and particularly in the university context.[45] In Easter Term 1278, a Jewess called Margarina, for instance, was sued by Oxford Carmelites for unlawful detinue of three books, "videlicet, epistolas pauli glosatas pretium xl s. matheum glosatum pretium vii s. et sententias pretium x s." (to wit, Paul's epistles, glossed, worth 40 shillings, Matthew glossed, worth 7 shillings, and a *Sentences*, glossed, worth 10 shillings). After an inquest was ordered and a mixed jury of Christian and Jews had investigated, Margarina "coram eis recognouit quod predictos libros a dictis fratribus in vadium recepit et postea per lapsum temporis eos vendidit" (acknowledged before them [the jury] that she had received the said books from the said brothers in pledge, and afterwards, because of the time elapsed, had sold them).[46] In 1281, the books of two female converts from Judaism, Belaset and Hittecote of Oxford, were the subject of a writ sent to the justices of the Jews by Edward I: he ordered their belongings sent to the Domus Conversorum in London "ad sustentacionem Conversorum ... eisdem Belassez et Hittecote faciat assignari" (for the maintenance of the converts ... to be assigned to the same Belaset and Hittecote); the Exchequer scribe thus listed their only movable belongings as duly delivered: nine Latin books, all concerning grammar, logic, and natural science.[47] This kind of interaction suggests a trade in books between Jewish women and religious and scholarly institutions, notably around Oxford.

Standard proclamations in synagogues concerning summary settlement of debts of Christian individuals (because they had died or were, for instance, going on crusade), in addition, suggest the regular presence of Jewish women in Jewish-Christian documentary interactions: the formula, frequently copied into the Exchequer rolls, reads, "If any Jew or Jewess [Jud' vel Judeam] have claim against X, he or she must be before the Justices by X day with chirographs, tallies, and all other instruments."[48] Licoricia of Winchester was individually summoned to appear before the court and "haberet chirographa" (have her chirographs);[49] the earliest mention of a Jewess that appears in the Henry III Fine Rolls, in April 1218, states simply, of a Jewish woman called Esterota, "habet brevem" (she has the writ).[50]

There is important emphasis to be placed on the idea that Anglo-Jewish women could be associated with "the letter of the law" just as much as Jewish men, and that they must have *seemed* to be literate and multilingual by virtue of their participation in documentary and book cultures. Clanchy has posited Hebrew as such an important "language of record" in England that "indebted magnates of the thirteenth century would probably have come across more writing in Hebrew than in English," and Olszowy-Schlanger's work on Anglo-Hebrew books and documents substantiates this and goes much further in showing collaboration and sustained interactions between Christians and Jews in both record-making, book making, and exegesis.[51] The people who produced and carried bonds to indebted magnates, and who traded and couriered books between scholars, were male and female. The figure of the Jew carrying letters (*judeus portans literas*), which Jocelin of Brakelond put to such effective figural and polemical use in his characterization of Abbot Samson of Bury St Edmunds, could just as well be a *judea*.

Interactions with Christian Women

In the final sections of the early Middle English spiritual guide for anchoresses known as *Ancrene Wisse* (ca. 1225), the author advises anchoresses, "ne wite ȝe in ower hus of oðer monne þinges—ne ahte ne claðes, ne boistes ne chartres, scoren ne cyrograffes" (don't guard other people's things in your house—don't keep clothes, nor chests nor charters, nor tally sticks nor chirographs).[52] The need to limit these women's guardianship of documents—in chests, as charters, as chirographs, with debts and payments accounted by tally—assumes some familiarity with financial and legal records, despite religious vows and enclosure, and we can hypothesize possible connections between anchoresses and Jewish neighbors too. Before the development of a state-regulated *archa* system for bonds related to Jewish transactions in the 1190s—a development that was still ongoing into the 1230s—"contracts drawn up by the Jews were deposited in a designated place, usually a church."[53] We know that anchorholds made good church storage rooms: the same passage in *Ancrene Wisse* also forbids storage of priestly vestments and chalices. Slightly earlier, moreover, the author allegorizes Christ as a knight who frees suitors of obligations to Jews: "Ne teleð me him god fere þe leið his wed i Giwerie to acwitin ut his fere? Godd almihti leide him-seolf for us i Giwerie, ant dud hi deorewurðe bodi to acwitin ut his leofmon of Giwene honden" (You tell me he is not a good friend who sells his pledge in the Jewry to acquit his friend of a pledge? God almighty sold himself in the Jewry for us, and he put up his precious body to acquit his beloved of a pledge in Jewish hands).[54] This allegorical evocation of Jewish debt and lending, and the complementary prohibiting of an anchoress's keeping of related documents, suggests a feminine connection to a common type of Jewish-Christian transaction that can be corroborated by national records.[55]

Even after the development of the Exchequer of the Jews, "it is difficult to claim that [accounts and debt bonds] were kept systematically,"[56] and the plea rolls record many cases in which Christians tried to help their neighbors during times of specific threat to Jews—the Barons' Wars, for instance—when Jewish documents were targets for destruction and sought in the storage areas of churches and homes. The *scoren* (wooden tally sticks) mentioned in the *Ancrene Wisse* passage quoted above are as important to this larger picture as the charters or chirographs that might confirm property rights and debts owed or paid: 280 such tally sticks survive recording Anglo-Jewish transactions, 58 with Hebrew inscriptions. While the majority of these record receipts for individuals' contributions to large tallages imposed on Jewish communities by Henry III, some show incremental Christian payments of debts to Jews. Nearly 50 of the surviving tally sticks are in Jewish women's names.[57]

Individual Christians or Christian couples, furthermore, protected the possessions, documents, and books of their Jewish neighbors in times of trouble, such that Jews sometimes brought complaints before the justices of the Jews concerning the unlawful detinue of property that should have been returned[58]— and many of these suits are of special interest because of women's involvement. Such cases, which feature questions of rightful possession of goods and documents, are evidence of meaningful Christian-Jewish interactions, seemingly the kind with which the *Ancrene Wisse* author expected his anchoresses to be familiar. In Trinity Term 1266, for example, Aaron of Sidingburn sued a Christian couple for "unlawful detinue of two mantles and cloaks of lawn and four silver buckles and other chattels."[59] Aaron had entrusted the Christians, Alan and Dionisia, with his belongings in early April 1264, just as Simon de Montfort raided and massacred London Jews at the start of the Second Barons' War. The couple claimed that they had provided a chest for Aaron's belongings and carried both Aaron's chest and their own goods to a nearby church, so "that there they [the goods] might be safeguarded from the pillagers that were gathering for the siege of Rochester castle" (which began 17 April 1264).[60] An originally cordial relationship between the Jewish and Christian families is evident: the Christian couple claimed that they gave up the whereabouts of Aaron's chest only when armed men pressed them to give up the location of Aaron himself. The ensuing conflict between them hinges on an unknown (to the husbands) private exchange between the women. Aaron was convinced that the Christian couple did not tell the truth because he had seen Dionisia with a buckle that should have been in the now-missing chest. Dionisia, however, testified that the buckle was separately given to her by Aaron's wife, as security for a small loan between them, and that it was therefore never in the chest.[61] The chest with Aaron's other possessions, the Christian couple claimed, was seized from the church; the pillagers did not hesitate to burgle the holy space.

In Trinity Term 1267, Isaac of Warwick and his wife Ivetta appeared before the justices of the Jews to claim that Alan le Hurer (i.e., the hatter) had "received of them for safe keeping goods and chattels to the value of £10, and a marked purse with chirographs under the names of him, Isaac, and divers Christians."[62] This Alan later appeared before the justices with a story similar to that of Alan and Dionisia: he claimed that "after the arrival of the Earl of Gloucester in London"—this is Gilbert de Clare, at this time loyal to Simon de Montfort and very recently responsible for the massacre of Jews at Canterbury in April 1264—men had entered his home and took away not only his Jewish neighbors' goods and chirographs but also his own belongings.[63] In the same term, a London Christian woman named Emma Sibeling appeared to answer a complaint from a Jewish man, Josce, in a similar case; an Isaac Scrovy sued a Christian herdsman for unlawful detinue of a household's worth of possessions, including "a psalter in the Hebrew character"; and another Jewish couple, Isaac and Slema, complained that they had given "divers chattels" to a Christian cook who should have protected them "at his peril," though Lovekin the Cook claimed that he did the best he could when he was seized and tied up by the Earl of Gloucester's men.[64]

The political trouble that produced these suits was the activities of Montfort and de Clare and the ensuing Barons' War, which was partly motivated by
Montfort's commitment to "alleviating the burden of Jewish debt" in England.[65]
The raids carried out by Montfort and his associates included the destruction of
both the official *archae*, those state-regulated chests that contained registered
chirographic documents of debts to Jews, and chests in church and domestic
storage areas, full of the kinds of documents and belongings we see Jews transferring to their Christian neighbors in the cases just described.[66] The cluster of
unlawful detinue suits around the war shows that it was not uncommon for
Christians to hold the goods and documents of Jews, nor for both Christian
and Jewish men and women to move belongings and records around as need
required. Jews might choose to deposit their goods with Christian women
alone (as in the case of Emma Sibeling), or Christian and Jewish women might
transact business privately (as in the case of Dionisia and Aaron's wife). For
both Jews and Christians, chattels and documents were thought best protected
if moved to Christian holy spaces (e.g., a church or an anchorhold). Such transfers implicate domestic space and include exchanges between women, as well as
the testimony of both husbands and wives.

Other records show us that Jewish and Christian women interacted in
England in more predictable and familiar ways, exactly as Baumgarten has surmised from northern French and German sources: Jews employed Christian
maidservants and wet nurses to their children.[67] Where Baumgarten argues
that "since halakhic responsa are our main source for examining this issue, . . .
it is impossible to evaluate . . . the quotidian reality,"[68] however, there is a
good deal of evidence of the quotidian reality in English sources. Indeed, Meyer
has examined Christian regulatory sources—papal, ecclesiastical, and royal
prohibitions on Christian nursing of Jewish infants—to reveal a range of English material that verifies Christian women's work in Jewish households into
the decade of the Expulsion. As she puts it, the "fears of corruption, transgression and subversion evident in official prohibitions," and in some narrative accounts in chronicles and literary materials too, "do not appear to have had that
much effect upon the employment of Christian women by medieval Anglo-
Jewish families," not least because there were no similar Jewish prohibitions.[69]
Anglo-Jewish women employed Christian women and shared domestic and familial space with them throughout the lifetime of medieval Anglo-Jewish communities.

Meyer takes care to emphasize the transactional nature and power dynamics at play in Anglo-Jewish employment of Christian women too: it was "money

for milk," as she says, and this transaction must be juxtaposed to other financial transactions and to the theological (supersessionist) anxieties of Christians serving supposedly inferior Jews. Where Baumgarten sees potential intimacy between Jewish and Christian women—"the close quarters of the home . . . allow[ing] Jewish and Christian women many intimate moments for the exchange of opinions and information"[70]—Meyer highlights the fact that the "use of Christian wet-nurses involved Jews, both male and female, in an employment contract . . . in which they [the Jews] had the powerful role," enabling a dynamic similar to a "creditor-debtor relationship"; this situation is not, in Meyer's view, "a reflection of neighbourliness or mutual assistance," because "Jewish families needed the services of a Christian nursemaid to enable the Jewish mother to continue her business activities . . . and the Christian nursemaid was evidently herself motivated by considerations of survival and economic need."[71] No doubt both Baumgarten and Meyer are correct, and *both* the resulting Christian-Jewish intimacy *and* the moral status or financial desperation of the employed women might influence how Christians perceived Jewish households, Jewish women, and their Christian servants together.

One Anglo-Jewish halakhic source allows a small window into the exigencies of such arrangements for Jews in predominantly Christian communities. In thirteenth-century discussions among rabbis about whether a Jewish child could be left alone with a Christian wet nurse or Jewish children left alone in Christian households, an English rabbi's response stands out. The rulings of French rabbis were, in general, that Christian caregivers must be supervised by Jews, and various *responsa* (i.e., the written decisions of rabbis on matters of religious law) suggest that it was not uncommon for Jewish women to leave their infants in Christian homes for some length of time, especially in cases where they did not have a wet nurse living with them. The most commonly cited ruling is that of R. Barukh: "A gentile woman may nurse an Israelite child if others are standing by, but not if she is on her own."[72] Rabbi Jacob of London, however, author of the Anglo-Jewish halakhic compilation *Sefer Etz Hayyim* (ca. 1287),[73] interpreted the requirement for Jewish supervision this way: "Even if there is no Jew in the house, if there is a Jewish home in the city . . . it is allowed."[74] Jacob's ruling is not incidental, of course, to the situation of the small Anglo-Jewish community in the late thirteenth century: it pragmatically allows that Christian homes must be safe spaces for Jewish children, even if, or perhaps especially if, a city or town hosts only a single Jewish home. Domestic interaction between Jewish and Christian women and children, for both Anglo-Jewish and Anglo-Christian officials, was a recognized, if problematic, norm.

Lists of Christian wet nurses and maidservants in Anglo-Jewish homes survive from York, Canterbury, and Lincoln. Receipts from the Canterbury Jewish community recorded by Kent sheriff Reginald of Cobham between 1250 and 1253 (35–38 Henry III) contain two notes pertaining to a wet nurse (French *norrice*) in the employment of Jewish women,[75] and surviving excommunication significations from 1276 (York) and 1278 (Lincoln) list twenty-five different Christian women working as a wet nurse (*nutrix*) and/or maidservant (*ancilla*) in eighteen distinct Jewish households, several of which had multiple Christian servants.[76] The excommunication documents are pro forma requests from local bishops for royal confirmation of ecclesiastical decisions; they list names and occupations without commenting explicitly on the reason for the excommunications. We see, for example, "Cecilia ancilla Mossi Iudei" (Cecily the maidservant of Mosse the Jew), "Elena ancilla Iossi Iudei" (Elena maidservant of Josse the Jew), "Cecilia nutrix Hakke Iudei" (Cecily wetnurse of Hake the Jew), "Emma nutrix Hakke" (Emma wetnurse of Hake), and the like.[77] The occupation in these cases surely constitutes the grounds for excommunication: English episcopal decrees (echoing papal ones) had repeatedly forbidden such practices throughout the thirteenth century.[78] The need for reissuance of prohibitions, naturally, says more about the prevalence of such employment than its successful regulation. Though they were larger than others, York and Lincoln and Canterbury did not, by the second half of the thirteenth century, have especially large Jewish communities—but babies continued to be born, and women were needed to nurse and raise them.

One of the Christian wet nurses mentioned in the Kent sheriff's receipt rolls has earned some special scholarly attention because of the exchange between women it implies: the sheriff received 40 shillings "por la norrice dame Avigaie et por nos doner congé à manger nostre aignel à Pasche" (for Lady Abigail's wetnurse and for us to grant [her] license to eat our lamb at Easter).[79] Meyer links this receipt notice to laws around Christian and Jewish butchers' practices in England, particularly to the idea that it was not uncommon for a Jewish ritual slaughterer (trained in accordance with laws of kashrut) to share space or sales with a Christian butcher. A Jewish butcher could follow religious law and then pass the treif discards to the Christian butcher for use or sale, as reflected in English prohibitions and fine records of the time, and the need to pay a fee for license to consume a particular meat makes some sense in this light: Meyer posits that since kosher lamb would not be restricted to the Jewish Dame Abigail, the fee is paid to allow her Christian wet nurse to eat.[80] The date (1253) corresponds, further, to Henry III's issuance of the Statute Concerning Jews, which prohibited Christian wet nurses and servants in Jewish homes and explicitly barred them from eating with Jews.[81] The personal pronoun "nostre," in Meyer's reading, is a quotation of what Abigail has requested: license for the wet nurse to eat *our* (i.e., the Jews') lamb, perhaps reflecting Abigail's concern that the wet nurse keep a kosher diet for the sake of her Jewish infant. Alternatively, Meyer suggests that the "aignel" may be the "lamb of God" and thus indicate a request that the wet nurse be permitted to take communion.

But another reading is possible, and much simpler. The phrase "à Pasche" may be translated as "at Passover," not "at Easter": both holidays are denoted by the same word in Anglo-French,[82] and Anglo-Jews are known to have paid for dispensations related to religious observance. Tower of London receipt rolls for 1275–78, for instance, include fees paid by Jews to observe Shabbat as they wished—"ut possint esse extra per sabbatum" (that they may be able to be outside throughout Shabbat)[83]—and to observe Rosh Hashanah, Yom Kippur, and Purim.[84] The fact that Passover fell during Lent in 1253 perhaps provides additional reason for Dame Abigail to seek license related to the seder, because Henry III's new 1253 statute also barred Jews from buying or eating meat during Lent. If we read the fee paid for the wet nurse to eat "our" lamb "à Pasche" (at Passover) this way, we do not require a reading that depends on fastidious concerns for kosher law in relation to a Christian, nor on a symbolic reading of "lamb." Reading "Pasche" as Passover/Pesach, rather, allows us to hypothesize that Abigail wanted to ensure her infant's wet nurse could be present during a long Passover meal and share the kosher-for-Passover lamb—a situation that seems quite humane for all involved. It suggests, moreover, how the employer-employee and Jewish-Christian relationship could work with domestic intimacy, even within a Christian system that was explicitly hostile to Jews. Abigail—wife of Salle of Canterbury, a leading member of the Canterbury Jewish community in the mid-thirteenth century—turned to her local sheriff more than once for domestic help. He also received payment from her "por lui aider" (for helping her) on another occasion, and, separately, for ten days of assistance "quant son baron fu outre mer et ele jut en gisine" (when her husband was across the sea and she was giving birth).[85] The interconnections of Christians and Jews in such scenes speak to porous and familiar relationships, even if they were inevitably marked by uneven power dynamics and biases.

Christian women also worked inside Jewries in trade-related capacities. Of nearly sixty Jewish-Christian interactions recorded in the Tower receipt roll for 1275–78, twenty-five involve Christian women, and two types of offenses mark their presence *in Judaismo*: they were either there at night ("Christiana noctanter in Judaismo" [a Christianess at night in the Jewry])[86] or caught exchanging ("ad faciendum escambium" or "pro suspicione excambii"), that is, trading, selling, or changing money.[87] One such woman is named "Emma escambiatrice" (Emma the Changer); another is fined "pro vadiis recuperandis" (for collecting sureties); another pays a fine "quia tradidit argentum in Judaismo" (because she spent money in the Jewry).[88] In two entries for 1277, the sergeant of the Tower collected easy money "de quadam Christiana venienti in Judaismo cum centum solidis que fugiit [*sic*] et dimisit argentum" (from a certain Christianess coming into the Jewry with 100 shillings, who fled and left her money behind her).[89] Such mixing in Jewish spaces must have made statutes that legislated the visible difference of Jews and Christians seem more urgent, even as it may have encouraged women to avoid visible difference precisely to avoid such expensive run-ins with local officials.

It is not difficult, in any case, to establish that Anglo-Christian and Anglo-Jewish women could be side by side, speak each other's languages, and interact in ways that men did not, for example, through private exchanges and wet-nursing. Christians nursed Jewish children, Jewish women employed Christian maidservants and loaned to Christian neighbors, and Christian women traded in the Jewry. English authorities dutifully reissued and refined the Lateran IV order for distinction in the clothing of Jews many times between 1218 and 1290, but regular reissuance suggests that such rules were never strictly obeyed. English statutes from 1222, 1253, 1271, 1275, and into the late 1280s show that concerns over miscegenation, shared domestic spaces, and Christian wet nurses in Jewish homes persisted.[90] In May 1279, Edward I sent letters to the justices of the Assize and the warden of the Cinque Ports demanding that Jewish women in particular comply with orders to wear identification badges: "The king wills that Jewish women shall henceforth bear a sign on their outer garment as Jewish men do."[91] The proclamation, which includes many other items pertaining to Jews but is nowhere else concerned with identification badges, suggests that Jewish women in particular were, or were thought to be, defying existing laws that insisted on the visible difference of Jewish and Christian women.

The two pre-Expulsion images of Jewish women that survive, furthermore, suggest little distinction. One is the famous illustration of a lending scene, often characterized as an early instance of medieval anti-Jewish caricature, drawn at the top of a 1233 Norfolk tallage roll, where Abigail ("Avegaye") of Norwich stands alongside Moses son of Abraham ("Mosse Mokke"), both facing each other below the prominent financier Isaac of Norwich, who is caricatured as a three-faced Antichrist (Figure 3).[92] The caricature of Abigail and Moses, however—they have extended noses to which a small devilish figure labeled "Colbik" draws attention—is more likely an indictment of the economic corruption of Henry III's courts than of Jews as such. As Lipton has persuasively argued, the image "is political satire,"[93] and Abigail looks like any Christian noblewoman of her time: she has "lovely long hair and a fashionable head-covering" that seem to evoke not Jewishness but "preachers' warnings about the deceptive and potentially corrupting power of [women's] beauty."[94] The visual criticism of Abigail in this notorious sketch, for Lipton, is of wealth, her association with the Norman elite, and perhaps her regular presence at court. The scholarly tendency to see Moses's and Abigail's noses as a mark of anti-Jewish caricature, Lipton clarifies, is a historical backreading that ignores details of the other figures in the scene: the costumed devil "Colbik" is a court jester figure who engages in a "medieval 'nose-dance,' a riotous revelry in which dancers grabbed each other by the nose, and which was often allegorized as a metaphor for folly and deceit," and the hooded figure at the left who weighs coins in a scale is not Jewish at all—though many interpretations have labeled him so—but more likely a Christian clerk assessing fines.[95] This scribe's sketch in fact conjoins Jews and Christians in a view of royal economic systems that, for the Jewish woman in the picture, does not require much visual distinction from Christians. The scribe perhaps criticizes Abigail's expensive (and very Christian-like) fashion, but she and Moses are, in this image, marked more for their roles in a drama of corruption than for their Jewishness.

The earliest known image of an Anglo-Jewish woman appears in the margin of a fine roll for 2 Henry III (1218), where the scribe has apparently sketched Mirabel of Gloucester, widow of Elias the Jew, alongside note of her appearance to gain confirmation of a grant from King John concerning taxes on her deceased husband's properties (Figure 4).[96] The grant relieved Mirabel from responsibility for paying a full third of Elias's estate to the king, as would normally happen after an English Jew's death. Early in Henry III's reign, Mirabel thus confirms the previous monarch's allowance, which in turn keeps her well positioned to maintain an inherited lending business. The scribe's tiny marginal doodle shows Mirabel in profile, just under the word "Gloucester," with wrapped or covered hair. Another woman is similarly sketched in the margin of a fine roll for 5 Henry III (1221), and she seems to be Heloise of Somerset, a Christian whose dowry case is noted just four lines below the image (Figure 5). The Christianess is also in profile, with wrapped or covered hair. Little distinguishes the two.

Figure 3. Isaac of Norwich, Abigail, and Moses ben Abraham
in Norfolk tallage roll, 1233. TNA E 401/1565.

Converts and Confusions

When an Anglo-Jewish woman converted to Christianity, as Alice of Worcester did, the process was not easy. Many medieval miracle stories end in Jewish women's conversions or suggest that Jewish women were simply more susceptible to conversion than men—just as the murderous Samuel in the *Passion of Adam of Bristol* sees in his wife and worries about in his sister—but there is no evidence that Jewish women converted more than men.[97] If they did convert, however, their conversions could cause extended debate and confusion. The question of whether such women were Jewish or Christian presented trouble from both Christian and Jewish perspectives. The case of Alice of Worcester is one remarkable survival, but other records show that she was not alone in her concerns over her family members, lodgings, belongings, and Christian men's attitudes toward her.

Throughout the 1270s and 1280s, another Jewish woman called Milcana (a variant of Milca or Malka), wife of Sakerel of London, *seemed* to have converted to Christianity. The Plea Rolls of the Exchequer of the Jews preserve four appearances concerning this Milcana's London property, all of which hinge on her apparent conversion. In Michaelmas Term 1275, London financier Aaron Crespin appeared to vouch to warranty the archpresbiter of the Jews, Hagin son of Master Moses. Hagin, whose role as archpresbiter meant that he was an intermediary for "the financial dealings between the King and 'his' Jews" and was to be "present at the Exchequer of the Jews . . . and advise the Justices of the Jews in

Figure 4. Mirabel of Gloucester
in Fine Roll for 2 Henry III
(1218). TNA C 60/9, m. 7.

Figure 5. Heloise of Somerset
(?) in Fine Roll for 5 Henry III
(1221). TNA C 60/15, m. 8.

legal matters regarding the Jewish community,"[98] would have to appear to answer for the rightful ownership of Milcana's house. She had apparently transferred the property to Hagin, and Hagin sold it to Aaron Crespin, but the king
now claimed it "per conversionem Milcane" (through the conversion of Milcana). Hagin did not appear at first, so the sheriff was ordered to summon him
and assess the value of Milcana's property.[99]

    In the same term, as a result, Aaron and Hagin both appeared before the
justices of the Jews. The king continued to claim ownership of the house "per
conversionem Milcane Judee" (through the conversion of Milcana the Jewess),
but Hagin produced Henry III's confirmation of the sale to prove that he had

acted legally in selling the house to Aaron. An attorney for the king argued that Milcana converted "per multum temporis ante" (a long time before) the sale, and that the sale and the confirmation of it were, therefore, forfeit. Hagin did not dispute her conversion, nor the law that would normally allow a convert's property to revert to the king (ostensibly for the convert's care), but he did assert that the sale happened before the conversion.[100] A further date was set for a judgment, but, in Trinity Term of the following year (1276), Hagin kicked the can down the road and vouched to warranty a certain Jurnin son of Abraham concerning the legality of the sale to Aaron. The king's attorney reiterated that Hagin had "iniuste deforciavit ad dampnum Regis" (unlawfully dispossessed [the king] to the king's damage), and this new player—Jurnin—was now summoned as well.[101] Still, at this point, all parties seem to agree that Milcana converted to Christianity sometime before Henry III's death in November 1272. The only point of contention is whether the sale of her house happened before or after her conversion.

But the final entry on the case—in the Plea Roll for Trinity Term 1277—turned everything on its head.[102] The memorandum includes a copy of a letter from Edward I to Aaron Crespin (to whom the property has been sold by Hagin) acknowledging that Milcana may not have converted after all, and so her home may not be owed to him, particularly since her husband Sakerel is still alive (and presumably never converted, therefore retaining rights to the house in any case). Edward ordered an inquest to ascertain whether Milcana was a convert, and a mixed jury of twelve Christian men and twelve Jewish men was convened to determine the facts. The jury finally reported that the woman "numquam fuit christiana nec conuersa set a tempore natiuitatis sue judea fuit et adhuc est" (never was a Christian nor a convert but since her birth has been and still is a Jew).[103] Her former London property would thus stay in Aaron Crespin's hands.

The story of Milcana's conversion, however, continues. Four years later, on 2 November 1281, Archbishop of Canterbury John Peckham wrote to the king with concerns about apostate Christians, that is, Jews who had converted to Christianity but later returned to Judaism. Peckham wanted royal support to investigate the matter under civil law, with the help of the archdeacon of Rochester, who was also warden of the Domus Conversorum at the time, John de St Denis. Peckham must have received support and permission, for a year later, on 14 November 1182, Edward I wrote to the mayor and sheriffs of London and ordered that thirteen apostates identified by Peckham, two men and eleven women, be arrested and imprisoned for their apostasy. Four days later, Peckham in turn wrote to request that the king punish *fifteen* apostates, two men and *thirteen* women, two of whom he identified by family relations only. One of the London women, on both men's lists, is "Milca uxor Sakerel," that is, Milca (a variant of Milcana), the wife of Sakerel.[104]

The king's order to round up the apostates was not obeyed. The mayor and sheriffs of London responded, in their endorsement of the writ, that they had no jurisdiction over London Jews, who were not subject to their authority within the Jewry and were, also, protected by the constable of the Tower. In consideration of this, on 9 January 1283, Peckham wrote to Robert Burnell, lord chancellor and bishop of Bath and Wells—the same man to whom Alice of Worcester felt captive—and asked him to draft a writ that would be more effective in finding and punishing the apostates.[105] Peckham pursued the issue until 1285, when he brought a complaint to the Easter Parliament, issuing a *gravamina* (i.e., the basis for a grievance) in connection to continuing debates over the relative authority of royal and ecclesiastical writs: it was difficult to find the apostates on his list because, within the London Jewry, they were protected in ways that were both legal (that is, under laws pertaining to Jews) and community-based, and, for these reasons, orders for their arrest were not heeded. Royal writs were further ineffective, he claimed, because of "the evasions of these false Christians," that is, these Jews.[106]

The sheer energy and time spent on Milcana's case—to resolve the question of whether she was a Jew or a Christian—is worth emphasizing here: in Trinity Term 1277, when a mixed jury decided emphatically that she was Jewish, the case regarding her property had been ongoing for two years and included evidence of a sale that was at least five years old. After a four-year interim, Peckham's efforts, which disproportionately targeted women and included Milcana, spanned five years again. Indeed, it may be that Milcana's archived presence in the Plea Rolls was part of the problem: Peckham—or more likely the archdeacon of Rochester and warden of the Domus Conversorum, John St Denis—seems to have been mining the Jewish Exchequer rolls for information about apostates. The man who sold Milcana's house, further, was part of a prestigious London family: Hagin son of Moses, also known as Hayyim ben Moses, was the son of Rabbi Moses of London and brother of the English Talmudists Berakhyah of Lincoln and Elijah Menahem.[107] His participation in Milcana's and other such cases is almost certainly linked to Peckham's preoccupations: in 1286, Pope Honorious IV, in a letter directed to the English Church (*Nimis in partibus anglicanis*), wrote to Peckham to support his views on apostasy and explicitly cited the meddling of English Talmudists in conversion cases.[108]

Another particularly lurid case from the Plea Rolls interacts with Peckham's lists as well. In Michaelmas Term 1274, Juliana the Convert claimed that she had been entrusted "per penitentiarum Sancti Pauli" (by the penitentiaries of St. Paul's) with the teaching of a more recent convert called Roesia. The two went walking near the London Jewry in the midst of the Jewish High Holidays,[109] and they were, she said, attacked, abducted, and tortured by London Jews.[110] Juliana named five men and four women among her attackers, beginning with Abraham and Rosa of Dorking, and detailed how she was kept "occulte" (secretly) imprisoned and tortured in the house of a widow named Antera: Antera, "precepto quadam corda circa collum eius voluta eandem Julianam minibatur suspendere" (having ordered a cord wrapped around her neck, had threatened to hang this Juliana) unless she returned to Judaism. After this, a man named Solomon took her on a boat on the Thames and nearly raped her, but a storm took the boat to the port of Sandwich so that, narrowly escaping him, she was able to make her way to Canterbury. The Jews of Canterbury carried a letter to the Jews of London on her behalf, demanding damages in the huge sum of 1,000 marks. During her imprisonment, Juliana said, she had lost track of her convert companion Roesia: she "vidit nec statum ubi posita sit nec si sum superstes uel ad incredulitatem Iudeorum reuersa uel interfaecta" (could not discern in what state she might be, whether she survives alive, or is returned to the disbelief of the Jews, or killed). The assembled accused—including Abraham and Rosa of Dorking—refuted all claims. After two further appearances before the justices, Juliana finally chose not to prosecute, and the court fined her for the trouble.[111]

For Peckham, however, Juliana's sensational testimony appears to have joined Milcana's case as mounting evidence of roaming women apostates: among the women listed in both documents that order the arrest and imprisonment of converts who had returned to Judaism is "Rosa de Dorkyng." The "Rosa" of Peckham's list is undoubtedly related to the Abraham and Rosa of Dorking whom Juliana accused. F. Donald Logan has suggested that Peckham's Rosa may even be Abraham's wife "done an astonishing volte-face," but more likely is that "Rosa de Dorkying" is Juliana's lost convert companion "Roesia," the daughter or granddaughter of the accused Abraham and Rosa. This would suggest that Juliana's companion did indeed return to her Jewish faith, if she had ever truly left it, or at least that Peckham expected that she was alive and somewhere hiding in the London Jewry. The telegraphed second- and third-hand reports of the Jewish Exchequer rolls, filtered through Christian scribes and the summarized interrogations of attorneys, provided the evidence for him. Though Juliana's case was dismissed and Juliana fined, officials like Peckham and the warden of the Domus Conversorum could still use its archived details to imagine women converts who might return to Judaism under pressure from other Jews—even pressure that might come most intensely from a Jewish widow, not unlike Samuel's sister in the *Passion of Adam of Bristol*, acting in secret.

Secrecy and unknowing run through many documents featuring Anglo-Jewish women. It is clear that women converts were especially difficult for Peckham to identify: the two unnamed women in his November 1282 request for their punishment—the ones identified only by their relations ("filia Cresse," "filia Vivos")—do not make it into the king's list, and two other women, including Milcana, are first listed as "dudum" (formerly) wives of their husbands, though the word *dudum* is struck out in the king's version of the list (because in fact these women were still married to their Jewish husbands).[112] Peckham found it impossible to verify the existence and relational status of some of his candidates, let alone arrest or imprison them. If they could be found, doubts might linger in any case. Also on the lists is Swetecote, the wife of Moses of Horndon, who appeared before a chancery court to testify that rumors that she had been baptized during the Second Barons' War were false, and that she was not a Christian; like Milcana's, her case prompted a mixed-jury inquest in 1288, despite the fact that the baptism apparently took place between the Battles of Lewes and Evesham (14 May 1264–4 August 1265).[113] Though Swetecote appeared to state her own identity, and at issue was a claim of forced baptism in wartime, it remained uncertain whether she was a Christian or a Jew. The doubt appears to have hung over her head, in both Jewish and Christian company, for more than twenty years.

These kinds of records could produce their own brand of anti-Jewish polemic, a widespread (and dual-edged) suspicion of female pliability and persuasion around conversion. Gendered anxieties over women's conversion, or, conversely, women's capacity to convert others, persisted during the thirteenth century, often linked to prohibitions against Christian wet nurses in Jewish homes, with continental Jewish sources likewise discussing the risks of conversion associated with keeping Christian wet nurses and servants.[114] Archbishop Peckham's lists (87 percent women), as well as cases like Milcana's and Swetecote's (for which there is no male comparison), reflect an ideology not that women might convert more frequently than men—they did not—but that women would be more prone to fickleness, backsliding, or dishonesty. Edward I's 1279 letters to the justices of the Assize and the warden of the Cinque Ports perhaps served as a catalyst for Peckham's search for apostates: there Edward had juxtaposed the problem of apostasy to Jewish women's failure to wear identifying badges. The fuller passage reads, "The king wills that . . . those who were baptized at any time when converted to the catholic faith and afterwards perverted to the Jewish wickedness [shall be punished similarly to blasphemers]. The king wills that Jewish women shall henceforth bear a sign on their outer garment as Jewish men do."[115] The problem of women's indistinguishability from Christians was connected to the problem of unfixed, suspect, or feigned conversions by the king himself.[116] If Peckham's preoccupation with female converts does not match what we can reconstruct of the reality of the number of English converts from Judaism in the thirteenth century, it does suggest the nature of certain preconceived ideas about Jewish women.

Women converts' stories, like the ones I have described, are intertwined with the last generations of medieval Anglo-Jewry, and they persist past the Expulsion too. More than one woman left behind letters and receipts attesting to her life's narrative, and some—most of them brief and financial in nature or connected to the Domus Conversorum—even provide evidence of converts' sustained interaction with both their former and current communities. These letters, like Alice of Worcester's, have not usually been noted among the survivals of medieval English Jewry, but, as I have argued for Alice, it is worth thinking of these women as Jews; they were Jews for part of their lives, and their postconversion lives are marked by labels and institutions that signal their former Jewishness. Including Alice of Worcester's, I know of eight letters by or about English women who converted from Judaism between 1270 and the early 1400s. Six were written by the women themselves.

One of these, not extant but summarized in the Edward III Close Rolls, was written by Claricia of Exeter, a convert who petitioned the king for readmission to the Domus Conversorum in 1327.[117] Claricia was the daughter of the financier Jacob Copin. From 1266 to 1280, Jacob had been the chirographer of the Exeter *archa*—the state-sanctioned depository of Exeter Jewish bonds—and in 1280 he was hanged for murdering a Christian.[118] Not much is known of Jacob's family, but he had at least one son who was imprisoned with him in the Tower of London from 1275 to 1278, a time when many English Jews were imprisoned for coin clipping.[119] From Claricia's enrolled letter, where she is identified in relation to her father, we also know that he had at least one daughter. Claricia converted to Christianity and resided in the Domus Conversorum in London on and off from around the time of her father's death until her own death in 1356, when she must have been quite elderly. She is the last recorded member of the pre-Expulsion Jews of England.

Surviving Domus records show that Claricia lived in London in 1280 but that her whereabouts were unknown in 1308; in 1327, as the Close Rolls attest, she asked the newly crowned Edward III for reentry and renewed financial support. In 1330, based on her petition, the king directed the warden of the Domus to readmit her and maintain her so long as it could be verified that she was a in fact a convert. Despite the king's doubting qualification, this must have happened, for ten years later her son Richard and daughter Katherine are recorded as inmates of the Domus with her.[120] Claricia, according to the Close Roll account, told the king that she was unjustly refused reentry because she had been absent in "distant parts" and was therefore unknown to the current warden.[121] Whether her conversion and travels had anything to do with her father's execution or the Expulsion are unknown, but it was apparently not impossible that such a woman *might* be Jewish (i.e., Edward III wanted to verify her conversion), nor that she might come and go from the Domus once admitted. Another surviving letter evidences the same kind of mobility: Margery (or Margaret) of Stanford, writing sometime after Edward II's accession to the throne in 1307, similarly petitioned the king for renewed support because, like Claricia, Margery had been absent for some reason when previous residents were registered.[122]

The post-Expulsion decades also give us a letter from one Juliana, a woman who wrote to King Edward II in 1320, petitioning him for support of her children. She may be the same Juliana the Convert who appeared before the justices of the Jews in 1274 to accuse London Jews of abducting her and her convert companion Roesia/Rosa, though Juliana was a common baptismal name for converts. Records show that there were two Julianas living in the London Domus in 1280, and three by 1308, one with her husband Martin, also a convert.[123] It is this Juliana, the wife of Martin, who writes in 1320, in the immediate wake of her husband's death: "por ce qentre les auanditz Martin et Juliane fut grant engendrure" (because there was much offspring between the said Martin and Juliana), and because their ancestors (presumably their Jewish family) are now gone—"a dieu commandetz," the letter says, a phrase that can mean "deceased" but is also used in Anglo-French for formal goodbyes[124]—she asks that her children be permitted to live in the Domus Conversorum with her. Her letter is endorsed in French in a remarkable way: "Les enfanz ne sont mie conuers mes pur ceo qe il sont fitz a conuers le Roi sauisera" (The children are by no means converts, but because they are children of a convert the king will consider it).[125] What does this mean? The simplest explanation is that the children of this union were not converts because their parents were already Christians when they were born. Why the children would not have already been residents of the Domus, as Claricia of Exeter's were, remains puzzling, but converts (and presumably their children), as we have already seen, might come and go from the Domus for extended periods of time.

In the next generation, the self-identified "Joan the Convert of Dartmouth," along with her daughter Alice, wrote a quarterly receipt for wages to the warden of the Domus on 16 April 1410; the two women's personal seals are still attached the document.[126] A corroborating 1409 letter from Henry IV to the warden tells us more: Henry asked for admission of

> noz bien amees Iohanne Conuerse de notre ville de Dertemuth' et Alice sa fille nadgairs esteantes Iuwesses mescreantes et desirantes destre de la secte cristiene refuserent touz lour bons et chateulx que eles auoient et arriuerent en port de notre dite ville et feurent conuertees et baptisees.[127]

> our good friends Joan the Convert from our city of Dartmouth and her daughter Alice who, recently remaining miscreant Jewesses but desiring to be of the Christian sect, have given up all their goods and chattels with which they set out and arrived at the port of our said city, and have been converted and baptized.

Why do Henry and Joan both firmly connect her identity to Dartmouth instead of whatever, presumably (though not definitively) continental, city she came from? And how long were Joan and her daughter living as Jews in Dartmouth? Joan stayed in the Domus for forty years, her daughter for at least forty-five; their friendship with Henry IV apparently sealed the arrangement. Their presence in England and claimed English identities, more than a century after the Expulsion, add to the documentable cases of those converts who remained and arrived in England after 1290, and who apparently could and did travel the country—from Dartmouth to, as Claricia of Exeter put it, "distant parts." Together with the pre-Expulsion cases of confusion and doubt over Jewish women's conversions, these cases help us to envision a type of the Jewish woman convert that persisted in England, and they sit provocatively alongside literary examples that imagine English Jewesses even into the late Middle Ages:[128] around the same time that Joan and Alice of Dartmouth converted from Judaism and claimed their (Christian) Englishness, Margery Kempe was asked whether she was "a Cristene woman er a Jewe."[129]

Forgers and Fighters

The Christian-Jewish interactions and conversion cases I have discussed thus far, in addition to establishing relationships and potential confusions, also suggest the extent to which Jewish women might be seen as threatening or dangerous to Christians. This danger did not manifest because of difference but because Jewish women were proximate to Christians (in courts, homes, and finance) or even became Christians (as converts) in ways that made officials and archivists anxiously uncertain. The roles that Anglo-Jewish women play in historical record—as literate businesswomen, as employers of Christian maidservants and wet nurses, or as converts, apostates, and confusions—adhered to the ways in which they could be viewed as suspect. Like their male counterparts, Jewish women were also sometimes suspected of defrauding Christians and could be brought to court to answer to charges of violence.

Jewish women's participation in documentary practices occasionally caused suspicions of forgery and had special implications for the validation of documents. In November 1277, for example, four men of York and two of Lincoln vouched for a Christian sheriff's clerk who was commanded to appear before the king to answer for his possession of "a writ sealed with a false seal, that of Belaset, wife of Abraham son of Joceus, a Jew of York, delivered to the sheriff of York, which Jewess he ought then to have arrested"—and Beleset too was summoned to answer for her forgeries.[130] In 1275, a starr of Belia of Bedford produced hesitancy among the justices of the Jews when a Robert Cave "came before the court and produced a certain starr of acquittance under the name of Belia" to show that he had already paid his debt to her. The fact of the starr in Belia's name seems to have caused worry about its validity: as the Exchequer scribe writes, "Because there was uncertainty whether the said starr that he produced was legal and valid, therefore the Justices commanded that the said Belia be made to appear before the court."[131] While it did not automatically invalidate the starr of acquittance, the presence of a woman's signature, or perhaps the fact of its being solely in her name, seems to have called its authenticity into question; the justices sought further confirmation from Belia herself, as was perhaps the scenario when Henna of York's signature "litera mea ebraica" (in my Hebrew script) necessitated her appearance before the Exchequer's court.[132] The document chest of Henna of Oxford also received special scrutiny after her death in June 1290, because a bond between herself and the abbot and Convent of Osney was found to be false and her seal forged.[133]

Jewish women were, of course, not exempt from prosecution, imprisonment, or suspicion because of their gender either. In the coin-clipping crisis of the late 1270s, Jewish women were sought, rounded up, or imprisoned along with Jewish men,[134] though the rates and circumstances of imprisonment and punishment do differ markedly by gender. Assessing the data available for coin-clipping offenses in this period, Zefira Rokéah found 62 women among the 481 Jews accused (roughly 13 percent), but only 10 of those 62 were subsequently imprisoned (i.e., 1 in 6 imprisoned Jews were women); of 39 Jews executed for the crime, no more than 5 were women.[135] More Christians than Jewish women were accused of clipping—a kind of complicated interaction and neighborliness—and, in general, Jewish women were able to avoid the harshest consequences: the Tower of London receipts show that Jewish women paid for ease of imprisonment more frequently than men, sometimes because they were pregnant.[136] The idea that Jewish women could avoid imprisonment and execution, however, alongside evidence that women might pay off sheriffs or be "false Christians," shaped stereotypes of the Jewess that were, at the same time, developing in English historiographical and literary narratives.

Michael Adler, in the same 1934 address on medieval Anglo-Jewish women that begins this chapter, felt compelled nonetheless to list several sensational cases in which Jewish women were suspected of murder or involved in woman-to-woman assault. This, he said, was their "darker side."[137] As an example, Adler and Dobson both wrote about the brutal beating of Bessa of Warwick by other Jewish women at the door of the Warwick synagogue.[138] The beating resulted in a miscarriage that a Jewish Exchequer scribe, writing a memorandum of the case in Michaelmas Term 1244, called "horrible to relate": Bessa's husband had testified that the fetus "was yet too young for its sex to be distinguished" and that, despite her attackers' claims to the contrary, Bessa "did not smear herself with the blood of animals, but . . . was bathed in her own blood as she held her [miscarried] infant."[139] Dobson used this case partly to confirm that Anglo-Jewish women "could freely walk the streets of provincial towns" and to make the point that "it would be unwise to assume that they usually lived either the secluded or gentle life advocated in Hebrew religious literature"[140]—though this is perhaps *the least* of the evidence that they, or indeed any medieval Jewish woman, were not as secluded and gentle as halakhic or Talmudic literature might impress. In response to Adler's idea of a "darker side," Dobson further speculated that cases in which Jewish women were the victims of anti-Jewish attacks were "no doubt much more common (but much less often recorded)" than cases in which a Jewess herself had committed any sort of assault.[141] I would suggest, however, that if indeed (and we cannot know for certain) such cases were "much less often recorded," that fact is itself important to an understanding of the (mis)representations of Jewish women in medieval Anglo-Christian eyes.

In any case, these women do not need our apologetics. Fraud or assault cases are not a distinguishing feature of the records about them, even if they do, individually, make an impression on the modern reader. Available accounts of their financial, legal, and domestic lives do more to underscore medieval Anglo-Jewish women's ability to "freely walk" (relatively speaking) than does a tragic fight outside a synagogue. As Dobson also points out, it is the apparent scribal reveling in such cases, "so vivid and so sanguinary," and consciousness that such accounts are "utterly dependant on the record compiled and preserved by Christian clerks," that are most worthy of our attention.[142] Anglo-Jewish women were not necessarily extraordinary by comparison with the activities of, and prejudices against, Anglo-Jewish men, but they were archived differently. "The Jew" and "the Jewess" may, equally, be examined in light of historical records and contexts, though related analysis must lead us to distinct conclusions. Anti-Jewish sentiment against women manifests disproportionately at permeated boundaries between Christians and Jews and is managed through fantasies of secret and intimate feminine spaces. Where Baumgarten's work with continental Hebrew *responsa*, for instance, shows that Jews worried that a Christian wet nurse, left unsupervised in a Jewish home, might kill a Jewish child or convert it with lullabies,[143] papal decrees and English statutes showed concern over whether the breast milk of a communicant (i.e., a Christian wet nurse in a Jewish home) might bring a Jewish child into false communion.[144]

The danger of the woman was secret, domestic, and unmarked. Circumcision too, as a marker of Jewish identity, was worryingly absent from Jewish women. No examination or performance like the ones imposed on Jurnepin/Odard of Norwich or Sampson son of Samuel of Northampton—anxious as those already were—was possible to determine a woman's Jewishness. The convert Petrus Alfonsi, a Spanish expatriate writing in England, imagined in his *Dialogue Against the Jews* (ca. 1109) that his postconversion Christian self

(Petrus) and preconversion Jewish self (Moses) argued about this feminine lack: "What do you think . . . about Jewish women, who cannot be circumcised and yet are still believed [by Jews] to be saved?" asks Petrus. And when Moses responds that Jewish women are saved because they are conceived by circumcised men, Petrus answers with pre-Christian models: "Then what do you say about Sarah and Rebekah, Rachel and Leah and Zipporah . . . and Ruth, who all, as you believe, were saved and who nonetheless were not born from Jews?"[145] The absence of circumcision is a question of salvation, and Petrus/Moses wants to have it both ways. He *uses* women to prove that salvation cannot, rationally, depend on circumcision—Jewish women before Christ "were all saved without circumcision but with a correct faith and good works"[146]—but their lack also means that they are more easily admitted to Christian salvation, since baptism is a "universal form."[147] This is even acknowledged by Jews, Petrus argues, who require only baptism (the mikveh) for female converts to Judaism and not the mark of circumcision.[148] More than a century later, Matthew Paris compared coin clipping to circumcision and thought that all Jews were clippers and forgers of charters and seals:[149] clipped coins were Judaized because, upon examination, it was evident that they had been "circumcised"— but Jewish women, of a tougher metal, could not be. Where circumcision could be revealed, considered, or imposed, the Jewishness of a woman could remain concealed.

The surviving records of medieval Anglo-Jewish life offer a mix of the quotidian and the remarkable—and they are often more formulaic than anything else—but they do reveal what was deemed worthy of record from an Anglo-Christian perspective. Jewish women certainly could be associated with the stereotypes and Christian prejudices that we commonly associate with (male) anti-Judaism—for instance, deception, trickery, violence, litigiousness, and usury—but they also challenged and crossed Christian boundaries. Their domestic and maternal roles allowed for gendered interactions with Christian women, evidence of their documentary literacy and multilingualism is imposing, and disproportionate resources went into detecting the status and identities of women converts. They had less (and perhaps no) distinguishing clothing—as noted by Edward I, who worried that women did not wear the mandated Jewish identification badges—and their bodily distinction could be theorized, as by Petrus Alfonsi, for its lack.

The evidence presented here must impact how we read fictionalized representations of Jewish women in the English context. It is, for instance, clearly in conversation with the *Passion of Adam of Bristol*, which is so unusual among the survivals of medieval anti-Jewish literature for its featuring of a multilingual widowed Jewess who, in addition to appearing to be Christian, is able to negotiate body-disposal fees with a priest and disappear without converting—though when we are talking about thirteenth-century England this must by now seem almost predictable. Bureaucratic and literary records *together* reinforce the English Jewess type I am sketching: unmarked, in both Jewish and Christian spaces, with financial and linguistic know-how that depends on and reiterates her indistinguishability. From a historical perspective, the Anglo-Jewish woman can be admired. From a medieval bigot's perspective, her sameness is both the problem and the attraction. Around Jewish women, tales of predictable conversions, evaded punishments, feigned Christianity, violence, and concealed or deceptive interactions coexisted with the Christian desire for, and usurpation of, Jewishness.

CHAPTER 4

Mothers and Cannibals

The hands of pitiful women have sodden their own children: they
were their meat in the destruction of the daughter of my people.
                                            —Lamentations 4:10

Except that you eat the flesh of the Son of man, and drink his blood,
you shall not have life in you. . . . For my flesh is meat indeed: and my
blood is drink indeed.
                                            —John 6:54–56

Reading for the Unmarked Jewess

Jewish women are legion in the Christian literature of medieval England. Any
impression that they are not comes mainly from the visual record, where their
lack of physical marking, striking in opposition to the caricatures of Jewish men
that developed in the High Middle Ages, suggests "almost no visually distin-
guishable Jewish women."[1] While the heroic Old Testament Jewess appears in
the Christian literature and art of this period and earlier, and much hagiographic and and historiographical literature includes the postbiblical Jewess, illustrations of "Jewish women can be identified only by context or by very
superficial cues: delete the setting, eliminate the male companions, or efface the
inscriptions, and they could be Christian matrons or nuns."[2] Sara Lipton's influential work on the Jewess in medieval art is careful to separate the visual and
textual evidence—she does note, by way of contrast, that the Jewess "as seductive femme fatale . . . , virtuous Christian convert . . . , or grieving mother of a

tender, Marian-loving son" is found in "myriad medieval fictional and historical texts"[3]—but the literary case, at least in England, is far more complex. It is fully entangled with the visual indistinguishability laid out by Lipton, and with the archived Jewish women detailed in the previous chapter.

The idea that the visual record may be in line with writers' disinterest in Jewish women, nonetheless, has bled into literary criticism. On the one hand, I agree to some extent with Steven Kruger that, in medieval Christian narratives, "Jewish women, unlike the obdurate men of their 'race,' seem particularly susceptible to Christianity's 'truth' and hence conversion"; with Miri Rubin that we often see Jewish women portrayed as femininely "pliant and impressionable" in medieval miracle tales, Jewish mothers "saved and converted at the price of the father's destruction"; and with Anthony Bale that, in anti-Jewish literature, "the real villain is the Jewish male; Jewish women are considered more pliant, more easily brought to the faith."[4] On the other hand, the Jewess in medieval English literature is far more than a predictable plot device or pliant foil for Jewish men. As Amy-Jill Levine might put it, she is "both more and less than 'Jew,'"[5] and her capaciousness includes the specific capacity to be or seem to be Christian. Pliancy, indeed, should not be understood as her primary attribute, nor should Jewishness. Her Jewishness, after all, can be a matter of invisibility, indistinguishable from or tending toward Christianity. Rather, we must read the Jewess for her sameness and look for her unmarking. It is, paradoxically, her Christianness that is primary.

Where Bale has summarized the "general gender dynamics of medieval antisemitic writing" as overwhelming masculine—when "medieval Christian texts present 'a Jew' they generally present an adult, male Jew, or groups of adult male Jews" or "female Christian intermediaries (in particular wet-nurses) . . . said to be in league with Jews"[6]—I insist that we recognize the Jewess as present throughout the life of medieval English literature, as a consistently utilized "Jew" type exploited by Christian authors in anti-Jewish texts and books. The sameness of the Jewess certainly *entails* malleability and uncertainty, but these are crafted. To engage idealized notions of Christian Jewishness, fear of Jewish infiltration, and the ingathering of Jews to Christianity, medieval Christian texts generally present an adult, female Jew as a doubled, passing, or ambiguous figure. The Jewess is not represented in Anglo-Christian literature only through the figures of the virtuous convert or the grieving mother of a son (i.e., as a type of Mary); she is also a sister, a cleaner, a cannibal, a mother, a wife, a daughter, and a go-between—and generally not a seductress or femme fatale.[7] In all cases, her polemical function is *to appear to be Christian.*

My final two chapters now turn to establishing a corpus of medieval Anglo-Christian texts that create and contend with the unmarked Jewess. By design, she is difficult to see, but reading for her reveals both a consistent polemic of sameness and a series of identifiable subtypes. The current chapter focuses on her (overlapping) characterizations as a mother, a convert, and a cannibal, which authors and artists entwine with intertestamental stories of the Virgin Mary or the matriarch Rachel. The next chapter, to address more directly the ambiguities that the unmarked Jewess produces, gathers go-betweens, sisters, daughters, and (so-called) femme fatales under the umbrella of "figures of uncertainty"—that is, the Jewish women authors and artists use to manipulate their (Christian) readers into uncertainties about self, faith, and neighbors.

Jewish Mothers

In his *Chronica majora* entries for the year 1250, Matthew Paris relates a now well-known libel concerning Abraham of Berkhamsted (d. ca. 1273), a financier and administrator who worked closely with Henry III's brother Richard, Earl of Cornwall, and was sometimes charged with assessing and collecting taxes and fines from other Jews.[8] Matthew says that Abraham stole an image of the Virgin Mary, shat on it, and then killed his wife Floria for sympathizing with the Virgin. His account is as follows:

> Erat quidam Judæus dives mediocriter, nomine non fide Abraham, apud Berkamestude et apud Walingeford habens frequentiam et mansionem. Erat enim comitis Ricardi ob aliam quam decuit, ut dicebatur, causam familiaris. Iste speciosam habuit uxorem et sibi fidelem, Floriam nomine. Ut igitur idem Judæus Christo dedecus majus accumularet fecit emi imaginem beatæ Virginis insculptam decenter et depictam, et ut moris est, filium suum in gremio confoventem. Hanc ipse Judæus in latrina sua constituit, et quod dedecus et ignominiosum est penitus exprimere, ipsi imagini, tanquam ipsi beatæ Virgini blasphemando, turpissimam et irrecitabilem rem diebus ac noctibus et irrogabat et irrogari ab uxore sua præcepit. Quod cum mulier aliquot dies videret, ratione sexus condoluit, et transiens clam sordes abstersit a facie imaginis enormiter deturpatae. Hoc autem cum Judæus vir ejus veraciter comperisset ipsam mulierem uxorem suam iccirco clam impie suffocavit.[9]

> There was a certain moderately wealthy Jew, Abraham by name but not in faith, who had a manor and retinue at Berkhamsted and at Wallingford, for by some fitting cause or other, as it is said, he was closely associated with Earl Richard. He had a wife who was beautiful and faithful to him, Floria by name. To heap more disgrace on Christ, this Jew had purchased a decently carved and painted image of the blessed Virgin, nursing her son at her bosom as is the norm. The Jew put this in his latrine, and—what is utter disgrace and shame to express, as if blaspheming the blessed Virgin—he inflicted, and ordered his wife to inflict, the most foul and unspeakable thing on it daily and nightly. So when the woman saw this for some days, she felt compassion because of her sex, and, going secretly, she wiped the filth from the face of the greatly befouled image. Now, when the Jew, her husband, learned this fact, for that reason he impiously suffocated the woman, his wife, in secret.

Bale has written persuasively about Matthew's use of Abraham's name as a negative reflection of the biblical Abraham, the alignment of scatalogical tropes with fantasized anti-Christian acts in this account, and the process by which an Anglo-Jewish person—that is, Abraham—becomes fantastical for Matthew because of "interaction and familiarity with the [institutional] structures and [cultural] images of medieval England."[10] However, nothing substantial has been said about Floria of Berkhamsted.

Not merely a sketch of the "Jewish wife as image desecrator," as Lipton has briefly described her, or a good example of the "pliant" Jewish woman trope, as Bale suggests,[11] Floria of Berkhamsted may indeed have died in 1250—though there is no corroborating evidence of her death, let alone by murder.[12] She had at least one child with Abraham. Her daughter, also called Floria, married Leo, the scholar son of Hamo of Hereford, whose estate Abraham had sued to claim inheritance rights for his daughter and granddaughter.[13] Record of the 1234 suit, in which Leo's books were at issue, also tells us that the younger Floria had a daughter by Leo (Contessa) and later remarried, thus maintaining familial ties between important Anglo-Jewish families.[14] In other words, Floria of Berkhamsted, like her husband Abraham, is the historical subject of a libelous fantasy. As he does with Abraham, Matthew Paris takes her from the "mundane, technical, [and] realistic" through a "process of fictionalisation and glossing," until Floria too shows "that it was not difference that made Jews threatening to medieval Englishmen, but rather the Jews' possible interaction and familiarity."[15] Bale's arguments about Abraham, edging toward sameness, are focused on the male Jew's interactions with "vectors of power" and a familiar Marian object,[16] but Floria's polemicized presence is arguably more insidious. Matthew's caricature of her depends not on her economic power or status as a wife, but on her motherhood and consequent likeness to the Virgin Mary.

Matthew sets Floria parallel to her husband in many ways, and, in my view, much of the significance of this little libel depends on Matthew's side-by-side descriptions of the male and the female Jew. The passage is crafted through verbal echoes and comparable actions that pit Abraham and Floria against each other. If Matthew uses Abraham's name figurally, for instance—"playing with" it to create "the 'bad', current Jew as contrasted with the 'good', antique Jew"[17]— he plays similarly with Floria's name. Floria or Fluria was an extremely common Anglo-Jewish woman's name,[18] and here it is used both to contrast Floria with her husband and to connect her to the Virgin Mary. Floria is faithful ("sibi fidelem") while Abraham is not ("non fide"). While Abraham is a poor reflection of his biblical namesake, Floria is like Mary and like her name (from French *fleur*, "flower" or "bloom"); she is beautiful ("speciosa," as in the hymn "Stabat mater speciosa"), and her name evokes common epithets for Mary: the fairest flower, the fleur-de-lis (lily), and the flower of the field.[19] Matthew establishes Floria's alignment with Mary through Abraham's actions as well: both women are the object of his violence and fiat, and both are mistreated by Abraham in similar ways. Where the image of Mary is drowned in a latrine as Abraham "accumularet" (heaps on) disgrace, Floria is impiously "suffocavit" by Abraham (i.e., suffocated, with secondary meanings of "drowned" or "choked").[20] Both Abraham and Floria act "clam" (secretly), but Floria's secret is her sympathy and maternal recognition of Mary. Matthew imagines that she feels compassion ("conduluit") for the nursing image of Mary because they are both women ("ratione sexus"), and, in an intimate exchange that momentarily relieves their mutual suffocation, Floria therefore "sordes abstersit a facie" (wipes the filth from [Mary's] face).

We see Matthew Paris here, at his most anti-Jewish—and he was that indeed—drawing a sharp line between his representation of Jewish men and women and inflecting his polemics against them differently. Where Abraham is dirty, violent, and faithless, Floria is faithful, compassionate, and cleansing. Because of her feminine similarity to another Jewish mother (Mary), Floria is the polemical inversion of her grotesque and abject husband, and the fictionalized "bad" male Jew responds to both women in the same way: Floria meets her death because she has become another image of Mary to desecrate. In Floria's "process of fictionalisation," to use Bale's apt term again, no conversion is necessary, because the sameness of the Jewess and her Jewish/Christian double is the point. Matthew simultaneously saves Mary from blasphemy and elevates Floria to be *like* Mary, precisely because she is neither like the male Jew nor able to act pliantly.

The popular Miracle of the Virgin known as "The Jewish Boy" functions very similarly. Often used as evidence for the malleability of Jewish women in Christian narratives, this miracle story, in wide circulation in the West from the late sixth century, likewise seems to make good evidence for the indistinguishability of Jewish women in medieval art.[21] It tells of a young Jewish boy who takes communion with his Christian playmates on Easter. When he returns home, his father is so angry that he throws him into the household oven. His mother wails through the streets, seeking Christian help, and, when help arrives, they find the boy safe inside the oven. The child claims that he was protected by Mary, the woman he saw in the church cradling her son. At this, the boy and his mother convert to Christianity, and the assembled crowd throws the Jewish father into the oven that he used in his attempt to kill his son. Many iterations of this story survive, in many languages, and illustrations of it are common in churches and devotional books.[22] Particularly in its English circulation, the tale is deeply concerned with Christian-Jewish interactions and Jewish passing among Christians.[23] It has rarely been noted, however, that its nameless Jewish mother, who seeks aid from Christian authorities and eventually becomes Christian, makes Jewish-Christian boundaries as permeable as her son does.

Through both its Jewish son and Jewish mother, "The Jewish Boy" rewards interaction and sameness even as it engages difference as a problem. English iterations make explicit that no one could tell that the young boy was a Jew, a fact already implicit in the plot that has him approaching a priest to take Easter communion. In the version that survives in Bod. MS Eng. poet. a.1 (The Vernon Manuscript), for example, the poet notes that the boy played with Christians so often "that riht as one of hem he were" (that it was just as if he were one of them).[24] The version in BL MS Additional 39996, similarly, reasons that the boy was "foled and torned" (baptized and converted) as a result of his being "*priuely / In cristen mannes company*" (*secretly* in the company of Christians).[25] While most versions of this miracle conclude with the burning of the Jewish father and conversion of all other Jews present, furthermore, the abridgment in Additional 39996 uniquely has the Christian crowd burn not only the father but also "all the oþere euerechone / Þat ever were at þat assent" (all the others, every single one, who ever agreed with him).[26] Such extremes of celebrated likeness and punished difference betray the double bind of ambiguous or conjoined Jewish/Christian identities in anti-Jewish texts: the boy and his mother become Christian because they were already indistinguishable from other Christians, able to interact with Christians without detection or hesitation. The desirability of this sameness, however, meets a competing desire for violent separation. In its succinct communication of the polemical point, the Additional 39996 version ensures that *all Jews* who maintain Jewish difference are executed, so that likeness and the violent enforcement of difference are means to the one oddly unifying end. These texts punish Jewish distinction in favor of an idealized blending of Jew and Christian, accomplished with conversions already predicated on likeness and enforced by the violent erasure of holdouts who are already aggressively distinct. "The Jewish Boy" suggests that distinction between Christians and Jews—geographically, visually, practically—is the offense. Sameness is as normal as children playing together.

The ability of the Jewish mother to summon Christian help and swiftly become Christian is part of this polemical position. Like her son, and like the Virgin Mary, the mother's ability to be both Jewish and Christian matters to the miracle's lessons about difference. Indeed, what we see in Christian illustrations of this woman, where she is unmarked and thus appears as any other (Christian) woman, betrays artists' understanding of her narrative utility. As Lipton has pointed out, one of the remarkable things about medieval depictions of Jewish women is that they "can be identified only by context,"[27] such that illustrative and narrative traditions *must* work together in representations of them. The function of sameness in such scenarios is, therefore, didactic and interactive: when Jewish and Christian women look the same in illustrations, it is impossible to know that you are looking at a Jewish woman unless you already know the story that the image reflects; if you learn the story, you also learn that the woman you are looking at is a Jew. The Jewess's indistinguishability is thus connected to processes of Christian knowing and recognition—and this process is a feature not a glitch.

Two English examples show us that artists sought to make the Jewish mother's similarity to Christian women a feature of her visual characterization. The first, in BL MS Egerton 2781 (The Neville of Hornby Hours), shows the Jewish mother standing behind and partially obscured by her husband, who is throwing their child into the oven, while the Virgin Mary stands nearby with protective and sorrowful gestures (Figure 6). With the Jewish father and his violent act between the two women, this artist—like Matthew Paris with Floria

Figure 6. Illustration of "The Jewish Boy" with Virgin Mary,
Jewish father, and Jewish mother. ©British Library Board.
BL MS Egerton 2781 (Neville of Hornby Hours), fol. 24r.

of Berkhamsted—composes the mothers as doubles of each other: the two
women frame the hook-nosed and angry-eyed man, who appears in profile
with his legs awkwardly in motion and extending out of the frame. The Jewish
mother mimics Mary's expression and gestures: the women's extended hands
and slightly tilted heads are at the same angle and height.

The Jewish mother in this image is so obscured by her marked male counterpart that she appears to grow out of his back: her image works with the
curves of his tunic, and whether her other hand or the draping of her clothing
might also mimic Mary's is unseeable. By contrast, the intentional space be-

tween Mary and the Jewish father, and the fact that the boy's struggling body touches and overlaps Mary's, suggest that the closeness and opposition of the male and female Jew should be read as purposeful. This artist, like Matthew Paris, has worked to highlight the contrast of his gendered characterizations of Jews. The Jewish mother is aligned with the model of Christian femininity and maternity in pointed contrast to the visible difference of the man who moves between them. And because there is no nearby text of the associated tale to gloss this image, nor any caption that tells who the characters are—only an *Ave Maria* prayer that continues from the initial *O* that contains the image—the didactic possibilities are dramatically evident in this instance. To see a Jewish woman, one must know or learn the story that the image depicts, and, in this process, one will first recognize a Jewess as a Christian, then discover that she is a Jewess, and then find that she is Christian again, through a conversion that is predicated on her likeness and access to Christians.

Another English illustration of "The Jewish Boy," in Bod. MS Eng. poet. a.1 (The Vernon Manuscript), provides a comparable example. However, in the Vernon collection of Miracles of the Virgin, an English verse version of each tale allows direct interaction between image and text: the Marian poems follow their related illustrations, and thus one can read the images with or against the explanatory stories.[28] "The Jewish Boy" and "The Child Slain by Jews"—sometimes called the "Miracle of the Boy Singer," best known in Chaucer's version as "The Prioress's Tale"—survive there in facing-page relation to each other (Figures 7 and 8).[29] Both tales, and both images, feature a male Jewish aggressor, the murder or attempted murder of a young boy, and a frantic mother who seeks help from Christian officials. In "The Child Slain by Jews," the boy and his mother are Christian, and a Jew murders the child for singing a Marian hymn; in "The Jewish Boy," the boy and his mother are Jewish, and the Jewish father attempts to murder the child for taking communion. In both, the mothers make noise and seek the help of local law enforcement. Both run "in everi stret[e]" (in every street) (147, 508), both lament loudly—one "criede in on" (cried out unceasingly), while the other was "ever hotyng out" (always shrieking out) (157, 507)—and both seek the "meir and bailifs" (mayor and bailiffs) (168, 511). The one substantive distinction between the Jewish and the Christian mother lies in their relative understanding of recourse to legal aid: where the Christian mother simply pleads with officials "to don hire lawe and riht" (to do legally and righteously by her) (176), the Jewess announces, "Mi cause I schal bifore you proven. . . . And I schal give ow gold to gloven" (I will prove my case before you. . . . And I will put gold in your palms) (526–30). This distinction is notable, for it shows lingering awareness of Anglo-Jewish women's careers before 1290, when, as we have seen, they might give testimony in court or pay fines for legal allowances. The Vernon texts thus maintain a specifically Anglo-Christian notion of the Jewess even as they purposefully highlight the sameness of Christian and Jewish mothers.

In all of their iterations, "The Jewish Boy" and "The Child Slain by Jews" invite comparison between Christians and Jews, and this is nowhere more evident than in the mothers' uncannily similar roles. The two tales are often juxtaposed, both historically and in modern scholarship. As in the Vernon Manuscript, they appear near each other in many medieval collections of Marian miracles.[30] Abbot Samson of Bury St Edmunds had at least two separate paintings of "The Jewish Boy" on a choir screen he commissioned, completed around the same time that Bury Jews were accused of murdering a Christian boy (1181/82), an accusation that had links to the 1255 case of little Hugh of Lincoln, which in turn inspired Chaucer's "Prioress's Tale" and several other iterations of "The Child Slain by Jews." The comparative place of the children's bodies in these stories—an oven, well, or latrine, all symbolically associated with wombs, eating, and/or bowels, all associated with domesticity and femininity—has garnered particularly careful discussions,[31] and the Vernon artist makes such connections visually plain. In the Vernon Manuscript illustrations, both the Jewish and the Christian mothers appear at the bottom of the frame, near the bodies of their sons, speaking animatedly to a mayor. The women are clothed similarly, in dress colors that match the mayors' tunics, kneeling, and gesturing alike too, with one hand at the face in sorrow and the other stretched toward the captive child. The Jewish man who seizes and attacks their sons is, visually, the same man: a hook-nosed Jew with a beard, wearing a brown robe and floppy hat. Without reading the accompanying poems, it is not immediately evident how these two women are distinct.

The accompanying Middle English poems provide some clarity on the matter, but only after significant delay and along with further parallels. "The Child Slain by Jews," which comes first in the manuscript, introduces the Christian mother and father very early, just eleven lines beneath its illustration, but "The Jewish Boy" poet does not mention the Jewish family unit until much later: the father appears after eighty-three lines, the mother after ninety-seven. That is to say, there are no immediate or easy glosses on the women's relative identities. Once the mothers begin to lament their sons' fates, indeed, the poems utilize repetitions and verbal echoes that further connect the women. Again, a didactic and interactive process of Christian recognition emerges: the women and their

Figure 7. Illustration of "The Child Slain by Jews" in Bod. MS Eng. Poet. a. 1 (Vernon Manuscript), fol. 124v. Reproduced by permission of The Bodleian Libraries, The University of Oxford.

foes appear more or less the same, while the texts allow simultaneous othering and saming of the Jewish mother. The Vernon artist, by featuring the moment at which the women make their cases to the mayor, both exploits the textual repetitions that draw the women together and highlights their similarity at a moment when their religious identities are distinct (for the Jewish woman, the illustration shows a *preconversion* episode). With the poems and images together, the Jewish mother must be both Jewish and Christian, even as both mothers reflect the Virgin Mary's care for her (Jewish) child. This sameness is so vital to the didactic utility of "The Jewish Boy" that the succinct Additional 39996 version I mentioned above—a bare-bones abridgment, thirty coupleted lines in total—makes it almost the sole characteristic of the tale's Jewess: there, she is simply "A Mayde þat loued þe child" (a young woman who loved the child) and "told þe cristen al þe cas" (told the Christians the whole situation).[32] Neither clearly Christian nor Jewish, the late medieval iteration *only* unmarks her.

Figure 8. Illustration of "The Jewish Boy" in Bod. MS Eng. Poet. a. 1 (Vernon Manuscript), fol. 125r. Reproduced by permission of The Bodleian Libraries, The University of Oxford.

Geraldine Heng, comparing "The Jewish Boy" and "The Child Slain by Jews" miracles, has remarked, "This Jewish mother . . . behaves like *all the Christian mothers of child-murder stories.*"[33] Heng's reading depends mainly on the Vernon version of "The Jewish Boy," and particularly on her comparison of it with the Vernon "Child Slain by Jews," Chaucer's "Prioress's Tale," and a thirteenth-century Anglo-French ballad ("Hugo de Lincolnia") that commemorates the 1255 murder of Hugh of Lincoln. Her observation about the sameness of the two mothers is generally true of all versions of "The Jewish Boy": the figure of the sorrowing mother who seeks legal assistance to find her missing or harmed son is, indeed, a stock character of anti-Jewish child-murder stories, such that her absence is notable when it occurs.[34] However, while Heng argues that the Vernon's Jewish mother is a post-Expulsion figure, because she goes outside on Easter and thus breaks Jewish curfew laws that must have been forgotten,[35] the Jewess's frantic running through streets on Easter is in fact a feature of even the earliest versions of the story. The oven that nearly burns the boy alive, likewise, cannot be a post-Expulsion "replacement of the privy," as Heng suggests: though a privy or well is a common place to hide a child's body in all anti-Jewish murder stories after *The Life and Passion of William of Norwich* (ca. 1173)—and this includes the story of Robert of Bury (ca. 1181), *The Passion of Adam of Bristol* (ca. 1290), Chaucer's "Prioress's Tale," and the Vernon "Child Slain by Jews" (ca. 1390)—"The Jewish Boy" and its oven vastly predate stories that feature latrines or wells; in its premedieval iterations, the father uses a glassblowing oven. Still, Heng's fundamental point—that the Jewish and the Christian mothers in these tales are *the same, but not quite*—gets precisely at how the Jewess functions in medieval English literature.

It is the comparative sequence that must be adjusted. I have argued elsewhere that, from its earliest Anglo-Latin adaptations in the pre-Conquest period to its late Middle English iterations, passing is the operative anxiety in "Jewish Boy" tales, and this anxiety is focused particularly on the Jewish mother and her son. Scribes copying the Anglo-Latin version of Dominic of Evesham (fl. ca. 1125) in the twelfth century, for instance, prefaced the story with an invective about how this kind of event might happen in any city with a synagogue.[36] Dominic was also the first writer to update the ancient tale's location from Constantinople to a medieval century and a European city, in the mixed population of Bourges in central France (close to England, but not quite),[37] and the earliest English-language version of the story, in the *South English Legendary* (ca. 1275), maintained the continental location and Dominic's commentary on the problem of Jewish-Christian mixing. Like the Vernon, and many earlier and later versions, the *South English Legendary* also has the Jewish mother running through the streets on Easter: "The moder as heo wod were, / . . . heo made a deoluol bere. / In the stret heo orn faste aboute & piteisliche cride" (The mother acted as if she were mad, / . . . she let out a sorrowful wail. / She ran frantically through the streets and cried out miserably).[38] In other words, the Jewish mother plays a consistent role in "Jewish Boy" tales and in English child-murder stories throughout the medieval period and in many genres, and, therefore, the pseudohistoriographical *Life and Passion of William of Norwich*, the historiographical and literary accounts of Hugh of Lincoln's murder, the Latin *Passion of Adam of Bristol*, the story of Robert of Bury that Jocelin of Brakelond says he wrote, and all versions of "The Child Slain by Jews" developed with *prior* knowledge of the "Jewish Boy." More bluntly: the Jewish mother wailed for her child first.

While I wholeheartedly agree, then, with Heng's assessment that the Jewish mother is "a doubled figure, a composite of two temporalities—the Christian woman she will become, and the Jewish woman she is,"[39] I must invert her observation about the Jewess's relationship to the Christian mothers of anti-Jewish child-murder stories. It is not that the Jewish mother behaves like all the Christian mothers, but rather, *these Christian mothers all behave like the Jewish mother*. This inversion is a significant corrective for how we understand the sameness of Jewish and Christian women in polemical literature. In comparing the mothers of the "Jewish Boy" and "Child Slain" stories, it is not the case that the Jewess is the pliant or malleable vessel—which she might seem if we focus solely on the "convert" subtype or the violent male counterpart—but that the *Christian* mothers are malleable: they are molded to the Jewess's shape. This is, of course, a typological impulse: the Jewish, and then the Christian, mothers are crafted in the traditions of the matriarch Rachel wailing for her children (Jer. 31:15), mothers witnessing the slaughter of the innocents (Matt. 2:16–18), and the Virgin Mary standing at the cross (John 19:25).[40] By calling the Christian mother "this newe Rachel" in his "Prioress's Tale," Chaucer simply drew the typological line more explicitly than other authors.[41] The mournful lament of Jewish mothers for Jerusalem and Jewish children is appropriated as Christian femininity and triumphalism.

As iterations of each other, Rachel and the Virgin Mary, and the Jewish mother of "The Jewish Boy" and the Christian mother of "The Child Slain by Jews," create "intertestamental" figures. This term, defined by Ruth Nisse, applies to women "occupying the liminal space between the Old Testament prophets and the fulfilment of their prophecies in the New Testament."[42] Nisse uses it in her discussion of medieval monastic understanding of "sexually powerful Jewish heroines" like Esther, Judith, Yael, and Asenath, all of whom had to maintain their Jewishness to function in Christian polemical literature.[43] Applying the term to Christian stories of the conversion of Asenath (the mother of Ephraim and Manasseh), where the converted woman "represents a refiguring of the [Jewish] feminine as knowable," as against historical characterizations of thirteenth-century Anglo-Jewish women converts as "radically passive and unknowable,"[44] Nisse sees associations of Asenath with Jerusalem serving "a double function, both reinforcing the ultimate conversion and salvation of the Jews . . . and recuperating the historical fallen Jerusalem."[45] The collective interpretation possible across multiple versions of "The Jewish Boy" and "The Child Slain by Jews" is that the mothers in these tales work similarly: since the wailing Jewish mother of "The Jewish Boy" simultaneously echoes the matriarch Rachel and reflects the Virgin Mary, she works intertestamentally for Christian readers. She occupies both Jewishness and Christianness, even if her Jewish identity is always prior and necessary. For the Jewess to become Christian, the Christian must already be the same as the Jewess.

The matriarch Rachel recast as the (Christian) Jewess, the sorrowing or converted mother and prophetess of violence, could also be used with devastating effect in Anglo-Jewish sources. As Nisse tells us, for example, Berekhiah ha-Nakdan (fl. ca. 1200) repurposed the Aesopic fable known as "The Wolf, the Dog, and the Sheep" in his *Fox Fables* (*Mishle Shualim*) by making the ewe (Hebrew *rekhelah*) a punning reference to Rachel: both the *rekhelah* of the fable and the matriarch Rachel wept for their children (Jer. 31:15) and "died by the way" (Gen. 35:19). In Berekhiah's version—closely aligned with Marie de France's—the ewe is falsely accused of theft, convicted on false testimony, shorn, and left to die, unable to care for her young children. For Berekhiah, Nisse argues, who was responding both to midrashic interpretation of the associated biblical passages and to contemporary legislation against Anglo-Jews, the *rekhelah* becomes "a victim of a predatory Christian 'Roman' society that is a condition of [Jewish] exile" in England, while Rachel remains "both the Israelite nation and intercessor for the nation's sins."[46]

Rachel's dual function as nation and intercessor was used in Jewish crusading discourses too, which consistently linked Rachel to the destruction of Jerusalem (as in the Bible) and to Christian hopes for the final conversion of Jews. As Jeremy Cohen has persuasively argued, Hebrew chronicles of the First Crusade (specifically the "Mainz Anonymous" and the *Solomon bar Simson Chronicle*) mobilize both Jewish and Christian interpretations of Rachel to make the connection. As a figure of tragedy,[47] the matriarch finds expression in these chronicles through Rachel of Mainz, a woman who chose to slaughter her four young children rather than allow them to be killed or baptized by encroaching crusaders. Cohen's analysis provides a useful parallel for my thinking about the polemical utility of Christian sameness in portrayals of medieval Jewesses. In his view, the Jewish chroniclers purposefully Christianize Rachel of Mainz, so that she serves both as a powerful Jewish martyr and as a recognizable figure of Ecclesia (the personified Church) and the Virgin Mary. They describe her sitting with her sacrificed children in her lap—creating a pietà-like image of maternal mourning[48]—and one account specifies that she catches her children's blood in her sleeves "instead of in the cultic chalice of blood," thus simultaneously evoking Levitical practices and commonplace medieval iconography of Ecclesia holding a chalice to catch Christ's blood at the Crucifixion.[49]

Cohen's litany of the Christian allusions connected to Rachel of Mainz in the Hebrew chronicles moves from evocation of crucifixion scenes, to multiple aspects of the Virgin Mary (textual and iconographic), to clear intertextual engagements with the slaughter of the innocents (Matt. 2:16–18), to related Christian liturgy and drama, and finally to the remarkable alignment of Rachel of Mainz with the matriarch Rachel as she appears in Christian iconographic traditions, at the center of the slaughter. Together, these citations amount to what Cohen calls "the 'Christian' identity of Rachel of Mainz."[50] The Jewish chroniclers craft the medieval mother Rachel as someone who chooses to sacrifice her children as "an exemplary Jewish heroine" only *in response to* the version of Jewish femininity already valorized by Christians. When Rachel "assumes the character of the Virgin Mary and of Holy Mother Church as well, she . . . respond[s] to the oppressive challenge of crusading ideology" and "boldly lays claim to the status of Christianity's two most important women-martyrs of all: none other than the Virgin and Holy Mother Church."[51] This kind of gathering of Christian and Jewish signs—in the mother, the virgin mother, the convert (or the one who refuses to convert), the woman who makes a scene—shows a Jewish awareness of the polemics of sameness at work in Christian uses of Jewish women, and particularly Jewish mothers. The Hebrew crusade chronicles invert the polemic, and in so doing they pointedly invert and exploit Christian notions of the pliant Jewess.

The Hands of Pitiful Women

It is not impossible that stories of Jewish women's martyrdom and slaying of their children in the face of the violence and forced baptisms of the First and Second Crusades reached England.[52] Such heroines could become, in the Christian imagination, terrifying responses to the fetishized changeability of the Jewess. If she did convert, she might apostasize. If she did not convert, she might feign Christianity. If she had been murdered, it was probably because she wanted to convert. If she would not convert, she might create a spectacular pietà of infanticide and faith. We see these scenarios—dependent on misogynistic expectations of feminine malleability in concert with anti-Jewish ideology—in the Jewish women of the *Passion of Adam of Bristol*, in Matthew Paris's account of Floria of Berkhamsted, in Archbishop Peckham's search for relapsed converts, and even in Alice of Worcester's letters, where the convert self-consciously fashions a dual identity out of desperation for the welfare of herself and her son. Most powerfully, we see them in medieval accounts of maternal cannibalism at the fall of the Second Temple.

After the First Crusade, the story of the Jewish cannibal mother at the 70 C.E. destruction of Jerusalem was told and retold in medieval literary reworkings. Both a reflection and an inversion of the mother of "The Jewish Boy," the starving mother who cannibalized her child during the first-century siege was, like Rachel of Mainz, understood as a woman who commited prophetically necessary violence. For the cannibal named Mary (sometimes called Miriam or Mary of Bethezuba), there are no "happy" Christian endings. No one saves her child from her. The return to the womb implied by the oven of "The Jewish Boy,"[53] and the association with digestion and bowels implied by the latrines of "Child Slain by Jews" stories, are just womb and bowels now. The eucharistic associations of such spaces, however, allow the conflation of feminized Christian and Jewish identities, and English authors' exploitation of the cannibal's link to the Virgin Mary create a difficult sameness. Cannibal Mary may seem a terrible parody of the Virgin Mary—consuming the flesh and blood of her sacrificial child—but, as medieval poets knew, her prophetic importance lay in the convergence of the cannibal and the Virgin.

Mary's starvation inside the besieged Jerusalem is a stock scene in chronicles and poems that narrate the siege of Jerusalem, and in the Vengeance of Our Lord tradition generally. She is a set piece in medieval illustrations of the siege too, and her story is ultimately derived from Josephus's *Jewish War*.[54] Everywhere she appears, moreover, she echoes various biblical scenes and prophecies that, like those that serve as this chapter's epigraphs, include parental cannibalism.[55] In the English language, the starving Jewish mother is evoked most memorably in the alliterative *Siege of Jerusalem* (ca. 1370), a romance that clearly engages in "crusade propaganda" and "contemporary crusading activities,"[56] but she also appears in John Lydgate's *Fall of Princes* (as derived from Boccaccio) and in the Middle English *Titus and Vespasian*.[57] In the alliterative *Siege*, she roasts and eats her infant son to save herself from death and commands her son to return from whence he came, thus conflating womb and bowels in a literalized (maternal) eucharistic meal.

The *Siege of Jerusalem* poet had four possible sources available to him: the medieval Latin redactions of Josephus's *Jewish War* first, but also Jacobus de Voragine's *Legenda aurea* (cannibal Mary's story appears in the *Life of St. James the Apostle*), Ranulf Higden's *Polychronicon*, and John of Tynemouth's *Historia aurea*, all of which, in turn, used Josephus directly or indirectly for their accounts of the siege of Jerusalem.[58] Some of the *Siege* poet's details clearly derive from reliance on the English chronicles, particularly Mary's command to her son, which in both Englishmen's accounts reads, "Redi in id secretum a quo existi" (Return to that secret place from which you came).[59] In the *Siege*, the episode is rendered as follows:

> On Marie, a myld wyf, for meschef of foode,
> Hire owen barn þat ʒo bare brad on þe gledis,
> Rostyþ rigge and rib with rewful wordes,
> Sayþ, "sone, vpon eche side our sorow is alofte:
>
> Batail aboute þe borwe our bodies to quelle;
> Withyn hunger so hote þat neʒ our herte brestyþ.
> Þerfor ʒeld þat I þe gaf and aʒen tourne,
> Entre þer þou out cam," and etyþ a schouldere. (1081–88)
>
> One Mary, a mild woman, because of absence of food,
> Cooked on the coals her own baby, whom she bore.
> She roasts the spine and the ribs, with pitiful words,
> Says: "Son, upon each side is our sorrow increased:
>
> Battle is outside the city to slaughter our bodies,
> Hunger is so hot within that our hearts nearly burst.
> Therefore give up what I gave you, and turn back again,
> Enter where you came out"—and she eats a shoulder.[60]

The poet's cinematic focus on the child's spine and ribs on the coals in this passage,[61] the momentary misdirection when "vpon eche side" seems to refer to the roasting meat rather than the sorrow of the siege, the poet's shift from past-tense description to the historical present tense, the internal and external violence that simultaneously describes the city and body in a concentric relationship—all of these bring the whole of the conquest of Jerusalem to the limits and permeability of a Jewish woman's body. The return of Jerusalem to righteous hands is aligned with the return of the son to the mother. The city walls are like the sides of the body, the bursting heart is like the starving city itself, and the son reenters the mother just as the avenging Christians reenter the place of Jesus's ministry and death. The dramatic placement of this episode at the end of the penultimate passus of the poem, just before Titus's triumphant entry into Jerusalem, means that the penetration of the city is signaled by the cannibal Jewess's act.

This mother compounds sameness and difference. Written first by Josephus, she is in some sense an authentic figure of Jewish history, but, in medieval Christian renderings, she is both a monstrous image of Jewish femininity *and* a Marian likeness. In the *Siege of Jerusalem*, she is simultaneously a sympathetic figure of sadness that betrays the cruelty and excess of the Romans/Christians, even as the poet argues that they justly avenge Christ, *and* an image of the Virgin, who likewise sacrifices, laments, and consumes her son (via the Eucharist). Her ability to be sympathetic, to echo the Virgin Mary in uncomfortable ways, and yet to maintain her Jewishness—a maligned category in *Siege*, where Jewish people suffer collective and individual violence in astonishingly graphic terms—means that she turns a mirror back to Christian readers. Her function in the poem is to hold Christian meaning and echo Christian women (in name and body) until she, by consuming her child, transcends her Jewishness to demonstrate how the suffering Jewish mother is at the heart of Christianity. The exile of Jews from Jerusalem and the destruction of the Temple are thus evoked as and occupied by Christian history. The cannibal Mary is not merely a grotesque inversion of the other Mary, for her meaning hinges on Christian recognition of her Christian sameness.

An important variation on the siege of Jerusalem story, popular in English vernaculars into the late medieval period, showed acute awareness of this cannibal Mary's primary identity and meaning. In these versions of the siege story, there are *two* cannibal women, both secretly Christians. The two well-known miniatures of the destruction that conclude BL MS Egerton 2781 (The Neville of Hornby Hours)—the same book that illustrates "The Jewish Boy" mother as a double of the Virgin Mary—clearly reflect this variant plotline. In the first full-page scene, just above the center line at the right and the left, we see twin women eating bloody babies inside the windows of Jerusalem battlements. The image and its caption, however, allow for confusion about these apparently monstrous women, their bloody mouths wide around naked children (Figure 9). For anyone familiar with the Josephan tradition, including the alliterative *Siege of Jerusalem* and its sources, the two devouring women will seem to be Jewish, their children Jewish boys. The doubling of the cannibal mother—in identical clothing, set at on both sides, creating a triangle formation with the one other woman in the

Figure 9. Illustration of the destruction of Jersualem with two cannibal mothers and patron Isabel de Byron. ©British Library Board. BL MS Egerton 2781 (Neville of Hornby Hours), fol. 190r.

scene, the book's patron Isabel de Byron, who is flanked by her family arms atop the ramparts—is either an oddity or a grotesque overabundance.

With Isabel de Byron overlooking the scene, however, the women might also seem to signal a comparative view of female agency, where "the juxtaposition of her [Isabel's] upright, serene form with the frenzied, pathetic figures of the cannibalizing mothers below" suggests that she is a "guardian of her families' interests and, by implication, her children's lives," while the "Jewish parents of Jerusalem are driven to kill and even consume their own offspring."[62] The French caption below the image offers no rebuttal. It reads: "coment titus et uaspazianus lemperour de rome destruit le iuzeus en la cite de ierusalem pur lamour de dieu. et coment le femmes mangerunt lour fiz et le fiz lour pere. e le pere lour fiz" (How Titus and the Roman emperor Vespasian slaughtered the Jews in the city of Jerusalem for the death of God. And how the women ate their sons and the sons their fathers and the fathers their sons). The inclusion of sons and fathers in this cannibalistic frenzy alludes to Ezekiel 5:10, a passage that also pertains to the exile from Jerusalem ("the fathers shall eat the sons . . . and the sons shall eat their fathers: and I will execute judgements in thee, and I will scatter thy whole remnant"). The only cannibals illustrated in the miniature, however, are mothers—and these mothers look like each other and, in general style, the colors of their clothing, and their hair coverings, like the Christian noblewoman standing calmly above them. Are we meant to see Jewish or Christian cannibals?

As I have already indicated—and despite the fact that the image and its caption do little to make this clear—it is almost certain that the Neville of Hornby miniature reflects a branch of the narrative tradition that turns the one cannibal Jewess mother into two secret Christians. As Kathryn A. Smith has pointed out, alongside her just-noted observations of the artist's juxtaposition of frenzied cannibal Jewish parents and Isabel de Byron's contrasting guardianship, the textual source for the image is very likely the Middle English poem *Titus and Vespasian* or a close but earlier analogue,[63] wherein the cannibal Mary has a companion called Clary (sometimes Clarice), and both women are *seemingly* Jewish but secretly Christian. In *Titus and Vespasian*, further, Mary and Clary consume not Mary's son but her daughter, a child who has already died of starvation. While the alliterative *Siege of Jerusalem* survives in nine manuscripts (three of which are small fragments), this contemporary alternative survives in twelve,[64] several of which seem to have been aimed at children's devotional educations.[65] While the earliest survival dates to around 1375, a copy made up to fifty years after the Neville of Hornby Hours, it is likely that *Titus*'s composition was contemporary with Isabel de Byron's book, or that an earlier English iteration, or perhaps the very similar Old French *Vengeance de Nostre-Seigneur*, was the artist's referent.[66] Though the *Siege* poet's desription of the lone cannibal Jewess is more refined and arresting, the *Vengeance* and *Titus* variants competed with, and were conflated with, the Josephan chronicle tradition throughout the fourteenth and fifteenth centuries in England.

The contagion of cannibalism that the Neville of Hornby miniature and its caption communicate are clearly reflected by the *Titus and Vespasian* account of events, where "Men and wymmen her children ete, / And yche man oþer by every strete" (Men and women ate their children, / and in every street each man [ate] the other).[67] In this poem, moreover, the idea that there are secret Christians among the Jews of Jerusalem goes right to the origin of the cannibal Mary story: amid Jerusalem's famine and suffering, the *Titus* poet reveals that Josephus himself was "a prive Cristen man" (a secret Christian), who mourned "for his kynde was not soo" (because his people were not thus [i.e., not Christian]) (3386–87). The source of the narrative tradition—as well as its ability to provide Christian meaning, and implicitly the right of this poet to adjust the polemical portraits—is thus retroactively justified by the Christianization of its originary author. However, the *Titus* poet presents the secrecy of the cannibal mothers' faith at much greater length. Mary and Clary are linked by their shared recourse to Christian space and prayer, and their decision to cannibalize Mary's daughter is explicitly sanctioned by Jesus, whose angel messenger reiterates the related (Jewish) prophecy.

Unlike the Josephan version of the cannibal mother, who in the *Jewish War* goes to Jerusalem for protection from invading Romans and warring internal factions, or in the *Siege of Jerusalem* (a poem interested in setting vengeance for the Crucifixion within the temporal space of the Crucifixion) to celebrate Passover,[68] the cannibal Mary of *Titus and Vespasian* seeks the Holy City for Christian companionship and finds shelter in a church:

> A riche lady of þat contre,
> Of large landes and eke of fee—
> Mary she hight sikerly,
> A Cristen womman priuely—
> She had acoyntance in Jerusalem
> And þerfore she þider cam.
> A gode lauedy [þat] she ded knowe,
> With whom she thought to dwell a throwe—
> Dame Clary was þe wommanes name,

> Of gode uirtues, of holy fame—
> Þei liueden þere togeder longe,
> Til þis woo bifell soo stronge.
> Oþer werkes þei couthe noon werke
> But dwellande mychel in holy chirch
> And ligge þere in afflicciones,
> In penance and in oresones. (3409–24)

> A wealthy lady of that country,
> A holder of a great amount of land and property—
> She was called Mary, certainly,
> A Christan woman secretly—
> She had a friend in Jerusalem
> And therefore she went there.
> A good lady whom she knew,
> With whom she intended to stay for a while—
> Lady Clary was the woman's name,
> Of good virtues, of holy reputation—
> They lived there together for a long time,
> Until this sorrow [the siege] became too horrible.
> There was nothing else they could do
> But stay for long stretches in a holy church,
> And lie there in misery,
> In penance and in prayers.

This Mary, like Isabel de Byron, is wealthy and landed. She seeks the companionship of another woman of her faith and rank (her friend is *Dame* Clary), and they both eventually pray for their salvation in a Jerusalem church. The consequent decision to eat Mary's lifeless child is then rationalized not through physical deterioration and madness—as it is in the Josephan tradition—but through the messenger sent from Christ:

> This Mary had a doughter dere
> Þat for hunger dyede þere, . . .
> "Ete we now þis childe anoon
> For the hongre þat is vs on."
> "Nay," quod Mary, "þat wil I noght.
> Er wolde I dye in my thoght.

Oure lorde god þat is soo hende
Of his grace he may us sende.
Be we not for þis sory.
Hit stande vs to purgatory. . . ."
In þis talkyng, right as þei sat,
Iesu Crist hem noght forgat.
An aungell come from heven shene,
As God hym sent hem bitwene,
And seide to hem: "Leteth þis strifes.
All þat ӡe may, holde ӡe ӡoure lifes.
Mary, loke þat þou doo
As Clarice here seide þe to.
God wil it soo er þan ӡe dye
To fulfillen the prophecie
Þat speketh of þis, 'by wey and strete'
Þat 'wymmen shulde her children ete.'
Grycceth ӡe noght to fulfille
All þat is to goddes wille. . . ."
Þei put þe childe vpon a spite
Agaynes a fuyre to roosten hit
And deden als þis aungell hem bad.
They ete þerof and made hem glad. (3431–32, 3437–44, 3446–
60, 3365–68)

This Mary had a beloved daughter
Who died of starvation there. . . .
"Let us eat this child right away
Because of the hunger that afflicts us."
"No," said Mary. "I won't do that.
I think I would rather die first.
Our Lord God who is so gracious
May yet send us his grace.
Let us not be sorry for this.
It would set us in purgatory. . . ."
Just as they were having this debate,
Jesus Christ did not forget them.
An angel arrived from bright heaven,
Since God sent him as an intermediary,

And said to them, "Stop this argument.
Hold to your lives with all you have.
Mary, take care that you do
As Clarice here has said to you.
God wishes it thus, rather than you die,
In order to fulfill the prophecy
That speaks of this, that 'in path and street'
'Women shall eat their children.'
Don't grumble against fulfilling
Anything that is according to God's wish. . . ."
They put the child on a spit
Over a fire, to roast it,
And did as this angel instructed them.
They ate from it, and it made them happy.

In this version of events, both the impulse to eat and the refusal to eat are presented as Christian virtues. Clary is a woman "of holy fame" (3418), and Christ and his messenger support her. Mary trusts that the God can assist them, fears purgatory, and is obedient to God's will once she knows it. The angel's argument that Mary must take her part in fulfilling the prophecies of Hebrew scripture—what he cites matches no biblical text exactly but seems to combine Ezekiel 5:10 and Lamentations 4:10—makes her another intertestamental figure. Though she exists in no Testament, and the siege ostensibly postdates the narrative of the New Testament, she is designed to occupy "the liminal space between the Old Testament prophets and the fulfillment of their prophecies in the New Testament,"[69] and her Christianity, revealed only to later Christian readers, must remain secret to allow her to function this way. Her Jewish sameness is required for the fulfillment of Jewish/Christian prophecy, and she must accept or even seize her gruesome role (it "made hem glad" to do so!) to move her people closer to salvation.

Most strikingly in the *Titus and Vespasian* account of events, this saming happens within a wholly feminine sphere: two women, alone and urged on by no one but Christ, consume a daughter. The *Titus* poet forecloses male presence in the scene in multiple ways. The women's decision to eat is between them: unlike Josephus's account, and unlike the *Siege of Jerusalem*, it is not a desperate response to attacks around the home or the sounds of battle outside, nor does it culminate in the entrance of an angry and horrified (male) mob who hungrily respond to the smell of the roast. In *Titus*, rather, the smell of the meat reaches Pontius Pilate "in his tour" (in his tower) (3469), and, though he does send men to retrieve the food for him, the outcome is narrated from the distance of Pilate's tower: his men report back, he orders them to seize the cannibalized body, and the women are left without further sustenance (3469–82). The Marian likeness suggested by the literalized eucharistic consumption in the alliterative *Siege*—where a Jewish Mary consumes a Jewish son—cannot function here. Neither, it turns out, is a male child essential to the sameness of Jewish and Christian mothers. The *Titus* variant suggests that the Jewess—whether she is a Christian-as-Jewess or a Jewess-as-Christian—is more dependent on intertestamental meaning than on her Marian or eucharistic signification.

In a similar way, the Neville of Hornby Hours miniature (Figure 9) forecloses Marian and eucharistic allusions to create a triangulation of the cannibal mothers with Isabel de Byron, the calm peak at the top of her ramparts. Of course the truth is that all women in the Neville of Hornby scene—Isabel and the two monstrous women with bloody infants in their wide mouths—are Christian. The secret Christianity of the mothers reveals itself, however, only with wider reading; the artist and the caption writer keep the possibilities open. The French caption tells us only that the destruction scene illustrates "le iuzeus en la cite de ierusalem" (the Jews in the city of Jerusalem); on the verso, where the visual story continues with a second full-page miniature of the Christian victory and its aftermath, we learn that "le cristiens geterent le iueus" (the Christians hurl the Jews) from the city walls and the emperor Titus sells "xxx iueus pur i diner" (thirty Jews for one penny). The identities of the women, thus, cannot be clarified by reading the image and captions alone, particularly when Isabel stands *within* the besieged Jeruselem. Indeed, the Christian patroness, as Smith has noted, might be interpreted not as one of the Christian conquerors but rather as the city's "principal defender"[70]—that is, as a Jew.

If Isabel should be read as a Jewess, however, her Jewishness can only be appropriative and aspirational; again, the cannibal mothers' Christian identities must remain hidden for polemics of sameness to function. Isabel cannot play Jewess beyond the level of simile—she is *like* the mothers and *like* the Jews defending Jerusalem—because she is flanked by her identifying family arms, the banner of Neville of Hornby on her right and Byron on her left. Whether the cannibals mothers are Christian or Jewish, however—and whether you think there should be one or two of them—depends entirely on which version of the story you know, while the French captions combat certainty in any case, because they repeatedly emphasize the Jewishness of the inhabitants of Jerusalem. The Neville of Hornby miniature and the Middle English *Titus and Vespasian* thus invert the deceptions of the Jewish sister in the *Passion of Adam of Bristol*: the devotional utility of these later artifacts depends on the ability of Christian women to pass as Jewish.

The Jewess is malleable, then, not in herself but through her readers and viewers. Her "true" identity and Christian meaning is internal, secret, potentially changeable, or a matter of perception. For a wealthy and devout Christian woman like Isabel de Byron, the cannibal Mary may be a figure of faith and courage: in the version presented in both Isabel's book and *Titus and Vespasian*, she performs a kind of feminized *akedah* (that is, the binding of Isaac by Abraham in Gen. 22:1–14); she is willing to commit a horrific and forbidden act against her own daughter because God commands her to do so—but the divine messenger does not stop her, and she does not falter. In this light, her apparent Jewishness is part of what makes her a model of faith and survival. In the (Christian) Josephan tradition, by contrast, the cannibal mother becomes a kind of Virgin Mary, a literalized figure of the Eucharist—but this too depends on her Jewishness, itself part of her Marian reflection. For a reader uncertain of the narrative connections, or acquainted with more than one, she may also vacillate or hold all in polysemy. The Neville of Hornby miniature, in particular, makes it difficult to understand the Jewess in either/ or terms at all. Rather, it successfully conjoins Jewess and Christianess so that the mother's meaning shifts with text-image relationships or readers' and viewers' interactions.

Mother, Cannibal, Convert

The *Passion of Adam of Bristol* clarifies that all of the above is insidious and dangerous. The unmarked Jewess should be understood as a problem in Christian literature, because Christian polemical investment in her sameness is anti-Jewish, and the two Jewesses of *Adam of Bristol*, both set in stark contrast to the man they serve, offer extreme cases in point. The murdering Samuel's sister, whom I have already discussed at length,[71] feigns Christianity to support and clean up after her violent brother, and his wife assists him with his murders before she almost converts to Christianity. Expectation of the malleability of the Jewess is used against Christians here: the tale's two Jewish women—the one a wife, mother, near convert, domestic, ultimately aligned with the Virgin Mary, and the other a sister, fixer, deceiver, aligned with urban money, negotiation, and seemingly Christian to outsiders—are not as much foils for the violent and unchangeable Jewish male as they are foils for each other. The anonymous author of the *Passion of Adam of Bristol* uses their extremes to explore the fissures they create in Christian fantasies of the pliant Jewess, and in Christian fantasies of self and community.

Adam of Bristol must test any thinking about medieval anti-Jewish discourses and their function for Christian readers, and it is especially important as an example of Christian identification of, and with, Marian Jewishness. Its position on the edges of pseudohistoriographical ritual murder and host-desecration libels, and of the Marian miracle genre, along with its refusal to fit these genres' modes of catharsis through sanctity and conversion, make it a useful oddity. Through its two Bristol Jewesses, *Adam of Bristol* offers the most thorough portrait of the fictionalized Anglo-Jewess available in medieval English literature. To my mind, it is, at its core, the story of these two women. Its proximity to the 1290 Expulsion, furthermore, suggests its relationship not only to the legacy of real violence and exclusion in England, but also, and at the same time, to a hardening English identification with Jewishness.[72] Through its Jewesses, *Adam of Bristol* transforms what Sylvia Tomasch has called "that forbidden identification" of English Christians with Jews into an open, essential, and gendered sameness.[73] So I return now to *Adam of Bristol*'s preoccupation with Jewish passing, and to the unmarked Jewess-as-Christian type that permeates it, with examination of the boy Adam's entrance into the Jewish home, the details of his murder, and the special role of the Jewish wife and mother in its narrative.

More than any other character in the *Passion of Adam of Bristol*, the unnamed wife and mother, despite her grisly and cannibalistic involvement in young Adam's murder, represents the text's Christian and Marian ideals. When Adam is lured to the Jewish home, his nominal status as a type of Christ or paradisal Adam joins immediately with his inability to discern Jewish difference. Adam does not know that Samuel and his son are Jewish when they invite him to their home, nor does he realize that he is in a Jewish home—even after he talks, plays, eats and drinks, and has been tied to a cross and called "deus christianorum" (god of the Christians)—until Samuel tells him explicitly, "Ego judeus puniam te hac nocte usque ad mortem" (I, a Jew, will torture you to death tonight).[74] This emphasis on passing is not superficial to the scene: Samuel and his family can appear to be Christian in public, and they are not understood as Jewish even in domestic spheres. There is apparently nothing visibly

Jewish about their homes, their food or drink, their child, their conversation, their language, or the location of their home, and this unsettling similitude is most elaborately exploited through shared Jewish and Christian tropes of sacrifice and maternity that involve both Samuel's wife and the Virgin Mary. Contained within the first third of the text—that is, within the story of the murders that Samuel narrates to his sister—the Jewish mother becomes a pivotal Christian presence. The Virgin Mary (herself a Jewish mother) appears in the story as well, to comfort Adam as the Jews roast him in a fire on the feast of her Assumption,[75] but the central role of Jewish women, and especially the intermittent ambivalence and ferocity of Samuel's wife, mark an uncanny Marian presence throughout the tale.

The issue here is not only that Mary's eventual appearance suggests that "the antidote to the demonic presence and deeds of the Jew is the Virgin Mary," as Harvey J. Hames has put it,[76] for this would suggest that we can read *Adam of Bristol* as parallel to any other Miracle of the Virgin (like "The Jewish Boy") in which a Jewish mother is sympathetic and a Jewish father unredeemable.[77] More fundamental to this tale's polemics is that, from the first folio, the Virgin Mary is doubled by Samuel's wife, and her "demonic presence," then, is always shadowed by Mary and presented as internal to Christianity. Among the first questions that Samuel's wife asks Adam when he enters her home, for instance, is whether his mother is living. Adam responds with information that seems either to interrupt connections between Adam and the Christ-child, by inviting a second male infant into the typology, or to be simply extraneous: he explains that his mother is alive, and that she has just given birth to a boy and is still convalescing (Cluse 306). This detail is in fact crucial to the text's Marian discourse, though we must think iconographically to make sense of it: the description of Adam's mother and her newborn on the childbed creates a Nativity scene, just at the moment that "Adam" has been lured to his death by the promise of apples (cf. Gen. 3:6–7); Samuel's son, in the opening lines of Samuel's account of events, promises that his mother will give Adam "poma plurima" (many apples) (Cluse 305). What we have, then, are familiar images of both the temptation and the redemption of humanity through women. The Jewish mother and her son are, from the start, set parallel to the Christian mother and her son, with the Christ figure (a second Adam) between them.

Christian knowledge of alleged Jewish blasphemies against Mary are relevant here too, as both Israel Yuval and Robert Stacey have noticed,[78] since the range of dates possible for this text (set in the twelfth century but written down in the last quarter of the thirteenth or so) places it in the context not only of the many ritual murder accusations that occurred in England during this period, but also of the 1171 accusation at Blois and the 1240 Paris Talmud trial. Yuval has asked whether there might be "a kind of circuitous dialogue" between *Adam of Bristol* and Jewish responses to the events in France, specifically through the Hebrew prayer *Alenu le-shabeah* that both Latin and Hebrew sources say the Jews at Blois sang as they were led to their execution.[79] Twelfth-century versions of the prayer included ridicule of Jesus and Mary that was consistent with "Jewish response to the growth of [Mary's] cult" and "the accusation made at the Talmud trial of 1240 charging Jews with cursing Mary."[80] One French version from the period included an anti-Christian addition that connected Jesus's flesh through Mary to bile (Hebrew *marah*). Medieval Christian etymologies of Mary's name routinely made the same connection, because of the "bitter" sorrow Mary experienced when her son died, but the wordplay in Jewish sources of course worked differently. Yuval quotes a letter from Obadiah ben Makhir that discusses the Blois case and links the *marah* of the French *Alenu le-shabeah* addition to the two harlots who appear before King Solomon to dispute the maternity of an infant son: "This is one of the two harlots who said she was his mother. . . . Therefore her name was called *Marah* [bile, with a pun on Mary]. And the shame of the daughters of Adam. And by our sins she placed her dead son in the bosom of the earth."[81] This anti-Christian invective turns the Virgin Mary into the lying harlot who "collocavit in sinu suo" (laid in her bosom) a stolen son and thus, according to Obadiah ben Makhir, became a figure of Jewish sinfulness (1 Kings 3:20).

But what can these twelfth-century trivia have to do with the Jewish wife and mother of *Adam of Bristol*? In the initial interrogative conversation between Adam and Samuel's wife—the same in which Adam describes his mother's Nativity scene—exactly this exegetical battle over Mary's identity takes place. At the literal level, the Jewess is simply deceiving the young boy in the course of orienting dialogue, but they have an exceptionally odd conversation, which appears to take part in the same Christian-Jewish discourse around the Virgin Mary as the Blois and Paris accounts, and to corroborate Yuval's and Stacey's suggestions that there is some knowledge of these cases at work in *Adam of Bristol*. Two moments of the dialogue pertain: first, when Adam tells Samuel's wife that he wants to go home, she responds, "Tu enim es, cum ceteris fratribus tuis, sanguis meus et caro mea, et ego ducam te domi ad patrem et matrem" (I am related to your father, for you are, along with your other brothers, my blood and my flesh, and I will lead you home to your father and mother); and second, when Adam insists on leaving, she continues, "Tota nocte ista *collocabo te in sinu meo*" (all of this night I will lay you in my bosom) (Cluse 307). In the first instance, by suggesting that the Christian child about to be crucified is "my blood and my flesh," the Jewess establishes a connection to the flesh and blood of Christ and Mary by echoing the eucharistic formula ("hoc est corpus meum, hic est sanguis meus"); she thus underscores the historically familial relationship between Christians and Jews, and suggests allegorically that she, like Mary, is a vessel for Christ (as Adam). This is a connection that the author works to ensure we understand: Adam later reports that the Virgin Mary has appeared and comforted him with an echo of the Jewess's words, "hac nocte venies ad patrem et matrem" (tonight you will go to your father and mother) (Cluse 312). In the second instance, the Jewess's offer to hold Adam in her bosom is clearly an allusion to the story of the two harlots before King Solomon, through which the Jewess aligns herself with the lying harlot who steals a living child to replace her own, as Obadiah ben Makhir did similarly with Mary/Marah. Consciousness of this Jewish ridicule of Mary provides an explanation for the Jewess's statement, and the *Adam of Bristol* author thus performs a stunning symbolic circle: he simultaneously aligns the Jewess with the child-stealing harlot of 3 Kings 3, connects her to known anti-Christian slurs against the Virgin Mary, and creates a Jewish image of the Virgin Mary. All of this requires not only contrast between the Jewess and Mary but also a profound recognition of likeness.

Both the horror of the Jewish mother's violence against Adam and her death at the hands of her husband further require this recognition. In the opening lines of Samuel's story, for instance, Adam tells Samuel's son that *his* mother would provide "panem album" (white bread) rather than the "poma" (apples) provided by the Jewess (Cluse 305), and this boast acquires deeper significance in connection to the Jewess's torture of Adam and her own death. It evokes an Eve/Mary dichotomy (from an apple to the bread of life) and aligns Adam with the consecrated host, making this a kind of proleptic host-desecration tale as well as a ritual murder libel, but it also connects Adam's body to the Jewish mother's later violence, again through an initial recognition of the parallelism crafted between Christian and Jewish mothers. The Jewess's most vicious attack on Adam, the only one she commits without explicit direction from her husband, should be read with this exchange in mind. In the mother's brutal mutilation of the boy, in fact, she is most clearly connected to other English literary representations of Mary:

Exclamaverunt dicentes: "Ecce deus christianorum!" Et ait Samuel: "Percuciamus eum et conspuamus eum!" Et accessit mulier et cultello

quo solebat incidere panem abcidit nasum pueri, et labia eius usque ad
dentes, et ait: "Ecce quam pulcre ridet deus christianorum!" (Cluse 309)

They shouted, saying: "Behold the god of the Christians!" And
Samuel said: "We will beat him and spit on him!" And the woman
approached, and, with a little knife that she was in the habit of using
to slice bread, cut off the boy's nose, and his lips, right down to the
teeth, and said: "Behold how beautifully the god of the Christians
smiles!"

The Jewess's use of a bread knife to cut the body labeled "god of the Christians"
by Jewish persecutors inverts the Christian mother who at the beginning of the
story would offer "white bread" to the Jews, even as it suggests a bloody version
of the eucharistic sacrifice and therefore a dark image of the Virgin Mary. Other
versions of this kind of medieval interpretation of Mary are evident in the *Siege
of Jerusalem*'s sympathetic portrayal of the cannibal Mary who roasts and eats
her own child, as discussed above, and in the *Book of Margery Kempe*'s description of the Virgin rejecting Margery's food because she will eat of "no mete but
myn owyn childe" (no food except my own child).[82]

The implication that the Jewess's intention is to ingest Adam—the Christ-
like sacrifice whose body "is meat indeed" (John 6:56)—is made stronger by the
several cannibalistic suggestions that occur elsewhere in *Adam of Bristol*. The
Jews roast Adam in imitation of the Passover sacrifice, and Samuel calls Adam
"porcellum meum" (my piglet), thereby connecting him to forbidden food
(Cluse 307). Samuel also claims that he roasts Adam "sicud gallina crassa" (like
a fat chicken) (Cluse 309), an eerie echo of which suggests that the visiting Irish
priest may be eating Adam later, when Samuel's sister claims that Bristol pork
("carnes porcine") is unclean and offers the priest, instead, a meal of "gallinas
crassas" (fat chickens) (Cluse 318). Claudine Fabre-Vassas has illuminated the
"complete turnaround" by which Jews in such stories could become associated
with cannibals and pig eaters:

Just as he is being presented to us in his role as a cannibal butcher . . .
the Jew shows his hidden face. With this porcine mark he sports the
secret of his "true nature." And this seemingly misplaced sign makes
the image of the piglet behind that of the slaughtered child all the
more obvious. . . . The accusation of ritual murder thus plays on the

relationships that . . . unite pigs, children, and Jews. For pig eaters the
Jew performs in reality the action that is always on the horizon of
their own pork consumption. . . . What is left unspoken is spoken
only with respect to the other and what he forbids himself.[83]

In this context, the Jewish declaration that Adam is "porcellum meum" is not
only a charge of Jewish cannibalism but of Jews' consumption of their own
children, since Jews were said not to eat pork because their own children (in
apocryphal stories of the childhood of Jesus) had been turned into piglets by
Christ.[84] Eating a piglet, in such a formulation, is eating one's own child, analogous to Christians eating the body and blood of the Eucharist, the flesh of their
own (Jewish) child. In this discourse, there is an anxiety both about real presence and about Christian-Jewish indistinguishability. While Fabre-Vassas discusses these connections in late medieval (continental) ritual murder stories,
and always with application to the Jewish father alone, the early appearance of
the motif in the *Passion of Adam of Bristol*, and connected to a Jewish mother
through her active participation in the butchering of a Christian child, suggests
that the cannibal (Virgin) Mary is what is left unspoken here.

This series of uncomfortable likenesses is hardly alleviated by the death of
Samuel's wife. Samuel kills her in a rage because, persuaded by miracles that occur
as they torture Adam together, she announces, "Crastina die baptismum recip-
iam, in nomine domini nostri Ihesu Christi" (Tomorrow I will receive baptism in
the name of our Lord Jesus Christ) (Cluse 313). Though she is murdered before she
has a chance to receive baptism, her death only serves to consolidate her unspoken
Marian sameness. As Samuel stabs his wife, his previous curses of the Virgin Mary
now apply likewise to the Jewess, whom he calls a "mentiris meretrix" (lying
whore),[85] and Jesus then appears with "Marie virginis" (the Virgin Mary) and
"anima pueri crucifixi" (the soul of the crucified boy [Adam]) to guide the Jewess
to heaven in posthumous acceptance of her faith (Cluse 313). Thinking iconographically again, this scene effects both a literal juxtaposition of the Jewess and
Mary *and* an image of Mary assumed into heaven to be with her crucified son.
The fact that the author specifies that the murders occur on the eve of the Assumption is especially important: the timing activates the Assumption story and
makes this image of Samuel's wife and the crucified boy unmistakably Marian.

The wife's final appearance in *Adam of Bristol*, moreover—in a vision to the
traveling companions of the Irish priest—explicates the sameness of the Jewess
and Mary. The priest's companions report this about their vision:

vidimus juvenes pulcherrimos nobis astantes. . . . Vidimus mulierem quondam egredientem et ingredientem indutam purpureo pallio cum quodam parvulo habentis indumentis eodem colore. . . . Species enim omnium erat sicud sol. . . . Mulier illa purpureis vestibus induta, cum filio suo subsequenter benedixit nobis ostendens nobis .3^{ia}. vulnera in corpore suo, duo in pectore et .3^{m}. in ventre. Parvulus autem sequens, unum vulnus ostendebat, sub mamilla, set et multi incedebant cum eis obsequentes eos. (Cluse 323)

We saw the most beautiful youthful figures standing near us. . . . We saw a certain woman going out and coming in, dressed in a purple robe, with a certain little boy wearing garments the same colour. . . . And their faces were wholly like the sun. . . . That woman wearing purple clothes, with her son very close behind, blessed us, showing to us three wounds in her torso, two in the chest, and a third in the stomach. But the little boy following showed one wound, under his breast. And a multitude walked with them, following behind them.

This passage has caused some interesting uncertainty in modern scholarship. Stacey has used it to emphasize the degree to which Mary is "the figure who stands at the devotional center of this tale," for not only does it take place on the feast of the Assumption, not only does Adam call upon Mary and she appear to protect him, but "it is Mary, dressed in purple, who leads the angelic procession to Adam's grave, accompanied by Jesus as a young boy."[86] Yuval, on the other hand, reads the passage as a vision of Jewish martyrs, "a vision of a woman and child dressed in the *porphyrion*, . . . one of the strongest symbols of Jewish martyrdom in Germany"; he points out, referring to the passage above, that in *Adam of Bristol* "the *porphyrion* is . . . specifically the garb of the Jews, not of the slain Christian child, but it also alludes to the garment worn by Jesus before the Crucifixion (Mark 15:17)."[87]

What makes Yuval right, and he mentions this too, is that the woman points to the wounds of her martyrdom, which seem to match the ones Samuel inflicted: "Concurrit post illam et percussit illam cultello, . . . percussa in ventre usque ad mortem, . . . tunc vir percussit eam tercio, et quarto, usque ad mortem, et sic mulier emisit spiritum" (He ran after her and stabbed her with a knife, . . . [she was] stabbed to death in the stomach, . . . then the man stabbed her a third time, and a fourth, until she was dead, and thus the woman gave up the spirit)

(Cluse 313). The wounds displayed in the vision—multiple wounds in the torso, chest, and "in ventre" (in the stomach, or womb)—certainly echo Samuel's attack, and the single wound on the boy likewise suggests Samuel's son (*not* Adam), whom he stabbed "statim" (at once, quickly) after he had killed his mother. What makes Stacey right, on the other hand, is the apparitions' clear imitation of Christ and Mary: a woman in royal robes, radiant like the sun (cf. Rev. 12:1), accompanied by a royal child with a wound beneath his breast, followed by an angelic multitude. The allusion to Mary and Jesus could hardly be stronger. What we have here, then, is both a (Christian) vision of Jewish martyrs and a vision of Mary and Christ, or, more specifically, a vision of Jewish martyrs *as* Mary and Christ. In her last appearance in the tale, the Jewess so explicitly inhabits Mary's place that it is difficult to distinguish her from Mary at all.

With the Jewish mother, the *Adam of Bristol* author uses sameness both to alleviate and to reinforce the danger of Jewish passing. Sameness is figuratively productive in the understanding of Mary and devotion to her—Mary becomes the operative figure in the story as a mediator between Jewish disbelief and Christian redemption—but it can also produce violence. Sameness affirms fantasized Jewish atrocities against Christ and Christians as ongoing, even as it halts those atrocities through the assumption (or Assumption) of the Jewish mother and son into heaven. This is most neatly seen in the moment that first forces Samuel's wife to question her adherence to her Jewish faith: an unconscious Adam, tied to a spit and roasting in a fire, miraculously speaks Hebrew, and he says, "Quare me comburis? . . . Ego sum deus Abraham, et deus Ysaac, et deus Iacob" (Why do you consume me? . . . I am the god of Abraham, and the god of Isaac, and the god of Jacob) (Cluse 311). The catalyst for the Jewess's decision to convert is thus the realization that her initial luring deception—her claim to be related to Adam's father and to share his flesh and blood—is reality. Her internal conversion is accomplished not only exegetically and iconographically but also linguistically, through an identification of a Christ-body with Jewish language and lineage and flesh that produces a symbolic remaking of the Jewess as Mary. The violence with which this saming happens is not evidence of contrast or impermeable boundaries, but rather evokes a language of shared Jewish and Christian suffering and violence, and it suggests intimacy and familial self-identification taken to extremes. I would not go so far as to draw a line between this narrative and the expulsion of the Jews from England that happened around the time it was written, but it is not too much to say that the narrative and the event evince similar sensibilities. Both imagine an intimacy so

Figure 10. The torture of Adam of Bristol alongside a portrait of the Bristol Jewish family in initial C. ©British Library Board. BL MS Harley 957, fol. 22r.

close to sameness that the Jew must be rendered absent to permit the Christian embodiment of the Jew(ess). The incorrect Jewess must be replaced with a correct one, not to walk the streets of Bristol—where she might simply feign Christianity undetected—but remade as a Marian vision.

We may close this chapter with what is, to my knowledge, the only pre- or para-Expulsion image of a medieval Jewess in an English literary text. The wife of the *Passion of Adam of Bristol*—mother, cannibal, near convert, Marian double—survives in a small historiated puzzle initial, opposite a much larger illustration of her husband Samuel killing the crucified Adam above a latrine, in BL MS Harley 957 (fol. 22r). These images appear at the top of the text's fourth folio (Figures 10 and 11). The tiny portrait of the Bristol Jewish family is set alongside the passage that narrates the wife's decision to convert and Samuel's murder of her and her son. The mother and her son are on their knees before Samuel in the family image, and he holds knives to both of them, one pointed toward his wife's stomach, the other his son's upper chest. The Jewess wears a fashionable head covering and green dress, trimmed with white. Both she and her son have white skin (painted in lead white, now blackened in some areas), which matches Adam's body and is distinct from the natural skin-tones used

Figure 11. The Jewish family in the *Passion of Adam of Bristol* (detail).
©British Library Board. BL MS Harley 957, fol. 22r.

for Samuel in both illustrations. As we come to expect, there is no visual indication that the woman is Jewish. Just as Lipton describes for such images, she "can
be identified only by context . . . : delete the setting, eliminate the male companions, or efface the inscriptions [or accompanying text], and [she] could be
Christian."[88] She is certainly drawn in stark contrast to her husband—who is in
profile, physically contorted, with a grotesquely elongated nose in the larger
image—and her hands are held in prayer.[89] The artist depicts her at the precise
moment of her death and last words: "percussa in ventre usque ad mortem, ait
voce magna, 'Jhesum fili Marie, miserere mei'" (stabbed to death in the stomach, she said in a loud voice, "Jesus son of Mary have mercy on me") (Cluse 313).
The artist illustrates her, that is, in the moment between her brutal cannibalistic torture of a Christian child and her Christian salvation.

It would be easy to argue that the family portrait shows the Jewish mother
as a Christian woman because it depicts her after her (internal if not formal)
conversion, or because her husband is turning her and her son into Christian

martyrs just as he does to the similarly white-skinned Adam in the larger image. But this is reductive. Rather, the artist chooses to display her in a liminal state, when she is *both* Jewish *and* Christian. Only a folio earlier, this woman had sliced off Adam's nose and lips with a bread knife; only lines earlier, her victim's use of Hebrew and claim to shared ancestry with her through Abraham, Isaac, and Jacob had moved her to Christian belief. In the passage next to her image, she prays to Jesus and Mary alongside her son; she is not quite Christian, but she believes in Christ and will soon be baptized in her own blood and assumed into heaven as Mary herself. When *Adam of Bristol*'s narrative frame and resolution depend so heavily on the feigned Christianity of another Jewess, and its devotional lessons depend on the persistent doubling of the Jewish mother and the Virgin Mary, an illustration that makes it hard to discern the Jewess's identity is, to understate the case, fitting.

This visual convergence of the Jewish and Christian self in the figure of a Jewish mother—along with the eventual triumph of Christianity through her assumption into heaven as Mary—reflects *Adam of Bristol*'s polemics of sameness. One identity cannot be erased in favor of the other: the Jewess's Christianity depends on her prior ability to pass (as it does for Samuel's sister), on her sense of the shared Hebrew "god of our fathers," and on her connection to the Virgin Mary as a Jewish mother. In the *Passion of Adam of Bristol*, as in other texts I have explored so far, the Jewess's ability to be (or be seen as) a Christian always presumes her Jewishness. It is the polemic—not the woman—that wants malleability, and in medieval Anglo-Christian books, text and image *together* emphasize the sameness of the Jewess because of the polemical utility she holds. Her gender, as Lipton has also argued, makes her an optimal vehicle for sameness, but not because "her femaleness trump[s] her Jewishness."[90] Rather, the unmarked Jewess works as a type, in both art and narrative, because her concomitant associations with feminine weakness, connections to female Christian readers (such as Isabel de Byron), and links to Old Testament heroines (like Rachel) coincide with her Jewishness. For Jewish mothers in particular, the intertestamental identities suggested by textual and visual associations with Old Testament prophecy and the Virgin Mary mean that the unmarked Jewess is never one or the other but always more than, and less than, both.

CHAPTER 5

Figures of Uncertainty

The woman answered . . . "I shall liberate you: above all, take care that
they do not perceive us to be Jews."

—*The Passion of Adam of Bristol*

A Jewess, More or Less

Both more than and less than "Jew" or "Christian," the Jewess in Anglo-
Christian polemical literature is marked by unmarking. She may be a martyr, a
convert full of sudden faith, a mother responding to the demands of prophecy,
or the Virgin Mary herself, but her unmarking, at the same time, permits invisibility, inscrutability, and deception. The Jewess may pass through Christian
and Jewish spaces, and the Christianess in Jewish spaces may do the same. These
figures of uncertainty are stock characters of medieval anti-Jewish literature.
Like the women who disappeared into the London Jewry, hidden from Archbishop Peckham the Jewess escapes reach and knowability. Like the women
who served throughout the thirteenth century as wet nurses, maidservants,
traders, and money changers in domestic and urban spaces, the Christianess in
Jewish space can seem to be Jewish. Like the seeming converts who prompted
years of lawfare before mixed juries and kings found that they were Jewish after
all, women of uncertain or conjoined identity crowd the literary record. Authors announce these women's ambiguity to warn against broken boundaries
run amok, and in so doing they also suggest a deep and long awareness—
manifest in stereotype—of Anglo-Jewish interactions with Anglo-Christian
homes and families.

That this should be the case, however, is neither an exclusively English nor an exclusively medieval phenomenon. Scholars working in Jewish studies have long noted the "transgressive possibilities" of the Jewess: "her femaleness, her *ess-ence*, makes her more assimilable" and "therein lies her threat, for she penetrates the dominant group easily, without its realization," notes Amy-Jill Levine.[1] "The stereotypical representation of Jewish women . . . seems often to be ambiguously identifiable," says Sander Gilman; it is a "'double vision' which constructs the image of the Jewish woman."[2] For Cynthia Baker, the "essentially ambiguous Jewess" is "in some respects like us, in other respects like them. . . . As a trope of indeterminacy and the promise and threat of openness, of permeable boundaries, she may be likened to a door or a window, to an open house or a bridge."[3] More recently, Baker has explained how this indeterminacy had developed over time because of the "easy separability of women from a collective ethnic identity" that is evident in scripture: "these categories, like *Jew* itself, are and always have been deeply gendered," partly because women's identities, religious choices, and religious practices have been traditionally and legally relegated to fathers and husbands.[4]

We should always have expected to find Jewish (or Judaized) women as uncertain and doubled presences in medieval sources too—the Jewess moves between "us" and "them," and theories of difference and opposition are insufficient to her—but we should also have expected to find that specific regional and temporal contexts will influence representations of the Jewess. Medieval English literary examples, both because of their place in a longer history of representations of women's Jewishness *and* their English particularity—especially in relation to English state, archival, and cultural attitudes toward Anglo-Jewish communities—carry more weight than has hitherto been recognized. Levine has called the Jewess "a heuristic model," that is, "a sign that signifies different cultural and gendered constructs for different times and places,"[5] and a heuristic Jewess is best left unmarked. Her function is to permit interpretations and recognitions suited to her immediate contexts.

Going Between and Passing Through

The Anglo-French commemorative ballad "Hugo de Lincolnia" (ca. 1260) provides an instructive instance of the interpretive potential of the Jewess's unmarking and simultaneity in an English setting. Memorializing the 1255 murder of young Hugh of Lincoln, this ballad makes poetic and propagandistic work of a crime for which nineteen English Jews were actually executed.[6] In the process, the poet describes a "noris" (wet nurse or nanny) who disposes of Hugh's body. When the boy's corpse has twice resisted burial and the Lincoln Jews discuss their predicament, an unnamed Jewish man comes forward to suggest that his *noris* carry it away. He has already bribed her for the purpose:

> Car, une femme que jo ai, privé,
> Me ad noris ad esté,
> Et pur dons l'a granté
> Le cors enporter en priveté.

> Indeed, a woman whom I have, a close friend,
> Was my nurse,
> And for gifts she has agreed
> To carry away the body secretly. (172–75)[7]

This characterization of a Lincoln *noris* plays on the expectation that Anglo-Jewish homes in the mid-thirteenth century employ Christian wet nurses and maidservants,[8] but of course it does so polemically. The poet suggests either that such women would serve Jews even in their darkest deeds or that they were corruptible and thus likely to betray their faith. The substantive noun "privé" (close friend, intimate) may also suggest sexual intimacy, though, in light of other English characterizations of Jewesses and this woman's role in the poem, it is more likely that "privé" suggests domesticity and secrecy, echoing "priveté" at line 175.[9] The woman does indeed carry away little Hugh's body, secretly and successfully, and she throws it into a well outside the bounds of the city.

But if readers at first understand this Lincoln wet nurse as a Christian once employed in a Jewish household, they are mistaken. The poet, having introduced her as above, then takes care to suggest her Jewishness:

> Le femme fu tenu cristien,
> Pur ceo se dota nule ren;
> Eschaper quidout mult ben.
> Puis fust tenu plus vil de chen.

> The woman was taken for a Christian;
> For this reason she feared nothing;

She expected to escape handily.
Afterwards she would be held more despicable than a dog. (184–87)

This stanza uses and confounds Christian expectations. The assumption that "la norriz maluré" (the wicked wet nurse) (180), as she is called elsewhere, was a Christian servant of Jews certainly makes sense: twenty-five women were excommunicated in York and Lincoln in the 1270s because of their employment in Jewish households, after all, and the real problem of Christian women's work in Jewish homes, which English and papal authorities unsuccessfully tried to prohibit in the period of this poem's composition,[10] constitutes part of the poet's commentary here. Yet the poet just as certainly implies that the woman is Jewish: she was only *taken for* a Christian. What is a reader to make of this? Perhaps she was always Jewish? Perhaps she became a Jew while in service and, as a result, has weaponized the expectation of her Christianity? As a former servant in a Jewish household, this woman is, in any case, able to mobilize uncertainty to criminal effect. Without explaining her identity, the poet lingers over how she was *perceived*. Whatever her identity, she ultimately turns out to be inhuman ("fust tenu plus vil de chen"), worse than a dog because of her association with Jews.

This *noris* appears again late in "Hugo de Lincolnia," after a Lincoln Jew called Jopin confesses to Hugh's murder before King Henry III and implicates his coreligionists. Hugh was murdered in his house, says Jopin, and he participated in the boy's torture, but it was other Jews who abducted him and inflicted killing blows. Retelling the events, Jopin repeats the previous claims about the *noris*:

L'enfant ne poeit estre enterré
Dedenz maison n'en priveté,
Purquei nus fumes esmerveillé
Et mult durement esponté.

L'enfant nutantre porté feu
Par la noriz de un Ju
Que pur cristien fu tenu
A une fontainne, jo sai be u,

Derere le chastel envers le west.
Mult ben sai que parfond est.

La fu plongé par la test.
Ore juge cum vus plest.

The child could not be buried
In the house or in secret,
So that we were amazed
And very sorely frightened.

The child was carried at night
By a Jew's nurse
Who was taken for Christian
To a well, I very well know where,

Behind the castle toward the west.
I very well know that it is deep.
There he was dropped head first.
Now judge as you please. (332–43)

Jopin's confession both repeats and adds new detail to the previous account. He suggests that others witnessed the disposal—the corpse went head first into a well of notable depth, behind the castle and to the west—and he reframes the woman's actions as the resolution of male Jewish fear. The men who tortured and killed the boy were too frightened to act, but this woman, "pur cristien fu tenu" (taken for Christian), solved the problem. Jopin's account prompts an outburst from Henry III: "Le rei Henri mult tost dist: / 'Pur la pité Jhesu Christ! / Mult mesfist que l'occist'" (King Henry immediately said: "For Christ's pity! It is a great crime that he [?] murdered him") (346–48). Henry, in response to Jopin, erases the ambiguous *noris*—or willfully forgets her—and seems to reimpose Jewish male guilt: while the subject of "l'occist" is unclear, the poet now continues to recount how Jopin alone was punished for the crime. No more of the ambiguous *noris* or her fate is offered, no judgment imposed on her. Having accomplished what no Jewish man could, she remains invisible—even to king and law.

Similar women feature in the *Passion of Adam of Bristol* and the *Life and Passion of William of Norwich*. They appear and disappear quickly and function in secrecy, but their momentary presence is critical to authors' polemical portraits of Jewish domesticity. The murderous Jewish couple of *Adam of Bristol*, to begin with, has a Christian maidservant who is complicit in their crimes: they send her into town "ut deferat nummatum pomorum, ut demus puero huic christiano, quia volumus hunc crucifigere" (to bring a pennyworth of apples, so we can give them to this Christian, because we wish to crucify him) (Cluse 305–6).[11] Samuel's sister, in turn, as a foil to her sister-in-law, has a Jewish maidservant, a *ministra* and *ancilla* "de genere suo" (of her people/kind) (Cluse 318). The Jewish maidservant is virginal and loyal and, like her mistress, appears to be Christian. She serves Christian guests—though draws the line at sleeping with them—and, in accordance with her mistress's wishes, she leads the gullible Irish priest between the story's two Jewish homes: "Vade et aperi hostium domus fratris mei et noli ingredi," Samuel's sister tells her, "dominus autem sacerdos subsequitur et ingredietur hostium quod te viderit aperire" (Go and open the door of my brother's house and do not enter it, but the lord priest will follow close and enter the door that he sees you open) (Cluse 321). The Jewish maidservant can hear divine singing inside Samuel's house, where angels surround little Adam's corpse, but she cannot answer the priest's questions about its source: "Ad hec ancilla: Nescio" (To this the maidservant, "I don't know") (Cluse 322). Instead of offering knowledge, that is, the woman performs a ritual of access and inaccess. She opens the way but remains at the threshold.

The ritualized servant-at-the-threshold scenes of *Adam of Bristol*, further, can be linked to counterparts in the *Life and Passion of William of Norwich* and thus give the impression of a motif. Thomas of Monmouth tells of a maidservant in the Jewish home where little William was allegedly murdered who likewise does not go through doors. In an extraordinary passage in his account of the 1144 event—the earliest example of a ritual murder narrative, completed roughly a century before *Adam of Bristol*—Thomas describes this servant as someone who unwittingly participated in the boy's torture:

> Muliercula quedam christiana que illis famulabatur, ab eisdem iussa feruentem aquam in coquina seorsum preparabat, ignorans quidem negotium, sed negotii plane audiens tumultum. Deintro autem acclamantibus: Aquam, aquam, mulier feruentissimam attulit, petentibus ministrauit. Sed dum deforis illa traderet ac deintus illi susciperent, hostio interaperto puerum posti affixum, quia duobus non potuit, oculo uno uidere contigit. Quo uiso exhorruit factum; clausit oculum, et illi hostium.

> A little Christian woman who worked as a servant for them, as she was preparing alone in the kitchen some boiling water, as ordered by

them, not knowing what was going on, nonetheless heard clearly the noise of it. When from inside they were calling out: "Water! Water!" the woman carried it, boiling fiercely, and served it to those who requested it. But while she handed it over from the outside and they received it from within, she happened to see through the open door—with one eye, since she could not with both—the boy fixed to a post. Having seen this she was horrified; she closed her eye and they shut the door.[12]

Like the Jewish maidservant in *Adam of Bristol*, this *muliercula* hears the sounds within but remains (at first) ignorant of their source. Like the Jewish maidservant, she has access to the inside—that is, to the place of male Jewish violence—but remains at the threshold. The movement from outside to inside is emphatic in Thomas's account, as is the simultaneous reinforcement of the boundary: the Christian eye and the Jewish door are synchronized in their opening and closing.

Such boundaries and thresholds, we may observe, are the special dominion of Jewish/Christian *muliercula*. The maidservant of *William of Norwich* reaches in "deforis" (from outside) but stays at the doorway; literally and figuratively, she sees only partially. The murderous Jews of *Adam of Bristol* order their Christian maidservant in and out of Jewish space: she carries apples from the Christian market back into the Jewish home, but the author does not place her at the center of the violence. The Jewish maidservant of *Adam of Bristol* moves between two Jewish homes, to mark a path for Christians, but she stays at the threshold and claims no knowledge of the inside. The wet nurse of "Hugo de Lincolnia" goes outside the boundaries of the city to dispose of Hugh's body, thus denoting a threshold past which Jewish men (and their violence) cannot go. These ambiguous figures carry weight for Jewish men—measured in water (baptism?), apples (the Fall?), or bodies (Incarnation?)—but they are associated with the boundaries between Christians and Jews *and*, importantly, with the boundaries between Jewish men and Jewish women.

This proves true even of an episode in the *Life and Passion of William of Norwich* that seems to make a man the figure of uncertainty. The messenger who abducts young William from his mother by pretending to be the Norwich archdeacon's cook serves as a go-between for the Norwich Jews, but Thomas of Monmouth renders him unknowable: "christianum nescio siue iudeum [erat]" (I know not whether he was a Christian or a Jew).[13] Functioning like the women go-betweens in other boy-martyr stories, his ambiguity not only transgresses Christian domestic boundaries, where Jewish men cannot or should not go, but also complicates the narrative roles of the story's mother and child: just as this messenger turns little William into a Christ, he turns William's otherwise pious and protective Christian mother into a Judas. Though Thomas first remarks that the ambiguous abductor is "fere per omnia Iude traditoris imitator" (an emulator in almost every way of Judas the traitor),[14] he ultimately casts the Christian mother as the Judaized traitor by transferring the Judas role from the messenger to the Christian woman in the process of their interaction: in the end, *she* is "argenti splendore corruptum" (corrupted by the glitter of silver) offered as "innocentis sanguinis precium" (the price of innocent blood), and, "preclaris tandem illecta argenteis cupiditate" (finally lured by her desire for the shining silver coins), she willingly hands her Christ-child to his tormentors.[15] Through his vacillating characterization of the Christian mother, who does not recognize Jewish difference nor realize her own proximity to Jewishness quickly enough, Thomas ultimately creates another ambiguous woman go-between. William's mother is both Christian and Jewish in her meaning, and her narrative function is not unlike the one-eyed maidservant, who *might have* reinscribed Jewish-Christian boundaries but instead let Jewish proximity shape her.

Around the body of young Robert of Bury, too, the ambiguous Jewish/Christian woman emerges. As I discussed in Chapter 2, Robert was supposedly killed in Bury St Edmunds in 1181, and Jocelin of Brakelond claimed to have written his *vita*: "fuit sanctus puer Robertus martirizatus, et in ecclesia nostra sepultus, et fiebant prodigia et signa multa in plebe, sicut alibi scripsimus" (the boy saint Robert was martyred and buried in our church, and there were many signs and wonders among the people, as I have written elsewhere).[16] Later sources clarify that Robert was reputedly killed by Jews and had a shrine at the Abbey of Bury St Edmunds from the twelfth century and into the late fifteenth.[17] John Lydgate (d. ca. 1451), a monk at Bury, wrote a "Praier to St Robert" to commemorate his martyrdom by Jews, perhaps citing Jocelin's now lost *vita*: "agayns the the Iewys were so wood, / lyk as thy story makyth mencyoun" (the Jews were so enraged against you [i.e., Robert], / as the account says) (5–6).[18] In this short prayer-poem, which survives only in Bod. MS Laud 683 (fol. 22v–23r), Lydgate also notes that Robert was so young that he was still in the care of a wet nurse: he was "a sowkyng child" (a nursing child) (11), "Fostrid with mylk and tendre pap" (nourished with milk and soft breast) (17), and, while his "purpil blood [was] allayd with mylk whiht" (purple blood was mixed with white milk), he remained "ffer ffro [his] norice, found no respight" (far from his wet nurse, found no reprieve) (26–28). Lydgate does not mark his *norice* as Christian or Jewish, but he makes her a significant part of the affective experience of Robert's passion.

A woman who seems to represent this Bury wet nurse appears in a late medieval illustration of Robert's passion. Roughly contemporary with Lydgate's "Praier to St Robert," a late fifteenth-century addition to Los Angeles, Getty Museum MS 101 (fol. 44r) depicts the discovery of Robert's body, a monkish patron, and a charter recording the Liberty of St Edmund (Figure 12). First in its sequence, however, is a woman in a reddish dress, apron, and fashionable head covering who holds Robert's small haloed corpse over a draw well. The *titulus* atop this woman provides additional information: "Voluit set non potuit anus abscondit lucerna dei" (The old woman wanted to, but could not, hide the light of God). Is this old woman the *norice* of Lydgate's "Praier to St Robert"? Or is she simply the stock Jewish/Christian servant that we have already seen in boy-martyr stories, now reimagined for a fifteenth-century patron?

The Getty 101 image appears to be cognate with both the nurse of the Anglo-French "Hugo de Lincolnia," because she carries the child's corpse to a well, and the wet nurse of Lydgate's "Praier," because of her close contact with the boy. The Latin word *anus* (old woman, matron) may contravene Lydgate's use of *norice* in Middle English, though *anus* is not necessarily a neutral descriptor: it sometimes denotes a sorceress and could be used as a term of contempt (similar to Modern English "hag").[19] In this light, the Getty 101 artist seems to share the "Hugo de Lincolnia" poet's contemptuous attitude toward the Lincoln *noris*. Lydgate's emphasis on the suckling Robert certainly connects the anti-Jewish account that undergirds his "Praier" to "feeding and nurturing, recalling both Marian devotion and maternity in general," as Anthony Bale has noted, and thus links the poem to similar ritual murder narratives that "evoke the sacrificial Christ-child" and "appeal to a particularly maternal sense of pity."[20] In Getty 101, moreover, a short Latin prayer facing the illustrative sequence likewise emphasizes Robert's infant vulnerability: "Ave dulcis puer beate Roberte qui infancie tempore floruisti martirii palma... in puerili corpusculo" (Hail, sweet boy, blessed Robert, who in infancy bloomed with the palm of martyrs... in a boyish little body).[21] But the wet nurse is not mentioned at all in this Latin prayer. Her identity, if it was ever more defined, is either lost with the Bury *vita* or present only as much as it is for the multiple similar women from analogous tales. The fifteenth-century artist's representation seems deliberately to confound certainty.

Figure 12. The story of Robert of Bury illustrated in Los Angeles, Getty Museum MS 101, fol. 44r (*olim* Dyson Perrins MS 1). The patron's prayer reads, "Meritis sancti Roberti hic et in eum misereatur mei," or "By the merits of St Robert, here and through him, have mercy on me." Image courtesy of the Getty's Open Content Program.

Still, Bale calls the Getty 101 woman "Robert's apparent murderess," though he puzzles over the fact that she is "not a 'Jewish' grotesque but a well-dressed gentlewoman."[22] Emily Rose sees definitive connections between this woman, Jocelin of Brakelond's lost *vita*, and Lydgate's "Praier," which she argues "suggests that Robert's nursemaid was in league with his oppressors": she reads Lydgate's line "ffer ffro thy norice, found no respight" to mean "*for* from your nurse [you] found no respite" instead of "*far* from your nurse, [you] found no respite."[23] For Rose, the woman in Getty 101 is "an early literary model of what was later stereotyped as the Wicked Woman (*mauvaise femme*), a Christian who serves as an intermediary for Jews in such narratives."[24] Bale, in summation, is more measured:

> Whether or not the woman is supposed to be Jewish is a moot point: is she the boy's wet nurse, the "norice" of Lydgate's "Praier", who has been co-opted by the Jews in their plan? Or is she a Jewish woman, who, unlike Jewish men, were often represented in later medieval English art as looking little different from Christian women? . . . The choice of a female protagonist in the narrative works as a negative *exemplum* to women and children in particular.[25]

Bale, seeing the woman as a murderess with a moot religious identity (in the legal sense, uncertain, open, conjectural), generally related to exempla aimed at domestic audiences, connects Robert's story to a range of miracle stories that involve women murdering children.[26] But this woman's *mootness* is also precisely what connects her to similar characters in earlier medieval English anti-Jewish narratives.

If the unmarked Christian/Jewish woman in ritual murder stories is moot—that is, an abstract case useful for discussion and pedagogy—she is necessarily a figure of uncertainty. She poses, by design, a problem that is difficult to resolve. She is supposed to be, as Geraldine Heng has put it in her discussion of mothers in English boy-murder stories, "a doubled figure, a composite."[27] Indeed, to conclude that the illustrated woman in Getty 101—a seeming Christian, dressed as a gentlewoman—is certainly Jewish, certainly Christian, or certainly in league with Jews goes against every other example we have of such figures in medieval English literature and art. Instead, we must admit, to use the "Hugo de Lincolnia" poet's phrase, that she may be "pur cristien fu tenu" (taken for Christian) but is ultimately unknowable. The Jewish/Christian go-between is part of the story of medieval Jews and Christians; her ambiguity is crafted and polemical. Even when she is just passing through, she warns Christian readers that not all Jewishness is discernible.

Close Encounters with the Jewess

The *Life of Christina of Markyate* includes a brief Christian encounter with a Jewish woman that, like the other brief episodes discussed above, turns out to be critically important to the text's structure and central characterizations. This fact is remarkable enough in a *vita* likely written shortly after Christina's death, sometime in the late 1150s, and in an episode set in the town of Huntingdon, otherwise unknown to have a Jewish population before 1226.[28] More remarkable, however, is the Jewess's ability to see and accept Christina's holiness, to Judaize her Christian mother, and to remain a trace presence in the visionary life of the would-be saint. The Huntingdon Jewess appears after a young Christina has refused to marry according to her parents' wishes, in the context of her mother Beatrix's physical and sexual abuse: Beatrix "iurabat quod non consideraret quis filiam suam corrumperet" (swore that she would not care who broke in her daughter) and "plurimum substancie dissipavit in annosas vetulas, que veneficiis et incantacionibus suis insanire facerent illam amore turpitudinis" (spent a huge amount of resources on hoary old women who, with their magic and charms, wanted to make her [Christina] go mad with love of shameful things."[29] When these tactics fail, she employs a Jewess:

> Voluit tandem iudea prestigiis contra solitum potentibus Christinam ledere. Intravit igitur in domum Aucti. Vidit virginem pretereuntem. dixit Beatrici ipsius genitrici. In vanum laboravimus. Video duo fata quasi duas candidas personas que cum illa iugiter gradiuntur et ab omnibus impugnacionibus hinc inde defendunt. Iccirco melius est vobis cessare iam quam ultra laborare nequicquam. Ceterum Beatrix obstinato animo persistebat in malicia. . . . Erat quando repente de convivio illam eduxit et in secreciori loco crinibus arreptam quamdiu lasata est verberavit. Scissamque rursus introduxit coram convivantibus ad ludibrium, relictis in dorso eius verberum vestigiis que nunquam potuerunt ipsa superstite deleri.[30]

At length a Jewess wanted to harm Christina with tricks more powerful than usual. So she entered [Christina's father] Autti's home.

She saw the virgin passing by. She said to her mother Beatrix: "We have laboured in vain. I see two phantoms, as two white figures, who continuously walk with her and protect her from all attacks on both sides. For that reason, it is better for you to stop now than labour further to no purpose." Nonetheless, Beatrix, with an obstinate spirit, persisted in malice. . . . Once she unexpectedly summoned her from a banquet and, in a hidden location, having grabbed her by the hair, beat her until she was weary. And, when she had been broken, she brought her back before the banqueters to be mocked, leaving marks of the beating on her back that would never disappear for the rest of her life.

Whether a Jewish woman—perhaps a physician or matchmaker—was in Huntingdon and available to assist Christians with unruly teenage daughters is beside the point. A twelfth-century hagiographer could imagine an Anglo-Jewish woman in this role, collaborating with a Christian mother in an early twelfth-century (likely English-speaking) home,[31] and he chose to align her with a Christian mother: "laboravimus," the Jewess says to Beatrix, that is, "*we* have labored."

This alliance affects the author's characterizations of both Beatrix and Christina. The Jewess may first be intent on harming Christina (though C. H. Talbot's reading is suspect on this point),[32] but she is nonetheless the exemplary woman in the scene: she refuses to participate further in the mother's abuse, and her ability to see Christina's divine protection associates her with the men in the *vita* who are privileged with similar sight, that is, with Christina's mentor Roger and her confidant Geoffrey, abbot of St Albans. The particulars of what the Huntingdon Jewess sees, moreover, align her with the adult Christina. Much later, Christina *also* sees "duabus venerandis et admodum speciosis albisque indutis . . . que collateraliter stantes nulla stature vel decoris differencia discrepabant" (two venerable and very beautiful figures, dressed in white, who, standing side by side, differed neither in height nor dignity).[33] This mature vision confirms Christina's spiritual authority over her male counterpart, Abbot Geoffrey, who, in the later episode, is barred from the chamber where Christina and the two divine figures stand. When Christina prays for him, a dove (the Holy Spirit) moves between her chamber and the outside room where Geoffrey remains, thus revealing that the white-robed figures who protect Christina are the other two persons of the Holy Trinity.[34] At the same time, Christina's vision creates a verbal and visual echo of the Huntingdon Jewess's vision, creating a link between the mature Christina and the Jewess's prior ability to recognize her holiness. The Jewess sees the Godhead before Christina does, in other words, and she understands its Christian meaning better than Christina's mother, Beatrix.

The cameo appearance of a Huntingdon Jewess, in this way, reveals an imagined Jewish sight that is privileged and associated with a specifically feminine (Christian) visionary truth. As the Jewess becomes Christianized in this way, however, the stubborn and violent Beatrix is both Judaized and masculinized by the Jewess's presence. Beatrix persists against her daughter "obstinato animo" (with an obstinate spirit) and tortures her in a way that loudly evokes the torture of Christ: she beats her, "scissamque rursus introduxit . . . ad ludibrium, relictis in dorso eius verberum vestigiis" (and, when she had been broken, she brought her back . . . to be mocked, leaving marks of the beating on her back."[35] The mother's obstinate refusal to accept Christian truth even after it has been revealed to her causes her to inflict a Passion on her own Christ(ina). And the author makes it clear that this conflation of the Christian mother and the torturers of Christ is not accidental: in the only other passage where Jews are explicitly mentioned in the *vita*, we learn why Christina, born Theodora, chose to take the feminine form of "Christ" as her name: "sicut Christus prius a Iudeis reprobatus . . . sic et hec virgo prius a parentibus afflicta" (just as Christ was first rejected by Jews . . . just so this virgin was first ill used by her parents).[36] The comparison asks us, very early in the narrative, to understand Christina's father and mother as the Jews who tortured Christ, and therefore to understand Christina's body, in feminine imitation of Christ's, as a Jewish body. Beatrix's beating and mocking of Christina in reenactment of Christ's Passion, along with her "Jewish" obstinacy, thus collapses Christian-Jewish stereotypes and gendered tropes around the Jewess and Christina.

When we understand Christina of Markyate as a figure affected by Jewish/ Christian sameness, we can also understand how and why "Jewess" becomes an exemplary Christian category in the *Life of Christina of Markyate*. The woman who should bestow blessings on Christina (the *beatrix*) simultaneously embodies a negative (notably masculine) model of Jewishness, while the Jewess (*judea* or *judit*) and Christina embody conjoined Jewish/Christian models of femininity through alignment with the Virgin Mary and the biblical Judith. Immediately after her Passion scene—in the manuscript, just half a folio later—Christina finds comfort in a vision of Christ and Mary, who offers her a branch of martyrdom and asks familiarly, "Quomodo tecum est" (How is it with you?).[37] Christina walks past her frustrated betrothed, who bangs his head against the ground in rage, and Mary lays her head in Christina's lap and reassuringly promises sisterhood with herself and Judith: "Et licet et contemplare postmodum ad

sacietatem: quando introduxero te in thalamum meum, te et Iudith una tecum"
(Later you will have as much as you wish of contemplation, to abundance, when I
bring you into my bedroom, you and Judith together with you).[38] The homoerotic
and domestic intimacy of these successive scenes—that is, the Jewess's vision, the
mother's torture of her daughter, Mary in Christina's lap, and the invitation to her
bedchamber—goads us to view the scenes and characters comparatively. Mary's
pledge to Christina is a future enclosure with the Israelite heroine who beheaded
Holofernes and the Jewess who gave birth to Jesus, while the narrative proximity
between the Huntingdon Jewess's vision and Mary's promise allows a linguistic
slip between *judea* (the word that describes the contemporary Huntingdon Jewess)
and *Judith* (i.e., *Iudit,* Hebrew for "Jewess"). The envisioned heavenly bedchamber,
thus, creates a typological circuit: the *vita's* author closes the spaces between the
contemporary Christianess (Christ-ina), the contemporary Jewess (jud-ea), and the
Israelite Jewess (Jud-ith) with Christina and the Virgin Mary, whose exemplary
Jewish maternal body replaces Christina's negatively Judaized mother.

In *Christina of Markyate*, the contemporary Anglo-Jewess is joined typologi-
cally to Judith, who by Christina's time was already understood in England as a
symbol of virginity, humility, and women's monastic life.[39] This happens through a
brief encounter, without a conversion narrative—the Huntingdon Jewess remains
Jewish—and without relief from the corresponding anti-Jewish rhetoric around
Christina's mother, Beatrix. On the one hand, recognizing that Beatrix has been
Judaized and masculinized by the presence of a Jewess reveals the text's coded anti-
Jewish language. The author uses the living, unconverted Jewess to emphasize Beatrix's failure—and this is similar to how "Jew" functions in the penitential lyric
from BL MS Harley 2253 discussed in Chapter 1, and to Orrm's redefinition of
"Jew" in the *Orrmulum*, where the idealized Christian definition coexists with
condemnation of living Anglo-Jews. Such strategies create Christian Jewishness
through simultaneous denigration of and aspiration toward the Jew. On the other
hand, the gendered aspect of this sameness presents a historical and figural swing
that moves from Christina of Markyate to the Virgin Mary to Judith, hinging on
Jewish women's bodies and spiritual understanding. Framed by two visions of
Christina's white-clad protectors, this temporal back-formation—the direction is
from the contemporary to the pre-Christian—works only with the assumption
that Jewish women are agents of Christian change and revelation.

But this too is a fantasy of Jewishness. Both the negative and the ameliorative approach depend on supersession, typology, and stereotype. In this way, the
Huntingdon Jewess of the *Life of Christina of Markyate* may be understood as
an exemplar for the Jewess's role in medieval Anglo-Christian texts more broadly.

Christina's encounter with her—momentary, amid charms and incantations, overshadowed by the cruelty of her mother's abuse—is not incidental. The Jewess is used to facilitate readers' recognition of, and identification with, the idealized Christian women of the *vita*, Christina and the Virgin Mary. At the same time, as with other English anti-Jewish narratives that feature such figures of uncertainty, the Jewess appears where and when identification and disidentification with Jewishness expose fault lines. Close encounters with the Jewess—nameless, appearing briefly, ambiguous, and out of public sight—are transformative to the Christians around them and to the narratives in which they appear.

This is true also of the thirteenth-century Judas Ballad, already discussed in Chapter 1 for its treatment of Pontius Pilate as a "rich Jew" who pays for Jesus's death, since the short poem hinges on Judas's brief interaction with his nameless pickpocket sister. An invention of the unique thirty-six-line Middle English poem preserved in Cambridge, Trinity College MS B.14.39, this Jewish sister has a literary existence nowhere else. She appears just after Jesus gives Judas thirty coins to buy food for the upcoming meal (i.e., the Last Supper), warning him that he may run into his "cunesmen" (kinsmen) along the way:

> Þou comest fer i þe brode strete fer i þe brode strete.
>   summe of þine cunesman þer þour meist imete.
> Imette wid is soster þe swikele wimon.
>   iudas þou were wrthe me stende þe wid ston.
> Iudas þou were wrthe me stende þe wid ston.
>   for þe false prophete þat tou bileuest upon.
> Be stille leue soster þin herte þe tobreke.
>   wiste min louerd crist ful wel he wolde be wreke.
> Iudas go þou on þe roc heie up on þe ston.
>   lei þin heued i my barm slep þou þe anon.
> Sone so iudas of slepe was awake.
>   þritti platen of seluer from hym were itake.
> He drou hymselue bi þe top þat al it lauede ablode.
>   þe iewes out of iurselem awenden he were wode.[40]

> "You will go into the broad street, go into the broad street.
>   You may meet some of your kinsman there."
> He met with his sister, the treacherous woman.
>   "Judas, I should hit you with stones:
> Judas, I should hit you with stones

> For the false prophet you believe in."
> "Be quiet, dear sister, your heart should break.
>   If my Lord Christ knew, he would be angry."
> "Judas, go to the rock, high up on the stone;
>   lay your head in my lap—you'll sleep quickly."
> As soon as Judas awoke from sleep,
>   Thirty pieces of silver were gone from him.
> He pulled at his scalp until it was bathed in blood.
> The Jews from Jerusalem thought he was mad.

Judas's sister, as created here, is a conflation of biblical types and stereotypes of the Anglo-Jewish woman financier. Irina Dumitrescu has proven that the poet uses a vocabulary of debt and lending that certainly had cultural currency in thirteenth-century England,[41] but, interestingly, she says little about how Judas's sister fits into this argument. Examination of a possible range of her figural and contemporary cultural connotations, however, is worthwhile in this context.

The poet calls Judas's sister a "swikele wimon" (treacherous woman), a thief who is stubborn in her disbelief. In the thirteenth century, the word *swikele* was used primarily to describe political traitors and devils[42]—and we should understand this figure in both registers. She robs Judas only after coaxing him into isolation on a "roc heie up on þe stone" (a rock high up on the stone), a barren landscape that evokes the Temptation of Christ in Luke 4:1–13, where the devil challenges Jesus to turn stones into bread and then leads him "into a high mountain" (Luke 4:5). In this parodic retelling of the Temptation of Christ, the wicked sister suggests that Judas be stoned before he buys food, and then takes him to a high place. The poet aligns her, in other words, both with Judas the Betrayer (responsible for the sale of Jesus) and with the tempting devil, while Judas, in the process, takes the place of Jesus on the high mountain. The siblings are also certainly designed to echo Samson and Delilah, the sister a deceitful Delilah and Judas a Samson asleep in her lap. The poet recreates Judges 16:19, where Delilah has Samson "sleep upon her knees, and lay his head in her bosom," with her theft echoing the Philistine promise of money for Samson's betrayal (Judges 16:5, 16:18). Though this biblical episode traditionally prompts typological readings of Samson as Jesus and Judas as Delilah,[43] Judas's violent hair pulling firmly sets him as Samson, who also loses his hair at Delilah's hands.

As I argued in Chapter 1 with regard to this poet's treatment of Pilate and Judas, the Judas Ballad is playful with its biblical allusions. As Bale has explained,

The poem presents a series of memorable moments of characters in contact and conflict, progressing through pairs of characters acting upon each other: Christ's command to Judas, Judas's betrayal by his sister, Pilate's deal with Judas [at lines 19–24, Pilate agrees to replace the lost coins if Judas forsakes Christ], Christ's identification of Judas [at the Last Supper, lines 28–30], Judas's contrast with Peter [lines 31–36]. Moving through these contrasts suggests a range of juxtapositions constituted by moral-emotional *tableaux*: Judas with his head in his sister's lap, Judas at the Passover table with Christ, the proleptic promise of the arrival of Pilate's men.[44]

However, as I have also noted, contrasts allow comparisons, and such doublings begs investigation of likeness as well as difference. The Judas Ballad ultimately asks how Peter is *like* Judas: in its final couplet, Jesus points out that Peter, for all his boasted loyalty, will also forsake him (35–36). The biblical allusions to the Temptation and to Samson and Delilah beg further: How is the sister like the devil who tempts Jesus? How is the sister's threatened stoning like the stones the devil uses to challenge Jesus? How is Judas like Jesus on the mountain? How is Peter, the rock on which the church is built, like the rock on which the sister's temptation happens? Use of biblical allusions to provoke such questions of likeness, and the intertextual knowledge they imply, in fact mark the poem's genre: such things are the common stock of Latin liturgical parodies from the same century. A typical parodic cento, for instance, inverts biblical passages as a form of intellectual and scriptural inquiry: "If thy enemy be hungry, give him iron and stones; if he thirsts, give him stones to drink," instead of "If your enemy hungers, put before him *bread*, and if he thirsts, give him *water* to drink" (Prov. 25:21, emphasis mine).[45] The parodic humor here depends on allusions that upset expectations and both require and prompt deep familiarity with scripture and typological exegesis.

The Judas Ballad, then, is a vernacular parody with a Jewess at its center. As Martha Bayless has defined it, medieval parody works either by "imitating and distorting the distinguishing characteristics of literary genres, styles, authors, or specific texts (*textual parody*)" or by "imitating . . . literary genres, styles, authors, or texts while in addition satirizing or focusing on nonliterary customs, events, or persons (*social parody*)."[46] In the Judas Ballad, the refrains, rhyming couplets, and scriptural allusions mark a textual parody of both secular songs and scriptural verses, a parodic mode that privileges "inversion and substitution of one tone for another."[47] This poet, for instance, makes the

Betrayal of Christ absurd by retelling it as a ballad about a hapless believer mugged by his sister while trying to purchase food at the marketplace. His scriptural allusions and typological substitutions, at the same time, upset exegetical expectations, a technique that Bayless argues more likely reifies standard typological doubles than produces anything "subversive or destabilizing."[48] The poet slips into social parody, however, when he adds a thieving Jewess near an urban marketplace.

To insert a previously unknown Jewess as centrally, secretly, and (once again) responsible for the fall of man is also to make the salvation of the world (once again) dependent on a Jewish woman's body. The sister's position in the poem, thus, *does* rely on upset scriptural and narrative expectations (i.e., on textual parody), but it relies equally on a specifically English understanding of Jewish women's cultural roles and involvement in Christian-Jewish financial transactions. The sister's theft of Judas's coins, that is, fits the poem's thirteenth-century social context, allows play with biblical allusion and inversion, *and* depicts a familiar English type of Jewess, one we have now seen again and again in Anglo-Christian literature. She appears without the notice of anyone but Judas, bracketed between Jesus's command that Judas go into the wide streets and the derisive gaze of all the Jews of Jerusalem who see only the aftermath. Her name, her origins, her motivations, and her afterlife are unknowable, even as she evokes an English bureaucratic understanding of Jewish women's positions within Jewish families and businesses. She is a polemical critique of Anglo-Jewish women financiers, traders, and alleged coin clippers—present in the urban centers of England at the time the Judas Ballad was copied—and, like caricatures of her male counterparts, she stands for the "Jewish" greed long associated with Judas. She intrudes on the story of Jesus's betrayal and transforms its narrative in the quiet of sleep. There is no conversion, no pliancy, no maternity here. This type of Jewess's narrative and didactic function, imagined through brief and intimate encounters, lies in her ambiguity and semantic excess.

The Myth of the Medieval Jewish Seductress

La norriz maluré of the Anglo-French "Hugo de Lincolnia" deserves further attention now, for she is a part of the history of *la juive fatale*, or the Jewess as femme fatale. The medieval Jewish seductress has become a scholarly commonplace: in Lipton's assessment, the Jewess "as seductive femme fatale" is one of three key types of medieval literary Jewess;[49] for Bale, late medieval literature yields eroticized "representations of the Jewish daughter" as "a fallen, sexy, secret and yet open body";[50] for Efraim Sicher, "the gendered difference of the Jew was . . . perceived in sexualized images of evil and promiscuity";[51] and Matthew Mesley lists "beautiful or exotic seductresses" first in his summary of how Jewish women appear in medieval anti-Jewish texts.[52] When the unnamed Jew who introduces *la norriz maluré* into "Hugo de Lincolnia" calls her "une femme que jo ai, privé" (a woman whom I have, a close friend [or intimate]) (172), the poem's most recent editor suggests a "hint at" the notion that such women might "engage in sexual relations with their employers."[53] Implications of a link between the ambiguous *noris*, her complicity in Hugh's murder, and the dangerous and alluring Jewess of the later English ballads known as "Sir Hugh" or the "Jew's Daughter" (Child Ballad no. 155), further, warrant full consideration of the Jewish seductress type.

Sources that engage the Hugh of Lincoln story have special importance to scholars of English literature. Chaucer famously had his Prioress—with her love of dogs, nasal Anglo-French, and self-infantalization—conclude her tale of a schoolboy killed by Jews with an apostrophe to "yonge Hugh of Lyncoln, slayn also / With cursed Jewes, as it is notable, / For it is but a litel while ago" (young Hugh of Lincoln, also killed / by damned Jews, which is worth mentioning / Because it was not so long ago).[54] Many scholars, in turn, have rightly linked Chaucer's use of Hugh of Lincoln to thirteenth-century accounts of his murder, including "Hugo de Lincolnia," most persuasively because the punishment Chaucer imposes on the Prioress's Jews (they are dragged behind wild horses and hanged) aligns them with the punishment that Lincoln Jews face in the Anglo-French ballad and in contemporary chronicle accounts of the case.[55] At the same time, the habit of reading "The Prioress's Tale" with the thirteenth-century ballad, and, as a consequence, with later ballads that may seem to adapt its story, has inflated the presence and importance of the medieval Jewish seductress—a figure few medieval English readers would have recognized. While the unmarked Jewess certainly could be sexualized in medieval Anglo-Christian literature, narratives in which a sexualized Jewess appear are more obviously entangled with the subtypes already discussed above than with later femme fatales.

As I have explained elsewhere,[56] the tale that Chaucer's Prioress tells is first and foremost a Miracle of the Virgin. In particular, it adapts the "Child Slain by Jews" story, discussed in previous chapters, and is influenced by "The Jewish Boy" as well. Chaucer's explicit connection of his Marian miracle with the historical Lincoln case is unique and purposeful: in addition to the Prioress's concluding apostrophe to Hugh, her punishment of the Jews recalls the actual execution of nineteen Lincoln Jews convicted of the 1255 murder, with an execution method that denotes treason.[57] As Sicher puts it, Chaucer thus "returns us to the historical status" of Jews " before expulsion."[58] He puts an English cap on a Marian miracle that he initially sets vaguely in "Asye, in a greet citee" and thereby interrogates the genre's anti-Jewishness and English responses in both literary and devotional modes.[59] Beyond this, however, any suggestion that the thirteenth-century sources provide a direct link to "The Prioress's Tale" is almost certainly false, and imputed connections, through mention of the Anglo-French ballad and iterations of the later "Sir Hugh" or "Jew's Daughter" ballad, are problematic.

The later ballads are Scottish in origin. In the earliest variants, a Jew's daughter kills young Hugh from "Linkim" or "Mirry-land" or "Merry-land Toune" after he plays ball with friends near her house. In the two earliest variants, the Jewess either comes out to invite Hugh in for a meal or he kicks a ball into her yard and must enter her home to retrieve it. In written form, the ballad emerges only in the second half of the eighteenth century, and there is no evidence for significantly earlier dates. D'Blossiers Tovey discusses the Hugh of Lincoln case at some length in his *Anglia Judaica* (1738)—including note of contemporary scholarship, related discoveries around the shrine, and cultural legacies in Lincoln and beyond—but he does not mention the ballads.[60] The earliest variant appears in Thomas Percy's *Reliques of Ancient English Poetry* (1765), where it is titled "The Jew's Daughter, a Scottish Ballad" and appears among "Ancient Songs." Percy claims that he had it "Printed from a MS. copy sent from Scotland."[61] In this version, the Jew's daughter uses an apple to lure Hugh, stabs him and dresses him like a pig, and then drops him into a well:

> Than out and cam the Jewis dochter,
> Said, Will ye cum in and dine?
> I winnae cum in, I cannae cum in,
> Without my play-feres nine.
>
> Scho powd an apple reid and white
> To intice the zong thing in:
> Scho powd an apple white and reid,
> And that the sweit bairne did win.
>
> And scho has taine out a little pen-knife,
> And low down by the gair [grass],

Scho has twin'd the zong thing and his life;
A word he nevir spak mair.

And out and cam the thick thick bluid,
And out and cam the thin;
And out and cam the bonny herts bluid;
Thair was nae life left in.

Scho laid him on a dressing borde,
And drest him like a swine,
And laughing said, Gae nou and play
With zour sweit play-feres nine.

Scho rowd him in a cake of lead,
Bade him lie stil and sleip.
Scho cast him in a deip draw-well,
Was fifty fadom deip.[62]

The well-known Percy Folio (BL MS Additional 27879), which contains many of the handwritten sources of Percy's *Reliques* and includes Middle English texts that he transcribed in the seventeenth century, *does not* contain this ballad. There is no reason to believe that Percy did not, as he claims, have a Scottish exemplar of unknown origin.

The earliest manuscript variant was recorded by David Herd in preparation for the printing of his *Ancient and Modern Scottish Songs, Heroic Ballads, Etc* (1776), in what is now BL MS Additional 22311. Herd called it "Sir Hugh" and labeled it "An old Ballad." He copied it just before another short song "wrote by Mr James Kerr of Kildrummy" (fol. 109r). In Herd's version, Hugh calls for the Jewess to throw back his ball, but she refuses unless he will enter her home. Again, she lures him with an apple, and the plot progresses similarly to the Percy variant:

H[e] keppit the Ba than wi his foot
And catch'd it wi his knee
And even in at the Jews window
He gart the bonny Ba flee

Cast out the Ba to me fair maid
Cast out the Ba to me

Ah never a bit of it she says
Till ye come up to me

Come up sweet Hugh come up dear Hugh
Come up and get the Ba
I winna come I mayna come
Without my bonny Boys a'

Come up sweet Hugh come up dear Hugh
Come up and speak to me
I mayna come up I winna come up
Without my bonny Boys three.

She's tain her to the Jews Garden
Where the grass grew lang & green
She's pu'd an apple reid & white
To wyle the bonny Boy in

She's wyl'd him in thro' ae Chamber
She's wyl'd him in thro' twa
She's wyl'd him till hir ain Chamber
The Flower out our them a'

She's laid him on a dressin board
Whare she did often dine
She stack a pen knife to his heart
And dress'd him like a swine

She row'd [him] in a Cake of Lead
Bad him lie still and sleep
She threw him i the Jews draw well
Twas fifty fathom deep.[63]

While these representations of a Jewish daughter do not clearly resonate with
any medieval Anglo-Christian text, several elements do recall the stories I have
examined in these chapters. The young boys playing ball, for instance, echo the
opening of most versions of "The Jewish Boy." The use of an apple as a lure and
cannibalistic implications managed through pig imagery echo the *Passion of*

Adam of Bristol. The disposal of the body in a deep draw well (the "cake of lead" weights the body and allows plumbing of depths) echoes the wet nurse's actions in "Hugo de Lincolnia" and the ambiguous woman in Getty 101's Robert of Bury illustrations.

None of these, however, is the echo that has concerned modern scholars. Lipton, for example, assigns the "murderous siren of *The Ballad of Sir Hugh, or, the Jew's Daughter*" to the category of "Jewesses who haunted the medieval Christian literary imagination" and claims that "Chaucer's 'Prioress's Tale' draws in part from this ballad but omits the villainous Jewess."[64] In her notes, she adds that the eighteenth-century ballads date "back to at least 1259,"[65] a claim that must either cite Matthew Paris's *Chronica majora* account of the 1255 Lincoln case or gesture to "Hugo de Lincolnia," written between 1255 and 1272.[66] Chaucer, of course, cannot have omitted a Jewess from a Scottish ballad tradition that appeared three centuries after his death, and it is unlikely that he knew "Hugo de Lincolnia,"[67] but Lipton's cited source is the great ballad scholar Francis James Child, who also mentions the thirteenth-century text in his account of the eighteenth-century ballads' history (Child no. 155A–E). When Sicher urges "pausing on the Middle Ages to ponder why the Jew's Daughter is invested with such sensuality," he likewise elides the thirteenth-century materials with the later ballad tradition by starting with "the first variant . . . found in the [*sic*] 'Sir Hugh, or the Jew's Daughter,' associated with the blood libel of Hugh of Lincoln (1255)" and cites the "Anglo-Norman French version."[68] Though he grants that there are "no extant medieval antecedents to the well-known eighteenth-century Scottish version," and that neither the Anglo-French poem nor contemporary chronicle accounts mention a Jew's daughter, he nonetheless focuses discussion of medieval English literature on his analysis of the later ballad, and, like Lipton, remarks that the Jewess is "missing from" Chaucer's "Prioress's Tale."[69] Bale, though he clarifies that the Scottish ballad tradition is "separate and later," also claims that the "association between the Jewish daughter and erotic carnality was evidently well established by the later Middle Ages" and offers as evidence the "range of ballads associated with the medieval cult of Little Hugh of Lincoln."[70]

Modern scholars, however, can be forgiven for having difficulty with the chronology. The medieval Jewess, as I have argued, is designed to hold all or no solutions, and the challenge of finding her *difference* has hampered modern assessments. Any search for gendered difference in line with medieval caricatures of Jewish men's carnality necessitates backreadings. Variants of the "Sir Hugh" or "Jew's Daughter" ballad, moreover, were associated with the Hugh of Lincoln case and Chaucer from the moment of their first appearance in print. Percy argued in his *Reliques* that the ballad he printed was

> founded upon the supposed practice of the Jews in crucifying or otherwise murthering Christian children, . . . [the] ballad is probably built upon some Italian Legend [Percy took "Mirry-land" to be a corruption of "Milan"], and bears a great resemblance to the Prior-esse's Tale in Chaucer: the poet seems also to have had an eye to the known story of HUGH OF LINCOLN, a child said to have been there murthered by the Jews in the reign of Henry III. The conclusion of this ballad appears to be wanting: what is probably contained may be seen in Chaucer.[71]

By 1857, when Child published five variants, he had explored all key medieval texts associated with Hugh of Lincoln, including "Hugo de Lincolnia" (of which Tovey, Percy, and Herd were apparently ignorant). Child did consider the Anglo-French poem to be an early English ballad, but he did *not* see it as a pre-cursor to the later tradition; the relationship, in his view, was one of overlapping topic.[72] Nonetheless, he titled his 1857 variants "Hugh of Lincoln" and provided an overview of the historical case by way of English literary traditions: "The ex-quisite tale which Chaucer has put into the mouth of the Prioress," he over-stated, "exhibits nearly the same incidents as the . . . [Anglo-French] ballad."[73] These suggestions of firm connection between the thirteenth-century poem and the later ballads have resulted in serious errors.

In all of the earliest iterations of the later ballad—by 1882, Child had catalogued eighteen—the young Jewess murders Hugh by sticking him with a knife, like a pig, and throwing him into a well, while Hugh's mother laments and searches for him like so many mothers of medieval boy-martyr tales.[74] Nonetheless, while general resemblance to medieval Anglo-Christian narra-tives exists in bare plot points, readings that use these to search for prototypes of a Jewess seductress err significantly, particularly if they emphasize canni-balistic tropes. The nineteenth-century edition of "Hugo de Lincolnia" by Francisque Michel—until recently the only one available—erroneously sug-gested that the thirteenth-century poet had made the Lincoln Jews cannibals, and this notion has persisted even into twenty-first-century scholarly transla-tions of the poem.[75] In the unique manuscript copy of the poem (Paris, Bib-liothèque national de France MS fr. 902), at the description of Hugh's torture, the scribe writes, "Agim le iu son kniuet prent . . . / E puis son quer en deus

defent / Dunques gurristrent les malueis gent" (fol. 135vb, 124–27), using the
unattested plural verb form *gurristrent* for the Jews' actions. With no explanation, Michel amended "Dunques gurristrent" to "Dont goûtèrent," so that
the lines mean "Hagin the Jew grasps his knife, . . . / And then he cleaves in
two [Hugh's] heart, / Of which the evil people tasted." As Roger Dahood has
proven, however, *gurristrent* is simply a scribal error for "*surristrent*, the per-
fect third plural of *surrire* (= *sorire*), 'to smile'"[76]—a typical sort of error,
where the scribe has either anticipated the word *gent* or miscopied a two-
compartment *s* in his exemplar. Dahood, quite rightly, is emphatic about the
consequences: the Jewish cannibalism long associated with the Anglo-French
ballad "springs neither from the anti-Semitism of the thirteenth-century author nor the carelessness of the medieval scribe but from the mistaken gloss of
the nineteenth-century editor. Flawed editing can lead to bad history, and
bad history exhibits a remarkable staying power."[77] And this error matters for
the story of the Jewish seductress type because, for the nineteenth-century
ballad anthologizers who were citing Michel's edition, the Jew's daughter
could be linked to the thirteenth-century poem through the cannibalistic implications of a Jewess inviting a boy to dine and then sticking and dressing
him like a pig.

The imputed cannibalism of the Jewish daughter—a trope that in any case
might have been more persuasively linked to the Jewish mothers discussed in
the previous chapter—has therefore played a role in establishing stronger connections between "Hugo de Lincolnia" and later English ballads than are war-
ranted. The Jewess of "Sir Hugh" or the "Jew's Daughter" is not a recognizable
medieval figure. Like the erroneous nineteenth-century emendation of the
thirteenth-century ballad, rather, she is a late accretion informed by postmedieval stereotypes. Chaucer did not distinguish himself by omitting the alluring
young Jewess from "The Prioress's Tale" because there was no such Jewess to
omit. If we want to examine the erotic and cannibalistic undertones of the later
ballads in relation to medieval English texts, then, we should not start with
Hugh of Lincoln or Chaucer's Miracle of the Virgin, as scholars since Percy
have done. Instead, we should ask how or why such a figure, as a late corruption
of medieval English Jewess types, could have developed at all. As Betrand Bronson concludes, "The [later] ballad-makers certainly worked at considerable remove from any dependence on chronicle or pious legend, and seem to have kept
nothing more than the nucleus: that Hugh of Lincoln was murdered by a Jew,
thrown into a well, sought by his mother, and discovered."[78] The Jewish seductress is not part of the medieval nucleus.

To the extent that the Jewess of "Sir Hugh" or the "Jew's Daughter" *does* evolve from medieval chronicles or pious legends, she is more clearly in line with the Jewish mother of the *Passion of Adam of Bristol*, who feeds Adam apples, uses a small bread knife to cut off his lips, and occasions a similar culinary vocabulary around the martyred boy, who is a "porcellum" (piglet) and "gallina crassa" (fat chicken) (Cluse 307 and 318).[79] She may also show traces of the mother(s) at the siege of Jerusalem, where cannibalism is related to eucharistic lessons, Marian likeness, prophecy, and supersession. A variant of "Sir Hugh" printed in 1806, in fact, makes this connection by specifying that Hugh's body was dropped into *"Our Lady's* deep draw-well."[80] Like many medieval versions of "The Jewish Boy" too, the later ballads begin with young boys playing together, likely because Matthew Paris's *Chronica majora* account of the Lincoln case had evoked and inverted the popular "Jewish Boy" tale by noting that Hugh was last seen "ludentem cum pueris Judæorum sibi coætaneis" (playing with Jewish boys of his own age).[81] Because the Jew's daughter throws Hugh's body into a well, we may also associate the story of Robert of Bury with her, along with others that feature an ambiguous woman who throws a boy's body into a well. These women *are* likely ancestors of the later ballads' Jew's daughter, but *not* because they were sexualized or understood primarily as temptresses. Rather, such figures reappear in anti-Jewish texts through the centuries because they blur the boundaries between Christian and Jew.

Prototypes of the Jewish seductress are more clearly visible in fifteenth-century exempla about Christian men who fall in love with Jewish daughters. Those that appear in the *Alphabet of Tales* and *Jacob's Well*, both dependent on the German Cistercian Caesarius of Heisterbach's thirteenth-century *Dialogus miraculorum*, have been used to discuss the seductress type more fruitfully.[82] But even in these cases the Jewess is not a femme fatale. These absurd narratives, rather, feature Jewish daughters as the love interests of canons or clerics in bumbling and foolish scenarios. The only one that Caesarius sets in England, for instance, casts a besotted canon, a close relative of a bishop, as a man who ignores his clerical responsibilities for his lover, a Jewish woman who has acquiesced to the canon's desires only in response to his dogged insistence. The Jewess affirms Christian fantasies of unnatural blood flow in Jews: she tells her lover that her father (and all Jews) must rest every year on Good Friday because of their bleeding, and she suggests that they may thus avoid her father by consummating their relationship at that time. But the plan leads to a furious encounter with the Jewish father, who finds the lovers together the next morning. As a result, the father and his coreligionists go to the local church to complain on the next day. The guilty canon is assisting the bishop at Mass, and, when he sees the Jews approaching, he quickly prays for forgiveness, miraculously silencing the Jews and therefore providing himself with enough time to confess his sins to the bishop after Mass. The bishop advises that he marry the Jewess, if she will receive baptism, and later both the canon and his once-Jewish wife take monastic vows. The lesson, says Caesarius, is the usefulness of contrition. In other words, Caesarius's tale focuses on the violation of observance of Good Friday and clerical duties related to assisting at Mass.

The English-language translation of this exemplum in *Jacob's Well* comprises a fairly accurate translation of Caesarius, though it omits his commentary on contrition, but the *Alphabet of Tales* version specifies that the events took place in Lincoln and treats clerical transgressions more emphatically.[83] The Jewish father chastises the canon for his lack of observance: "O! þou fals Christen man! what duse þou here in syn þis day? Whar is þi faith?" (Oh, you false Christian! what are you doing here engaging in sin on *this* day? Where is your faith?).[84] Where Caesarius emphasizes the canon's youthfulness and mentions only his reading of the epistle during Easter Mass, the Englisher elaborates: "he went home & happend þat day, þat is to say Pasch-even, to be assigned to þe bisshopp to be his dekyn in serves tyme & rede þe pistle" (he went home and happened that day, which was Easter evening, to be assigned to the bishop, to be his deacon during the service and read the epistle). The English version, unlike Caesarius, further specifies that the canon did not make confession before the Mass and thus celebrates unshriven of not just the one sin but all, and it is less concerned with the Jewess: the canon does not marry her and instead becomes a Cistercian monk immediately after his confession. While the Jewess does convert and take orders, a nondescript "they" imposes this fate on her: "þai garte cristen þis damsell, & made hur a non of þe same ordur" (they made this young woman a Christian and made her a nun of the same order). The Jewess is assigned her sameness with the Christian canon not by a bishop or through her own will but by an Anglo-Christian populace who forces the synchronicity.

One other tale of a sexualized Jewish daughter in an English setting appears in the *Alphabet of Tales*. This time, a clerk impregnates a Jewess and, fearing the consequent wrath of her parents, uses a reed straw to pipe his voice into the Jewish home and announce that their daughter is pregnant with the Messiah. Since the Jewish parents believe their daughter is a virgin, they rejoice at this prophecy and spread the news. When other Jews come to celebrate the Messiah's birth, however, the young Jewess gives birth to a daughter. Enraged, one of the assembled Jews "tuke þis childe be þe legg & threw it agayn þe wall & killid it, etc" (took this infant by the leg and threw it against the wall and killed it, etc.).[85] In Caesarius's template, which the *Alphabet* author mainly follows, the clerk is the seducer of the Jewess; the novice monk who serves as Caesarius's interlocutor in the *Dialogus* laments that she was "ab homine fideli seducta ac corrupta" (seduced and ruined by a man of [our] faith) when she might have been converted.[86] As Bale points out, this tale also sets the pregnant Jewess as a mirror of the Virgin Mary.[87] The dishonest clerk acts as a Gabriel in parody of the Annunciation, while the Marian figure does as her mock Gabriel commands, and the infant Jewess—doomed by genitals that are not what a Messiah's should be—is violently destroyed by a male Jew. The murder "makes sense within medieval ontologies of ritual murder, blood sacrifice, [and] violence against the Christ child,"[88] and it may allude to the final verse of Psalm 137 (Vulgate 136:9): "Blessed be he that shall take and dash thy little ones against the rock." The English text's "etc"—the angry Jew "killid it, etc"—is doing a lot of work in this regard. However, within an ontology of ritual murder, the infant Jewess also becomes *like* a Christ-child, and her sacrifice thus turns the Annunciation parody back on itself: with a conclusion that reifies the violent difference of the Jewish male against an innocent Christ figure, the Jewish daughter—initially a parody of the Virgin Mary—becomes *like* Mary again. With the allusion to Psalm 137, moreover, wherein exiled Israel sings of postexile vengeance against Babylon, the infant Jewess becomes both an allegorical representation of Babylon (a metonym for temptation) *and* a figure through which Christian readers can imagine Jews as both oppressor and oppressed.

Indeed, this messianic story—which the *Alphabet of Tales* author moves from Worms to London—concerns a Jewish femininity that goes far beyond any focus on the sexualized Jewish daughter. The narrative includes three generations of Jewish women: a wife, her pregnant daughter, and finally a newborn. In both the Englished version and Caesarius's Latin, the role of the wife is to dispute the deceitful clerk's prophecy. In both versions she speaks a single word in response to her husband's inquiry about whether she hears the "divine" voice: "No."[89] Her resistance forces the clerk to repeat his deception and command that the daughter go along with his plan, which she does until her newborn daughter is murdered. This multigenerational triad thus responds to and enacts masculine fantasies about both women *and* Jews—at the hands of both Christian *and* Jewish men—and sexuality and (female) seduction are not primary in these fantasies. Though Bale suggests that the feelings of the Jewish daughter are "not commented on" because "her sexual appetite is a given,"[90] this seems to me only a given of modern scholarship. The Jewesses of this exemplum, rather, do double duty as Christians and Jews: they hear *and* do not hear the Annunciation, they parody the Virgin Mary *and* become her, they are not the Messiah *and* they suffer like Christ, they are the oppressors *and* the oppressed in exile, while their sex and sexuality signify only through male deceit, violence, and difference. Carefully positioned as figures of *simul*taneity, the Jewesses affirm the alterity of only the male Jews in this tale. By contrast, readers or hearers must continuously remember, as *Piers Plowman* reminds us, that even "Jesu Crist on a Jewes doghter lighte" (Jesus Christ alighted in a Jew's daughter).[91]

Perhaps the Jewish seductress or femme fatale type can be traced, instead, to thirteenth-century English historiography? Recall that worries about miscegenation were codified by Lateran IV and statutes against Christian women working in Jewish homes appeared in England as early as 1222—and that these statutes were part of a larger state concern with the relative invisibility and malleability of Jewish women, as outlined in previous chapters.[92] Relationships between Jewish women and Christian men could and did occur, and there are two known cases of the conversion of Christian men who married Jewish women: one in 1222 from Oxford and one in 1275 from London (these two have often been wrongly conflated[93]). The 1222 case involved an unnamed Oxford deacon and is still most ably and thoroughly discussed by Frederick Maitland,[94] while the 1275 case involved a Dominican friar and Hebraist called Robert of Reading. According to the *Chronicle of Bury St Edmunds*, and several other chronicle accounts of the same period, the 1275 case happened as follows:

> Londoniis quidam de ordine Predicatorum dictus frater Robertus de Redingge, predicator optimus linguaque Hebrea eruditissimus apostavit et ad Iudaismum convolavit atque Iudæam ducens uxorem se circumcidi atque Aggeum fecit nominari. Quem accercitum et contra legem Christianam audacter et publice disserentem rex archiepiscopo commendavit Cantuariensi.[95]

> At London a certain member of the Order of Preachers [i.e., Dominicans], Brother Robert of Reading by name, a most skillful preacher and extremely learned in the Hebrew language, apostatized and flew headlong into Judaism, and, taking a Jewess as a wife, had himself circumcised and named Haggai. He repeatedly spoke boldly and publicly against Christian law, and the king delivered him to the Archbishop of Canterbury.

The archbishop of Canterbury in this case is the same man who devised the punishment (*penitencia*) of the Jewish friar Sampson son of Samuel of Northampton—the Dominican Robert Kilwardby—and the cases are oddly similar.[96] There is no evidence of Haggai's fate after he was handed over to Kilwardby, however, and it is not clear that Haggai's conversion or arrest was related to his marriage. If it was, the chronicler is not much interested; he subordinates the Jewish wife and does not imply that the conversion was a result of the relationship. Instead, Haggai's misuse of his considerable oratory and linguistic skills is the focus. As Robert Stacey has put it, if in 1222 "a Christian deacon converted to Judaism . . . [for] the beauty of his Jewish lover," in 1275 Haggai "was seduced into apostasy by his study of the Hebrew language."[97]

But the 1222 case is more complicated as well. Historiographical accounts of it have been cited, most recently by Lipton, as precocious manifestations of the Jewish seductress type, with a focus on the deacon's grisly death: he was defrocked and burned alive outside the meeting of the Provincial Council of Canterbury at Oxford, and almost all thirteenth-century iterations connect his marriage to and love of a Jewess to this fate. Lipton cites the deacon's story as one of "numerous contemporary tales of dangerously beautiful Jewish women who through deceit and seduction lure Christians to their ruin"[98]—though, as should be clear by now, such tales, by and large, are not found in England. Whether the deacon's story even fits the category is a real question. It was repeated in numerous thirteenth-century texts: in four contemporary chronicles (the *Annals of Waverly Abbey*, the *Dunstable Annals*, the *Annals of the Abbey of Coggeshall*, and the *Memoriale* of Walter of Coventry), then by Matthew Paris several decades after the fact, then by Thomas of Wykes near the end of the thirteenth century, and it was cited by Henry de Bracton.[99] In most of these, the deacon's conversion is connected to his wife only in the barest terms: he apostatized "for a Jewess" (Bracton); he married a Jewess and then "was degraded and afterwards burnt" (Waverly); he converted "for the love of a Jewess" (Dunstable, Coggeshall, Thomas of Wykes). Walter of Conventry's account, written within five years of the event, mentions neither the marriage nor the Jewess. None mentions the Jewish woman's beauty or deceitfulness, nor any active role she plays in the events that resulted in her husband's death. The case *was* polemically and sensationally exaggerated by Thomas Wykes, who cast the deacon as a host desecrator who used his position to steal the host, but even Wykes says little of the woman.

Only Matthew Paris, who mentions the Oxford deacon in his *Chronica majora* and then more elaborately in his *Historia Anglorum*, provides a characterization of the Jewess that arguably fits Lipton's suggestion that Jewish seductress types find an early model in the Oxford deacon's wife. Matthew—hardly a historian when it comes to Anglo-Jewish history—gives the Jewess a voice, casts her as a temptress, imagines that the affair included the ritual murder of a Christian boy, and notes that the woman easily escaped the Oxford sheriff who executed her husband. Here is Matthew's extended account, from the *Historia Anglorum*:

> Quidam diaconus Anglicus quandam Judæam illicito amore dilexerat, et ejusdem amplexus ardenter postulavit. Cui illa, "Faciam quod hortaris, si apostata factus circumcidaris, et Judaismo fideliter adhæreas." Quod cum ipse quicquid mulier hortabatur complevisset, potitus est amore illicito. Quod cum diu celari non posset, nunciatum est archiepiscopo Cantuariensi Stephano, ant quem cum constanter et graviter accusaretur et convinceretur super hiis omnibus, confessus est se palam interfuisse cuidam sacrificio, quod Judæi fecerant de puero quodam crucifixo . . . Et ejectum ex ecclesia, statim Falcasius, qui semper pronus fuit ad effundendum sanguinem, arripuit [e]um. . . . Et ducens raptim in loco secreto extra villam, decollavit eum. . . . Judæa autem clanculo evasit, unde Falco doluit dicens, "Doleo, quod iste solus descendit ad inferos."[100]

> A certain English deacon loved a certain Jewess with unlawful love, and he ardently desired her embrace. "I will do what you urge," she said, "if you, having apostatized, will be circumcised and adhere faithfully to Judaism." When he had done what the woman urged, he seized her unlawful love. When this could no longer be hidden, it was reported to Stephen [Langton], Archbishop of Canterbury, before whom he was accused resolutely and solemnly, and he was convicted in all these matters; he confessed that he had openly participated in a certain sacrifice that the Jews made of a certain crucified boy. . . . And when he had been cast out of the church, Fawkes [the Oxford sheriff], who was always inclined to spill blood, grabbed him . . . and dragged him quickly to a secret place outside the city and decapitated him. . . . The Jewess, however, secretly escaped, which grieved Fawkes, who said, "I lament that this man descends to hell alone."

The incidentals of this passage in part convinced Maitland that the Oxford deacon, appropriately defrocked after his conversion, was executed *not* by any order of the Provincial Council, nor for violations of religious statutes related to interactions with Jews or a Jewish woman, but rather without writ or trial by the Oxford sheriff Fawkes de Breauté, who had a contemporary reputation for violence and rash behavior.[101] In other words, Matthew Paris alone fantasized that a Jewess actively seduced a deacon, persuaded him to convert and take part in a ritual murder, and then made a wily escape. In a process of fictionalization, influenced no doubt by the other anti-Jewish tales he circulated, Matthew turned an oft-repeated story into a viciously polemical one.

It is worth noting that it would not have been difficult for a Jewish woman and a deacon to interact in thirteenth-century Oxford: several cases document such interactions, including through the pledging of scholars' books, debt bonds between Jewish women and religious institutions, and the rental of property.[102] Further, it is not unlikely that such interactions raised the ire of some members of monastic, ecclesiastical, and (related) scholarly communities. Matthew's fantasy, however, is about what goes on in the domestic spaces of Jewish Oxford, and his inclusion of a ritual murder libel and a Jewess's escape coincides with other tales we have seen from the same century. It is these characterizations of the Jewess that had greatest currency in the English Middle Ages. We see the same deception and escape with the wet nurse of "Hugo de Lincolnia," the sister of the *Passion of Adam of Bristol*, and the sister of the Judas Ballad, and a proleptic echo in Archbishop Peckham's complaint that he cannot arrest his predominantly female London apostates because of "the evasions of these false Christians."[103] The medieval Jewish seductress, however, is the singular contribution of Matthew Paris. The rest of his story—of an unnamed Anglo-Jewess who could interact with Christians but also disappear or blend in well enough to evade detection or punishment—is the standard stuff of medieval English representations of Jewish women.

One final addition to the English evidence of a medieval Jewish seductress type may be considered here. In BL MS Royal 8 A VI—a late thirteenth-century Latin miscellany full of scholarly, theological, scientific, and preaching materials intended for clerical use—an English scribe records a previously unedited exemplum, set in France, about a priest who loved a Jewess. The two have a sexual relationship that affects observance of their respective religious holidays, and the priest's body then manifests a strange miracle as he celebrates Mass:

Fuit sacerdos quidam in partibus gallie: diligens insano amore
quandam iudeam. quam sepe cognouerat. vnde in quodam festo die

iudeorum cum vellet accedere ad eam. et commisceri ei. Ipsa primo
pro sua festiuitate contradixit. at ille nichilominus instabat. quae
tandiu uicta est. . . . at illa in paschali die accessit ad sacerdotem
dicens. volo ut commiscearis mihi in tuo festo. sicut fregi meum
festum pro te. At ille dicebat se non posse. quia debebat tunc parrochianis suis celebrare. et illa propius accessit. et tandiu hinc et inde
palpauit quod ille uictus est. qui prius intratus ecclesias suas assumpsit indumenta sacerdotalia. Illa non uideri cupiens quid sacerdos
faceret retro hostium omnia prospexit. Sacerdos primo induit
supplicium. quod antequam induissus album erat. et tunc super eum
factum est nigrius carbone. post accepit albam. et statim in corpore
eius facta est nigerrima. et sic accidit omnibus que induit. preter altare
et corporalia. et ea que fuerunt super eucaristiam. et ipse totus
nigerrimus apparuit. Quibus omnibus visis. ipsa conuersa statim . . .
et currit cum lacrimis festinans baptizari ab illo. qui uidens eius
uisitationem et predicationem. et ipse conuersus est penitens. vnde
statim nigredo a uestibus et a corpore aufugit.[104]

There was a certain priest in France who loved a certain Jewess with a
mad desire. He often knew her. Accordingly, when he wanted to go to
her on a certain Jewish feast day and have intercourse with her, she
objected on account of her holiday. But he nonetheless insisted.
Eventually she was defeated. . . . But she approached the priest on
Easter, saying, "I want you to have intercourse with me on your feast
day, just as I broke my holiday for you." But he told himself it was not
possible, for he was supposed to be celebrating with his parishioners
then. And she approached nearer, and she stroked him here and there,
so that eventually he was defeated. Before he entered his churches, he
picked up his priestly vestments. Not wanting to be seen, she watched
everything the priest did from behind a door. First, the priest put on
the surplice that before it was donned was white, and then on him
became blacker than coal. Next, he picked up the alb, and immediately on his body it became even blacker. And thus it happened with
everything that he put on (with the exception of the altar and
corporals and things that covered the Eucharist), and he himself
appeared very black all over. When she saw these things, this woman
immediately converted . . . and ran forward in tears, rushing to be
baptized by him. He, seeing her visitation and teaching, repenting,

was himself also converted. Accordingly, the blackness immediately
fled from his vestments and from his body.

This, however, is not a story of a Jewish femme fatale. The careful balance between the Jewess and the priest—they are already in a relationship, he pressures
her on a holiday and is conquered, she pressures him on a holiday and is
conquered—and the incidental way in which it becomes clear that the Jewess is
present as her lover celebrates Easter Mass tell us that the exemplum's lessons
are not about a Jewish threat. The priest is madly in love with the Jewess, and he
acts first; her actions answer his original transgressions—my holiday for your
holiday, my insistence for your insistence—and she does little but match him in
a game that he started. The miraculous punishment of the priest punishes his
transgression of his priestly duties, not the fact that those transgressions were
committed with a Jewess. From a Christian perspective, indeed, the Jewess has
a tremendous amout of positive rhetorical power: the Christian lesson is provided by her "uisitationem et predicationem"—that is, her "visitation," a word
most often used to describe the Virgin Mary's meeting with John the Baptist's
mother Elizabeth in Luke 1:39–56, and her teaching or preaching—and she is
not punished at all. Rather, she is the beneficiary of her own desire to remain
invisible ("illa, non uideri cupiens") and thus to occupy public and private
Christian space. In the end it becomes clear that she is with her priest in his
church as he celebrates because she witnesses the blackening of his body and
vestments at the altar; she is able to burst forward to become a Christian because
she is already amid the Christians. This outcome depends entirely on the Jewess's ability to blend in, the *only* ability she has in pointed opposition to her
lover, who, at the altar, is wholly unable to do so.

A racialized miracle, the Royal 8 A VI tale may also participate in what Irven Resnick has called the "primitive cultural anthropology" of some medieval
medical and scientific materials engaged in anti-Judaism. The notion that
women could affect the color or size of bodies through force of imagination
during sexual intercourse did hold some sway: Resnick cites the thirteenth-
century theologian Albert the Great's readings of Aristotle's *On Animals*, for
instance, where Albert tells how a "woman, whom Avicenna described, imagining the shape of a demon or a dwarf (or, according to others, an Ethiopian), bore
children resembling them, because her own power succumbed at the moment of
conception owing to the violent imagination, and the natural power was altered
according to the kind of thing she was imagining."[105] An early fourteenth-
century pseudo-Aristotelian text similarly held that "a child will particularly

receive the disposition or the color of the thing imagined" if a woman has a "strong imagining."[106] With miscegenation laws and identification badges that reflected medieval worries that Christian men might unknowingly sleep with women of different religious identities, combined anxieties about women's invisible powers of imagination, men's inability to discern religious or ethnic difference in women, and the responsibility of clergy and monks to avoid sexual encounters in any case certainly could account for the miracle recorded in Royal 8 A VI. But even if one argues that the blackening of the priest's body communicates that he has been Judaized by sexual contact, it remains crucial to the Jewess's part in the miracle that she is not thus marked.[107]

Medieval Anglo-Christian characterizations of a sexualized (still unmarked) Jewess, when they occurred, were not primarily concerned with her ability to seduce, deceive, or harm Christian men. Only Matthew Paris implies this in his fictionalization of the 1222 Oxford deacon's wife. Where the Jewess might impose a sexual danger or temptation, moreover, she was specifically a danger to clergy and the administration of clerical duties. The medieval Jewess is not Jean-Paul Sartre's *belle juive* with her "very special sexual signification" and "aura of rape and massacre,"[108] nor is she the murderess Jewess of the eighteenth-century ballads of "Sir Hugh" or the "Jew's Daughter," enticing young boys into her bedchamber. When her Jewishness made her a taboo focus of Christian desire, it also gave her access to Christian space and the ability to appear and disappear within in it, whether through indistinguishability, escape, or conversion, as a go-between or as a Marian likeness. The Jewess's ability to move through these roles, in fact, makes her crucial to the narratives in which she appears. It defines her *as against* masculine caricatures (of both Jewish and Christian men) and makes her a doubled figure of Judaism and Christianity, most difficult to discern in the domestic spaces traditionally associated with women.

Sameness and the Jewess

To return to Levine's formulation, "a heuristic model" of the Jewess pertains across many times and places: from biblical apocrypha to the present, Jewesses "provide the stage upon which the anxieties of the communities that display them can be expressed, mapped, and alleviated," and "narratives depict the Jewess as negotiating [diasporic] borders."[109] Medieval English visual and textual narratives are no different, though their specific cultural contexts—in the long wake of the 1290 Expulsion or within the pre-1290 state bureaucracy that documented and archived Anglo-Jewry—inflect their range of interpretive possibilities. That Jewish women are made to look and act the same as Christian women should not be construed as an absence of feminized tropes of Jewishness in England, nor in the Middle Ages more broadly. The need to find or discern the Jewess, rather, aligns her with a range of diasporic engagements with Jewish women across time and, in the English context, denotes an observable branch of anti-Jewish polemics that exploit similarity and ambiguity to incorporate or erase the Jew. In the medieval English setting, the Jewess may be part of a sleeper cell, play a disappearing act, or serve as a Jewish/Christian go-between, a potential Christian, or an uncanny goad to self-reflection.

Once this is understood, the notion of the indistinguishability of Jewish and Christian women in medieval representations becomes its own kind of caricature, an exaggeration used to didactic or polemical effect. Unlike caricatures of Jewish men, the exaggerated feature is not carnal or (visible) racial difference. Instead, caricature of a Jewess exaggerates her versatile social and religious capacity, and her quality or potential of being the same. Not a "benign visual neglect" connected to medieval antifeminist discourses generally,[110] the lack of difference between Jewish and Christian women in English art can thus be viewed as a conscious and purposeful representation of Christian hopes for and fears about the Jewess, wholly consistent with the textual record. Where the vicious fictionalization of Jewish men manifests in grotesque physical features and images of violence, for Jewish women it manifests in their *likeness* to Christian women, which argues visually and narratively for sameness and exploits it for Christian good or ill. This process of saming is not, of course, disconnected from antifeminist tropes—that is, certainly the Jewess's femaleness is part of why polemics of sameness work especially well with women—but it is also not mere womanhood that marks the Jewess. It is Jewish womanhood in the Christian eye.

The literature from medieval England that is explicitly concerned with postbiblical and contemporary Jewish women is a substantial corpus, and the Jewess, resting in an uncanny valley between the familiar and the monstrous, is significant to medieval Anglo-Christian understandings of the self and other, and to the development of English anti-Judaism. Miri Rubin, discussing the many medieval versions of "The Jewish Boy" story, has suggested that the relative animus of the Jewish father in narratives and visual depictions stands in opposition to "the earthly Jewish mother," a figure "whose maternal quality outstrips her quality as a Jew."[111] Lipton has argued that "the religiously unmarked representation of Jewish women" in medieval illustrations—many of the earliest ones English—is the consequence of tropes of femininity outstripping tropes of Jewishness: "Christian artists already had a venerable sign with which to signify the pliant, unstable form of carnality: the female body."[112] But neither of these influential readings sufficiently theorizes how the Jewess's supposed universal maternity, pliancy, and indistinguishability might function in their own right. When we foreground the Jewish woman in medieval English sources, we see that unmarking and versatility (*not* pliancy) are essential *in relation to* her Jewishness. Authors and artists use the Jewess strategically, as a focal point of Christian attention, and the reactive or interactive Christian ability to empathize with her, inhabit her, be attracted to her, repelled by her, or fooled by her likeness *is* her polemical role. This is so repetitive—and so thoroughly connected to the historical remains of Anglo-Jewish women and their interactions with English institutions—that it functions as a dominant stereotype. Jewishness in these cases is not outstripped by but rather working in concert with whatever stereotypes of femininity accompany it (e.g., pliancy, inconstancy, maternity, submissiveness, or sexual availability). Polemics of sameness permit the Christian fantasy of ritual and ancestral identification with Jewishness to turn back on itself in fantasies that Jews might be or become Christians. The supposed pliability of the feminine is suitable to the double bind.

The word "Jewess" itself, as Levine argues, "perpetuates the almost abandoned practice of gendering people according to ethnic, religious, and racial categories"; it is "derived from a normative category 'Jew'" even as it is used to label a category of people and representations "at the borders of Jewish and gentile society."[113] Levine pronounces here exactly what we see in medieval Anglo-Christian representations of Jewish women: "Her 'Jew'ness becomes yet again ambiguous, and ambiguity is a threat. Brandishing her dangerous supplemental 'ess,' the Jewess is an ideal sign for conveying cultural anxieties. . . . She outstrips the category of analysis even as she reinforces it."[114] I have used the word "Jewess" throughout this book to denote precisely this aspect of medieval representations of the Jewish woman, though I think, finally, that we do not need the Jewess to outstrip or be outstripped by anything. Instead, we may pause on her versatility, uncertainties, and ambiguities and understand that her lack of marking is what we seek. The voice of Alice of Worcester, who begged Robert Burnell to take pity on her as a Mary Magdalene and yet knew herself to be the captive daughter of Zion in gentile lands, rings more loudly now. Alice knew the threshold on which she stood: restricted and archived by a Christian state, she would signify as both Jew and Christian. She embraced her sameness before they did it anyway.

Sameness and Sympathy

> The distinctions of actual creed were too subtle and too carefully
> made the study of churchmen alone to be understood or cared for by
> the multitudes. . . . By the multitudes, the Jews are still considered
> aliens and foreigners, supposed to be separated by an antiquated creed
> and peculiar customs from sympathy and fellowship. . . . Yet they are,
> in fact, Jews only in their religion—Englishmen in everything else.
>   —Grace Aguilar, "History of the Jews in England"

Grace Aguilar (d. 1847) was the first author to attempt a history of medieval English Jewry. She imagined that recognition of a common Englishness—rather than familial relationships of creed or scripture—might resolve a long heritage of anti-Jewish sentiment that continued to affect her in the mid-nineteenth century. In medieval Anglo-Christian law, art, and letters, sustained engagement with Jewish sameness had emerged as historically generative, gendered, and polemically motivated, encompassing developing notions of both Englishness and English Christianity. Aguilar responded with the hope that English Jews might be brought into "sympathy and fellowship" with their gentile countrymen.[1] The threat and presumption of sameness that she gleaned from her reading of pre- and post-Conquest legal prohibitions against Jewish-Christian interaction may indeed have some resolution in her notion of sympathy. As Rae Greiner has explained, "The desire to fuse with others—or lack thereof—distinguishes empathy from sympathy," and much nineteenth-century literature "entail[ed] a commitment to sympathetic, more than empathetic, relations":[2]

Sympathy served an important purpose for realist novelists [of the long nineteenth century] precisely because the fusion of self with other . . . remained largely if not entirely impossible. If their efforts to maintain a border between self and other has [sic] seemed prudish or reactionary, a moralistic response to Romantic or sentimental [or medieval?] excesses, the realists had powerful aesthetic and ethical reasons for creating forms of narrative that could generate experiences of sympathetic connection without requiring that others' feelings and minds be known or identically shared.[3]

When Aguilar, a young nineteenth-century Anglo-Jewish poet and novelist, expressed a wish for a previously absent "sympathy" with English Jews, she was reacting against polemics of sameness—though of course she would not have called them that. Polemical use of sameness, however, highlights a desire for fusion, and often accomplishes it rhetorically. Sameness allows a metaphor of the self with or within the other. Aguilar rejected this kind of sameness, just as Audre Lorde did from her different but still marginalized perspective, as a destructive myth.[4] Gendered investments in sameness, and later rejections of it, betray that processes of saming and misogynistic discourses have long been intertwined.

Medieval English poetry famously memorializes Judith and Susanna—in the Old English *Judith* and the Middle English *Pistel of Swete Susan*—as righteous (Christianized) Jewesses, and Joseph's Egyptian wife Osnat (Asenath) takes her place among matriarchal Old Testament Jewesses in the Middle English *Storie of Asneth* too, where she is "Of stature semeli as Sare, specious as Rebekke, / Fair formed of feturis as semblyng to Rachel" (as attractive in body as Sarah, lovely as Rebecca, in features so beautifully formed as to resemble Rachel).[5] Delilah could be a negative figure of Jewishness in English traditions, and the personified Synagoga and destroyed Jerusalem could be the feminized mirror images of Ecclesia and the heavenly Jerusalem.[6] Instead of these and other relatively well-understood typological figures, however, I have ultimately focused on representations of postbiblical and contemporary medieval Jewish women. Their representations do intersect with figural thinking about biblical Jewesses—one ought not divorce stories of mourning Jewish or Judaized mothers, for example, from "Rachel weeping for her children" (Jer. 31:15) or, in turn, from the Jewish mothers of the Holy Innocents (Matt. 2:18)—but more often the sameness of Jewish and Christian women is of the moment, a feminine and contemporary proficiency. A focus on nonbiblical Jewish women,

therefore, alters the view of medieval Christian identifications and disidentifi-
cations with Jewishness and creates a new, and newly urgent, centrality of the
Jewess in anti-Jewish narratives. The observable sameness of the Jewess, by way
of connection to and evolution from polemics of sameness as applied to the Jew,
promotes the erasure of continuing Judaism and living Jews.

What I hope this book has accomplished in documenting the gendered
uses and effects of polemics of sameness in medieval Anglo-Christian books,
and in English national definition with and against Jewishness, is a paradigm
shift. I offer an entry point into medieval and later Christian texts that engage
with Jews and the Jewess. When medievalists have previously focused on contrast and difference in English anti-Jewish materials, they have done so by looking primarily at the male Jew. The Jewess, however, reveals rhetorical and visual
arguments that erode difference between Christians and Jews to absorb Jewishness into Christianity. If we had rejected pretense to Jewish-Christian sameness
either as insincere (at work only within or as otherness) or as sympathetic in the
modern colloquial usage (i.e., somehow more humane than other kinds of anti-
Jewish expression, expressing sincere identification), we have been mistaken.
Pausing where and when authors elaborate on Jewish-Christian sameness or
dwell on the meaning of "Jew" as a Christian denotation—and pausing at
points where saming and othering coexist and remain mutually affirming—
reveals much. Distinct representations of Jewish men and women emerge, as
does the didactic flexibility of "samed" definitions and figures of Jewishness.
We see a polemical mode through which stories of supersession are predicated
on an accompanying Jewish-Christian sameness that is implicated in narratives
of Jewish difference, carnality, or violence. When Christian authors define
"Christian" as "Jew," they engage in expulsion and dispossession. As I asked at
the end of Part I, where was the space for living Jewish bodies in medieval
England when the Christian was the Jew?

Sameness, as an assimilative mode, speaks to more recent Christian-Jewish
discourses around land, identity, and nationalist politics as well. In October 2018, for example, U.S. Vice President Mike Pence invited a Christian rabbi
associated with Messianic Judaism (more popularly known as "Jews for Jesus")
to pray for the eleven Jews who were murdered while attending Shabbat services
at the Tree of Life synagogue in Pittsburgh, Pennsylvania. The self-identified
rabbi, Loren Jacobs, used a smattering of Hebrew and wore a tallit (a Jewish
prayer shawl); he prayed for the victims of anti-Jewish violence "*b'shem Yeshua*,
in the name of Jesus" after Pence introduced him as a "leader in the Jewish community."[7] On the day the U.S. Embassy opened in Jerusalem in May 2018, for-

mer governor of Arkansas Mike Huckabee, also a former Baptist minister, invited viewers to join him for an appearance on Fox News where he would "begin the show by blowing a shofar and speaking Hebrew" to celebrate the event.[8] Donald Trump, while campaigning for the office of U.S. president in September 2016, donned a tallit gifted to him by Bishop Wayne T. Jackson of Great Faith Ministries International in Detroit, Michigan—a Christian congregation that has introduced Jewish holidays into its liturgical observance and wears tallitot regularly. When asked about this practice by a journalist working for the *Times of Israel*, the pastor responded, "Of course the founder of our faith is the messiah Jesus, and he wore a tallit."[9] Christian polemics of sameness, when they apply to Jews, openly embrace the Jewish Jesus as the model and the end of Judaism. To imitate and embody Christ, in this view, is to imitate and embody the Jew in a pre-Christian state but also, necessarily, to embrace a fantasy of union with the living Jew. The hope of Jewish ingathering articulated by Christian Zionism requires Christian-Jewish sameness through union, conversion, and eschatological fiat. In medieval English anti-Jewish literature and its contexts, saming coheres in similar ways. It works within a nexus of religious, national, and political or economic concerns, even while it unabashedly erases continuing Jewishness as anything other than Christian desire.

When Lorde denounced the "myth of sameness which I think can destroy us,"[10] she saw her denunciation as a refusal to "settle" for something "easy," a rejection of the notion that unity (as opposed to "real coalition") is ideal or even effective in producing sympathy between different peoples, groups, or even aspects of oneself.[11] When Homi Bhabha described colonial mimicry as an engagement with a "recognizable Other, *as a subject of difference that is almost the same, but not quite*," he critiqued the "narcissistic demand" of the colonial mind-set.[12] To think seriously about the truism that like and unlike require each other, we must also acknowledge that likeness is both constructive and destructive. Acknowledgment that "us" is the same as "them" is necessarily prior to the construction of difference, but difference, then, may be badly or incompletely constructed, or it may be resolved by removing "them" from the equation. In polemical or disingenuous engagements with "them," one may argue that "us" *is* "them," or that "them" has already become "us," until no sincere discussion of difference, let alone tolerance, remains. This is what happens when Robert Kilwardby implies that Sampson son of Samuel of Northampton is the prodigal son, or when Matthew Paris uses the "Jewish" body of Jurnepin/Odard of Norwich to create a model of Christianity. It is what happens when Orrm redefines "Jew" and "Israelite" to mean "Christian," or when Jocelin of Brakelond *sames* Abbot Samson figuratively, typologically, and physically with the expelled Jewish financiers of Bury St Edmunds.

Because of their positions in biblical and English history, Jewish women become central to this insidious assimilation found in medieval Anglo-Christian literature. Uncircumcised, at the borders, converts or possible converts, unwilling to wear the identification badge, archived as literate businesswomen by Christian institutions, and set alongside Christian women in domestic contexts, Anglo-Jewish women seem to necessitate laws that legislate difference and separation, even as their literary representations announce their similarity to the Virgin Mary and good Christian women more broadly. While Sampson of Northampton and Jurnepin/Odard of Norwich could be manipulated because of their circumcisions, while Jocelin could structure Abbot Samson's sameness around the documents and seals that bore the mark of his authority within a masculine institution, Jewish women were more difficult to handle. They were lettered *and* unmarked, ambiguous *and* full of Christian potential; they seemed to have extraordinary access to Jewish *and* Christian space, whether masculine or feminine, private or public. As tools of an anti-Jewish polemic, then, visual and narrative strategies that emphasized their sameness could stoke Christian fears of, and eschatological hopes for, the Jewish other, to justify and forget expulsion.

Most importantly, articulation and recognition of the historical uses of anti-Jewish polemics of sameness provide us with a better understanding of how anti-Judaism develops. And we better be paying attention. The trap that polemics of sameness set is in their relative invisibility. Practitioners want to persuade you that it is less insidious and more sympathetic than the violence and dispossessions that so often accompany it.

Sampson Son of Samuel of Northampton

Record of Sampson son of Samuel of Northampton and his conviction for impersonating a Franciscan appears in TNA E 9/24 (m. 5d), a Plea Roll of the Exchequer of the Jews for Trinity Term 5 Edward I (1277). The case is among the roll's "memoranda," a heading that describes "entries of . . . purely administrative nature plus all litigation of interest to the king,"[1] and it comprises a summary after the fact of the alleged crime, the Northampton sheriff's actions, liaison between different authorities (ecclesiastical and royal), a writ from the king, and orders for the following term. While the memorandum tells us that Sampson's unusual sentence was upheld, and that Sheriff Gilbert de Kirkeby was put to judgment for his mishandling of the matter, no further record of the case has yet been discovered. Whether Sampson or his mainpernors ever returned to Northampton or suffered the imposed punishment, or what judgment if any Gilbert received, is thus unknown.

Hilary Jenkinson published an English translation of the entry printed here in 1929, when he calendared TNA E 9/24 for *PREJ* 3 (311–12), though the new translation below substantially corrects and updates Jenkinson's. The Latin has never before been printed. In what follows, medieval punctuation and capitalization are maintained, expanded abbreviations are marked by italics, and square brackets indicate editorial intervention.

TNA E 9/24, m. 5d (ca. July 1277)

Northt'.[2] Cum quidam Sampson fil*ius* Samu*elis* iudeus capt*us* fuit *et* detent*us* in p*ri*sona Northt' *per* uic*ecomitem* Northt' ac Samu*el* fil*ius* Simon*is et* Isac fi-lius Leuy Iud*ei* manuc*eperunt* p*re*di*ctu*m Sa*m*pson ad habe*ndum* corpus eius coram In Oct*abis* s*anct*i Ioh*ann*is Bapt*iste* pr*oximo* preter*ito* ad respondend*um* omnib*us* de eo conqueri volentib*us* propt*er* quod precept*um* fuit eidem vice*com*item quod ips*um* deliberaret pre*dictos* manu*captores* nisi capt*us* fuisset p*er* speciale precept*um* Reg*is*. uel pro tall*agio* Reg*is*. uel pro auro m*atris* uel consort*is* Reg*is*. uel pro aliqua alia re coronam Reg*is* tangente [et] q*uo*d scire faceret qu[i]d occ*asi*one capt*us* fuit. Et idem vic*ecomes* mandauit q*uo*d Samps*on* fili*us* Samue*lis* capt*us* fuit eo q*uo*d assumpsit habitum f*ratris* minoris p*re*dicando quedam in contemptu*m* fidei *christ*iane *et* p*re*dic*t*i ordinis de quo nup*er* conuictus fuit co*ram* Archiep*iscop*o Cant' p*er* quod sentencial*iter* adiudicatu*m* fuit q*uo*d iret nudus p*er* tres dies p*er* medi*um* q*ui*nque Ciuitatum sc*ilici*t. London' Cant' Oxon' Linc' *et* Northt' portando in manib*us* suis viscera cuiusdam vituli *et* vitulu*m* excoriatu*m* in collo quod no*n* permisit fieri sine speciali precepto Reg*is*. retinendo ips*um* iude*um* in castro don*ec* d*omi*n*us* Rex aliud inde mandauerit. pr*o* quo Archiep*iscopu*s scripsit Reg*i*. Et p*er* idem Samps*on* non uenit ad pred*ictam* diem ad respondend*um* *etc'* nec aliquid inde f*actum* fuit. ac *etiam* datum fuit intelligi prefa*tis* Iustic*iariis* quod d*omi*n*us* Rex p*er* breu*em* suu*m* de magno sigillo mandauit eidem vice*comit*i q*uo*d prefatu*m* iude*um* subire faceret prim*us* condemnatione*m* supra*dict*am sibi iniunctam p*er* Archiep*iscopu*m Cant'— Precept*um* fuit eide*m* vice*comit*i quod sec*und*um tenorem illius mandati debitam execu*cion*em faceret sup*er* hoc. Ita q*uo*d prefat*us* Samps*on* predictam punic*ion*em sustineret. Et *etiam* pro eo q*uo*d dat*um* fuit intelligi eisde*m* Iustici*ariis* quod prefat*us* Samps*on* deliberat*us* fuit a prisona Lic*et* idem vice*comes* pri*us* significasset q*uo*d ips*um* non deliberaret sine precepto d*omi*ni Reg*is* speciali. simil*iter* precept*um* fuit eide*m* quod si ide*m* iud*eus* fuisset absens. tunc attach*iatus* faceret pre*dictos* Samu*elem* *et* Is*acum* iudeos q*u*i ips*um* iude*um* pri*us* manuceperant. sicut pre*dictum* est. Ita q*uo*d h*ab*eret corpora eor*um* coram *etc'*. in Crastino s*anct*i Iacobi ad standu*m* recto *et* faciendu*m* pro eode*m* iudeo penitenciam sibi iniunctam. Ad que*m* diem vic*ecomes* mandauit q*uo*d breu*em* illud sibi uen*it* die Lune In Crastino s*anct*i Iacobi. Et nich*il*omin*us* Samu*el* fili*us* Symon*is* *et* Isac fili*us* Leuy no*n* fueru*nt* inuenti in balliu*a* sua nec aliquid h*ab*ueru*nt* ibidem. Et q*uo*d Samps*on* fili*us* Samuel*is* non fuit inuent*us* postqu*am* misit corp*us* ei*us* p*er* precept*um* Iusticiariorum coram eisde*m* Iustici*ariis* in Oct*abis* Ioh*ann*is Bapt*iste* pr*oximo* preter*ito* Et ide*m* ips*um* ad penitencia*m* illam faceret compellere no*n* potuit donec ad p*artes* Northt' redierit. Et quia ide*m* vice*comes* pri*us* significasset q*uo*d ips*um* h*ab*uerit in prisona. *et* sine precepto Reg*is* speciali ips*um* non deliberaret *et* nu*n*c significa*uit* q*uo*d no*n* est inuent*us* set eu*m* tradidit pre*dict*is manucaptorib*us* quod in priori mandato no*n* significasset Ideo ipse vice*comes* sc*ilic*et *etc'* aud*iendum* Iudic*ium* suu*m* a die

sancti micheli*s* in .xv. dies. Et q*u*od corpus p*re*fati iud*e*i u*e*l p*re*di*ctorum* manu-
c*ap*torum duci fac*er*et Archiep*iscop*o ad stand*um* ordinacio*n*i suo *et* id q*uo*d
ide*m* Archiep*iscop*u*s* ei scire fac*iat* sine dil*a*cione exequat*ur*.

Northampton. Whereas a certain Jew, Sampson son of Samuel, was seized and
detained in prison at Northampton by the sheriff of Northampton,[3] and the
Jews Samuel son of Simon and Isaac son of Levi mainperned the said Sampson
to have his body present on the octave of St John the Baptist just past [1 July] to
respond to all wanting to complain about him, on this account the same sheriff
was ordered to release him to the aforesaid mainpernors—unless he had been
seized by special order of the king, or because of the king's tallage, or because of
the king's mother's or consort's gold, or for whatever other matter touching the
king's crown—and to make known for what reason he was seized.

And the sheriff sent word that he had seized Sampson son of Samuel
because he assumed the habit of a Friar Minor, preaching certain things in contempt of the Christian faith and the aforesaid Order, of which he was recently
convicted before the Archbishop of Canterbury,[4] whereby it was adjudged as
sentence that he should go naked for three days through the middle of five
cities—namely London, Canterbury,[5] Oxford, Lincoln, and Northampton—
carrying in his hands the entrails of a certain calf and the calf flayed around his
neck, which he, holding the same Jew in the castle until the king command
something different on the matter, would not allow to be done without special
order of the king, concerning which the archbishop wrote to the king.

And since this Sampson did not appear on the aforementioned day to respond etc., nor was anything done after that, and also the presiding justices were
made aware that the lord king through his writ under the Great Seal had ordered this sheriff that the aforementioned Jew should in the first place be made
to undergo the previously noted punishment enjoined on him by the Archbishop of Canterbury, the sheriff was commanded to enforce the pending
judgement in this matter according to the tenor of that order, such that the
aforementioned Sampson should suffer the aforesaid punishment. In addition,
because the same justices were made aware that the aforementioned Sampson
was released from prison, even though the same sheriff previously indicated
that he would not release him without special order of the king, likewise he was
commanded that if this Jew should be absent he should attach the aforesaid
Jews Samuel and Isaac, who had previously mainperned the same Jew, as has
been said, so as to have their bodies present etc. on the morrow of St James to
stand to right and do for that Jew the penance enjoined on him. On that day,

the sheriff sent word that that writ had come to him on the Monday of the morrow of St James [26 July],[6] and nonetheless Samuel son of Simon and Isaac son
of Levi were not found in the area of his bailiwick, nor did they have anything
there, and indeed Sampson son of Samuel was not found, ever since his body, by
order of the justices, went before the justices on the octave of St John the Baptist
past, as mentioned, and so he could not force him to do that penance until he
returned to the Northampton area.

And because the sheriff previously had indicated that he had him in prison
and would not release him without special order from the king and now indicated that he was not found and in fact he handed him over to the aforementioned mainpernors, which he did not indicate in the previous message,
therefore the sheriff, namely etc., [is ordered] to hear his judgement on the quin-
dene of St Michael [13 October]. Moreover, he should have the body of the
aforementioned Jew or the aforesaid mainpernors escorted to the archbishop to
stand for his judgment and execute whatever the archbishop should tell him to
do without delay.

Jurnepin/Odard of Norwich

Record of testimony concerning the alleged forced circumcision of a young Norwich boy named Odard in 1230 survives in a Curia Regis Roll for 18 Henry III (TNA KB 26/115B, rot. 22, *olim* rot. 21). The inquest was conducted four years after the supposed event (1234), when six of thirteen accused Jewish men had already been either outlawed or imprisoned.[1] By 1241, at least four had been executed.[2] Several other extant records provide evidence of how arrests and convictions unfolded.[3]

The Latin text printed below was previously presented by William Prynne, in an abridged and corrupted form, as part of his anti-Jewish *Short Demurrer to the Jewes* (London: Edward Thomas, 1656), 19–21, where he included a mix of Latin excerpts, French translations of the Latin, and English summary. The first scholarly edition was completed by J. M. Rigg, in *Select Pleas*, xliv–xlvii, though Rigg relied overmuch on Prynne and made several (minor) errors. A reliable modern edition is available in *CRR 1233–37*, 333–35 (item no. 1320).[4]

The single rotulus on which this text appears is severely damaged, especially at its edges, and shows evidence of past conservation attempts and use of chemical reagents that have further contributed to its damaged state. In what follows, illegible or amended text is transparently noted. Medieval punctuation is maintained, expanded abbreviations are marked by italics, interlinear scribal additions are marked by angled slash marks (\ /), and square brackets indicate editorial intervention. Interventions supply text that is missing or unreadable, with likely abbreviations indicated (commensurate with space) where possible, as determined in consultation with previous editions and through in situ examination with ultraviolet light. Explanation of decisions that differ markedly from the available twentienth-century editions may be found in the notes. The English translation presented here is new.

TNA KB 26/115B, rot. 22 (ca. December 1234–January 1235)

[Dorse:] Recordum loquele de Iudeis Norwic' qui sunt in prisona apud Lond'[5]

[Benedictus fisicus] appellat Iacobum de Norwic' iudeum quod cum Odardus filius suus puer etatis .v. annorum iuit ludendo I[n via villate Norwic'] vigilia sancti
Egidii quatuor annis elapsis venit idem Iacobus iudeus et cepit eundem Odardum
et eum porta[uit usque] ad domum suum et circumcidit eum in membro suo et
uoluit [ipsum] facere iudeum et eum retinuit per unum diem et [unam noct]em in
domo sua. quousque per clamorem vic[inorum uenit ad quan]dam domum et illum inuenit in manibus ip[sius Iacobi] et sic ipsum puerum circumcisum mon-
strauit Officiali [Archidiaconi et Corona]toribus ipso die qui presentes sunt et hoc
d[ie testantur et qui] dicunt quod uiderunt predictum puerum circumcisum et
qui h[abuit] membrum suum grossum et ualde infl[atum et ita aturnat]um sicut
predictum est. Et quod hoc nequiter fecit et in felonia et in dispectu crucifixi et
christianitatis et [in pace domini regis] et quod \ipse/ non potuit habere ipsum puerum nisi per forciam christianorum [et] offert \disracionare/ uersus eum sicut
Curia consider[auerit. Et postquam] circumciderat eum vocauit eum Iurnepin. Et
puer visus est coram Iusticiariis et liquidum est [quod circumcisus] erat.

 [Idem appella]t de forcia et consilio Leonem filium margarete Senioretem
filium Ioscei Deodone Ioppe filium Chere[6] [Eliam] filium Viuonis. Mosse fil-
ium Salomonis. Simonem Koc filium Sarre Sampsonem filium Vrsel Benedictum filium Avigay [Mosse] filium Abraham. Isaac paruum. Dyay Le Kat. qui
omnes uenerunt preter. Dedone. Ioppe. Bene[dictum] Mosse et Isaac.[7] et hoc
totum defendunt sicut Iudei uersus christianum.

 [Poste]a predictus puer qui tunc fuit etatis .v. annorum et modo est etatis
.ix. annorum requisitus quomodo circum[ciderunt] eum dicit quod ceperunt
eum et adduxerunt eum usque ad domum ipsius Iacobi. et unus illorum tenuit
[eum et] cooperuit oculos suos et quidam alius circumcidit eum quodam cultello
et postea ceperunt peciam [illam] quam sciderant de membro suo et posuerunt
in quodam bacyno cum sabelone. et quesierunt [ipsam] illam cum paruis fusselletis quousque quidam Iudeus qui vocabatur Iurnepin inuenit eam primo. Et
[quia] idem Iurnepin inuenit eam primo. vocauerunt eum Iurnepin.

 [Et] Officialis Archidiaconi uenit coram Iusticiariis cum magna secta sacerdotum qui omnes dixerunt in uerbo dei quod predictus puer ita circumcisus
fuit sicut predictum est. et per predictos Iudeos. et quod uiderunt predictum puerum recenter circums[isum habentem membrum] \suum/ grossum et ualde
inflatum et sanguinolentum.

Et Coronatores de Com*itatu et* Coronatores de Ciuitate Norwic.' *et* xxxvj. hom*in*es de villata de Norwic' Iura[ti] veniu*n*t *et* dicu*n*t super sacrame*n*tum suu*m* precise qu*o*d pr*edic*tus puer ita c*ir*cumcis*us* fuit sic*ut* pr*edictu*m est [et hoc] sciu*n*t pr*o* certo q*uia* qua*n*do ita fuit c*ir*cumcis*us* idem puer euasit de mani-b*us* iudeor*um et* inuent*us* fuit sede[ns iuxta] Ripam Norwic' per qua*n*dam Matilde*m* de Bernha*m et* filia*m* eius *et* que i*n*uenerunt eum plorante*m et* vlulan-te*m* [et dicente*m*] qu*o*d erat Iudeus. Ita qu*o*d eadem Matild*is* cepit eunde*m* pu-er*u*m pr*o* amore dei *et* duxit eu*m* ad domu*m* suu*m* [et] hospitata est eu*m* tota nocte usq*ue* in crastinu*m et* cu*m* Iudei hoc adiuer*un*t vener*un*t ad domu*m* pre-d*ic*te Matill*dis* [et voluer]unt vi capere eum q*uia* dixer*un*t ipsum esse iudeu*m* suu*m et* vocauer*un*t eu*m* Iurnepi*n* audientib*us* pr*edic*tis matill*de* [et filia] sua *et* pl*u*rib*us* aliis tu*n*c presentib*us*. *et* cum no*n* potuer*un*t *h*abere eu*m*. vener*un*t postea cu*m* magna m*u*ltitudine [iudeorum] ad pr*edictu*m domu*m et* magna vi uoluer*un*t adducere eu*m* secum. Et cu*m* hoc audiuer*un*t vicini scil*icet* circa m[atilde*m*][8] vener*un*t ad domu*m* illam *et* bene audiuer*un*t qu*o*d pr*edic*ti Iudei vocauer*un*t pr*edictu*m Iudeum pueru*m* suu*m*.[9] *et* qu*o*d vocauer*un*t eu*m* Iurne-pi*n*. *et* qua*n*do Iudei no*n* potuer*un*t *h*abere eu*m* prop*ter ch*ris*t*ianos. prohibuer*un*t eide*m* Matill*di* ne [daret] ei carne*m* porcina*m* \ad/ manducandu*m*. q*uia* dix-er*un*t ipsum esse iudeu*m*. ita qu*o*d per vim vener*un*t c*h*ris*t*iani *et* [abstu]ler*un*t pueru*m* pr*edictu*m a manib*us* iudeor*um*.

[Et] pr*edic*ta Matill*dis* in cui*us* domo puer inuent*us* fuit uenit cora*m* Iusti-ciariis *et* cum ea filia ei*us* simil*iter* Iurate *et* hoc [cogno]scunt dicentes qu*o*d ita inuener*un*t pr*edic*tum pueru*m* plorante*m* sic*ut* pr*edictu*m est *et* qu*o*d pr*o* amore dei tenuer*un*t eu*m* [in domo] sua q*uia* nescier*un*t cui*us* filius puer ille erat *et* q*uia* vider*un*t eundem pueru*m* ita i*n*firmum qu*o*d esti[mauer*un*t] eu*m* cito mori *et* qu*o*d Iudei ita vener*un*t in crastinu*m* sic*ut* pr*edictu*m est. Set nescier*un*t cui*us* fili*us* puer [ille esset nisi p*er*] qua*n*dam mulierem que dixit eu*m* esse filiu*m* mag*ist*ri Bened*ic*ti fisici. *et* ad mandatu*m* pr*edic*tarum [mulierum] uenit pr*e*-d*ic*tus Benedictus fisic*us et* abscondit se i*n* camera ipsius Matill*dis* ut audiret quid [pr*edic*ti Iudei] l[oc]uti essent cu*m* filio suo. *et* cu*m* audiret q*uo*d uocau-er*un*t eu*m* filium suu*m et* Iurnepi*n et* [iudeum suu*m*] statim exiuit de camera co*n*tradicens eis *et* quesiuit a puero quomodo uocar*etur*. qui dixit prop*ter* timo-rem Iu[deus][10] uocabat*ur* Iurnepin. *et* percepto p*at*re suo gauis*us* dixit qu*o*d fuit Odardus filius suus. N*un*c om*n*es [Iudei] sunt i*n* prisona ap*u*d Norwic'. preter illos q*ui* fuer*un*t ap*u*d Lond' qua*n*do h*ec* inquisicio *fac*ta fuit.

[Et omnes] Iuratores requ*i*siti qui i*n*terfuer*un*t ad circumsicione*m* illam dicu*n*t qu*o*d omnes pr*edic*ti Iudei fuer*un*t con[sentientes facto] illo preter mossy fili*u* Salom*on*is.

[Hec autem omnia] facta fuerunt in curia domini regis apud Norwic' coram Iusticiariis presentibus Priore Norwic' et fratribus pre[dicatori]bus et fratribus minoribus et pluribus aliis tam clericis quam laicis.

[Postea] apud Catteshill' venit coram Iusticiariis apud Cattishill' Ricardus de frensingfeld' qui tunc temporis fuit constabularius [Norwic' et] cognouit coram eisdem Iusticiariis quod cum ipse fuit ad Castrum Norwic' venerunt Iudei ad eum et que[sti fueru]nt quod christiani uoluerunt auferre eis iudeum suum. et audito iuit ipse ad querelam eorum ad domum [predicte Ma]tilldis et inuenit ibi congregationem magnam christianorum et Iudeorum et predicti Iudei ostenderunt ei quod christiani [voluer]unt auferre eis Iudeum suum. Et cum hoc audiuit predictus Benedictum fisicus contradixit eis dicens quod [era]t Odardus filius suus. et vnde bene dixit quod vidit predictum Odardum filium predicti Benedicti habentem [membrum suum] abscisum. sanguilentem et grossum inflatum. et bene dixit quod cristiani ceperunt eundem Odardum et [eum abstule]runt a manibus eorum.

[Si]mon de Berstrete et Nicholas Chese qui tunc fuerunt Ballivi Norwic' venerunt coram Iusticiariis et [cognouer]unt quod ad querelam predictorum Iudeorum venerunt ad predictam domum et dixerunt quod hoc \totum/ uiderunt de predicto [facto sicut] predictum est.

[Postea] coram domino Rege et domino Cant' et maiori parte Episcoporum Comitum et Baronum Anglie quia casus iste nun[quam prius ac]cidit in Curia domini Regis. et preterea quia factum illud \primo/ tangit deum et sanctam Ecclesiam eo quod circumcisio et [bapti]smum sunt pertinentia ad fidem. et preterea non est ibi talis felonia nec amissio \menbri/ nec mahemium nec plaga [mortalis] vel alia felonia laica que possit hominem dampnare sine mandato sancte Ecclesie. Consideratum est quod [factum] istud in primo tractetur in Sancta Ecclesia. et per ordinarium \loci/ inquiratur rei ueritas et mandetur domino Regi vt [quid]quid faciat quod facere debet.

[Super] hoc uenerunt omnes Iudei in communi et optulerunt domino Rege vnam marcam auri per sic quod puer uid[eatur coram ipsis] Iudeis si circumcisus fuit vel non. et recipitur.

[E]t visus est puer et menbrum eius uisum est pelle coopertum ante in capite. et in tali statu liberatur patri suo ut eum [habeat] coram Iudicibus ecclesiasticis. et ipsi Iudei remanent in prisona.

Record of testimony concerning Norwich Jews who are imprisoned in London:

Benedict, a physician, appeals Jacob of Norwich, a Jew, that whereas four years ago on St Giles' eve when his son Odard, a boy of five years, went playing in a Norwich street, the same Jew, Jacob, came and took Odard and carried him to his house and circumcised his penis and wanted to make him a Jew and held him for a day and a night in his house until, because of the report of neighbours, he went to a certain house and found him in this Jacob's hands; and accordingly he showed the same circumcised boy on that day to the Archdeacon's official and the coroners, who are present and testify today and who say that they saw the aforesaid boy circumcised and with a large and very swollen penis and maltreated as aforesaid, and that he did this wickedly and feloniously as an insult to the Cross and Christianity and against the Lord King's Peace, and that he [Benedict] could not have the boy except through an act of force by the Christians; therefore he [Benedict] offers to provide proof against him as the court will decide. And after he circumcised him, he called him "Jurnepin." And the boy was seen in the presence of the justices, and it is clear that he had been circumcised.

Likewise he appeals, as aiders and abetters to the crime, Leo son of Margaret, Senioret son of Josce, Deudone, Joppe son of Chera, Elias son of Vives, Moses son of Solomon, Simon Cok son of Sarah, Sampson son of Ursel, Benedict son of Abigail, Moses son of Abraham, Isaac Parvus, Diaie Le Chat—who all came, except for Deudone, Joppe, Benedict, Moses, and Isaac. And they deny this in its entirety as Jews against a Christian.

Subsequently the aforesaid boy, who then was five years old and now is nine years old, when asked in what manner they circumcised him, says that they took him and led him up to the house of this Jacob, and another one of them held him and covered his eyes, and a certain other circumcised him with a certain little knife, and then they took the piece they had cut from his penis and put it in a certain basin lined with sable fur, and they searched for it with little sticks until one Jew, who was called Jurnepin, found it first. And because this Jurnepin found it first, they called him [the boy] Jurnepin.

And the Archdeacon's official came before the justices with a large group of priests, who all said by God's word that the aforesaid boy was circumcised in this way, as was said, and by the aforesaid Jews, and that they saw the aforesaid boy when he was recently circumcised, with his penis large and very swollen and bloody.

And the coronors of the county [of Norfolk] and coroners of the city of Norwich and thirty-six men from the town of Norwich come as jurors,[11] and they say on their oath without reservation that the aforesaid boy was thus circumcised, as was said, and they know this as fact because when this boy was thus circumcised he escaped Jewish hands and was found sitting near the Norwich river by a certain Matilda of Bernham and her daughter; and they found him crying and wailing and saying that he was a Jew, such that this Matilda took the boy, for God's love, and led him to her house and gave him lodging for the whole night until morning; and when the Jews heard this they came to the aforesaid Matilda's house and wanted to take him by force because, they said, he was their Jew, and they called him "Jurnepin" in the hearing of the aforesaid Matilda and her daughter and the many others then present; and, when they could not have him, they came afterwards to this aforesaid house with a great multitude of Jews, and they wanted, with great force, to take him away with them. And when the neighbours heard this, namely those living around Matilda, they came to that house and heard well that the aforesaid Jews called the aforesaid Jew their boy and that they called him "Jurnepin." And when the Jews could not have him on account of the Christians, they forbade Matilda to give him pork to eat—because, they said, he was a Jew—such that the Christians came and removed the aforesaid boy from Jewish hands by force.

And the aforesaid Matilda in whose home the boy was found came before the justices, and with her daughter, similarly sworn, and they acknowledge this, saying that they found the aforesaid boy thus, crying as was said, and that, for God's love, they kept him in their house because they did not know whose son the boy was, and because they saw the same boy in such bad condition that they thought he would soon die, and that the Jews came in the morning thus, as was said. And further, they did not know whose son the boy was except through a certain woman who said he was the son of Master Benedict the physician. And so at the command of the aforesaid women [Matilda and her daughter], the aforesaid physician Benedict came and hid himself in Matilda's bedroom so that he could hear what the aforesaid Jews would say to his son. And when he could hear that they called him their son and "Jurnepin," he immediately came out of the bedroom contradicting them, and he asked the boy what he was called, who said, because of fear, "A Jew called Jurnepin." And once he had seen his father, he rejoiced and said that he was his son, Odard. Now all of the Jews are in prison at Norwich, except those who were at London when this inquest was conducted.

And all of the jurors, when asked who was involved in this circumcision, say that all of the aforesaid Jews agreed to the deed except for Moses son of Solomon.

All of this was undertaken before justices in the Lord King's Court at Norwich with the Prior of Norwich and Dominican friars and Franciscan friars, and many others, both clergy and laity, present.

Subsequently at Cattishall,[12] Richard of Fressingfield, who at that time was Constable of Norwich, came before the Cattishall justices and acknowledged before those justices that the Jews came to him when he was at Norwich Castle and made complaint that the Christians wanted to steal their Jew from them, and, upon hearing this, he himself went at their suit, to the aforesaid Matilda's house, and found a great crowd of Christians and Jews there, and the aforesaid Jews explained to him that the Christians wanted to steal their Jew from them, and when the aforesaid physician Benedict heard this he contradicted them, saying that Odard was his son. And accordingly, he [Richard] also said well that he saw the aforesaid Odard, son of the aforesaid Benedict, with his penis cut, bleeding and swollen big, and he said well that the Christians took this Odard and removed him from their hands.

And Simon of Ber Street and Nicholas Chese, who were then the bailiffs of Norwich, came before the justices and acknowledged that they went to the suit of the aforesaid Jews, to the aforesaid house, and they said that they saw all of this aforesaid deed, as was said.

Subsequently, before the Lord King and Lord [Archbishop] of Canterbury and a great part of the Bishops, Earls, and Barons of England: because this type of case had never before fallen to the Lord King's Court, and also because such a deed firstly touches God and Holy Church, in that circumcision and baptism pertain to the faith, and also because there is no such felony, neither loss of limb nor mayhem nor mortal wounding or any other secular felony that may condemn men without order of Holy Church, it was decided that such a deed should first be handled in Holy Church and the truth of things investigated by the ordinary of that place and [the truth] be sent to the Lord King so that he may do whatever he ought to do.

Furthermore, all the Jews came as a group and proffered one mark's worth of gold to the Lord King so that, through this, the boy might be viewed before these Jews as to whether he was circumcised or not. And it was accepted.

And the boy was seen, and his penis was seen covered with skin [only] before the head. And in this condition, he was released to his father so that he might have him before the ecclesiastical judges. And the Jews remain in prison.

Alice the Convert of Worcester

The three known letters by and about Alice of Worcester, a convert from Judaism to Christianity, date between August 1274 and, at the latest, March 1282. Two are by Alice (items 1 and 2 below), the third by King Edward I to Worcester Cathedral Priory in response to Alice's complaints. Alice's letters, one in French to Edward I and one in Latin to Robert Burnell, are in different scribal hands, and the first attests to the fact that her son (John) has acted as a courier for her. Edward I's letter survives only in a late medieval copy by John Lawerne, a Worcester monk and lecturer at Gloucester College, Oxford. Item 1 has been printed on four previous occasions: in F. J. Tanquerey, ed., *Recueil de lettres anglo-françaises (1265–1399)* (Paris: Édouard Champion, 1916), no. 61; with an English translation in Michael Adler, *Jews of Medieval England* (London: JHSE, 1939), 347–48; in English translation only in Anne Crawford, ed., *Letters of the Queens of England, 1100–1547* (Thrupp: Sutton, 1994), 246–47; and, as below, in Adrienne Williams Boyarin, "Anglo-Jewish Women at Court," in *Women Intellectuals and Leaders in the Middle Ages*, edited by Kathryn Kerby-Fulton, Katie Ann-Marie Bugyis, and John Van Engen (Cambridge: D. S. Brewer, 2020), 55–70, at 67. Items 2 and 3 have not appeared in print except as below in Williams Boyarin, "Anglo-Jewish Women at Court," 67–69. In the transcriptions that follow, medieval punctuation is maintained, expanded abbreviations are marked by italics, and square brackets indicate editorial intervention.

1. TNA SC 1/16/63, Alice the Convert of
Worcester to King Edward I, ca. 1274–1275

A nostre seygnur le Rey si li pleyt Alice la conuerse de Wyrecestr' monstre cum
el aueyt par le graunt le Rey Henri ke fu vostre pere ke deu de sa alme eyt merci
charite en la Priorie de Wyrcestr' e pus par vostre graunt ke vos ly grauntates en
Gascoyne la ele vaya sun fiz kaunt vos fuces en ses parties e la vos ly grauntates
vne Lecter ke ele dute ressayuer la charite ieskes a [v]ostre venue en Engletere
cum ele aneyt ressu deuaunt ses oures / dunt pus ke vos estes venu en Engletere
mercie seyt nostre seygnur ele vos pri pur deu e par seynte charite si vos pleyt ke
vos ly grauntes vostre lecter au Priour e au Couent de Wyrecstr' deauer e ressey-
ure la charite cum ele a ressu deuaunt ses oures kar le Priour e les bone gent de la
mesun le volunt ben .

       To our Lord the King, if it please him, Alice the Convert of Worcester
shows how she had charity in the Priory of Worcester by the grant of King
Henry who was your father (may God have mercy on his soul), and then by your
grant that you gave her in Gascony, where she sent her son when you were in
those regions and where you granted him a letter that she ought to receive the
charity until your coming into England, as she had received it formerly. Wherefore, since you have arrived in England (thanks be to our Lord), she begs you for
the sake of God and holy charity, if it please you, that you grant her your letter
to the Prior and Convent of Worcester that she might have and receive the charity as she received it formerly, for the Prior and the good people of the house
truly desire it.

2. TNA SC 1/24/201,[1] Alice the Convert of
Worcester to Robert Burnell, Bishop of Bath and Wells and
Chancellor of England, ca. 1275–1280

Viro venerabili et discreto Roberto dei gratia Episcopo de Baa . necnon et domini
Edwardi regis nostri Cancellario. sua captiua Alicia de Wyrcestr' conuersa si
placet salutem. pontificali Excellencie vestre notifico. quod domus Coventrenc'
que me cum filio meo latore presentium mandasti. literatorie vt mihi victus
meos donec mihi melius prouideretis tribueret. literas vestras mihi sub sigillo
vestro tributas nullo modo suscipere dignantur. Quapropter vobis conuolo

tamquam ad refugium meum lacrimabiliter exorando. quatinus super hiis mihi
aliquid remedium volitis tribuere. Sciatis me commorantem apud Cestr' donec
non valentem itinerando laborare. sumptibus carendo. donec mihi aliquid ben-
eficium si vobis placuerit per latorem presentium mittere dignenum. Tamen super hiis faciatis ne in infirmitate mea vos petere agar et si pedibus ac manibus
oportet incedere. valete. Miserere mei captiue pro maxima misericordia quam
dominus iesus christus misertus fuit super beatam mariam magdalen'. valete.

To the venerable and prudent man Robert, by God's grace Bishop of Bath
and likewise Chancellor of our lord king Edward, from his captive Alice of
Worcester, a convert, if it please, greetings. I notify your pontifical excellency
that the Coventry house to which you assigned myself with my son, the bearer
of the present document, in writing, to contribute to my sustenance until you
provide better for me, in no way deigns to receive your letters, which were
granted to me under your seal. Therefore, I fly to you as to my refuge, praying
tearfully, that you might give me relief in the matter of these desired things.
Know that I am staying at Chester for as long as I cannot manage travelling,
lacking means, until it pleases you to send some worthy benefice to me through
the bearer of the present document. Would that you act on these things, lest in
my weakness I am driven to beg and, if necessary, go on feet and hands. Farewell. Have mercy on me, a captive, according to the great mercy with which
Lord Jesus Christ showed mercy to the blessed Mary Magdalene. Farewell.

3. Bodleian MS Bodley 692 (fol. 89v), King Edward I to the Prior and Convent of Worcester, 18 March 1282(?), as copied in 1446 by John Lawerne, Worcester monk and D.Theol. (Gloucester College, Oxford)[2]

[In margin:] Litera domini rege pro Aliciam la conuerse ad priorem et conuen-
tum Wygornensis

Edward dei gratia Rex Anglie. Dominus Hibernie et Dux Aquitania. dilec-
tis sibi in Christo Priori et Conuentui Wygornensis salutem. Ex graui querela
Alicie la conuerse de Wygornia et Iohannis filii eius nobis est ostensum. quod
cum ipsi habere debeant quandam certam sustentacionem de domo vestra que
eis ad mandatus domini et quondam regis Anglie patris nostri. Ad totam vitam

eorumdem Alicie *et* Ioh*annis* percipiendam *per* vos extit*it* assignata.ʾ quam qui-
dem sustentacio*n*em. iidem Alicia *et* Ioh*ann*es ta*m* d*ic*ti *p*atris *n*o*s*tri tempo*re*
quam *n*o*s*tro iux*t*a forma*m* assignacio*n*is p*redic*te diutius p*er*ceperu*n*t *et*
h*a*buerun*t*.ʾ Vos nichi*l*omi*n*us d*ic*tam sustentacio*n*em eisd*e*m Alicie *et* Ioh*ann*i
subtrahit*is* ia*m* de nouo. *et* ea*m* eis sic*ut* asseru*n*t renuitis amplius exhibere. in
ip*s*oru*m* Ali*c*ie *et* Ioh*ann*is dampnu*m* *et* depaup*er*acio*n*em ma*n*ifesta*m*. Et q*u*ia
nolum*us* qu*o*d eisd*e*m Alicie *et* Ioh*ann*i iniuri[ari] aliqua*liter* in hac p*ar*te vobis
mandam*us* sic*ut* alias ma*n*dauim*us*. q*uo*d si ita e*s*t eisd*e*m Alicie *et* Ioh*ann*i
t*a*l*e*m sustentacio*n*em de domo *ve*st*r*a p*redic*ta exhiberi faciat*is*. quale*m* eis in
tempo*re* d*ic*ti *p*atris *n*o*s*tri exhibuist*is*. Et tallit*er* vos habeat*is* in hac p*ar*te qu*o*d
n*o*n oporteat ip*s*os in *ve*st*r*i def*ec*tus ad nos it*er*ato req*ui*rere ex hac c*au*s*a*. vel
c*au*sa*m* nobis si*g*nificat*is*. quare ma*n*dato *n*o*s*tro alias vobis inde directo minime
paruistis. T*es*te me ip*s*o ap*u*d Westm*onisterium* xviii*mo* die Martii anno regni
n*o*s*t*ri [x]°

Letter from the Lord King for Alice the Convert to the Prior and Convent of
Worcester:

Edward, by God's grace King of England, Lord of Ireland, and Duke of
Aquitaine, to his beloved in Christ, the Prior and Convent of Worcester, greetings. On the grievous complaint of Alice the Convert of Worcester and her son
John, it was shown to us that they should have had certain guaranteed support
from your house that was set for them by order of the Lord and once-King of
England our father. It was assigned to you in order to secure the whole life of
the said Alice and John; indeed, the same Alice and John secured and held this
support both in the time of our father and in our own time, according to the
form of the aforesaid assignment, for a long time. You nevertheless withhold
the said support from this Alice and John even now, and, as they assert, refuse
to pay it to them further, to the manifest damage and impoverishment of this
Alice and John. And because we do not wish to do injustice to the same Alice
and John, so we command you in this matter, as we have commanded before,
that you are to effect such support of the same Alice and John from your aforesaid house as you did for them in the time of our said father, and so deal in this
matter that they need not inquire at us for this reason again because of your
failure, or show us cause why you have not previously performed our direct order to you. Witness myself at Westminster on the 18th day of March in the
[tenth?] year of our reign.

The Jewess and the Priest

This exemplum about a French priest in love with a Jewess appears in BL MS Royal 8 A VI (fol. 15v), within a fragmentary booklet of homiletic material written in the same late thirteenth-century English hand (fols. 12–16). It is part of a sermon (fols. 14v–16v) on Psalm 62:2 ("Deus, Deus meus, ad te de luce vigilio"), which also includes a story about how Saladin prepared for death (fol. 14v). The manuscript belonged to St Augustine's Abbey, Canterbury: a flyleaf note identifies it as one of the books that William de Clara brought to St Augustine's in 1277 after studying at the University of Paris.[1] Including work in various hands, the book is a miscellany of homiletic, theological, grammatical, and scientific texts (evincing a particular interest in logic and astronomy) and shows evidence of readership into the late sixteenth century. This text has not appeared in print before.[2] In what follows, medieval punctuation is maintained, expanded abbreviations are marked by italics, and square brackets indicate editorial intervention.

BL Royal MS A VI, fol. 15, ca. 1275

Fuit sacerdos quidam in partibus gallie: diligens insano amore quandam iudeam. quam sepe cognouerat. vnde in quodam festo die iudeorum cum vellet accedere ad eam. et commisceri ei. Ipsa primo pro sua festiuitate contradixit. at ille nichilominus instabat. quae tandiu uicta est hac interiecta condicione. vt ille quando uellet consentiret ei. at illa in paschali die accessit ad sacerdotem dicens. volo ut commiscearis mihi in tuo festo. sicut fregi meum festum pro te. At ille dicebat se non posse. quia debebat tunc parrochianis suis celebrare. et illa propius accessit. et tandiu hinc et inde palpauit quod ille uictus est. qui prius intrat[u]s ecclesias suas assumpsit indumenta sacerdotalia. Illa non uideri cupiens quid sacerdos faceret retro hostium omnia prospexit. Sacerdos primo induit supplicium. quod antequam induissus album erat. et tunc super eum factum est nigrius carbone. post accepit albam. et statim in corpore eius facta est nigerrima. et sic accidit omnibus que induit. preter altare et corporalia. et ea que fuerunt super eucaristiam. et ipse totus nigerrimus apparuit. Quibus omnibus visis. ipsa conuersa statim credidit sacrificium altaris verum esse. et a malo ministro non posse deteriorari. et currit cum lacrimis festinans baptizari ab illo. qui uidens eius uisitationem et predicationem. et ipse conuersus est penitens. vnde statim nigredo a uestibus et a corpore aufugit.

There was a certain priest in France who loved a certain Jewess with a mad desire. He often knew her. Accordingly, when he wanted to go to her on a certain Jewish feast day and have intercourse with her, she objected on account of her holiday. But he nonetheless insisted. Eventually she was defeated, though she set this condition: that he, whenever she might want, would consent to her. But she approached the priest on Easter, saying, "I want you to have intercourse with me on your feast day, just as I broke my holiday for you." But he told himself it was not possible, for he was supposed to be celebrating with his parishioners then. And she approached nearer, and she stroked him here and there, so that eventually he was defeated. Before he entered his churches, he picked up his priestly vestments. Not wanting to be seen, she watched everything the priest did from behind a door. First, the priest put on the surplice that before it was donned was white, and then on him became blacker than coal. Next, he picked up the alb, and immediately on his body it became even blacker. And thus it happened with everything that he put on (with the exception of the altar and corporals and things that covered the Eucharist), and he himself appeared very black all over. When she saw these things, this woman immediately converted and believed the sacrifice of the altar to be true, and, not able to be held back by the bad servant of God, she ran forward in tears, rushing to be baptized by him. He, seeing her visitation and teaching, repenting, was himself also converted. Accordingly, the blackness immediately fled from his vestments and from his body.

NOTES

INTRODUCTION

1. Influential studies of anti-Judaism in medieval and early modern England from recent decades include Anthony Bale, *The Jew in the Medieval Book: English Antisemitisms, 1350–1500* (Cambridge: Cambridge Univ. Press, 2006), and *Feeling Persecuted: Christians, Jews, and Images of Violence in the Middle Ages* (London: Reaktion, 2010); Geraldine Heng, *England and the Jews: How Religion and Violence Created the First Racial State in the West* (Cambridge: Cambridge Univ. Press, 2018); Miriamne Ara Krummel, *Crafting Jewishness in Medieval England: Legally Absent, Virtually Present* (New York: Palgrave, 2011); Lisa Lampert-Weissig, *Gender and Jewish Difference from Paul to Shakespeare* (Philadelphia: Univ. of Pennsylvania Press, 2004); Kathy Lavezzo, *The Accommodated Jew: English Antisemitism from Bede to Milton* (Ithaca: Cornell Univ. Press, 2016); Robin R. Mundill, *England's Jewish Solution: Experiment and Expulsion, 1262–1290* (Cambridge: Cambridge Univ. Press, 1998), and *The King's Jews: Money, Massacre, and Exodus in Medieval England* (London: Continuum, 2010); and Ruth Nisse, *Jacob's Shipwreck: Diaspora, Translation, and Jewish-Christian Relations in Medieval England* (Ithaca: Cornell Univ. Press, 2017). Important books on anti-Judaism in medieval Europe more broadly include Jeremy Cohen, *The Friars and the Jews: The Evolution of Medieval Anti-Judaism* (Ithaca: Cornell Univ. Press, 1982), and *Living Letters of the Law: Ideas of the Jew in Medieval Christianity* (Berkeley: Univ. of California Press, 1999); Joan Young Gregg, *Devils, Women, and Jews: Reflections on the Other in Medieval Sermon Stories* (Albany: State Univ. of New York Press, 1997); Sara Lipton, *Dark Mirror: The Medieval Origins of Anti-Jewish Iconography* (New York: Metropolitan, 2014); Steven F. Kruger, *The Spectral Jew: Conversion and Embodiment in Medieval Europe* (Minneapolis: Univ. of Minnesota Press, 2005); David Nirenberg, *Anti-Judaism: The Western Tradition* (New York: Norton, 2013); Irven M. Resnick, *Marks of Distinction: Christian Perceptions of Jews in the High Middle Ages* (Washington, DC: Catholic Univ. of America Press, 2012); and Miri Rubin, *Gentile Tales: The Narrative Assault on Late Medieval Jews* (Philadelphia: Univ. of Pennsylvania Press, 2004). Many of these—and particularly Bale, Heng, Kruger, Lavezzo, Nisse, and Resnick—have discussed issues of Jewish-Christian contact and sameness in sensitive ways, though none has presented sameness as a primary frame of analysis for understanding anti-Jewish polemics.

2. My previous work on doubled Jewish/Christian identity in English Miracles of the Virgin—texts that frequently align the Virgin Mary with Jews or evoke the historical fact of her Jewishness in order to make her both the ideal Jewish convert and the ideal Christian woman— is important background to this study. In part, the current project explores more thoroughly the dynamics of identification and disidentification that I first noticed around Mary and other

Jewish women in medieval English texts. See my *Miracles of the Virgin in Medieval England: Law and Jewishness in Marian Legends* (Cambridge: D. S. Brewer, 2010); "Inscribed Bodies: The Virgin Mary, Jewish Women, and Medieval Feminine Legal Authority," in *Law and Sovereignty in the Middle Ages and Renaissance*, ed. Robert S. Sturges (Turnhout: Brepols, 2011), 229–51; and "Desire for Religion: Mary, a Murder Libel, a Jewish Friar, and Me," *Religion & Literature* 41, nos. 1–2 (2010): 23–48, especially 30–42, where I first articulated two of the readings featured in this book. I discuss pedagogical uses of sameness in "Difficult Sameness and Weird Time: Starting with *The Siege of Jerusalem*," in *Jews in Medieval England: Teaching Representations of the Other*, ed. Tison Pugh and Miriamne Ara Krummel (New York: Palgrave Macmillan, 2017), 311–28.

3. Sylvia Tomasch and Krummel, for instance, both use "absent presence" or "present absence" to describe the figural likeness of the absent that continues to signify in the present. See Tomasch's "Post-Colonial Chaucer and the Virtual Jew," in *Chaucer and the Jews: Sources, Contexts, Meanings*, ed. Sheila Delany (New York, 2002), 69 and passim (with a useful bibliography of the concept in n. 2); and Krummel, *Crafting Jewishness*, 8 and passim.

4. Tamsin Barber, "The Plasticity of Diasporic Identities in Super-Diverse Cities," in *The Routledge Handbook of Diaspora Studies*, ed. Robin Cohen and Carolin Fischer (New York: Routledge, 2018), 268–75, at 269.

5. Gilles Deleuze and Félix Guattari, *A Thousand Plateaus: Capitalism and Schizophrenia*, trans. Brian Massumi (London: Continuum, 1987), 415.

6. H. J. Schroeder, ed. and trans., *Disciplinary Decrees of the General Councils: Text, Translation, and Commentary* (St. Louis: B. Herder, 1937), 290.

7. The English *tabula* mandated in the 1275 Statute of the Jewry was notably different from the more usual yellow circle mandated on the continent: "a badge on the outer garment, that is to say, in the form of two tables joined, of yellow felt, of the length of six inches, and of the breadth of three inches." In compliance with Lateran IV, a version of this badge was instituted in England by 1218, but it is difficult to know how widespread compliance was; Jews could pay waiver fees, and multiple statutes reinstituted the badge throughout the second half of the thirteenth century. See Mundill, *England's Jewish Solution*, 56–59 and 291–93 (here 292), and *DMAJH*, s.v. "Badge," 46–47.

8. Bale, *Feeling Persecuted*, 72.

9. Bale, 77 and 78.

10. For these terms, see, respectively, Bale, *Jew in the Medieval Book*, 13, where the "mutable Jew" is one that "resists or escapes . . . containment"; Cohen, *Living Letters of the Law*, 65, where Cohen connects the "hermenuetical Jew" to the Augustinian "idea of the Jew as witness" and later exegesis; Tomasch, "Post-Colonial Chaucer and the Virtual Jew," 77–78, where "virtual Jew" expresses "the integral connections between imaginary constructions and actual people, even when they exist only in a fabricated past or a phantasmatic future"; Denise Despres, "The Protean Jew in the Vernon Manuscript," in Delany, *Chaucer and the Jews*, 145–64; Brian Cheyette, *Constructions of "The Jew" in English Literature and Society: Racial Representations, 1875–1945* (Cambridge: Cambridge Univ. Press, 1993), 8, where English characterizations reveal "the protean instability of 'the Jew' as a signifier"; and Kruger, *Spectral Jew*, 5, where spectrality evokes Derrida's *Spectres of Marx* and describes "strong ambivalence" in Christian representations and voicing of Jews.

11. Kathleen Biddick, *The Typological Imaginary: Circumcision, Technology, History* (Philadelphia: Univ. of Pennsylvania Press, 2003), 2. "Typology Never Lets Go" is Biddick's title for the Introduction in this book (1–20).

12. Tomasch, "Post-Colonial Chaucer and the Virtual Jew," 75.

13. Biddick, *Typological Imaginary*, 6. See also Steven F. Kruger, "The Times of Conversion," *Philological Quarterly* 92, no. 1 (2013): 19–39, at 20, where Kruger explores the medieval experience of Jewish conversion to Christianity as one that "echoes in miniature the larger historical trajectory that the Christian dispensation constructs for itself," and thus always engages a kind of temporal doubling.

14. Denise Despres, "Mary of the Eucharist: Cultic Anti-Judaism in Some Fourteenth-Century English Devotional Manuscripts," in *From Witness to Witchcraft: Jews and Judaism in Christian Thought*, ed. Jeremy Cohen (Wiesbaden: Harrassowitz, 1996), 388.

15. For example, Geraldine Heng, in "England's Dead Boys: Telling Tales of Christian-Jewish Relations Before and After the First European Expulsion of the Jews," *MLN* 127, no. 5, supp. (2012): 54–85, argues for a post-Expulsion shift through examination of similar anti-Jewish boy-martyr narratives before and after the Expulsion; and Krummel, in *Crafting Jewishness*, suggests that more tolerant views of Jews begin to appear after the Expulsion. See my review of Krummel's book for an assessment of how this post-Expulsion argument develops: Adrienne Williams Boyarin, review of *Crafting Jewishness in Medieval England*, by Miriamne Ara Krummel, *JEGP* 112, no. 3 (2013): 382–85. In my view, it is more likely that observed changes are responses to regional trends (e.g., the spread of boy-martyr narratives and cults in East Anglia), wider European historical and intellectual trends (e.g., crusading sentiment, *kiddush ha-shem*, the twelfth-century rise of *Adversos Judaeos* literature), and shifts in genre and language. As Bale notes in *Jew in the Medieval Book*, 16, "The *punctum* of 1290 is of little importance in terms of representation."

16. Nicholas Howe, *Migration and Mythmaking in Anglo-Saxon England* (New Haven: Yale Univ. Press, 1989), 105 and 72–73. More recent books that build on Howe's argument and explore pre-Conquest British identity-making in relation to Jews and Israel more thoroughly are Andrew Scheil, *The Footsteps of Israel: Understanding Jews in Anglo-Saxon England* (Ann Arbor: Univ. of Michigan Press, 2004); and Samantha Zacher, ed., *Imagining the Jew in Anglo-Saxon Literature and Culture* (Toronto: Univ. of Toronto Press, 2016).

17. Janet Adelman, *Blood Relations: Christian and Jew in "The Merchant of Venice"* (Chicago: Univ. of Chicago Press, 2008), 105. See also Achsah Guibbory, *Christian Identity, Jews, and Israel in Seventeenth-Century England* (Oxford: Oxford Univ. Press, 2010); and Jeffrey Shoulson, *Fictions of Conversion: Jews, Christians, and Cultures of Change in Early Modern England* (Philadelphia: Univ. of Pennsylvania Press, 2013).

18. Lampert-Weissig, *Gender and Jewish Difference*, 143. On the complex construction of feminine Jewishness and conversion in the *Merchant of Venice*, see also M. Lindsay Kaplan, "Jessica's Mother: Medieval Constructions of Jewish Race and Gender in *The Merchant of Venice*," *Shakespeare Quarterly* 58, no. 1 (2007): 1–30; and Michelle Ephraim, *Reading Jewish Women on the Elizabethan Stage* (Aldershot: Ashgate, 2008), 133–52.

19. Sara Lipton, "Isaac and the Antichrist in the Archives," *Past & Present* 232, no. 1 (2016): 3–44, at 22.

20. Krummel, *Crafting Jewishness in Medieval England*, 132–33.

21. Krummel, 134 and 158.

22. Andrew S. Jacobs, *Christ Circumcised: A Study in Early Christian History and Difference* (Philadelphia: Univ. of Pennsylvania Press, 2012), 4.

23. Jacobs, *Christ Circumcised*, 6.

24. *OED*, s.vv. "sameness, *n.*" 1 and "same, *adj., pron.,* and *adv.*" 7a.

25. *MED*, s.v. "samnen (v.)" 1 and 2.

26. Audre Lorde, "Audre Lorde: Claudia Tate/1982," in *Conversations with Audre Lorde*, ed. Joan Wylie Hall (Jackson: Univ. Press of Mississippi, 2004), 86. Hall's volume reprints Lorde's interview with Tate as it appeared in *Black Women Writers at Work*, ed. Claudia Tate (New York: Continuum, 1983), 100–116.

27. Lipton, *Dark Mirror*, 219, and "Where Are the Gothic Jewish Women? On the Non-iconography of the Jewess in the *Cantigas de Santa Maria*," *Jewish History* 22 (2008): 139–77, at 158.

28. Lampert-Weissig, *Gender and Jewish Difference*, 2.

29. Respectively, Kruger, *Spectral Jew*, 85; Rubin, *Gentile Tales*, 43; and Anthony Bale, "Fictions of Judaism in England Before 1290," in *Jews in Medieval Britain: Historical, Literary, Archaeological Perspectives*, ed. Patricia Skinner (Woodbridge: Boydell, 2003), 129–44, at 137.

30. Sander L. Gilman, "Salome, Syphilis, Sarah Bernhardt, and the 'Modern Jewess,'" *German Quarterly* 66, no. 2 (1993): 195–211, at 196 and 210.

31. The *Cronicon* of Richard of Devizes (written at Winchester ca. 1190–1200) may seem a notable absence in this context: I choose to exclude it from the present study because of its satirical tone—other sources considered here are unambiguously sincere in their theological, devotional, or political commitments—and because the work has been so ably discussed in the recent past. Most notably, see Heather Blurton, "Richard of Devizes's *Cronicon*, Menippean Satire, and the Jews of Winchester," *Exemplaria* 22, no. 4 (2010): 265–84, which gives thorough attention to the tone and genre of the *Cronicon*; and Anthony Bale, "Richard of Devizes and Fictions of Judaism," *Jewish Culture and History* 3, no. 2 (2000): 55–72, which argues that Richard's account of a Winchester ritual murder accusation is a satirical fiction that critiques other such narratives.

32. For a good summary of the development of medieval caricatures of Jews, see Lipton, "Isaac and the Antichrist in the Archives," 14–17, where she summarizes the timeline and explains that few of the features now associated with anti-Jewish stereotypes were well established before 1250. Resnick, with *Marks of Distinction*, challenges this assessment, if mainly on textual bases.

33. Scholars who have included the Adam of Bristol story among historical ritual murder accusations include Joe Hillaby and Caroline Hillaby, *DMAJH*, s.v. "Ritual-Child-Murder Accusations," 323–30; John M. McCulloh, "Jewish Ritual Murder: William of Norwich, Thomas of Monmouth, and the Early Dissemination of the Myth," *Speculum* 72, no. 3 (1997): 698–740, at 712; Heng, "England's Dead Boys," 55, where the murder is even given an unqualified secure date; and Mundill, *England's Jewish Solution*, 52.

34. Schroeder, *Disciplinary Decrees*, 290.

35. A medieval compilation of restrictions around Jewish-Christian interaction, sharing of resources, and employment can be found, for instance, in the *Omne Bonum*, a massive encyclopaedia ascribed to James le Palmer and compiled in the mid-fourteenth century (now housed in two volumes as BL MS Royal 6 E VI and BL MS Royal 6 E VII). The entry for "Jews" (s.v. *Iudei*, fols. 341r–345r in Royal 6 E VII) begins with an illustration of two Jewish men who do not look remarkably different from other men depicted throughout the work, and its text is for the most part a list of rules and regulations regarding interactions between Christians and Jews, culled from various theological and legal texts (including papal pronouncements) and ranging from the patristic to the contemporary. Though Jews had been exiled from England for more than fifty years at the time of its production, the *Omne Bonum* codifies a continuing concern with how and when to distinguish Jews from Christians and

other non-Christian groups; Jews' ability to look the same or blend into other groups is the primary delimiter of the entry.

PART I. *HISTORIAE*

1. The full record, in Latin and Modern English, can be found in Appendix 1. All citations and translations are from this new transcription and translation (my own).

2. The account of Samuel's case is in TNA E 9/24, m. 5d (a Plea Roll of the Exchequer of the Jews for 5 Edward I). It follows a large blank space and fills the end of the membrane, suggesting that room had been reserved for later copying from notes, as was not unusual practice for Exchequer scribes. On the institutional history of the Exchequer of the Jews, see Paul Brand's introduction to *PREJ* 6, Hilary Jenkinson's introduction to *PREJ* 3, and J. M. Rigg's introduction to *Select Pleas*.

3. *DMAJH*, s.vv. "Coinage and Coin-clipping Crises, 1238–47 and 1276–76," 105–8, and "Ritual-Child-Murder Allegations," 326–27; *CCR 1272–79*, 565; Robin R. Mundill, *England's Jewish Solution: Experiment and Expulsion, 1262–1290* (Cambridge: Cambridge Univ. Press, 1998), 69 and 275.

4. Ivan G. Marcus, "A Jewish-Christian Symbiosis: The Culture of Early Ashkenaz," in *The Cultures of the Jews: A New History*, ed. David Biale (New York: Schocken, 2002), 2:185.

5. Marcus, "Jewish-Christian Symbiosis," 159.

6. Most notable is Jeremy Cohen, *The Friars and the Jews: The Evolution of Medieval Anti-Judaism* (Ithaca: Cornell Univ. Press, 1982)—still a standard. See also Mundill, *England's Jewish Solution*, 270–75; and Christoph Cluse, "Stories of Breaking and Taking the Cross: A Possible Context for the Oxford Incident of 1268," *Revue d'histoire ecclésiastique* 90, no. 3 (1995): 396–442, which has much to say on the friars and the Jews at Oxford. For an interesting and somewhat critical response to Jeremy Cohen's thesis and the assumption of widespread anti-Jewish preaching by fraternal orders, see Jussi Hanska, "Sermons on the Tenth Sunday After Holy Trinity: Another Occasion for Anti-Jewish Preaching," in *The Jewish-Christian Encounter in Medieval Preaching*, ed. Jonathan Adams and Jussi Hanska (New York: Routledge, 2014), 195–212.

7. See *DMAJH*, s.v. "Converts, House of," 119; and Mundill, *England's Jewish Solution*, 275.

8. Mundill, *England's Jewish Solution*, 272–73. On Kilwardby and the Jews more generally, see Ellen M. F. Sommer-Seckendorff, *Studies in the Life of Robert Kilwardby O.P.* (Rome: Istituto Storico Domenicano, 1937), 56–66, and *A Companion to the Philosophy of Robert Kilwardby*, ed. Henrik Lagerlund and Paul Thom (Leiden: Brill, 2012), 5.

9. For the full text of Kilwardby's letter about Elijah Menahem ("Magister Helias Judaeus") and his excommunication case, see Sommer-Seckendorff, *Studies in the Life*, 64 n. 135. The case is also discussed in Donald F. Logan, "Thirteen London Jews and Conversion to Christianity: Problems of Apostasy in the 1280s," *Bulletin of the Institute of Historical Research* 45, no. 112 (1972): 214–29, at 217 and 224.

10. Both Logan and Sommer-Seckendorff discuss Kilwardby's collaborations with Burnell (see notes 7 and 8 above), but see also Joan Greatrex, "Monastic Charity for Jewish Converts: The Requisition of Corrodies by Henry III," *Studies in Church History* 29 (1992): 133–43. Burnell's role in the case of an Anglo-Jewish woman convert is discussed at length in the *Historiae* that begin Part II, below.

11. This incident is recorded in the continuations of Florence of Worcester's *Chronicon ex Chronicis, Florentii Wigorniensis Monachi Chronicon ex Chronicis*, ed. Benjamin Thorpe (London: English Historical Society, 1848), 2:214, and is discussed further in Chapter 5, at 213–16.

12. A medieval midrashic compilation makes the same connection between the sacrificial calf (the "red heifer") and the golden calf of Exodus. See *Yalkut Shim'oni: Midrash 'al Torah, Neviim u-Khetuvim*, Ḥukat (para. 759), commenting on Numbers 19:2: "Regarding the red heifer: Why is it that all sacrifices come from male [animals] while she is female? Rabbi Aybo said, 'It is like the son of a servant who soiled the floor of a king. The king said, Let his mother come and clean the defecation.' So said the Holy One, blessed be He: 'Let the cow come and atone for the deed of the calf.'" In other words, the sacrifice of the red heifer (the cow) is atonement for the sin of the calf.

13. On the status of medieval English Jews in relation to the Crown, see Robin R. Mundill, *The King's Jews: Money, Massacre, and Exodus in Medieval England* (London: Continuum, 2010), and his *England's Jewish Solution*, especially 45–71. On sheriffs, and particularly their part in the administration of the Exchequer of the Jews, see *DMAJH*, s.v. "Sheriffs," 333–37; and Brand, *PREJ* 6:6–16.

14. *PREJ* 3:312.

15. *PREJ* 3:188, 204, and 209 respectively.

16. *PREJ* 3:133.

17. This is TNA KB 26/115B (18–19 Henry III), rot. 22. The Norwich circumcision case occupies the face, with only a descriptive label of content on the dorse ("Recordum loquele de Iudeis Norwici qui sunt in prisona apud Lond'," confirming that several of the Jews named in the document were in prison at the time of recording). The damaged text was first edited by Rigg (in *Select Pleas*, xliv–xlvii), who admittedly relied on William Prynne's 1656 *Short Demurrer to the Jews* for unreadable portions. While Prynne did provide some of the text in an abridged format, and surely had access to the text in a less damaged state, the *Short Demurrer* is viciously anti-Jewish, and Prynne relied on Matthew Paris's libelous fictionalization for his understanding of the case. For a new transcription and Modern English translation, as well as complete information on editions and corroborating documents, see Appendix 2 below.

18. Jeffrey Jerome Cohen, *Hybridity, Identity, and Monstrosity in Medieval Britain: On Difficult Middles* (New York: Palgrave Macmillan, 2006), 29.

19. Cohen has rewritten and reframed some of the material from *Hybridity, Identity, and Monstrosity* in a series of posts on his scholarly blog *In the Middle*. I quote here from "Stories of Blood 2: The Blood of Race," *In the Middle*, 17 April 2017, http://www.inthemedievalmiddle .com/2017/04/stories-of-blood-2-blood-of-race.html.

20. See Appendix 2; *Select Pleas*, xlvii; V. D. Lipman, *The Jews of Medieval Norwich* (London: JHSE, 1967), 59–62; and H. R. Luard, ed., *Matthæi Parisiensis Monachi Sancti Albani Chronica majora* (London: Longman, 1877), 4:30–31.

21. All citations (both Latin and Modern English) are from Appendix 2.

22. See *Select Pleas*, xlvii; and *CCR 1237–42*, 168 (18 January 1240) and 175 (21 February 1240).

23. By February 1231, Senioret of Norwich had been banished from Norwich for his part in the circumcision, and his property was given to the harmed boy's father by order of the king. See *Calendar of Inquisitions Miscellaneous (Chancery) Preserved in the Public Record Office* (London: HMSO, 1916), 1:171, item no. 522.

24. Luard, *Chronica majora*, 4:30–31, and *CT* VII.628–34. See also Roger Dahood, "The Punishment of the Jews, Hugh of Lincoln, and the Question of Satire in Chaucer's Prioress's Tale," *Viator* 36 (2005): 465–91, and his "The Anglo-Norman 'Hugo de Lincolnia': A Critical Edition and Translation from the Unique Text in Paris, Bibliothèque nationale de France MS fr. 902," *Chaucer Review* 49, no. 1 (2014): 1–38, lines 353–64 of the poem in particular. I discuss the Hugh of Lincoln case in more detail in Chapter 5, at 185–209.

25. See Lipman, *Jews of Medieval Norwich*, 60–61.

26. See Sara Lipton, "Isaac and the Antichrist in the Archives," *Past & Present* 232, no. 1 (2016): 3–44. Lipton argues convincingly that the well-known images of Mosse and Avegaye are not anti-Jewish caricatures, as has been often repeated, but satirical illustrations that connect the Norwich Jews to Norman royal officials who, along with Jewish moneylenders, were thought to contribute to state economic oppression.

27. This story, in which a Jewish boy is thrown into an oven by his angry father for taking communion with his Christian companions, circulated in England from at least the early twelfth century, when it was used in the Marian miracle collections of Dominic of Evesham and William of Malmesbury. On "The Jewish Boy" in the Western tradition, see Miri Rubin, *Gentile Tales: The Narrative Assault on Late Medieval Jews* (Philadelphia: Univ. of Pennsylvania Press, 2004), 7–39. On its transmission in England in particular, see Adrienne Williams Boyarin, *Miracles of the Virgin in Medieval England* (Cambridge: D. S. Brewer), 63–70 and 87–90.

28. On the "Child Slain by Jews," sometimes called the "Miracle of the Boy Singer," see Anthony Bale, *The Jew in the Medieval Book* (Cambridge: Cambridge Univ. Press, 2006), 55–103; and Williams Boyarin, *Miracles of the Virgin*, 26–29 and 149–64. The attention of neighbors and law enforcement in both of these story types is drawn by distraught mothers (not fathers); I will also discuss the gendered dimensions of these and similar tales in Chapters 4 and 5.

29. See Miri Rubin, ed. and trans., *The Life and Passion of William of Norwich by Thomas of Monmouth* (London: Penguin, 2014), 16–18; and for the Latin, Augustus Jessop and M. R. James, eds. and trans., *The Life and Miracles of St William of Norwich by Thomas of Monmouth* (Cambridge: Cambridge Univ. Press, 1896), 19–23.

30. See Appendix 2: "Ceperunt peciam illam quam sciderant de membro suo et posuerunt in quodam bacyno cum sabelone, et quesierunt ipsam illam cum paruis fusselletis quousque quidam Iudeus qui vocabatur Iurnepin inuenit eam primo. Et quia idem Iurnepin inuenit eam primo, vocauerunt eum Iurnepin."

31. Luard, *Chronica majora*, 4:30.

32. Lipman, *Jews of Medieval Norwich*, 62. Lipman cites Walter Rye, ed., *The Norfolk Antiquarian Miscellany*, vol. 1, no. 2 (Norwich: Samuel Miller, 1877), 312–21. Interestingly in the context of the current discussion, Rye admits that his assumptions about the conversion of Jurnepin/ Odard's father are based on his own ideas of racial difference between Jews and Norwich Christians: "We may be tolerably sure . . . that the Jews would never have had the hardihood to go to the house of a Christian woman and clamorously demand a boy as 'their Jew,' if he bore on his face the evidence of Saxon or Danish blood" (320)!

33. Several such conversion cases are discussed in detail in Chapter 3, at 132–41. It is also worth noting, in relation to Rye's and Lipman's reading, that while there were indeed Jewish physicians in England (and at least one, Petrus Alphonsi, known to serve the court of Henry I), the stereotype does not seem to have been widespread in medieval England, possibly because the Anglo-Jewish community was never very large (see *DMAJH*, s.v. "Physicians and Surgeons," 306–8). Judith Olszowy-Schlanger's *Hebrew and Hebrew-Latin Documents from Medieval England: A Diplomatic and Palaeographical Study*, 2 vols. (Turnhout: Brepols, 2015), further,

finds only two Jews identified as physicians in its 258 documents and fifty-eight tally sticks: Isaac and Solomon of Norwich (father and son). The document that names them is dated 1266 (item 62 in vol. 1) and cites their joint property at Norwich—i.e., Solomon and his father's careers would have overlapped with the Jurnepin/Odard circumcision case.

34. In the thirteenth century, Ashkenazi boys did not wear tzitzit before the age of thirteen: see Elisheva Baumgarten, *Mothers and Children: Jewish Family Life in Medieval Europe* (Princeton: Princeton Univ. Press, 2004), 186–87; and only in 1275, with the infamous Statute of the Jewry, did English law specify that Jewish children should wear an identifying badge (though even there the requirement is for children seven and older). For the text of the 1275 Statute of the Jewry, see Adrienne Williams Boyarin, ed. and trans., *The Siege of Jerusalem* (Toronto: Broadview, 2014), 174–77.

35. Andrew S. Jacobs, *Christ Circumcised: A Study in Early Christian History and Difference* (Philadelphia: Univ. of Pennsylvania Press, 2012), xi. While Jacobs is concerned primarily with Christians before the sixth century, he cites medievalists' studies in his discussion of libels.

CHAPTER 1

1. Newman spoke as a respondent to a session on her *Medieval Crossover: Reading the Secular Against the Sacred* (Notre Dame: Notre Dame Univ. Press, 2013) and was, in this moment, interrogating the fundamental questions of her chapter "Mocking Mass Murder: *The Passion of the Jews of Prague*" (181–200). Her article "The Passion of the Jews of Prague: The Pogrom of 1389 and the Lessons of a Medieval Parody," *Church History* 81, no. 1 (2012): 1–26, discusses the same poem, "a polished literary text that parodies the gospel of Christ's Passion to celebrate the atrocity" (1) and therefore, perforce, utilizes likeness, contradiction, and inversions to vilify its Jews.

2. See Lynne Staley, ed., *The Book of Margery Kempe* (Kalamazoo: Medieval Institute, 1996), lines 2010–15: "Sche [Margery] was so meche affectyd to the manhode of Crist that whan sche sey women in Rome beryn children in her armys, yyf sche myth wetyn that thei wer ony men children, sche schuld than cryin, roryn, and wepyn as thei sche had seyn Crist in hys childhode."

3. See, for instance, Lee Edelman, *No Future: Queer Theory and the Death Drive* (Durham: Duke Univ. Press, 2004); Miri Rubin, *Gentile Tales: The Narrative Assault on Late Medieval Jews* (Philadelphia: Univ. of Pennsylvania Press, 2004), 7–39; Denise Despres, "Adolescence and Sanctity: *The Life and Passion of Saint William of Norwich*," *Journal of Religion* 90, no. 1 (2010): 33–62; and Geraldine Heng, "England's Dead Boys: Telling Tales of Christian-Jewish Relations Before and After the First European Expulsion of the Jews," *MLN* 127, no. 5, supp. (2012): 54–85. Many of the essays collected in Albrecht Classen, ed., *Childhood in the Middle Ages and Renaissance* (Berlin: Walter de Gruyter, 2005) also speak to this issue.

4. J. Allan Mitchell explicates this particularly well in *Becoming Human: The Matter of the Medieval Child* (Minneapolis: Minnesota Univ. Press, 2014).

5. Despres, "Adolescence and Sanctity," 41–43.

6. Despres, 45.

7. On this initiation rite, see Ivan G. Marcus, *Rituals of Childhood: Jewish Acculturation in Medieval Europe* (New Haven: Yale Univ. Press, 1996), 18–34 and 107–16.

8. Carolyn Dinshaw, "Pale Faces: Race, Religion, and Affect in Chaucer's Texts and Their Readers," *Studies in the Age of Chaucer* 23 (2001): 19–41, at 25. Dinshaw is here citing and paraphrasing Kruger's celebrated essay "Conversion and Medieval Sexual, Religious, and Racial Cat-

egories," in *Constructing Medieval Sexuality*, ed. Karma Lochrie, Peggy McCracken, and James A. Shultz (Minneapolis: Univ. of Minnestoa Press, 1997), 158–79.

9. Erich Auerbach, "Figura," trans. Ralph Manheim, in *Scenes from the Drama of European Literature* (Minneapolis: Univ. of Minnesota Press, 1984), 11–76, at 68.

10. See *DMAJH*, s.v. "Northampton," 276–79, at 278. For an overview of the *archae* system more generally (i.e., the chests that held records of Jewish bonds in cities with significant Jewish populations, as mandated in 1194 by Richard I's Justiciar Hubert Walter), see the same work s.vv. "1194, Form of Proceeding in Pleas of the Crown," 20–21, and "Chests," 95–97.

11. Latin quotations of Thomas of Monmouth's text follow Augustus Jessop and M. R. James, eds. and trans., *The Life and Miracles of St William of Norwich by Thomas of Monmouth* (Cambridge: Cambridge Univ. Press, 1896), here 17. English translations are those of Miri Rubin, ed. and trans., *The Life and Passion of William of Norwich by Thomas of Monmouth* (London: Penguin, 2014), here 14.

12. Jessop and James, *Life and Miracles*, 111; Rubin, *Life and Passion*, 72.

13. See Irven M. Resnick, *Marks of Distinction: Christian Perceptions of Jews in the High Middle Ages* (Washington, DC: Catholic Univ. of America Press, 2012), 181–82, 188–91, and 203–5. Caesarius of Heisterbach's thirteenth-century *Dialogus miraculorum* includes a miracle story set in England that claims all Jews suffer from a debilitating "fluxus sanguinis" on Good Friday. See Chapter 5 below, 210–11, and Book II, Chapter 23 in *Caesarii Heisterbacensis monachi ordinis Cisterciensis Dialogus miraculorum*, ed. Josephus Strange (Cologne: H. Lempertz, 1851), 1:92–94.

14. Jessop and James, *Life and Miracles*, 111; Rubin, *Life and Passion*, 72. The allusion is to Matthew 27:24.

15. Jessop and James, 58; Rubin, 40.

16. Jessop and James, 25; Rubin, 19.

17. This is CUL MS Additional 3037, perhaps copied at Sibton Abbey, Suffolk. For detailed information on the manuscript's date and history, see Rubin, *Life and Passion,* xxxi and li–lxiii.

18. For an overview of medieval Christian stories of the destruction of Jerusalem and the *Vengeance of Our Lord* tradition (presented as context and background for later English poems), see Adrienne Williams Boyarin, ed. and trans., *The Siege of Jerusalem* (Toronto: Broadview, 2014), 15–26.

19. Rubin, *Life and Passion*, xxvii. Rubin here makes this point with reference to Thomas's composition of a new kind of anti-Jewish story that imagines Jews as "acting in a concerted, knowing, planned, collective and cruel manner"; I extend it to the structure of his Christ/child narrative.

20. Homi K. Bhabha, *Location of Culture* (London: Routledge, 1994), 86. For a full articulation of the concept, see 85–92.

21. Bhabha, *Location of Culture*, 86.

22. Bhabha, 86.

23. Bhabha, 91.

24. Cynthia Baker, *Jew* (New Brunswick, NJ: Rutgers Univ. Press, 2017), 2.

25. Baker, *Jew*, 4.

26. Leonard Cohen, "Not a Jew," *Book of Longing* (Toronto: McLelland and Stewart, 2006), 158. A later online iteration of the poem, printed with Cohen's permission on a tribute site, alters it slightly (deleting "this decision" and changing line breaks) and adds a list of identifying titles for Cohen in "an editor's note." See "Not a Jew," *The Leonard Cohen Files*, ed. Eija Arjatsalo and Jarkko Arjatsalo, 2008, www.leonardcohenfiles.com/jew.html.

27. Adele Reinhartz, "The Vanishing Jews of Antiquity," *Marginalia Review of Books*, 24 June 2014, http://marginalia.lareviewofbooks.org/vanishing-jews-antiquity-adele-reinhartz/.

28. Timothy Michael Law and Charles Halton, eds., "Jew and Judean: A *Marginalia* Forum on Politics and Historiography in the Translation of Ancient Texts," *Marginalia Review of Books,* 26 August 2014, http://marginalia.lareviewofbooks.org/jew-judean-forum/.

29. Jonathan Klawans, "An Invented Revolution," in Law and Halton, "Jew and Judean." The claim that English words in particular provide their own problems (or solutions) is further discussed in Daniel Boyarin's contribution to the 2017 *Marginalia* Forum on Cynthia Baker's *Jew*, "Yeah Jew!" (see note 30 below).

30. Annette Yoshiko Reed and Shaul Magid, eds., "A Forum on Cynthia Baker's *Jew*," *Marginalia Review of Books,* 6 May–4 July 2017, http://marginalia.lareviewofbooks.org/introduction -forum-on-cynthia-baker-jew/; in Baker's book, this sentence appears on pp. 14–15. In addition to Baker's response essay, "One Final Word on *Jew*: A Response," the Forum includes an introduction by Annette Yoshiko Reed and Shaul Magid and essays by Daniel Boyarin, Matthew Chalmers, Michael Pregill, Naomi Seidman, Shaul Magid, and Susannah Heschel.

31. David Nirenberg, *Anti-Judaism: The Western Tradition* (New York: Norton, 2013), 1–2.

32. A good investigation of similarities between medieval crusader and twenty-first-century American evangelical dispensationalists, for instance, is Matthew Gabriele, "The Chosen Peoples of the Eleventh and Twenty-First Centuries," *Relegere: Studies in Religion and Reception* 2, no. 2 (2012): 281–90.

33. See Zygmunt Bauman, "Allosemitism: Premodern, Modern, Postmodern," *Modernity, Culture, and "The Jew,"* ed. Bryan Cheyette and Laura Marcus (Stanford: Stanford Univ. Press, 1998), 143–56.

34. I discuss several such miracle tales (in text and illustration) in Chapters 4 and 5.

35. Michael Clanchy, *From Memory to Written Record: England 1066–1307,* 2nd ed. (Oxford: Blackwell, 1993), 215.

36. See Malcolm Parkes, "On the Presumed Date and Possible Origin of the Manuscript of the 'Orrmulum': Oxford, Bodleian Library, MS Junius 1," in *Five Hundred Years of Words and Sounds,* ed. E. G. Stanley and Douglas Gray (Cambridge: D. S. Brewer, 1983), 115–27. The most recent full edition currently accessible is still that of Robert Holt, *The Ormulum with the Notes and Glossary of Dr. R. M. White,* 2 vols. (Oxford: Clarendon, 1878), who based his updated work on R. M. White's *The Ormulum, Now First Edited from the Original Manuscript in the Bodleian with Notes and Glossary* (Oxford: Oxford Univ. Press, 1852). Both Meg Worley and Nils-Lennart Johannesson (before his death in June 2019), however, have been at work on new (online and print) editions of the text. I cite line numbers according to Holt's edition (here line 2) but see note 41 below for further commentary on how I print Orrm's lines.

37. Estimates of the full length of the *Orrmulum* vary, as do numbers for the amount of surviving and planned sermons, because the manuscript is now imperfect, and Orrm often writes double homilies that combine two lections from his contents list. We can be sure, however, that the work was in volumes, because a second, contemporary hand adds to Orrm's contents the note "hucusque .j. uol*umen*" (first volume up to here) at the fiftieth pericope noted on fol. 5v (center margin). See also note 39 below.

38. See, for example, Christopher Cannon, "Spelling Practice: The *Ormulum* and the Word," *Forum for Modern Language Studies* 33, no. 3 (1997): 229–44, at 229, which calls the work a "homiletic life of Christ." This characterization persists in Cannon's influential *The Grounds of English Literature* (Oxford: Oxford Univ. Press, 2004), 82.

39. Orrm's contemporary list of Latin pericopes (those related to his sermons) are recorded in Bod. MS Junius 1, fols. 5r–9v, following his note that the list constitutes "Þa goddspelless alle þatt icc her in þiss boc ma33 findenn" (printed in Holt, *The Ormulum,* following the "Dedica-

tion," n.p.). The list is incomplete but likely missing only a small scrap-parchment fold-in, of the type that Orrm used regularly for corrections and additions; it breaks off around Acts of the Apostles 20 (exact chapters and verses for Acts are hard to know, because Orrm begins summarizing content to save room). My observation that we have simple chronology through to the end of the Acts of the Apostles in Orrm's plan disrupts the main rationale for Parkes's placement of Orrm at Bourne Abbey in "On the Presumed Date and Possible Origin," and so possibly arguments that rely on his residence at Bourne Abbey. Parkes chooses Bourne because Orrm's contents list ultimately focuses on Peter and Paul, and Bourne was an Augustinian house dedicated to Saints Peter and Paul; Orrm's focus, however, is likely an accident of the fact that Acts 1–20 feature Peter and Paul. None of this, however, changes Parkes's expert assessment of the date of Orrm's hand, the dialect of the work, and the Lincolnshire origin in general—nor does it preclude Bourne Abbey.

40. James Morey, *Book and Verse: A Guide to Middle English Biblical Literature* (Urbana: Univ. of Illinois Press, 2000), 79.

41. Holt, *Ormulum*, 1118–21. In quotations of the Middle English, I do not print Orrm's septenaries in half lines as Holt does (and so almost all editors and scholars after him); I also alter Holt's punctuation and capitalization of the text and on occasion make minor corrections based on my own examination of the manuscript. It is clear that Orrm intended long lines, as Holt himself emphasizes in his preface (lxv–lxvi): "Ormin . . . has composed his Homilies in verses of fifteen syllables, in two sections distinguished by the metrical point which is placed at the end of the eighth syllable or fourth foot. . . . In strictness the long line is more correct for [Orrm's] unrhymed metre. . . . The editor has risked the adoption of the couplet for the greater convenience of the reader." Holt's decision, however, has contributed to the feeling that Orrm's work is excessively long (approximately 20,000 instead of 10,000 lines), when in reality its length is similar to other encyclopedic compositions, chronicles, or indeed homily collections of the era. In situ examination of the manuscript makes Orrm's long lines even clearer: while he writes across his pages to conserve space, the capitals at the beginning of each long line are large and written in thick-laid ink, as if he has gone over them twice (or more) to mark the start of each line. Orrm's meter, orthography, and manuscript are discussed further in the next chapter.

42. See Guzmán Mancho, "Considering *Orrmulum*'s Exegetical Discourse: Canon Orrmin's Preaching and His Audience," *English Studies* 6 (2004): 508–19. Mancho also suggests that Jews are the primary audience of the homilies in "Is the *Orrmulum*'s Introduction an Instance of Aristotelian Prologue?," *Neophilologus* 88 (2004): 477–92, at 487.

43. In the manuscript (fol. 93v, col. a), "þatt witt tu wel to soþe" is Orrm's marginal replacement for the deleted phrase "swa summ þe boc uss kiþeþþ" (just as the book tells us). Orrm consistently deletes such adversions to a notional source and replaces them with general affirmations of spiritual knowledge or broad appeals to Christian truth.

44. All in-text citations of the *Orrmulum* follow the line numbering of Holt, *Ormulum*. On my long-line presentation of block-quoted text, see note 41 above.

45. David Lawton, "Englishing the Bible, 1066–1549," in *Cambridge History of Medieval English Literature*, ed. David Wallace (Cambridge: Cambridge Univ. Press, 1999), 454–82, at 464.

46. Parkes, "On the Presumed Date and Possible Origin," proposed the Augustinian Bourne Abbey near Stamford as the location of composition (though see note 39 above). Parkes also surmised that Orrm was working on the text over a prolonged period of time (decades), probably beginning in the 1150s.

47. *DMAJH*, s.vv. "1218, The Re-establishment of the English Jewry by Henry III's Council of Regency," 23–25, and "Stamford," 340–43.

48. For the dedication, see Holt, *Ormulum*, 1–342 (numbered first and separately from the homilies). Debt enrollments from the Rutland area survive from the reign of Henry II in TNA E 101/249/1, which records obligations to various Jewish moneylenders, including "Deulesalt' judeo de Stamfort" (Stamford); debts include those taken by parsons and clerics of local churches, as well as one by Richard, prior and canon of Brooke, a small Augustinian Priory. Datable entries put this roll ca. 1183–85. Jocelin of Brakelond also details interactions with Jews in his Benedictine monastery at Bury St Edmunds (about sixty miles southeast of Bourne) in the 1180s, including the abbey's indebtedness to Jewish lenders, its sheltering of Jewish families during times of political unrest, and an apparent ritual murder accusation. See *CJB*, especially 1–46. I discuss Jocelin's *Chronicle* and its treatment of Jews in the next chapter.

49. *Anglo-Saxon Chronicle* MS E's annal for 1137 is printed in any number of anthologies, e.g., *Old and Middle English, c. 890–1450: An Anthology*, ed. Elaine Treharne, 3rd ed. (Malden, MA: Wiley-Blackwell, 2010), 301–07 (here 306, line 118). For a critical edition, see Cecily Clark, ed., *The Peterborough Chronicle 1070–1154*, 2nd ed. (Oxford: Oxford Univ. Press, 1970).

50. *MED*, s.vv. "Jeu," "Judeu," "Judeish," "Ebreu," and "Jeuerie," which also provide many samples of usage, including the ones I mention as the earliest instances.

51. *DMLBS*, s.v. "Judaismus."

52. *MED*, s.v. "Jeuesse." The document that the *MED* entry cites for "Gywes" as a surname ("Christina Gywes") is printed in the *Court Rolls of the Abbey of Ramsey and the Honor of Clare*, ed. Warren Ortman Ault (New Haven: Yale Univ. Press, 1928), 177. Christina Gywes is named in the records of the leet court of Walsoken (Norfolk), as one of several men and women who sold beer illegally. Many women who converted from Judaism took the name Christina in the decades after the Expulsion, however, and elsewhere in Ault's edition (77), in the records of the 1308–9 honor court of Clare (Suffolk), a "Galfridus le Jeu et Juliana uxore eius" appear concerning a land dispute; Geoffrey and Juliana were likewise common names for Anglo-Jewish converts in this period. For lists of pre- and post-Expulsion converts, see Michael Adler, *Jews of Medieval England* (London: JHSE, 1939), 342–46 and 350–52. As a counterpoint, Robert Stacey, contra Hillaby and Hillaby in *DMAJH*, is "doubtful" that surnames "can be reliably presumed to indicate that the individual was a convert from Judaism" because such surnames are "too common, too rural, and too long-lived": see his review of *DMAJH* in *Jewish Historical Studies* 48 (2016): 257. As Baker notes in *Jew*, 14, the word "*Jewess* calls for a book of its own."

53. Child Ballad no. 22. See Francis James Child, *The English and Scottish Popular Ballads* (Boston: Houghton Mifflin, 1882), 1:242–44. This manuscript is no. 323 in M. R. James's *The Western Manuscripts in the Library of Trinity College, Cambridge: A Descriptive Catalogue*, 4 vols. (Cambridge: Cambridge Univ. Press, 1902), now bound with Trinity MS B.14.40, and the Judas Ballad occupies all of fol. 34r. For more information on the poem's categorization as a ballad, and an up-to-date edition and translation, see Irina Dumitrescu, "Debt and Sin in the Middle English 'Judas,'" *Anglia* 131, no. 4 (2013): 509–37.

54. I discuss Judas's sister and her role in this ballad at some length in Chapter 5.

55. I follow the lineation of Dumitrescu, "Debt and Sin," where she edits and translates the text as an appendix at 531–33. Dumitrescu's edition has thirty-six lines (by expanding the refrains), as opposed to the thirty-three lines written out on the manuscript page. Otherwise, while I am generally guided by Dumitrescu, I amend text, punctuation, and translation based on my own examination of the manuscript.

56. *MED*, s.v. "riche (adj.)."

57. Anthony Bale, *Feeling Persecuted: Christians, Jews, and Images of Violence in the Middle Ages* (London: Reaktion, 2010), 83.

58. Dumitrescu, "Debt and Sin," 523. Dumitrescu's understanding of Pilate is crucial to her reading of the poem's credit economy, which ultimately suggests that, in a strange inversion, Judas is slowly Judaized by his association with Pilate's credit. The footnotes and bibliography of her article, furthermore, are crucial for anyone who might want to do further work on the poem.

59. A. O. Belfour, ed., *Twelfth-Century Homilies in MS. Bodley 343* (London: Kegan Paul, 1909), 100, lines 29–31. For an updated edition, see Susan Irvine, ed., *Old English Homilies from MS Bodley 343* (Oxford: Oxford Univ. Press, 1993).

60. Charlotte D'Evelyn and Anna J. Mill, eds., *The South English Legendary* (London: Oxford Univ. Press, 1956), 2:694, lines 64–66, and 701, line 100.

61. D'Evelyn and Mill, *South English Legendary*, 2:703, line 151.

62. Richard Morris, ed., *An Old English Miscellany* (London: N. Trübner, 1872), 47, lines 347–52.

63. Morris, *Old English Miscellany*, 40, line 110.

64. Scholarship on Jewish conversion to Christianity is a useful corollary here, as authors could use similar rhetoric in association with contemporary converts as well. Learned Jews who converted and then wrote Christian treatises on or relating to their conversion, such as Petrus Alphonsi and Hermann of Cologne, could appropriate these devices and frame their conversion in light of their past Jewishness and Hebrew/Arabic learning. Authors like Thomas of Monmouth, who takes evidence of Jewish conspiracy from a (possibly fictional) former Jew named Theobald, and ecclesiastical authorities judging cases related to new or lapsed converts (like those I will discuss around female converts in Part II), could use such arguments as well. In these cases, the convert's Jewish past becomes essential to the construction of Christian identity. See, for instance, Steven F. Kruger on Hermann of Cologne in *Dreaming in the Middle Ages* (Cambridge: Cambridge Univ. Press, 1992), 154–65, and his "The Times of Conversion," *Philological Quarterly* 92, no. 1 (2013): 19–39; Irven M. Resnick, trans., *Petrus Alfonsi: Dialogue Against the Jews* (Washington, DC: Catholic Univ. of America Press, 2006); Robert C. Stacey, "The Conversion of Jews to Christianity in Thirteenth-Century England," *Speculum* 67 (1992): 263–83; and F. Donald Logan, "Thirteen London Jews and Conversion to Christianity: Problems of Apostasy in the 1280s," *Bulletin of the Institute of Historical Research* 45 (1972): 214–29.

65. Theresa Tinkle, "Jews in the Fleury Playbook," *Comparative Drama* 38, no. 1 (2004): 1–38, at 28 and 26–27. While the Fleury Playbook, named for its association with the Abbaye St Benoît de Fleury, is a Latin northern French production, it dates before 1290, as does the Judas Ballad. Wider comparison of such uses of Jews and Jewishness with those in northern France would, I am sure, prove fruitful.

66. I follow Susanna Fein, who sees Harley 2253 as a six-booklet structure. See Susanna Fein, David Raybin, and Jan Ziolkowski, ed. and trans., *The Complete Harley 2253 Manuscript*, 3 vols. (Kalamazoo: Medieval Institute, 2015). I also use Fein's edition for lineation of this poem (in vol. 3, pp. 82–85, art. 73), though I alter her translation and provide commentary on the manuscript layout (where the poem is copied in long lines). So, for instance, the line quoted here is 29–30 in Fein's edition but 15 on the manuscript page. Fein's line numbers are hereafter cited parenthetically in text.

67. See Fein, *Complete Harley 2253*, vol. 1, arts. 2, 3, 3a, and 3b (pp. 208–373), and vol. 3, art. 115 (pp. 298–305).

68. Fein, *Complete Harley 2253*, vol. 3, art. 71 (*Estoyres de la Bible*), 62, lines 728–29, and 62, lines 732–33 (I also use Fein's facing-page translation in this case). Authorship of this text is attributed to the main scribe (the "Ludlow scribe"), fols. 92v–105r in manuscript.

69. This is generally true of the entire manuscript: though the word "Jew" appears frequently in its French texts (as *judeus, judeux*, or variants of *gyw*) and once in a Latin text (in the plural form *iudei*), all of these uses apply to scenes of Christ's Passion (where Jews are cast negatively and violently as torturers and mockers, actively rejecting Christ) or to contemporary, post-Crucifixion Jews. In positive roles (e.g., praising Christ as he enters Jerusalem on Palm Sunday) or as Old Testament figures, or in reference to the language, *ebreu* or *hebreus* appears. It could be, indeed, that the later glossator was struck by the unique appearance of the word in English.

70. On the figure of "Stephaton" the sponge-bearer, and his attribute's connection to Jewishness in medieval English iconography, see Bale, *Feeling Persecuted*, 79–81.

71. Fein, in *Complete Harley 2253*, vol. 3, art. 73, translates line 45 as "False I was in every way." It is also worth noting that "in crop ant rote" suggests a temporal claim—where a crop belongs to the future, a root to the past—an idea that resonates with Orrm's temporalities, as discussed above. My thanks to Stephanie J. Lahey for this point.

72. *MED*, s.v. "rote" 6.

73. See Caroline Walker Bynum, *Holy Feast and Holy Fast: The Religious Significance of Food to Medieval Women* (Berkeley: Univ. of California Press, 1987). I am referring to chapter 10 (278ff.), where Bynum borrows the anthropological term "symbolic reversal" to frame her discussion of gendered symbols in medieval theological discourse, as used distinctively by male and female authors to signal an ascent to holiness that assumes a preexisting (female) weakness or inferiority, itself desirable in the Christian scheme.

74. Nirenberg, *Anti-Judaism*, 3.

75. See Sean Eisen Murphy, "Concern About Judaizing in Academic Treatises on the Law, c. 1130–c. 1230," *Speculum* 82, no. 3 (2007): 560–94. Rubin, *Life and Passion*, xxix, also notes the tendency in twelfth-century English monastic contexts: "Monks were particularly preoccupied with Judaism. . . . Monastic ideas were not solely prompted by interactions with contemporary Jews . . . but rather through reflection on the precarious relationship of affinity and supersession between Judaism and Christianity."

76. Bale, *Feeling Persecuted*, 74.

CHAPTER 2

1. Michael Clanchy, *From Memory to Written Record: England 1066–1307*, 2nd ed. (Oxford: Blackwell), 215.

2. Orrm's brother Walter is the dedicatee of, and apparent motivating force behind, the *Orrmulum* ("Nu broþerr Wallterr, broþerr min affterr þe flæshess kinde / . . . icc hafe don swa summ þu badd 7 forþedd te þin wille. / icc hafe wennd inntill Ennglissh goddspelless hallзhe lare" [D 1–14]), and some have seen Orrm's dedicatory directives to Walter as an invitation to edit the text (e.g., D 65–79: "te bitæche icc off þiss boc heh wikenn alls itt semeþþ / all to þurrhsekenn illc an ferrs 7 to þurrhlokenn offte / þatt upponn all þiss boc ne be nan word зæn Cristess lare"). Orrm's vocabulary, as Henry Sweet summarized in his *First Middle English Primer: Extracts from the "Ancren Riwle" and "Ormulum" with Grammar and Glossary* (Oxford: Clarendon, 1884), 43, "shows hardly any French, but considerable Norse, influence." See also E. S. Olszewska, "Alliterative Phrases in the *Ormulum*: Some Norse Parallels," in *English and Medieval Studies: Presented*

to J.R.R. Tolkien on the Occasion of His Seventieth Birthday, ed. Norman Davis and C. L. Wrenn (London: George Allen & Unwin, 1962), 112–27. Meg Worley's "Using the *Ormulum* to Redefine Vernacularity," in *The Vulgar Tongue: Medieval and Postmedieval Vernacularity,* ed. Fiona Somerset and Nicholas Watson (University Park: Penn State Univ. Press, 2003), 19–30, persuasively argues that Orrm's phonetically driven orthography and avoidance of French loanwords is carefully aimed at directing Francophone speakers of English—a scenario that in fact shows fairly profound understanding of French.

3. Guzmán Mancho, "Considering *Orrmulum*'s Exegetical Discourse: Canon Orrmin's Preaching and His Audience," *English Studies* 6 (2004): 508–19, at 518. Mancho suggests the same argument in "Is *Orrmulum*'s Introduction an Instance of an Aristotelian Prologue?," *Neophilogus* 88 (2004): 477–92, at 483–88.

4. Mancho, "Considering *Orrmulum*'s Exegetical Discourse," 515.

5. On the composition date of the *Orrmulum,* see M. B. Parkes, "On the Presumed Date and Possible Origin of the Manuscript of the 'Orrmulum': Oxford, Bodleian Library, MS Junius 1," in *Five Hundred Years of Words and Sounds,* ed. E. G. Stanley and Douglas Gray (Cambridge: D.S. Brewer, 1983), 115–27. On the early French of English Jews and the possibility of the development and influence of other vernaculars in the Anglo-Jewish community, see Judith Olszowy-Schlanger, *Hebrew and Hebrew-Latin Documents from Medieval England: A Diplomatic and Palaeographical Study* (Turnhout: Brepols, 2015), 1:97–98.

6. James Morey, *Book and Verse: A Guide to Middle English Biblical Literature* (Urbana: Univ. of Illinois Press, 2000), 78 and 77.

7. On the rise of *contra* (or *adversus*) *Judaeos* exegesis and treatises in the late eleventh and twelfth centuries, particularly in England and France, see Jeremy Cohen, *Living Letters of the Law: Ideas of the Jew in Medieval Christianity* (Berkeley: Univ. of California Press, 1999), especially pt. 3 (147–270), which still provides a masterful overview.

8. According to Stephen Morrison, "Orm's English Sources," *Archiv* 221 (1984): 54–63, at 54: "Ælfric and Orm, alone among early medieval homilists, adopt the exegetical method as their norm."

9. For a relatively recent summary of Orrm's prosody, along with a variety of his linguistic features, see R. D. Fulk, *An Introduction to Middle English* (Peterborough, ON: Broadview), 163–65. J. A. W Bennett, *Middle English Literature* (Oxford: Clarendon, 1986), 30–32, also provides a good overview (with some disapproval) of Orrm's "jog-trot fifteener."

10. Orrm writes in double columns except in the case of some of the singletons he added for prefatory material (fols. 1–7) and small added scraps he inserted for editorial changes. For an up-to-date summary of his use of parchment (which corrects previous descriptions), see Erik Kwakkel, "Discarded Parchment as Writing Support in English Manuscript Culture," in *English Manuscripts Studies, 1100–1700,* vol. 17, *English Manuscripts Before 1400,* ed. A. S. G. Edwards and Orietta Da Rold (London: British Library, 2012), 238–64, at 254.

11. As in the previous chapter, all quotations of the *Orrmulum* cite the line numbers (though not the punctuation or capitalization) of Robert Holt, *The Ormulum with the Notes and Glossary of Dr. R. M. White,* 2 vols. (Oxford: Clarendon, 1878), though I print the text in long lines instead of Holt's half lines. The Dedication and Preface are numbered separately in Holt's edition and are thus marked in parenthetical citations with a D or P.

12. I diverge from other numerical summaries of Orrm's surviving work here, based on my own examination of the manuscript and inspection of its structural divisions in terms of both content and visual markers (as indicated, for instance, by decorated capitals, heavy inking of opening lines or letters, and Latin pericope cues written in a second, contemporary hand). These

do not always correspond to the divisions in Holt, *Ormulum*, nor to Orrm's bare list of pericopes, which is incomplete and should be treated as a "contents list" only with caution. Many of the surviving homilies are double homilies (i.e., one homily on two pericopes), and the contemporary hand that adds pericope cues also marks the end of the first volume ("Huc usque .i. uolumen," fol. 5v) at a point in the opening pericope list that likely corresponds to the original end of the surviving codex.

13. Parkes, "On the Presumed Date," 116–20; Christopher Cannon, *The Grounds of English Literature* (Oxford: Oxford Univ. Press, 2004), 104–7.

14. Parkes, "On the Presumed Date," 125.

15. Worley, "Using the *Ormulum*," 20.

16. Worley, 23–26.

17. Cannon, *Grounds of English Literature*, 83. Cannon's chapter on the *Orrmulum* subtly reworks and expands his "Spelling Practice: The *Ormulum* and the Word," *Forum for Modern Language Studies* 33, no. 3 (1997): 229–44. Both the book chapter and the article are interested, as I am, in Orrm's deployment of "sameness"—a correlation that I will discuss further below.

18. Katharine Breen, *Imagining an English Reading Public, 1150–1400* (Cambridge: Cambridge Univ. Press, 2010), 119.

19. Bennett, *Middle English Literature*, 32.

20. David Lawton, "Englishing the Bible, 1066–1549," in *The Cambridge History of Medieval English Literature*, ed. David Wallace (Cambridge: Cambridge Univ. Press, 1999), 454–87, at 466; Morey, *Book and Verse*, 74.

21. Cannon, *Grounds of English Literature*, 101 and 103.

22. Breen, *Imagining an English Reading Public*, 120.

23. Cannon, *Grounds of English Literature*, 110.

24. Cannon, "Spelling Practice," 237 and 240. Interestingly, the latter phrase is absent in *Grounds of English Literature*, though it is closely associated with "sameness" as a formal, linguistic, and semantic constraint in this context.

25. Cannon, *Grounds of English Literature*, 102.

26. See Worley, "Using the *Ormulum*," 20–21.

27. Morey, *Book and Verse*, 79.

28. Erich Auerbach, "Figura," trans. Ralph Manheim, in *Scenes from the Drama of European Literature* (New York: Meridian, 1959), 11–75, at 67–68.

29. A search of Holt, *Ormulum*, reveals exactly 100 uses of the word, spread widely throughout the text.

30. *DMLBS*, s.v. "litteralis, literalis" 1 and 2. This denotation also existed in later Middle and early Modern English: see *OED*, s.v. "literal" I.1.a.

31. See *MED*, s.v. "stafi"; and J. R. Clark Hall, *A Concise Anglo-Saxon Dictionary* (Cambridge: Cambridge Univ. Press, 1960), s.v. "stæflic," where it is marked as part of Ælfric's lexicon.

32. R. M. White, "Preface," *The Ormulum with the Notes and Glossary of Dr. R. M. White* (Oxford: Clarendon, 1878), 1:vii–lxxv, especially l–lx. This introduction to the *Orrmulum* as part of the history of pre-Conquest learning was reworked by Holt and John Earle, whom Holt thanks for "revising, and adding somewhat to the completeness of, the continuation of Dr. White's History of Anglo-Saxon Literature [i.e., the scholarly preface], which in this edition is brought down to the present time" (vi).

33. Lawton, "Englishing the Bible," 466.

34. For other examples, see Morrison, "Orm's English Sources"; Worley, "Using the *Ormulum*," 24–26; and, less kind to Orrm, J. A. W Bennett and G. V. Smithers, eds., *Early Middle*

English Verse and Prose (Oxford: Clarendon, 1968), 174, where Orrm's work is "freakish" unless we understand that "his purpose is not essentially different from that of Ælfric in his *Catholic Homilies.*"

35. Bella Millett, "Change and Continuity: The English Sermon Before 1250," in *The Oxford Handbook of Medieval Literature in English*, ed. Elaine Treharne and Greg Walker, with William Green (Oxford: Oxford Univ. Press), 221–39, at 231.

36. Millett, "Change and Continuity," 232.

37. Clanchy, *From Memory to Written Record*, 215 and 329–30; Cannon, *Grounds of English Literature*, 82–110; and Breen, *Imagining an English Reading Public*, 121.

38. Lawton, "Englishing the Bible," 464; Cannon, *Grounds of English Literature*, 83; Bennett and Smithers, *Early Middle English*, 174.

39. Elizabeth Salter, *English and International: Studies in the Literature, Art, and Patronage of Medieval England* (Cambridge: Cambridge Univ. Press, 1988), 7 and 2.

40. Stephen Morrison's articles on Orrm's sources include "Orm's English Sources"; "Sources for the *Ormulum*: A Re-examination," *Neuphilologische Mitteilungen* 84, no. 4 (1983): 419–36; and "New Sources for *The Ormulum*," *Neophilologus* 68 (1984): 444–50. Nils-Lennart Johannesson's work on the *Orrmulum* is vast, but articles and essays that speak specifically to Orrm's sources include "Bread Crumbs and Related Matters in the *Ormulum*," in *Selected Proceedings of the 2005 Symposium on New Approaches in English Historical Lexis (HEL-LEX)*, ed. R. W. McConchie et al. (Somerville, MA: Cascadilla, 2006), 69–82 (see nn. 8, 19–20, and 26 in particular); "Orm's Relationship to His Latin Sources," in *Studies in Middle English Forms and Meanings*, ed. Gabriella Mazzon (Frankfurt: Peter Lang, 2007), 133–43; "'Icc Hafe Don Swa Summ Þu Badd': An Anatomy of the Preface of the *Ormulum*," *SELIM* 14 (2007): 107–40; "The Four-Wheeled Quadriga and the Seven Sacraments: On the Sources of the 'Dedication' of the *Ormulum*," in *Bells Chiming from the Past: Cultural and Linguistic Studies on Early English*, ed. Isabel Moskowich-Spiegel and Begoña Crespo-García (Amsterdam: Rodopi, 2007), 227–45; and "'Þurrh be33ske 7 sallte tæress': Orm's Use of Metaphor and Simile in Exegesis of John 1:51," in *Selected Papers from the 2006 and 2007 Stockholm Metaphor Festivals*, ed. Nils-Lennart Johannesson and D. C. Minugh (Stockholm: University of Stockholm, 2008), 85–96.

41. White, "Preface," lx.

42. This point is also supported by two recent articles on Orrm's creative use of, and movement beyond, his sources: Laura Ashe, "The Originality of the *Orrmulum*," *Early Middle English* 1, no. 1 (2019): 35–54; and Samuel Cardwell, "Wurrþlike shridd: *Cossmós, Mycrocossmós*, and the Use of Greek in Orrm's Exegesis of John 3:16," *Early Middle English* 1, no. 2 (2019): 1–12.

43. Morrison, "Orm's English Sources," 64.

44. See Marcia L. Colish, "Another Look at the School of Laon," *Archives d'histoire doctrinale et littéraire du moyen âge* 53 (1986): 7–22. This article is reprinted as the third chapter of her *Studies in Scholasticism* (Aldershot: Ashgate Variorum, 2006).

45. For information on the authorship, dates, and development of the *Glossa ordinaria*, see Lesley Smith, *The "Glossa Ordinaria": The Making of a Medieval Bible Commentary* (Leiden: Brill, 2009).

46. See Johannesson's "Orm's Relationship to His Latin Sources," 135, and "Anatomy of a Preface," 126–36. I am, however, summarizing information spread across several of the works cited in note 40 above.

47. Johannesson, "Anatomy of a Preface," 126.

48. Johannesson, 126.

49. Parkes, "On the Presumed Date."

50. Worley, "Using the *Ormulum*," 23; Johannesson, "Anatomy of a Preface," 134–35; Colish "Another Look at the School of Laon," 7.

51. See note 40 above for the works from which I am compiling this selective list; I am not, in this context, interested in Orrm's several late antique or early medieval souces.

52. Johannesson, "Orm's Relationship to His Latin Sources," 133.

53. Morrison, "New Sources of *The Ormulum*," 449.

54. Clanchy, *From Memory to Written Record*, 215.

55. On medieval Augustinian conceptions of Jewishness and the "doctrine of Jewish witness"—the conviction, gleaned from a variety of Saint Augustine's writings, that Jews must be protected and remain unharmed as witnesses of Christian revelation and proof of Christian prophecy—see the foundational work of Cohen, *Living Letters of the Law*, 23–71. For a reading that applies this doctrine to medieval English literature, see Elisa Narin van Court, "*The Siege of Jerusalem* and Augustinian Historians: Writing About Jews in Fourteenth-Century England," in *Chaucer and the Jews: Sources, Contexts, Meanings*, ed. Shiela Delany (New York: Routledge, 2002), 165–84.

56. Cohen, *Living Letters of the Law*, 151–52 and 153–54.

57. Cohen, 158; Johannesson, "Orm's Relationship to His Latin Sources," 141.

58. Cohen, *Living Letters of the Law*, 158.

59. In the manuscript (fol. 25r, col. a), "affterr gastlike lare" is Orrm's marginal replacement for the deleted phrase "swa summ þe boc uss kiþeþþ" (just as the book tells us). In addition to his orthographic and other more minor corrections, Orrm consistently deletes such initial adversions to a notional source and replaces them with more general affirmations of spiritual knowledge or appeals to broad Christian truth. The singular "boc" is likely, in any case, an authority trope (rather than a real source), not unusual in homiletic or hagiographic genres, though scholarly expectation that an author's use of such tropes indicates the presence of a findable source has led researchers down many a rabbitless rabbit hole. See, for example, Johannesson, "On Orm's Relationship to His Latin Sources," 133–35; and Adrienne Williams Boyarin, *Miracles of the Virgin in Medieval England: Jews and Jewishness in Marian Legends* (Cambridge: D.S. Brewer, 2010), 13–19.

60. *DOE*, s.v. "hæþen" (note the adjectival use at I.B.1.b in particular).

61. Cohen, *Living Letters of the Law*, 157, where, to support his own perspective, Cohen is summarizing and quoting the arguments of R. I. Moore's *The Formation of Persecuting Society: Power and Deviance in Western Europe* (Oxford: Oxford Univ. Press, 1987).

62. Cannon, *Grounds of English Literature*, 102.

63. Cannon, 99 and 103.

64. Cohen, *Living Letters of the Law*, 153; Clanchy, *From Memory to Written Record*, 215.

65. All quotations and translations of *The Chronicle of Jocelin of Brakelond* come from *CJB*, here 40 (hereafter cited parenthetically in text). The sole surviving manuscript copy of Jocelin's *Chronicle*, which dates to the third quarter of the thirteenth century, is in the *Liber albus* of Bury St Edmunds: BL Harley 1005, fols. 127–70. Another copy, probably earlier, existed in BL Cotton Vitellius D XV, but it was almost entirely burned in the 1731 Ashburnham House fire.

66. See R. M. Thomson, *The Archives of the Abbey of Bury St Edmunds* (Woodbridge: Boydell and Brewer, 1980); and R. Sharpe et al., ed., *English Benedictine Libraries: The Shorter Catalogues* (London: British Academy, 1996).

67. In addition to his own English preaching and commissioned pulpit, Jocelin records Samson's support of his new prior, who attempted to decline the position in 1201 because of his inability to compose learned sermons. According to Jocelin, *CJB* 128, Samson "multa respondit,

dicens quod bene posset recordari et ruminare alienos sermones . . . [et] dicens quod in multis ecclesiis fit sermo in conuentu Gallice uel pocius Anglice, ut morum fieret edificacio, non literature ostensio."

68. On Robert of Bury and his likely connection to the little William of Norwich case, see Anthony Bale, "'House Devil, Town Saint': Anti-Semitism and Hagiography in Medieval Suffolk," in *Chaucer and the Jews: Sources, Contexts, Meanings*, ed. Sheila Delany (New York: Routledge, 2002), 185–210; and Geraldine Heng, "England's Dead Boys: Telling Tales of Christian-Jewish Relations Before and After the First European Expulsion of the Jews," *Modern Language Notes* 127, no. 5, supp. (2012): 54–85. Bale's article is substantially reworked and expanded in *The Jew in the Medieval Book: English Antisemitisms, 1350–1500* (Cambridge: Cambridge University Press, 2006), 105–44.

69. The choir screen Samson commissioned, and for which he composed elegiac verses to accompany painted images (see *CJB* 9), likely participated in his anti-Jewish program. The paintings and verses Samson arranged are recorded in London, College of Arms MS Arundel 30, a Bury miscellany made up primarily of thirteenth- and fourteenth-century texts, a large portion of which describe abbey items, buildings, and payments. M. R. James, *On the Abbey of S. Edmund at Bury* (Cambridge: Cambridge Univ. Press, 1895), 192–93 and 202, showed that several items in MS Arundel 30 closely match Jocelin's account of the work completed during Samson's tenure, including the choir screen. This assertion is accepted by Butler, *CJB*; Lisa Lampert-Weissig, "The Once and Future Jew: The Croxton *Play of the Sacrament*, Little Robert of Bury, and Historical Memory," *Jewish History* 15 (2001): 235–55; and Bale, "'House Devil, Town Saint,'" and *Jew in the Medieval Book*, 105–44. In the choir screen's design are several Miracles of the Virgin, including the story of Theophilus, a clerk who contracted his soul to the devil through a Jewish intermediary (depicted twice), and the story of the Jewish boy thrown into an oven by his father (depicted three times). In addition, Arundel 30 notes a contemporary altar table with three lines of verse on "The Jewish Boy," set with roundlets of images and verses related to the Virgin Mary's symbolic status as the body that closed the Old Law and made the Synagogue new. On the history of these two Marian legends and associated anti-Jewish rhetoric in medieval England, see Williams Boyarin, *Miracles of the Virgin in Medieval England*.

70. See *DMAJH*, s.v. "Bury St Edmunds," 69–70. On the Richard I coronation riots more generally, see Robin R. Mundill, *The King's Jews: Money, Massacre, and Exodus in Medieval England* (London: Continuum, 2010), 75–83. For more on the historical contexts of anti-Judaism in late twelfth-century Bury St Edmunds, see also Daniel Gerrard, "Jocelin of Brakelond and the Power of Abbot Samson," *Journal of Medieval History* 40, no. 1 (2014): 1–23; and James, *On the Abbey of S. Edmund at Bury*, which remains an invaluable resource.

71. This is something that Thomas Carlyle understood well when he wrote about Jocelin, Samson, and the Bury *Liber albus* (BL MS Harley 1005) in his 1843 work *Past and Present*. Carlyle remarked on the "evil" of the abbey's indebtedness to "usurious insatiable Jews; every fresh Jew sticking on him [Abbot Hugh, Samson's predecessor] like a fresh horseleech, sucking his and our life out; crying continually, Give, Give!" and made clear that Jocelin set up the fundamental question of the narrative as "How to quiet your insatiable Jew" in the face of "papers" and "so many parchments." Carlyle also easily (and viciously) connected the *Chronicle* to the 1190 York massacre of Jews. See Richard Altick, ed., *Past and Present by Thomas Carlyle* (New York: New York UP, 1965), here 64 and 65.

72. An overview of scholarly attitudes toward the *Chronicle of Jocelin of Brakelond* since the nineteenth century (as well as further details on manuscripts, editions, and translations) can be found in Gerrard, "Jocelin of Brakelond and the Power of Abbot Samson," 1–7.

73. Antonia Gransden, "Realistic Observation in Twelfth-Century England," *Speculum* 47, no. 1 (1972): 29–51, at 29.

74. Gransden, "Realistic Observation," 29–30.

75. See, for instance, Lampert-Weissig, "Once and Future Jew"; Anthony Bale, "Fictions of Judaism in England Before 1290," in *Jews in Medieval Britain: Historical, Literary, Archaeological Perspectives*, ed. Patricia Skinner (Woodbridge: Boydell, 2003), 129–44; and Michael Widner, "Samson's Touch and a Thin Red Line: Reading the Bodies of Saints and Jews in Bury St Edmunds," *JEGP* 111, no. 3 (2012): 339–59.

76. Gerrard, "Jocelin of Brakelond and the Power of Abbot Samson," 16.

77. Gerrard, 16–17.

78. On Benedict and Jurnet of Norwich and their families, see V. D. Lipman, *The Jews of Medieval Norwich* (London: JHSE, 1967), passim; and *DMAJH*, s.vv. "Norwich," "Norwich, Isaac of," and "Norwich, Jurnet of," 282–89.

79. See, for a few examples, *CJB* 37–38 (on Samson's own fear of raging like a wolf, with Jocelin's commentary on his wrathful nature); 42 (where the monks call him "hominem iracundum"); 62 (the "abbas . . . turbatus et iratus"); 79 ("nolumus ei contradicere, nec ad iracundiam prouocare"); 111 (Samson "ualde iratus est et comotus"); and 131 (Samson "cito commotus respondit").

80. For example, *CJB* 59–60, where Samson razes the Haberdun windmill and threatens to tear down the whole mill until it is actually dismantled and moved.

81. I owe the concept of "activated" biblical stories, and the effects of this kind of activation on narrative and interpretive possibilities, to Shamma A. Boyarin.

82. Greti Dinkova-Bruun, "Biblical Thematics: The Story of Samson in Medieval Literary Discourse," in *The Oxford Handbook of Medieval Latin Literature*, ed. Ralph Hexter and David Townsend (New York: Oxford Univ. Press, 2012), 356–75, at 358.

83. Dinkova-Bruun, "Biblical Thematics," 361. This Delilah type is also discussed by Irven M. Resnick, *Marks of Distinction: Christian Perceptions of Jews in the Middle Ages* (Washington, DC: Catholic Univ. of America Press, 2012), 37.

84. Robert Scheller, *Exemplum: Model-Book Drawings and the Practice of Artistic Transmission in the Middle Ages, ca. 900–1450*, trans. Michael Hoyle (Amsterdam: Amsterdam Univ. Press, 1995), 26. For an edition of the *Pictor in carmine*, with further information on manuscripts and the critical tradition, see Karl-August Wirth, ed., *Pictor in Carmine: Ein Handbuch der Typologie aus der Zeit um 1200 nach MS 300 des Corpus Christi College in Cambridge* (Berlin: Gebr. Mann, 2006).

85. Quoted and translated in Dinkova-Bruun, "Biblical Thematics," 364–65.

86. For a useful discussion of this narrative device in thirteenth-century historiography, see Bale, "Fictions of Judaism," especially 137.

87. Jocelin's full description of Samson's personality and physical appearance is several pages long, at *CJB*, 39–41.

88. Red hair, for instance, could also be a mark of wrath or denote the god Mars, as is the case with Chaucer's later use of a red beard to characterize the Miller in the General Prologue of *CT* (GP 552), or his description of "myghty Mars the rede" in "The Knight's Tale" (*CT* I.1969). Walter Clyde Curry's "Chaucer's Reeve and Miller," *PMLA* 35 (1920): 189–209, and *Chaucer and the Mediaeval Sciences* (Oxford: Clarendon, 1926), 71–90, as well Jill Mann's *Chaucer and Medieval Estates Satire* (Cambridge: Cambrige Univ. Press, 1973), 160–67 and 282–83, remain useful sources on later medieval literary uses of physiognomy in general and red hair in particular.

89. This resemblance is not necessarily an argument against the nose as, also, a Jewish sign: a triangulation of the bodies of Jews, Samson, and Saint Edmund in the *Chronicle* has been persuasively argued by Widner, "Samson's Touch and a Thin Red Line."

90. A miniature of Samson and the lion in BL MS Arundel 157, fol. 65r (an English book that dates to the first quarter of the thirteenth century) in fact depicts the biblical hero in exactly this way: Samson atop the lion is adorned with black wavy hair, flowing out behind him, and a full beard that is distinctly touched with red.

91. See Anthony Bale, *Feeling Persecuted: Christians, Jews, and Images of Violence in the Middle Ages* (London: Reaktion, 2010), 65–89, here 73.

92. Resnick, *Marks of Distinction*, 268–69. Resnick is here relying on Robert Bartlett's influential "Illustrating Ethnicity in the Middle Ages," in *The Origins of Racism in the West*, ed. Miriam Eliav-Feldon, Benjamin Isaac, and Joseph Ziegler (Cambridge: Cambridge Univ. Press, 2009), 132–56.

93. This has been widely and ably discussed, for instance, in Ruth Mellinkoff, "Judas's Red Hair and the Jews," *Journal of Jewish Art* 9 (1982): 31–46; Bale, *Feeling Persecuted*, 65–79; Denise Despres, "Mary of the Eucharist: Cultic Anti-Judaism in Fourteenth-Century English Devotional Manuscripts," in *From Witness to Witchcraft: Jews and Judaism in Medieval Christian Thought*, ed. Jeremy Cohen (Wiesbaden: Harrassowitz, 1996), 375–401; and Claudine Fabre-Vassas, *The Singular Beast: Jews, Christians, and the Pig*, trans. Carol Volk (New York: Columbia Univ. Press, 1997).

94. Bale, *Feeling Persecuted*, 84–85.

95. Mellinkoff, "Judas's Red Hair and the Jews," 32.

96. Despres, "Mary of the Eucharist," 397.

97. Bale, *Feeling Persecuted*, 85. Note that I am silently modernizing Bale's incorporated quotation of a Middle English physiognomy handbook, including his gloss on "freting wretthe" (biting wrathfulness).

98. Bale, *Feeling Persecuted*, 85.

99. Kathleen Biddick, *The Typological Imaginary: Circumcision, Technology, History* (Philadelphia: Univ. of Pennsylvania Press, 2003), 6. Note that Biddick summarizes key arguments of Jeffrey Librett's *The Rhetoric of Cultural Dialogue: Jews and Germans from Moses Mendelssohn to Richard Wagner and Beyond* (Stanford: Stanford Univ. Press, 2000).

100. For the William de Brailes image, see Claire Donovan, *The de Brailes Hours* (Toronto: Univ. of Toronto Press, 1991), 78–80 and pl. 8. The *Chronica majora* accounts and illustration are discussed in Suzanne Lewis, *The Art of Matthew Paris in the "Chronica Majora"* (Berkeley: Univ. of California Press, 1987), 300–304 and fig. 188.

101. Henry Richards Luard, ed., *Matthæi Parisiensis monachi Sancti Albani, Chronica majora* (London: Longmans and Trübner, 1876 and 1880), 3:161–62 (the main account) and 5:340–41 (the later account). In neither instance does Matthew call Joseph Cartaphilus a Jew, though Luard's marginal notes label him the "Wandering Jew" in each case.

102. The figure had been styled "an anonymous Jew" by a Bolognese chronicler in 1223. See Lewis, *Art of Matthew Paris*, 300–302, at 302; and George K. Anderson, *The Legend of the Wandering Jew* (Providence: Brown Univ. Press, 1965), 18.

103. For more information on the development of the Wandering Jew legend and related terminology, see Galit Hassan-Rokem and Alan Dundes, eds., *The Wandering Jew: Essays in the Interpretation of a Christian Legend* (Bloomington: Indiana Univ. Press, 1986); Anderson, *Legend of the Wandering Jew*; and, more recently, with sensitive assessments of the figure's development within English literary traditions, Lisa Lampert-Weissig's "The Wandering Jew as Relic,"

English Language Notes 53, no. 2 (2015): 83–96, and her "Chaucer's Pardoner and the Jews," *Exemplaria* 28, no. 4 (2016): 337–60.

104. Luard, *Chronica majora*, 3:162.

105. Luard, 3:162.

106. Luard, 3:161 and 163.

107. For discussion of the anti-Jewish visual register evoked in the Matthew Paris depiction, and its interaction with his narrative accounts, see Lewis, *Art of Matthew Paris*, 302–4. In conversation with Lewis's reading is Lampert-Weissig, "Chaucer's Pardoner and the Jews," 340–43, who is particularly clear-eyed on the uses and manipulations of the figure in the early English iterations: she bluntly (and unusually) acknowledges that he "is not specified as Jewish" (342) and explains connected tropes of Jewishness alongside that fact. Donovan, *De Brailes Hours*, 79, suggests that William de Brailes painted the figure in "the robe of the High Priest."

108. Cohen, *Living Letters of the Law*, coined the now oft-evoked term "hermeneutical Jew," which denotes "constructions of Jews [that] continued to emerge [after Augustine] at the juncture of biblical hermeneutic, the philosophy of history, and anthropology" (68). A number of useful terms for the Jew as a Christian concept have emerged in recent scholarly history (summarized well in the first paragraphs of Lampert-Weissig, "Chaucer's Pardoner and the Jews" and in the Introduction above). None maps onto "sameness" perfectly, as I explain in the Introduction, but Cohen's "hermeneutical" does relate to the kinds of engagements and exegesis I have highlighted in this chapter. It is notable that all hitherto-proffered terms and related theories refer almost exclusively to Jewish men.

PART II. *HISTORIAE*

1. These are TNA SC 1/16/63 and SC 1/24/201, respectively.

2. On Jewish converts in thirteenth-century England generally, see Michael Adler, *Jews of Medieval England* (London: JHSE, 1939), 277–379; and Robert Stacey, "The Conversion of Jews to Christianity in Thirteenth-Century England," *Speculum* 67, no. 2 (1992): 263–83. Stacey finds that in the "king's [Henry III's] 1255 assignments of converts to monasteries . . . a very obvious effort was made to assign converts to a religious house in or around the convert's hometown" (279).

3. On the Worcester and Gloucester communities, see *DMAJH*, s.vv. "Gloucester" and "Worcester," 147–53 and 412–17; and Joe Hillaby, "The Worcester Jewry, 1158–1290: Portrait of a Lost Community," *Transactions of the Worcestershire Archaeological Society*, 3rd ser., no. 12 (1990): 73–122.

4. Monica Green, "Conversing with the Minority: Relations Among Christian, Jewish, and Muslim Women in the High Middle Ages," *Journal of Medieval History* 34, no. 2 (2008): 105–18, at 116 and 117.

5. A (French) transcription and Modern English translation of the full letter is available in Appendix 3.

6. See Appendix 3 for text and translation.

7. Edward I's letter is copied in Bod. MS Bodley 692, fol. 89v. Full text and translation are in Appendix 3.

8. The other possibility, given the shape and angle of the ascender by comparison to others in the same hand, is the fifth year (i.e., the roman numeral v), which would date the letter to March 1277. The same comparative process, however, suggests that the tenth (x) is more likely.

9. Adler prints the surviving 1308 Domus Conversorum inventory in *Jews of Medieval England*, 350–52; he discusses the situation of extant wardens' and inquiry records at 307–10.

10. In 1255, Henry III made provision for about 150 converts to be maintained at monasteries across England, as recorded in TNA C 60/52, mm. 2d, 12d, 13d, and 14d. Digital images of these records are available online through the *Henry III Fine Rolls Project* (TNA and Kings College London, 2009). On these provisions, see Adler, *Jews of Medieval England*, 341–47; and Joan Greatrex, "Monastic Charity for Jewish Converts: The Requisition of Corrodies by Henry III," *Studies in Church History* 29 (1992): 133–43. Greatrex calls 1255 "a turning point in the billeting of *conversi* in monastic establishments" (137) but notes that "there is sufficient evidence [Alice's letters among them] to show that the allocation of places for both *conversi* and other royal nominees continued through the remaining years of Henry's reign and beyond" (140).

11. *DMAJH*, s.v. "London, Abigail and Family of," 235–39, where the Giffard siblings' profits from debt trafficking are incidentally discussed.

12. *DMAJH*, s.v. "London, Abigail and Family of," 235–39. See also *ODNB*, s.vv. "Giffard, Walter (c. 1225–1279)" and "Giffard, Godfrey (c. 1235–1302)"; and material related to John Giffard's inheritance in Francis Joseph Baigent, ed., *A Collection of Records and Documents Relating to the Hundred and Manor of Crondal in Southampton* (London: Simpkin, 1891), 1:xxv and 416–20.

13. See Stacey, "Conversion of Jews to Christianity," 268; and Adler, *Jews of Medieval England*, 344.

14. See note 3 above. Barrie Dobson also discusses the dower-town expulsions in "The Jews of Medieval Cambridge," in *The Jewish Communities of Medieval England: The Collected Essays of R. B. Dobson*, ed. Helen Birkett (York: The Borthwick Institute, Univ. of York, 2010), 101–26, especially at 115–18.

15. See Adler, *Jews of Medieval England*, 277–379 ("History of the Domus"); Stacey, "Conversion of the Jews"; and F. D. Logan, "Thirteen London Jews and Conversion to Christianity: Problems of Apostasy in the 1280s," *Bulletin of the Institute of Historical Research* 45 (1972): 214–29. There is lengthy back-and-forth and confusion (on both Jewish and Christian sides), for example, evident in the Jewish Exchequer rolls and royal documents (cited by Logan) concerning a certain Milcana, a Jewish woman who apparently converted to Christianity but later claimed she had always been Jewish. Her case and others similar are discussed in some detail in the next chapter, at 132–37.

16. On resistance to Henry III's placements, see Greatrex, "Monastic Charity for Jewish Converts."

17. Stacey, "Conversion of the Jews," 268.

18. Adler published Alice's French letter to Edward I (with a translation) in *Jews of Medieval England*, 347–48; the same letter also appears (in French) in *Recueil de lettres anglo-françaises (1265–1399)*, ed. F. J. Tanquerey (Paris: Édouard Champion, 1916), no. 61, and (translated) in *Letters of the Queens of England, 1100–1547*, ed. Anne Crawford (Thrupp: Sutton, 1994), 246–47. The new texts and translations I provide in Appendix 3 can also be found in my "Anglo-Jewish Women at Court," in *Women Intellectuals and Leaders in the Middle Ages*, ed. Kathryn Kerby-Fulton, Katie Ann-Marie Bugyis, and John Van Engen (Cambridge: D. S. Brewer, 2020), 55–70, at 67–69. For the incorrect summary of the content of Alice's letter to Robert Burnell, see Greatrex, "Monastic Charity for Jewish Converts," 141: "She [Alice] likened herself first to Hagar, the bondwoman in the Old Testament, who was persecuted and driven into exile."

19. Ruth Nisse, *Jacob's Shipwreck: Diaspora, Translation, and Jewish-Christian Relations in Medieval England* (Ithaca: Cornell Univ. Press, 2017), 116.

20. Nisse, *Jacob's Shipwreck*, 116–17, where a useful summary of Robert Grosseteste's place in this tradition of reading the Hebrew Hagar as "the stranger" (*ha-ger*) can also be found. Nisse's wider discussion of conversion and apostasy, 114–26, is also relevant.

21. Nisse, *Jacob's Shipwreck*, 116.

22. See BL MS Harley 957, fol. 1v (contemporary contents list); and *A Catalogue of the Harleian Manuscripts in the British Museum* (London: British Museum, 1808), 1:484. Scholars who list the Bristol story among historical accusations of ritual murder in medieval England include Joe Hillaby and Caroline Hillaby, *DMAJH*, s.v. "Ritual Child-Murder Accusations," 323–30; John M. McCulloh, "Jewish Ritual Murder: William of Norwich, Thomas of Monmouth, and the Early Dissemination of the Myth," *Speculum* 72, no. 3 (1997): 712; Geraldine Heng, "England's Dead Boys: Telling Tales of Christian-Jewish Relations Before and After the First European Expulsion of the Jews," *MLN* 127, no. 5, supp. (2012): 55, where the murder is given an unqualified date; and Robin R. Mundill, *England's Jewish Solution: Experiment and Expulsion, 1262–1290* (Cambridge: Cambridge Univ. Press, 1998), 52.

23. Harvey J. Hames, "The Limits of Conversion: Ritual Murder and the Virgin Mary in the Account of Adam of Bristol," *Journal of Medieval History* 33 (2007): 43–59, at 56.

24. All quotations of the *Passion of Adam of Bristol* are from Christoph Cluse, ed., "'Fabula ineptissima': Die Ritualmordlegende um Adam von Bristol nach der Handschrift London, British Library, Harley 957," *Ashkenas* 5 (1995): 293–330, here (and throughout this paragraph) 305. Cluse's edition is hereafter cited parenthetically in text. Translations are my own, though I lean on the unpublished translation of Robert Stacey, who generously shared his draft with me. The text survives only in BL MS Harley 957 (fols. 19r–27r), where it is part of a small miscellany of mainly Latin texts. Summaries are available in Hames, "Limits of Conversion," 49–54; Robert Stacey, "'Adam of Bristol' and the Tales of Ritual Crucifixion in Medieval England," in *Thirteenth-Century England XI: Proceedings of the Gregynog Conference, 2005*, ed. Bjorn K. U. Weiler and Janet E. Burton (Woodbridge: Boydell, 2007), 2–15, at 3–7; Stacey, "From Ritual Crucifixion to Host Desecration: Jews and the Body of Christ," *Jewish History* 12, no. 1 (1998): 11–28, at 15–19; and Anthony Bale, *The Jew in the Medieval Book: English Antisemitisms, 1350–1500* (Cambridge: Cambridge Univ. Press, 2006), 133–34.

25. See Robert Alter, ed. and trans., *Strong as Death Is Love: The Song of Songs, Ruth, Esther, Jonah, and Daniel: A Translation with Commentary* (New York: Norton, 2015), Esther 10:1, note 1.

26. On the manuscript and the somewhat difficult dating of the tale's hand, see Stacey, "'Adam of Bristol,'" 8–9. Stacey looks at the codicological unit containing the story as "a two-quire booklet" (8), but I am not sure about this designation. The tale fills the third quire (8 + 1) and the recto of its added singleton (fols. 19r–27r), and Anglo-French verses ("The 33 Folies") on fol. 27v are apparently written by the same scribe. The fourth gathering (fols. 28–33), however, is more complicated: it is written in two other contemporary scribal hands and framed by two more singletons (1 +4+1). Fol. 28 begins a new text, and it is thus my opinion that the third and fourth gatherings cannot confidently be conceived of as an originary codicological unit.

27. Stacey, "'Adam of Bristol,'" 3, notes that the "other Henry" here is probably Henry II's eldest son, but it is also possible that this refers to Henry I (1100–1135), sometimes mistakenly thought to be Henry II's father. The potential confusion may be deliberate, a device that purposefully subverts secure positioning of the tale in historical time. This is much more subtle than, but similar to, the manipulations of sacred and secular time noted by Lisa Lampert-Weissig in "The Once and Future Jew: Little Robert of Bury, Historical Memory, and the Croxton *Play of the Sacrament*," *Jewish History* 15, no. 3 (2001): 235–55.

28. As discussed in the Introduction, Canon 68 of the Fourth Lateran Council (1215) mandated that Jews and Muslims of both sexes wear an identifying badge on their clothing, but English authorities reissued and refined the order for Jews many times between 1218 and the 1290 Expulsion, including in the well-known 1275 Statute of the Jewry. More detail, including discussion of Edward I's perception that women were ignoring the statutes, is provided in the next chapter, at 130.

29. Irven M. Resnick, *Marks of Distinction: Christian Perceptions of Jews in the High Middle Ages* (Washington, DC: Catholic Univ. of America Press, 2012), 254–55. See also Adrienne Williams Boyarin, "Desire for Religion: Mary, a Murder Libel, a Jewish Friar, and Me," *Religion and Literature* 42, nos. 1–2 (2010): 23–48, at 31–33.

30. For brief discussions of the linguistic and (related) issues of national identity in the tale, see Stacey, "'Adam of Bristol,'" 13–14, as well as his "Jews and Christians in Twelfth-Century England: Some Dynamics of a Changing Relationship," in *Jews and Christians in Twelfth-Century Europe*, ed. Michael A. Signer and John Van Engen (Notre Dame: Univ. of Notre Dame Press, 2001), 340–54, at 344–45; and Hames, "Limits of Conversion," 50.

31. The Jewess's interactions with the Irish priest suggest that *Adam of Bristol* can also be read in the context of anti-Irish material in English and Welsh literature of the period. The related linguistic complexities—and associated political, legal, and literary echoes and negotiations—in Irish and Welsh border regions and archives are discussed by Kathryn Kerby-Fulton in her "Competing Archives, Competing Languages: Office Vernaculars, Civil Servant Raconteurs, and the Porous Nature of French During Ireland's Rise of English," *Speculum* 90, no. 3 (2015): 674–700.

32. The Jewish wife and mother, and all of the horrifying details, are more thoroughly discussed in Chapter 4, at 172–83.

33. The one other instance comes from Samuel's wife, who asks Samuel "in secreto" if he is certain that no one saw the Christian boy Adam enter their Jewish home. Cluse, "'Fabula ineptissima,'" 306.

34. See Cluse, "'Fabula ineptissima,'" 316, where Samuel proposes that they "refer omnia bona que sunt in domo mea ad domum tuam," and 317, where he remarks, "O soror, .xlᵃ. marcas habeo in hac domo sub custodias tua."

35. See Cluse, "'Fabula ineptissima,'" where English is spoken to the Jews at 309, 312, 318, and (around the Jewish house) 322.

36. Cluse, "'Fabula ineptissima,'" 319.

37. Miri Rubin, *Gentile Tales: The Narrative Assault on Late Medieval Jews* (Philadelphia: Univ. of Pennsylvania Press, 1999), 5.

38. The identifying badges imposed on European Jews by Lateran IV were, of course, involved in this kind of nervousness about indistinguishability, already feminized with its rationale concerning miscegenation. The English *tabula* that resulted—"a badge on the outer garment, that is to say, in the form of two tables joined, of yellow felt, of the length of six inches, and of the breadth of three inches"—was distinct from the more usual yellow circle mandated on the continent, and it was instituted in England by 1218. There is some dispute over how widespread it was because of the multiple statutes reinstituting it throughout the thirteenth century. See Mundill, *England's Jewish Solution* 54–59 and 291–93.

39. Zygmunt Bauman, "Allosemitism: Premodern, Modern, Postmodern," in *Modernity, Culture, and "The Jew,"* ed. Bryan Cheyette and Laura Marcus (Stanford: Stanford Univ. Press, 1998), 143–56, at 143–44.

CHAPTER 3

1. Anthony Bale, *The Jew in the Medieval Book: English Antisemitisms, 1350–1500* (Cambridge: Cambridge Univ. Press, 2006), 134. Bale does note the role of women and maternity tropes in *Adam of Bristol*—which I will also discuss in the next chapter—but his focus is the "masculine Jewish potency, to which Samuel is repeatedly connected."

2. Irven M. Resnick, *Marks of Distinction: Christian Perceptions of Jews in the High Middle Ages* (Washington, DC: Catholic Univ. of America Press, 2012), 255. Resnick's argument about the importance of passing in *Adam of Bristol* are similar to my own, though I am shifting discussion toward the tale's female characters.

3. I borrow the term "uncanny valley" from robotics, where it refers to the point at which near resemblance to the human causes discomfort or revulsion. For an early explication, see Jasia Reichardt, *Robots: Fact, Fiction, and Prediction* (New York: Viking Penguin, 1978).

4. Michael Adler, *Jews of Medieval England* (London: JHSE, 1939), 15; Barrie Dobson, "The Medieval York Jewry Reconsidered," in *The Jews of Medieval Britian: Historical, Literary, and Archaeological Perspectives*, ed. Patricia Skinner (Woodbridge: Boydell, 2003), 145–56, at 153; Hannah Meyer, "Female Moneylending and Wet-Nursing in Jewish-Christian Relations in Thirteenth-Century England" (PhD diss., University of Cambridge, 2009), 293.

5. Elisheva Baumgarten, *Mothers and Children: Jewish Family Life in Medieval Europe* (Princeton: Princeton Univ. Press, 2004), 6, and *Practicing Piety in Medieval Ashkenaz: Men, Women, and Everyday Religious Observance* (Philadelphia: Univ. of Pennsylvania Press, 2014), 4.

6. Sara Lipton, *Dark Mirror: The Medieval Origins of Anti-Jewish Iconography* (New York: Metropolitan, 2014), 219, and "Where Are the Gothic Jewish Women? On the Non-iconography of the Jewess in the *Cantigas de Santa Maria*," *Jewish History* 22 (2008): 139–77, at 158.

7. Baumgarten, *Mothers and Children*, 188–89.

8. See Anna Rich Abad, "Able and Available: Jewish Women in Medieval Barcelona and Their Economic Activities," *Journal of Medieval Iberian Studies* 6, no. 1 (2014): 71–86; William Chester Jordan, "Jews on Top: Women and the Availability of Consumption Loans in Northern France in the Mid-Thirteenth Century," *Journal of Jewish Studies* 29 (1978): 30–49; and Meyer, "Female Moneylending and Wet-Nursing," 176–212. For a broad comparative picture of the continental situation, see also Joseph Shatzmiller, *Cultural Exchange: Jews, Christians, and Art in the Medieval Marketplace* (Princeton: Princeton Univ. Press, 2013), 7–44. For a compelling and dissenting view of both the role of medieval Jews in England and Anglo-Jewish women's position, see Julie L. Mell, *The Myth of the Medieval Jewish Moneylender*, vol. 1 (New York: Palgrave Macmillan, 2017), who critiques the scholarly historiography via its roots in nineteenth-century antisemitism. As I am primarily interested in the rhetoric and narrative that can be gleaned from the historical records, I am not at odds with Mell's conclusions. Indeed, as Pinchas Roth notes, her book both highlights "the significance of gender roles" and identifies "the dangers of skewed perspective" that result from using only Christian sources. See his "Who Speaks for the Jews? Latin and Hebrew Sources," in "The Myth of the Medieval Jewish Moneylender: A Forum," ed. Nina Caputo, *Marginalia Review of Books*, 8 May 2020. https://marginalia.lareviewofbooks.org/who-speaks-for-the-jews-latin-and-hebrew-sources/.

9. A list of essoins in the earliest extant plea roll of the Exchequer of the Jews (TNA E 9/1), for instance, lists six different cases brought by two prominent Jewish women—four by Chera of Winchester, two by Antera of Coventry—while a case brought by one of Chera's sons mentions only that he is "fil Chere" (m. 2); and a 1267 record of inquest regarding the debts of a Thomas de Bromwyz includes the Hebrew signature of Moses son of Avigail (TNA C 255/18/5B). See also Suzanne Bartlet, "Women in the Medieval Anglo-Jewish Community," in Skinner, *Jews of Medieval Britian: Historical, Literary, and Archaeological Perspectives*, 114–27, at 116–19, where she discusses matronymics and expresses frustration with past editors of the *PREJ* because they often omit lists of debts or essoins and thereby "possible evidence of the whereabouts or even the continuing existence of the male and female individuals being traced" (116). On Anglo-Jewish women's names and naming practices more generally, see Simon Seror, "Les noms des femmes juives en Angleterre au moyen âge," *Revue des études juives* 154, nos. 3–4 (1995): 295–325.

10. On the "embedded autonomy" of Jewish courts and authorities in medieval England, see Judith Olszowy-Schlanger, *Hebrew and Hebrew-Latin Documents from Medieval England: A Diplomatic and Palaeographical Study* (Turnhout: Brepols, 2016), 1:21–22 and 24–29. For an English rabbi's consideration of marriage law, see Pinchas Roth and Ethan Zadoff, "The Talmudic Community of Thirteenth-Century England," in *Christians and Jews in Angevin England: The York Massacre of 1190, Narratives and Contexts*, ed. Sarah Rees Jones and Sethina Watson (Woodbridge: Boydell and Brewer, 2013), 184–203, at 193–200. Several of Pinchas Roth's articles, moreover, establish distinct aspects of Anglo-Jewish halakha and jurisdiction: see his "Medieval English Rabbis: Image and Self-Image," *Early Middle English* 1, no. 1 (2019): 17–33; "Jewish Courts in Medieval England," *Jewish History* 21, nos. 1–2 (2017): 67–82; and "New Responsa by Isaac ben Peretz of Northampton," *Jewish Historical Studies* 46 (2014): 1–17.

11. Barrie Dobson, "The Role of Jewish Women in Medieval England (Presidential Address)," *Studies in Church History* 29 (1992): 145–68, at 146.

12. Quoted in R. B. Dobson, "A Minority Within a Minority: The Jewesses of Thirteenth-Century England," in *The Jewish Communities of Medieval England: The Collected Essays of R. B. Dobson*, ed. Helen Birkett (York: The Borthwick Institute, Univ. of York, 2010), 149–66, at 150.

13. Olszowy-Schlanger, *Hebrew and Hebrew-Latin Documents*, 1:26–27 (emphasis mine).

14. On the institutional history of the Exchequer of the Jews, see Olszowy-Schlanger, *Hebrew and Hebrew-Latin Documents*, 1:22–24; Paul Brand's introduction to *PREJ* 6:1–51; J. M. Rigg's introduction to *Select Pleas, Starrs,* ix–xliii; and Hilary Jenkinson's introduction to *PREJ* 3:xi–lii.

15. Victoria Hoyle, "The Bonds That Bind: Money Lending Between Anglo-Jewish and Christian Women in the Plea Rolls of the Exchequer of the Jews, 1218–1280," *Journal of Medieval History* 34, no. 2 (2008): 119–29, at 122. In my own continuing surveys of the unpublished rolls, I have so far found an additional fifty-four cases featuring Jewish women. For information on what is and is not published, see *PREJ* 6:57–68.

16. Suzanne Bartlet, "Three Jewish Businesswomen in Thirteenth-Century Winchester," *Jewish Culture and History* 3, no. 2 (2003): 31–54, at 31.

17. Suzanne Bartlet, *Licoricia of Winchester: Marriage, Motherhood, and Murder in the Medieval Anglo-Jewish Community* (London: Vallentine-Mitchell, 2009), edited by Patricia Skinner after Bartlet's death in June 2008.

18. Dobson, "Minority Within a Minority," 151.

19. Dobson, 123.

20. See note 8 above for recent and influential work on the comparative contexts.

21. Dobson, "Minority Within a Minority," 122.

22. The king retained some prerogative, however, and Jews could invite the "law of the land" into disputes where a *beit din* decision was opposed. See Olszowy-Schlanger, *Hebrew and Hebrew-Latin Documents*, 1:24–26.

23. *PREJ* 1:49–55.

24. *PREJ* 1:152.

25. For information on how Christian and Jewish courts interacted in medieval England, as well as on the limits of Jewish autonomy and laws related to Jewish women, see Olszowy-Schlanger, *Hebrew and Hebrew-Latin Documents*, 1:20–29.

26. I use Shamma Boyarin's translation of Ephraim of Bonn's *Book of Historical Records*, in the appendices of *The Siege of Jerusalem*, ed. and trans. Adrienne Williams Boyarin (Toronto: Broadview, 2014), 156–58. The Hebrew can be found in A. M. Habermann, ed., *Sefer Gezerot Ashkenaz ve-Zorfat* (Jerusalem: Tarshish, 1945), 127.

27. Since the Latin "suis" is grammatically masculine in this passage only because it modifies "libris," I translate the phrase to remove a gendered pronoun. See Henry Richards Luard, ed., *Bartholomaei de Cotton monachi Norwicensis Historia anglicana* (London: Longman, Green, Longman, and Roberts, 1859), 178. Bartholomew is an independent authority for the years 1285–91, writing nearly contemporaneously with the 1290 Expulsion.

28. I quote here from Olszowy-Schlanger's lecture "Hebrew Documents in Medieval England," delivered at the Hebrew and Jewish Studies Centre of the University of Oxford, 8 December 2014, now posted on the Oxford Jewish Heritage website, Oxford Jewish Heritage Committee, 2014, https://www.oxfordjewishheritage.co.uk. See also her *Hebrew and Hebrew-Latin Documents*, 1:97–98, as well as her many other works on the larger topic of medieval Anglo-Hebrew books: *Les manuscrits hébreux dans l'Angleterre médiévale: Étude historique et paléographique* (Paris: Peeters, 2003); "A School of Christian Hebraists in Thirteenth-Century England: A Unique Hebrew-Latin-French and English Dictionary and Its Sources," *European Journal of Jewish Studies* 1, no. 2 (2007): 249–77; "Robert Wakefield and His Hebrew Manuscripts" *Zutot* 6, no. 1 (2009): 25–33; "Christian Hebraism in Thirteenth-Century England: The Evidence of Hebrew-Latin Manuscripts," in *Crossing Borders: Hebrew Manuscripts as a Meeting-Place of Cultures*, ed. Piet van Boxel and Sabine Arndt (Oxford: Bodleian Library, Univ. of Oxford, 2009), 115–22; and, with Patricia Stirnemann, "The Twelfth-Century Trilingual Psalter in Leiden," *Scripta* 1 (2008): 103–12. Pinchas Roth's work on medieval Anglo-Jewish rabbinic culture is also worth noting: see his "Medieval English Rabbis," "Jewish Courts in Medieval England," "New Responsa by Isaac ben Peretz of Northampton, and (with Ethan Zadoff) "Talmudic Community of Thirteenth-Century England."

29. Olszowy-Schlanger, *Hebrew and Hebrew-Latin Documents*, 1:97. See also Michael Clanchy, *From Memory to Written Record: England 1066–1307*, 2nd ed. (Oxford: Blackwell, 1993), 201–3, discussed in further detail below. An interesting comparative case for the participation of Christian women in legal-documentary and epistolary culture in the late Middle Ages is Malcolm Richardson, *Middle-Class Writing in Late Medieval London* (London: Pickering and Chatto, 2011), especially Chapter 4.

30. Clanchy, *From Memory to Written Record*, 202.

31. *PREJ* 1:270; TNA E 9/11, m. 10. For close rolls and plea rolls, I lean on previous translations where possible (only inconsistently available in *PREJ* 1–4), though all translations have been modified by me. Latin text is included wherever possible—i.e., when previous publications include it or when I have been able to examine a roll in situ—and, when not otherwise noted, Latin is quoted from my own transcriptions.

32. *PREJ* 1:149; TNA E 9/8, m. 2.

33. *PREJ* 3:305; TNA E 9/24, m. 4d.

34. See Olszowy-Schlanger, *Hebrew and Hebrew-Latin Documents*, 1:26: "Jews took their oath on a Torah scroll also in non-Jewish courts." For this reason, justice Hamo Hauteyn amerced the sergeant of the York Jewry Meyrot of Stamford for contempt in Hilary Term 1278, when "he did not have the book of Judaic Law on which Jews could make an oath" (non habuit librum legis judaice super quem judei potuerunt sacraementum facere). See *PREJ* 5:46; and cf. Dobson's confused assessment of the same entry in "Medieval York Jewry Reconsidered," 151–52.

35. *PREJ* 5:17.

36. Dobson, "Medieval York Jewry Reconsidered," 154.

37. For brief discussion of this document and seal, see Charlotte Newman Goldy, "Muriel, a Jew of Oxford: Using the Dramatic to Understand the Mundane in Anglo-Norman Towns," in *Writing Medieval Women's Lives*, ed. Charlotte Newman Goldy and Amy Livingstone (New York: Palgrave, 2012), 227–45, at 232–33. It is also included in Daniel M. Friedenberg's *Medieval*

Jewish Seals from Europe (Detroit: Wayne State Univ. Press, 1987). On Anglo-Jewish seals more generally, see Olszowy-Schlanger, *Hebrew and Hebrew-Latin Documents*, 1:60–64.

38. Olszowy-Schlanger, *Hebrew and Hebrew-Latin Documents*, 1:67.

39. Olszowy-Schlanger, 1:69–70 and 1:67–68.

40. I use the translation (from Hebrew) of Olszowy-Schlanger, in *Hebrew and Hebrew-Latin Documents*, 1:300–301 (item no. 66, Westminster Abbey Muniments 6797). This *shidduch* was also translated by Adler in *Jews of Medieval England*, 42–43, from the Hebrew in M. D. Davis, ed., *Hebrew Deeds of English Jews Before 1290* (London: Jewish Chronicle, 1888), 299–302.

41. Olszowy-Schlanger, *Hebrew and Hebrew-Latin Documents*, 1:300–301.

42. *PREJ* 3:112; TNA E 9/49, m. 9d.

43. This infamous libel is discussed in more detail in the next chapter, at 148–51.

44. *DMAJH*, s.v. "Hereford, Hamo of, and his Family," 167.

45. On Jewish participation in the Latin book trade, see Collette Sirat, "Looking at Latin Books, Understanding Latin Texts: Different Attitudes in Different Jewish Communities," in *Hebrew to Latin, Latin to Hebrew: The Mirroring of Two Cultures in the Age of Humanism*, ed. Giulio Busi (Berlin: Institut für Judaistik, Freie Universität Berlin, 2004), 7–22; and Shatzmiller, *Cultural Exchange*, 22–42.

46. *Select Pleas*, 103–4; TNA E 9/27, m. 7.

47. *Select Pleas*, 114. The books listed are "unus liber Prisciani Constr', . . . unus Grecismus, . . . una Logica vetus, . . . unum Doctrinale magnum, . . . quidam liber Institutionum, . . . quidam Codex, . . . quoddam Inforciatum, . . . liber Nature, . . . [et] quidam Grecismus." This collection supports evidence of Jews' participation in the medieval Oxford University book trade in Malcom Parkes, "The Provision of Books," in *The History of the University of Oxford*, vol. 2, *Late Medieval Oxford*, ed. J. I. Catto and Ralph Evans (Oxford: Clarendon, 1992), 407–83, at 410. Kathryn Kerby-Fulton's "Afterword: Social History of the Book and Beyond: *Originalia*, Medieval Literary Theory, and the Aesthetics of Paleography," in *The Medieval Manuscript Book: Cultural Approaches*, ed. Michael Johnston and Michael Van Dussen (Cambridge: Cambridge Univ. Press), 243–54, at 247, emphasizes that Parkes demonstrated that some books "were even owned by Jewish women."

48. Such proclamations can be found in *PREJ* 1:89, as well as 91, 115, 193, 194, 197, 200, and passim through all six *PREJ* volumes.

49. *Select Pleas,* 19. This is just one convenient example, however. Licoricia was frequently in court with her documents. For more on her long career and business dealings, see Bartlet, *Licoricia of Winchester.*

50. *CFR 1217–18*, no. 47; TNA C 60/9, m. 6.

51. See note 28 above. Also relevant is Ruth Nisse's *Jacob's Shipwreck: Diaspora, Translation, and Jewish-Christian Relations in Medieval England* (Ithaca: Cornell Univ. Press, 2017).

52. Middle English as edited by Bella Millett and Jocelyn Wogan-Browne in *Medieval English Prose for Women: Selections from the Katherine Group and "Ancrene Wisse"* (Oxford: Clarendon, 1993), 134, lines 32–34.

53. Olszowy-Schlanger, *Hebrew and Hebrew-Latin Documents*, 1:22–23, at 23.

54. Millet and Wogan-Browne, *Medieval English Prose for Women*, 116, lines 23–26.

55. It is worth noting that the probable location of the composition and early readership of the *Ancrene Wisse*, near Wigmore and Lingen in Herefordshire, is nearby Hereford, an *archa* town with a firmly established Jewish community as early as 1179, and an important Jewish moneylending family from about 1218. See E. J. Dobson, *The Origins of "Ancrene Wisse"* (Oxford: Clarendon, 1976). On the Hereford Jewish community, see the work of Joe Hillaby, particularly

"Hereford Gold: Irish, Welsh, and English Land—The Jewish Community at Hereford and Its Clients, 1179–1253: Four Case Studies, Part 2," *Transactions of the Woolhope Naturalists Field Club* 45, no. 1 (1985): 193–270, and "A Magnate Among the Marchers: Hamo of Hereford, His Family and Clients, 1218–1253," *Jewish Historical Studies* 31 (1990): 23–82.

56. Olszowy-Schlanger, *Hebrew and Hebrew-Latin Documents*, 1:23.

57. Adler, *Jews of Medieval England*, included forty-two women's tallies in his assessments, with nine cases of gender ambiguity. Olszowy-Schlanger, *Hebrew and Hebrew-Latin Documents*, adds fifty-eight tallies to Adler's knowledge, ten of which are in women's names. On the use of tally sticks in Anglo-Jewish business more generally, see her overview at 1:46–47.

58. See also Bartlet, "Women in the Medieval Anglo-Jewish Community," 120. I previously discussed the cases of unlawful detinue listed in these paragraphs, as well as their connection to *Ancrene Wisse*'s passages on Jewish bonds and document storage, in "Inscribed Bodies: The Virgin Mary, Jewish Women, and Medieval Feminine Legal Authority," in *Law and Sovereignty in the Middle Ages and Renaissance*, ed. Robert S. Sturges (Turnhout: Brepols, 2011), 229–51.

59. *PREJ* 1:132–33.

60. *PREJ* 1:133.

61. This is an interesting case of a loan *from* a Christian *to* a Jew, and apparently a private one between the women. The idea of small consumption loans between Jewish and Christian women going in *both* directions runs counter to the French evidence: see Jordan, "Jews on Top."

62. *PREJ* 1:142.

63. *PREJ* 1:146.

64. *PREJ* 1:142 and 145, respectively.

65. J. R. Madicott, *Simon de Montfort* (Cambridge: Cambridge Univ. Press, 1996), 360. Madicott discusses the associated London massacre of the Jews at 268ff.

66. In 1264–65, Montfort offered cancellation of Jewish debts partly in an attempt to alleviate the raids of the *archae* that were resulting in massacres. See Madicott, *Simon de Montfort*, 315–16; and Robin R. Mundill, *England's Jewish Solution: Experiment and Expulsion, 1262–1290* (Cambridge: Cambridge University Press, 1998), 259.

67. In 1277, Licoricia of Winchester was stabbed to death at home, along with her Christian maidservant Alice of Bicton. See the eighth chapter of Bartlet, *Licoricia of Winchester*, which provides details about the murders and their aftermath. For a continental Jewish perspective on such relationships, see Elliott Horowitz, "Between Masters and Maidservants: The Jewish Society of Europe in Late Medieval and Early Modern Times" [in Hebrew], in *Sexuality and the Family in History*, ed. Isaiah Gafni and Israel Bartal (Jerusalem: Zalman Shatar Center, 1998), 193–211.

68. Baumgarten, *Mothers and Children*, 133.

69. Meyer, "Female Moneylending and Wet-Nursing," 265. Meyer also includes an overview of the role of the wet nurse in anti-Jewish libels and literature (245ff.), some of which I discuss in the next chapter.

70. Baumgarten, *Mothers and Children*, 144.

71. Meyer, "Female Moneylending and Wet-Nursing," 291.

72. Quoted in Baumgarten, *Mothers and Children*, 141.

73. On Jacob of London and his *Sefer Etz Hayyim*, see Olszowy-Schlanger, *Hebrew and Hebrew-Latin Documents*, 1:28; and Roth and Zadoff, "Talmudic Community," 187 and 197–202.

74. Quoted in Baumgarten, *Mothers and Children*, 142.

75. *PREJ* 4:142.

76. Meyer, "Female Moneylending and Wet-Nursing," 274. Unlike Meyer, I take Floricote and Malecote to be women's names, and I include an unnamed woman in my count.

77. TNA C 85/99/33.

78. Meyer, "Female Moneylending and Wet-Nursing," 261. The 1275 English Statute of the Jewry expressly mandated that no Christian live among Jews.

79. *PREJ* 4:142.

80. Meyer, "Female Moneylending and Wet-Nursing," 270.

81. *DMAJH*, s.v. "1253, Statute Concerning the Jews," 29.

82. *AND*, s.v. "pasche." Misconstrual is understandable given that nearby entries (see *PREJ* 4:142) mention Henry III's Easter tallage, but the juxtaposition is simply temporal: the holidays are at the same time of year and often overlap.

83. *PREJ* 4:170.

84. *PREJ* 4:153; TNA E 101/249/22, m. 3. The Christian scribe uses the words Josana (probably transliterated strangely from השנה), Enna (Yom Kippur?), and Purim.

85. *PREJ* 4:142.

86. *PREJ* 4:152. This is occasionally the case for Christian men and boys as well: one similar case for a "puero" (*PREJ* 4:160) is glossed by the editor as a "prostitute," though this is probaby unnecessarily sensational. Other kinds of interactions, including those between friends, playmates, or childcare providers, are certainly possible.

87. *PREJ* 4:150 and 152.

88. *PREJ* 4:152, 161, and 149, respectively.

89. *PREJ* 4:156 (and cf. 150).

90. This includes the 1275 Statute of the Jewry, which specified that children wear the badge from age seven. The English badge—"two tables joined, of yellow felt, of the length of six inches, and of the breadth of three inches"—was distinct from the more usual yellow circle mandated on the continent. See Mundill, *England's Jewish Solution*, 291–93.

91. *CCR 1272–79*, 565–66; TNA C 54/96, m. 6d.

92. TNA E 401/1565, now used popularly as an early example of anti-Jewish caricature even in primary school contexts. See, for example, "A Medieval Mystery," The National Archives: Classroom Resources, accessed 24 September 2019, http://www.nationalarchives.gov.uk /education/resources/medieval-mystery.

93. Sara Lipton, "Isaac and the Antichrist in the Archives," *Past & Present* 232, no. 1 (2016): 3–44, at 28.

94. Lipton, "Isaac and the Antichrist," 22.

95. Lipton, 28 and 12.

96. *CFR 1217–18*, no. 17; TNA C 60/9, m. 7.

97. See Robert Stacey, "The Conversion of Jews to Christianity in Thirteenth-Century England," *Speculum* 67 (1992): 263–83, at 272 and 278–81; F. D. Logan, "Thirteen London Jews and Conversion to Christianity: Problems of Apostasy in the 1280s," *Bulletin of the Institute of Historical Research* 45 (1272): 214–29, at 222; Joan Greatrex, "Monastic Charity for Jewish Converts: The Requisition of Corrodies by Henry III," *Studies in Church History* 29 (1992): 133–43; and Adler, *Jews of Medieval England*, 283–84 and 287–90 (with his editions and translations of Henry III's 1255 lists of converts assigned to monastic houses and Edward II's inquisition records for the London Domus Conversorum at 341–47 and 350–52, respectively). These resources document a roughly even number of men and women converts.

98. Olszowy-Schlanger, *Hebrew and Hebrew-Latin Documents*, 1:27. Hagin held his position 1268–80.

99. *PREJ* 3:22; TNA E 9/21, m. 4d.

100. *PREJ* 3:34–35; TNA E 9/21, m. 6d.

101. *PREJ* 3:177; TNA E 9/22, m. 6d.

102. TNA E 9/24, m. 7.

103. *Select Pleas*, 99–100; TNA E 9/24, m. 7.

104. Edward I and Peckham's 1282 lists of apostates are preserved in TNA C 85/3/71 and C 255/18/5B. My thanks to Paul Dryburgh for helping me track down the latter, which has been reclassified since the time of the most recent publications to discuss it. Logan, "Thirteen London Jews" also discusses Milcana's case in some detail and edits the two documents at 227–28.

105. Logan, "Thirteen London Jews," 216 and 228–29.

106. Quoted in Logan, "Thirteen London Jews," 219.

107. On Elijah Menahem and his family, see Roth and Zadoff, "Talmudic Community," 188–200; and Roth, "Jewish Courts in Medieval England."

108. *Registres d'Honorius IV*, ed. Maurice Prou (Paris: Ernst Thorin, 1886), 563, no. 809. The idea that a rabbi might intervene in such cases is not implausible. Milcana, in any case, was still married to Sakerel in 1282.

109. They went walking on Coleman Street on 22 September, in that year between Rosh Hashanah and Yom Kippur, and thus were near the Great Synagogue that sat at the intersection of Coleman and Lothbury. See *DMAJH*, s.v. "London," 219 (Plan 7).

110. *PREJ* 2:209–10.

111. TNA E 9/21, m. 4 and m. 8d.

112. TNA C 255/18/5B. See also Logan, "Thirteen London Jews," 228 and 229 n. 1.

113. Logan, "Thirteen London Jews," 218.

114. See Baumgarten, *Mothers and Children*, 119–53.

115. *CCR 1272–79*, 565–66; TNA C 54/96, m. 6d.

116. It should be noted that there are, also, records of Jewish women who refused to convert. Women who resisted despite the conversion of their husbands or fathers appeared in court because when the norm was that a convert's property reverted to the king, women's status in relation to male family members could cause administrative confusion. The Pipe Roll for 9 Richard I (1198), for instance, includes Gentilia, daughter of Samson of York, who appeared to claim her inheritance at a postmortem inquisition of her father's property; he had converted, but she had not (TNA E 372/43, rot. 4, m. 2). In 1234, Chera of Canterbury attempted to claim her marriage portion from the man to whom her property had been sold after her husband's conversion; her plea was refused, on the grounds that she should have followed her husband into Christianity (*CCR 1231–34*, 555; TNA C 54/45, m. 27d). While not as prevalent as the types of cases listed above, these instances can be connected to confusion around Jewish women's status, or, polemically, to the kind of resistance characterized by Samuel's sister in the *Passion of Adam of Bristol*.

117. *CCR 1330–33*, 64. On Claricia more generally, see Adler, *Jews of Medieval England*, 313–20.

118. Jacob Copin is discussed further in Alder's overview of Claricia's case, *Jews of Medieval England*, 313–20. See also *DMAJH*, s.v. "Exeter," 136–37; and Zafira Entin Rokéah, "Money and the Hangman in Late Thirteenth-Century England: Jewish, Christians, and Coinage Offences Alleged and Real (Part II)," *Jewish Historical Studies* 32 (1992): 159–218, at 194.

119. Mundill, *England's Jewish Solution*, 172–74.

120. Adler, *Jews of Medieval England*, 350–52.

121. *CCR 1330–33*, 64.

122. TNA SC 8/158/7875.

123. See Adler, *Jews of Medieval England,* 356–57, where he prints the letters of Juliana and her husband (TNA SC 8/103/5120 and SC 8/4/154). He discusses their case at 313, and presents the lists of the Domus residents compiled by inquisitors in 1280 and 1308 at 350–52.

124. *AND,* s.v. "comander" 4.

125. Adler, *Jews of Medieval England,* 357; TNA SC 8/103/5120.

126. TNA E 101/251/11. Joan and Alice's signet-sized, green-wax seals are attached to a single parchment tongue. They are now too damaged to discern the impressions or legends.

127. Adler, *Jews of Medieval England,* 324, 367, and 370–71; TNA E 101/251/11.

128. Adler, 324.

129. Lynn Staley, ed., *The Book of Margery Kempe* (Kalamazoo: Medieval Institute, 1996), line 2933. This mocking question might be taken seriously as a historically savvy (and particularly English) barb in a place that certainly could have had long-standing notions of the Jewess as someone who, like Margery Kempe, was a businesswoman, traveling without a husband, handling her own money, appearing before courts, and laden with documents. It is also probable, I will note, that Margery's "wedding" ring with the inscription *Ihesus est amor meus* was a signet ring: several personal seals with the same legend survive; e.g., TNA DL 25/3546.

130. *CCR 1272–79,* 487.

131. *PREJ* 4:53 and 178.

132. *PREJ* 1:270; TNA E 9/11, m. 10.

133. BL MS Harley 79, fol. 1r. In this case, a mixed jury of Christians and Jews determined that the forgery was not done by Henna but rather by Vives and Hagin of Gloucester, who had accepted payment from a Christian man to create the forgery after Henna's death.

134. See *DMAJH,* s.v. "Coinage and Coin Clipping," 105–7; and Zafira Entin Rokéah, "Money and the Hangman in Late Thirteenth-Century England: Jewish, Christians, and Coinage Offences Alleged and Real (Part I)," *Jewish Historical Studies* 31 (1990): 83–109.

135. Rokéah, "Money and the Hangman (Part II)," 159–218.

136. See *PREJ* 4:139–94.

137. Adler, *Jews of Medieval England,* 34.

138. Alder, 34–36, at 36; Dobson, "Role of Jewish Women in Medieval England," 145–68, at 148–49.

139. *PREJ* 1:103–4, at 104; TNA E 9/4, m. 4d.

140. Dobson, "Role of Jewish Women in Medieval England," 149.

141. Dobson, 149 n. 12.

142. Petrus Alfonsi, *Dialogue Against the Jews,* ed. and trans. Irven M. Resnick (Washington, DC: Catholic Univ. of America Press, 2007), 149–60.

143. Baumgarten, *Mothers and Children,* 136–37.

144. Baumgarten, 138–39.

145. Resnick, trans., *Dialogue Against the Jews,* 252–53.

146. Resnick, 254.

147. Resnick, 254.

148. Resnick, 254.

149. See Resnick, *Marks of Distinction,* 286; and Willis Johnson, "Textual Sources for the Study of Jewish Currency Crimes in Thirteenth-Century England," *British Numismatic Journal* 66 (1996): 21–32, at 28–29. The relevant primary texts are in Henry Richards Luard, ed., *Matthæi Parisiensis monachi Sancti Albani Chronica majora* (London: Longmans and Trübner, 1877 and 1880), 4:608–9 and 632–33, and 5:15–16.

CHAPTER 4

1. Sara Lipton, *Dark Mirror: The Medieval Origins of Anti-Jewish Iconography* (New York: Metropolitan, 2014), 203.

2. Lipton, *Dark Mirror*, 203.

3. Lipton, 203–4.

4. Respectively, Steven F. Kruger, *The Spectral Jew: Conversion and Embodiment in Medieval Europe* (Minneapolis: Univ. of Minnesota Press, 2006), 85; Miri Rubin, *Gentile Tales: The Narrative Assault on Late Medieval Jews* (Philadelphia: Univ. of Pennsylvania Press, 2004), 43 and 73–78; Anthony Bale, "Fictions of Judaism in England Before 1290," in *Jews in Medieval Britain: Historical, Literary, Archaeological Perspectives*, ed. Patricia Skinner (Woodbridge: Boydell, 2003), 137. See also Anthony Bale, "The Female 'Jewish' Libido in Medieval Culture," in *The Erotic in the Literature of Medieval Britain*, ed. Amanda Hopkins and Cory James Rushton (Cambridge: D. S. Brewer, 2007), 94–104.

5. Amy-Jill Levine, "A Jewess, More and/or Less," in *Judaism Since Gender*, ed. Miriam Peskowitz and Laura Levitt (New York: Routledge, 1997), 149–57, at 151.

6. Bale, "Female 'Jewish' Libido," 95.

7. Lipton, in *Dark Mirror*, 205–6, is careful to note that the femme fatale type is a postmedieval development in the art historical tradition, but she nonetheless suggests (as does Bale in "Female 'Jewish' Libido") that this is not the case for literature. As I will argue in the next chapter, however, the illustrative and narrative traditions are not far removed from each other on this issue: the medieval Jewish femme fatale type is a myth born of backreading.

8. *DMAJH*, s.vv. "Berkhamsted, Abraham of" and "1241, Worcester 'Parlaiment,'" 50–52 and 27–29, at 29; for Abraham's marriage to Floria and their children's links to other prominent families, see also the family tree s.v. "Hereford, Hamo of, and his Family," 166.

9. Henry Richards Luard, ed., *Matthæi Parisiensis monachi Sancti Albani, Chronica majora* (London: Longmans and Trübner, 1880), 5:114–15.

10. Bale, "Fictions of Judaism," 135–37.

11. Lipton, *Dark Mirror*, 342 n. 9; Bale, "Fictions of Judaism," 137. Interestingly, Bale and Lipton use Floria to argue opposing points: Lipton sees her as one of the female villains who occupy medieval narratives in contrast to art historical traditions, while Bale sees her pliancy in contrast to the "real villain" Abraham.

12. Bale, "Fictions of Judaism," 138, claims that "the 'real' Abraham was indeed in trouble in the 1250s, both for financial misdeeds and for murdering his wife." However, no indication of a murder case exists, and Bale's source—Gavin Langmuir, "The Knight's Tale of Young Hugh of Lincoln," *Speculum* 47, no. 3 (1972): 459–82, at 463—says only that Matthew Paris's "story is highly dubious because, although Abraham was on trial in this period on some charge, he was released on pledge before his trial and was finally condemned to lose his chattels but freed on condition that he avoid the king's presence for a year—hardly the penalty one would expect for murder or striking blasphemy." *DMAJH* gives details of the relevant case (or cases), all financial in nature, s.v. "Berkhamstead, Abraham of," 51. See also *CCR 1247–51*, at 235, 263, 284, 299, 320, 339, 360, and 375.

13. See my discussion of Abraham's suits for his son-in-law's library above, at 122.

14. An Isaac of Berkhamstead, son of Manser, whose name appears in records from the 1270s, may also be a relation. See *DMAJH*, s.v. "Berkhamstead, Abraham of," 50; and Suzanne Bartlet, "Women in the Medieval Anglo-Jewish Community," in *Jews in Medieval Britain: Historical, Literary, Archaeological Perspectives*, ed. Patricia Skinner (Woodbridge: Boydell, 2003),

113–27, at 124, who notes that in 1270 Isaac of Berkhamsted married "Porun, widow of Josce fil Abraham of Worcester" and "not only acquired all of her late husband's bonds and chattels, but three years later carried off her ex-father-in-law's estate before it could be assessed for the king's [postmortem] share."

15. Bale, "Fictions of Judaism," 138.

16. Bale, 137.

17. Bale, 137.

18. See Simon Seror, "Les noms des femmes juives en Angleterre au moyen âge," *Revue des études juives* 165, nos. 3–4 (1995): 295–325, especially 309–10.

19. The hymn "Stabat mater speciosa" dates to the thirteenth century and is traditionally attributed to the Franciscan Jacopone da Todi (d. 1306). "Quasi oliva speciosa in campis" (Eccles. 24:19) is also commonly used as a Marian antiphon, and Song of Songs 1:1–2 read typologically in relation to Mary: "Ego flos campi, et lilium convallium" (I am the flower of the field, and the lily of the valleys). Related English-language epithets can be found, for instance, in the Marian poems of Bod. MS Eng. poet. a. 1 (The Vernon Manuscript), where the Virgin is "flour of alle," "of alle fruytes feirest flour," or "fayrore then the flour delys": see Adrienne Williams Boyarin, ed. and trans., *Miracles of the Virgin in Middle English* (Toronto: Broadview, 2015), 142, lines 11, 42, 68, and 146.

20. *DMLBS*, s.v. "suffocare" 1a, 1b, and 3a.

21. See, for instance, Rubin, *Gentile Tales*, 11 and 27; Lipton, *Dark Mirror*, 207–9; and Geraldine Heng, "England's Dead Boys: Telling Tales of Christian-Jewish Relations Before and After the First European Expulsion of the Jews," *MLN* 127, no. 5, supp. (2012): 54–85, at 79–81. I return to Heng's important argument about the Jewess's Christian likeness below.

22. For detailed information on "The Jewish Boy" and its development in the West from Gregory of Tours's *De gloria martyrum*, see Rubin, *Gentile Tales*, 1–39. For its history in England specifically, see Adrienne Williams Boyarin, *Miracles of the Virgin in Medieval England: Law and Jewishness in Marian Legends* (Cambridge: D. S. Brewer, 2010), 63–70 and 87–90; and Denise Despres, "Mary of the Eucharist: Cultic Anti-Judaism in Some Fourteenth-Century English Devotional Manuscripts," in *From Witness to Witchcraft: Jews and Judaism in Medieval Christian Thought*, ed. Jeremy Cohen (Wiesbaden: Harrassowitz, 1996), 375–401 (note especially her list of English manuscript illustrations of "The Jewish Boy" at 385).

23. See Williams Boyarin, *Miracles of the Virgin in Medieval England*, 63–70.

24. All quotations of the Vernon Manuscript Miracles of the Virgin come from Williams Boyarin, *Miracles of the Virgin in Middle English*, 57–92, which provides the most recent edition of the all surviving miracles, with continuous line numbering for the whole set (1–1139), here at 437. Citations by line number appear hereafter in the text.

25. See Ruth Wilson Tryon, ed. "Miracles of Our Lady in Middle English Verse," *PMLA* 38, no. 2 (1923), 308–88, here at lines 351–52 (emphasis mine).

26. Tryon, "Miracles of Our Lady," 352, lines 28–29.

27. Lipton, *Dark Mirror*, 203.

28. On the Vernon collection of Marian miracles, see Carole M. Meale, "The Miracles of Our Lady: Context and Interpretation," in *Studies in the Vernon Manuscript*, ed. Derek Pearsall (Cambridge: D. S. Brewer, 1990), 115–36; as well as Williams Boyarin, *Miracles of the Virgin in Medieval England*, 29–32 and 146–49, and *Miracles of the Virgin in Middle English*, 56–92 and 158–59.

29. "The Child Slain by Jews" illustration appears near the top of col. a on fol. 124v, and its text occupies cols. a–c; "The Jewish Boy" illustration is the only image on fol. 125r, set at a central position in col. b, and the tale's text continues through col. c and onto the verso.

30. This is true primarily after 1300: "Jewish Boy" tales circulated in the West from the sixth century, and in English Marian miracle collections from the early twelfth century, while the earliest "Child Slain" story dates to the first quarter of the thirteenth century. See Anthony Bale, *The Jew in the Medieval Book: English Antisemitisms, 1350–1500* (Cambridge: Cambridge University Press, 2006), 55–103, and Williams Boyarin, *Miracles of the Virgin in Medieval England*, 63–70.

31. See Rubin, *Gentile Tales*, 25, where the oven is read as "the womb, the place where children were 'cooked', a secret place . . . as well as a destructive place where children were destroyed"; and Heng, "England's Dead Boys," 80, where the oven is "resignified by the intervention of the Virgin as female space, a matrix, a womb" that works as "a replacement of the privy" in "Child Slain" stories. In Figure 6, in this light, it is notable that the child's body is placed in front of the Virgin Mary's belly.

32. Tryon, "Miracles of Our Lady," 351, lines 11–13.

33. Heng, "England's Dead Boys," 79.

34. As noted just above, the mother is absent in the abridged version of "The Jewish Boy" in BL MS Additional 39996—she is replaced by a "A Mayde þat loued þe child"—but the expected sorrowing mother is also absent from the *Passion of Adam of Bristol*, which breaks its genre's gendered conventions with Samuel's expectation that Adam's *father* may come searching for him.

35. Heng, "England's Dead Boys," 79: "The poem has forgotten that pre-expulsion Jews were not allowed to be publicly outdoors in the streets during Holy Week, let alone at Easter." In fact, however, there is little evidence that this (papal) restriction was ever well enforced in England.

36. Williams Boyarin, *Miracles of the Virgin in Medieval England*, 66.

37. Williams Boyarin, 65.

38. Charlotte D'Evelyn and Anna J. Mill, eds., *The South English Legendary* (London: Oxford Univ. Press, 1956), 1:228, lines 223–25. The text is also available, with a facing-page Modern English translation, in Williams Boyarin, *Miracles of the Virgin in Middle English*, 32–35.

39. Heng, "England's Dead Boys," 80.

40. See Jeremy Cohen, *Sanctifying the Name of God: Jewish Martyrs and Jewish Memories of the First Crusade* (Philadelphia: Univ. of Pennsylvania Press, 2006), 124–27.

41. *CT* VII.627.

42. Ruth Nisse, *Jacob's Shipwreck: Diaspora, Translation, and Jewish-Christian Relations in Medieval England* (Ithaca: Cornell Univ. Press, 2017), 125.

43. Nisse, *Jacob's Shipwreck*, 124–26.

44. Nisse, 124 and 115–17, where she refers to Alice of Worcester and the London apostates who were pursued by John Peckham. See also my discussion in Chapter 3 above, at 134–38.

45. Nisse, *Jacob's Shipwreck*, 125. Nisse discusses Asenath (or Osnat), the Egyptian/Jewish wife of the biblical Joseph, as she is portrayed in medieval Anglo-Latin versions of the Hellenistic Jewish romance *Joseph and Aseneth*, which circulated in the thirteenth century among Robert Grosseteste's circle and then through the *Speculum historiale* of Vincent of Beauvais (see *Jacob's Shipwreck*, 103). The fifteenth-century Middle English *Storie of Asneth*, which survives uniquely in Huntington Library MS Ellesmere 25.A.13, is derived from these. On the Middle English version, see Russell Peck, ed., *Heroic Women from the Old Testament in Middle English Verse* (Kalamazoo: Medieval Institute, 1991); and Heather A. Reid, "Female Initiation Rites and Women Visionaries: Mystical Marriage in the Middle English Translation of *The Storie of Asneth*," in *Women and the Divine in Literature Before 1700: Essays in Memory of Margot Louis*, ed. Kathryn Kerby-Fulton (Victoria, BC: ELS Editions, 2009), 137–52.

46. Nisse, *Jacob's Shipwreck*, 95–96, at 96.

47. Cohen, *Sanctifying the Name of God*, 111–12.

48. Cohen, *Sanctifying the Name*, 123, emphasizes that Solomon bar Samson's twelfth-century chronicle even calls Rachel "marat Rachel ha-baḥurah" (Mistress Rachel the maiden), echoing biblical words for unmarried or virginal women (*baḥurah* and *betulah*) and thereby making connections to the Virgin Mary more explicit.

49. Cohen, *Sanctifying the Name*, 108. This allusion to Ecclesia's chalice also puts Rachel in pointed opposition to Synagoga as portrayed in Christian art: Rachel is upright, holding her own children's blood, not broken and blinded. On Ecclesia and Synogoga in high medieval Christian art, see Nina Rowe, *The Jew, the Cathedral, and the Medieval City: Synagoga and Ecclesia in the Thirteenth Century* (Cambridge: Cambridge Univ. Press, 2011).

50. Cohen, *Sanctifying the Name of God*, 124.

51. Cohen, 128.

52. See Israel Jacob Yuval, "Jewish Messianic Expectations Towards 1240 and Christian Reactions," in *Toward the Millenium: Messianic Expectations from the Bible to Waco*, ed. Peter Schäfer and Mark Cohen (Leiden: Brill, 1998), 105–21; and Israel Jacob Yuval, *Two Nations in Your Womb: Perceptions of Jews and Christians in Late Antiquity and the Middle Ages*, trans. Barbara Harshaw and Jonathan Chipman (Berkeley: Univ. of California Press, 2006), 161–89.

53. On the oven as womb, see note 31 above.

54. See Merrall Llewelyn Price, "Imperial Violence and the Monstrous Mother: Cannibalism at the Siege of Jerusalem," in *Domestic Violence in Medieval Texts*, ed. Eve Salisbury, Georgiana Donavin, and Merrall Llewelyn Price (Gainesville: Univ. Press of Florida, 2002), 272–98. On the Vengeance of Our Lord tradition—which incorporates stories of the Passion, the life of Saint Veronica and the Vernicle, and the siege of Jerusalem by Titus and Vespasian—see Steven K. Wright, *The Vengeance of Our Lord: Medieval Dramatizations of the Destruction of Jerusalem* (Toronto: PIMS, 1989); Alvin A. Ford, ed., *La Vengeance de Nostre-Seigneur: The Old and Middle French Prose Versions*, 2 vols. (Toronto: PIMS, 1984–93); and the introductions to Adrienne Williams Boyarin, ed. and trans., *The Siege of Jerusalem* (Toronto: Broadview Press, 2014), and Michael Livingston, ed., *Siege of Jerusalem* (Kalamazoo: Medieval Institute, 2004).

55. For example, Deuteronomy 28:53–57, Leviticus 26:29, 2 Kings 6:26–29, and Ezekial 5:10, as well as Jeremiah 19:9 and Lamentations 4:10 (cited in the epigraphs of this chapter).

56. Kathryn A. Smith, *Art, Identity, and Devotion in Fourteenth-Century England: Three Women and Their Books of Hours* (London and Toronto: The British Library and Univ. of Toronto Press, 2004), 37. On the *Siege of Jerusalem* as a crusade poem, see Suzanne Akbari, "Erasing the Body: History and Memory in Medieval Siege Poetry," in *Remembering the Crusades: Myth, Image, and Identity*, ed. Nicholas Paul and Suzanne Yeager (Baltimore: Johns Hopkins Univ. Press, 2012), 146–73; John Finlayson, "The Contexts of the Crusading Romances in the London Thornton Manuscript," *Anglia* 130, no. 2 (2012): 240–63; Mary Hamel, "*The Siege of Jerusalem* as a Crusading Poem," in *Journey Toward God: Pilgrimage and Crusade*, ed. Barbara N. Sargent-Baur (Kalamazoo: Medieval Institute, 1992), 177–94; and Suzanne Yeager, *Jerusalem in Medieval Narrative* (Cambridge: Cambridge Univ. Press, 2008), 78–107.

57. See Henry Bergen, ed., *Lydgate's Fall of Princes: Part III* (London: Oxford Univ. Press, 1924), 7, lines 1482–88; and J. A. Herbert, ed., *Titus and Vespasian, or The Destruction of Jerusalem in Rhymed Couplets* (London: Roxburghe Club, 1905), lines 3395–504. I discuss the *Titus and Vespasian* account in more detail below, at 166–71.

58. For Josephus's originary version of the story, see William Whiston, trans., *The Complete Works of Flavius Josephus* (London: Nelson, 1860), at *War of the Jews* VI.3.4. A very readable more

recent translation is available in Gaalya Cornfeld, ed. and trans., *Josephus: The Jewish War* (Grand Rapids, MI: Zondervan, 1982). On Josephus and his works more generally, see Louis H. Feldman and Gohei Hata, eds., *Josephus, Judaism, and Christianity* (Detroit: Wayne State Univ. Press, 1987). For discussion of the circulation of Josephan texts in medieval England, see Karen Kletter, "The Uses of Josephus: Jewish History in the Medieval Christian Tradition" (PhD diss., University of North Carolina, Chapel Hill, 2005); and Nisse, *Jacob's Shipwreck*, 19–48.

59. See Ralph Hanna and David Lawton, eds., *The Siege of Jerusalem* (Oxford: Oxford Univ. Press, 2003), 164–69, at 168 (the relevant excerpts of Higden's *Polychronicon*); and Andrew Galloway, "Alliterative Poetry in Old Jerusalem: The *Siege of Jerusalem* and Its Sources," in *Medieval Alliterative Poetry: Essays in Honour of Thorlac Turville-Petre* (Dublin: Four Courts Press, 2010), 90–91 and 96–106 (which includes the relevant portion of John of Tynemouth's *Historia aurea*). Hanna and Lawton make a detailed case for the poet's primary reliance on Josephus for the cannibalism episode (xl–lii), while Galloway's essay argues that John of Tynemouth is more likely the direct source.

60. Citations of the Middle English alliterative *Siege of Jerusalem* follow Hanna and Lawton, *Siege*, with line numbers noted parenthetically in text. Translations follow Williams Boyarin, *Siege of Jerusalem*.

61. It is worth noting that the rack (spine with ribs) and the shoulder are among the best cuts of lamb, so that the child is no doubt acting as a kind of *agnus dei* here. My thanks to Stephanie J. Lahey for pointing out the *Siege* poet's grisly specificity about the cuts of meat in this passage!

62. Smith, *Art, Identity and Devotion*, 137.

63. Smith, 131–39, at 136. For more on *Titus and Vespasian*, see Herbert's introduction to his *Titus and Vespasian*, v–xlvi (though Herbert's manuscript data require significant updating, as he was aware of only seven of the twelve manuscripts now known). See also Bonnie Millar, *The Siege of Jerusalem in Its Physical, Literary, and Historical Contexts* (Dublin: Four Courts Press, 2000), 100–140; and Maija Birenbaum, "Affective Vengeance in *Titus and Vespasian*," *Chaucer Review* 43, no. 3 (2009): 330–44.

64. Smith, *Art, Identity and Devotion*, 131, notes that *Titus* must "have circulated widely among the nobility and gentry: Guy de Beauchamp, Earl of Warwick, owned two copies of this work, as his 1305 will reveals"—which suggests that the poem significantly predates extant manuscripts. *Titus and Vespasian* (in full or part) can be found in Cambridge, Magdalene College MS Pepys 2014; Coventry, City Record Office MS 325/1; BL MSS Additional 10036, Additional 36523, Additional 36983, and Harley 4733; New Haven, Beinecke Library MS Osborn A.11; New York, Pierpont Morgan Library MS M 898; and Bod. MSS Digby 230, Douce 78, Douce 126, and Laud Misc. 622.

65. I draw this conclusion from my own examinations of the *Titus and Vespasian* manuscripts held at the Bod. and BL. In general, these manuscripts suggest a lay domestic readership. BL MS Additional 36523, for instance, combines *Titus* with English translations of the penitential psalms and the "Lay Folk's Mass Book"; Bod. MS Douce 78 puts *Titus* with short English Marian poems and a selection of medical recipes for women attributed to "þe woman of Penyton"; and BL MS Harley 4733 is a schoolboys' book, including mnemonics, moral lessons, proverbs, pen trials, and children's doodles—a flyleaf inscribed in a fifteenth-century hand reads "Master Iohannes Penyngton schole master of Wurcestur' ys possessesed of thys booke" (fol. 2v).

66. That *Titus and Vespasian* may be the source is likely for the usual reasons (i.e., extant manuscript copies do not represent the poem's composition dates or full circulation history), but

more particularly because a 1305 will suggests ownership of two copies of the English poem before 1305 (see note 64 above). A late thirteenth-century abridged copy is also extant in Cambridge, Magdalene College MS Pepys 37, edited by Rudolf Fischer as "Vindicta Salvatoris Mittlenglisches Gedicht des 13. Jahrhunderts, zum erstenmal herausgegeben," pts. 1 and 2, *Archiv für das Studium der neuren Sprachen und Literaturen* 111, no. 11 (1903): 285–98; 112, no. 12 (1904): 24–45.

67. Herbert, *Titus and Vespasian*, lines 3406–7, hereafter cited parenthetically in text. Though I rely on Herbert for all quotations of *Titus*, I have modified his text in minor ways based on my own transcriptions of several *Titus* manuscripts, including BL MSS Additional 10036, Additional 36523, Additional 36983, Additional 39996 (excerpts), and Harley 4733; and Bod. MSS Digby 230, Douce 78, Douce 126, and Laud Misc. 622.

68. See Whiston, *Complete Works*, at *War of the Jews* VI.3; and Hanna and Lawton, *Siege*, lines 317–20.

69. Nisse, *Jacob's Shipwreck*, 125.

70. Smith, *Art, Identity, and Devotion*, 137.

71. See above, at 104–10.

72. For other discussions of the idea that medieval and early modern notions of Englishness were bound up in medieval (Christian) notions of Jewishness, see Bale, *Jew in the Medieval Book*, 1–21; Denise Despres, "Immaculate Flesh and the Social Body: Mary and the Jews," *Jewish History* 12, no. 1 (1998): 47–69, at 62–64, where she explicates Margery Kempe's self-fashioning as ambiguously Jewish; Lisa Lampert-Weissig, *Gender and Jewish Difference from Paul to Shakespeare* (Philadelphia: Univ. of Pennsylvania Press, 2004), 138–40; Colin Richmond, "Englishness and Medieval Anglo-Jewry," in *Chaucer and the Jews: Sources, Contexts, Meanings*, ed. Sheila Delany (New York: Routledge, 2002), 213–27; and Sylvia Tomasch, "Post-Colonial Chaucer and the Virtual Jew," in Delany, *Chaucer and the Jews*, 69–85, at 69: "'The Jew' was central not only to medieval English Christian devotion but to the construction of Englishness itself."

73. Tomasch, "Post-Colonial Chaucer and the Virtual Jew," 73.

74. All quotations of the *Passion of Adam of Bristol* are from Christoph Cluse, ed., "'Fabula ineptissima': Die Ritualmordlegende um Adam von Bristol nach der Handschrift London, British Library, Harley 957," *Ashkenas* 5 (1995): 293–330, here at 308, hereafter cited parenthetically in text. Samuel's threatening declaration in the passage cited here echoes Philippians 2:8, in which Paul praises Christ for obedience "usque ad mortem, mortem autem crucis." This is another instance of saming: Samuel echoes (or uses?) Paul's convert voice even as he announces his Jewish identity, while the Pauline allusion makes Adam, destined to be tortured on a cross, more obviously the type of Christ whom Paul praises with the same words. My thanks to Jonathan Juilfs for pointing out this scriptural connection.

75. For a reading that focuses on the Virgin Mary's role in the tale, see Harvey J. Hames, "The Limits of Conversion: Ritual Murder and the Virgin Mary in the Account of Adam of Bristol," *Journal of Medieval History* 33 (2007): 43–59. Hames also notes that many components of the story are analogous to "The Jewish Boy."

76. Hames, "Limits of Conversion," 44.

77. "The Jewish Boy," as discussed above and in the previous chapter, obviously provides the prime comparative case, but "The Child Slain by Jews" story is another. For a detailed reading of other English versions of "The Child Slain by Jews" that includes iterations circulating in England around the same time, see Bale, *Jew in the Medieval Book*, 55–103. As should be clear, I do not think that *Adam of Bristol* follows the gender conventions of these related stories, though it certainly evokes them.

78. See Yuval, *Two Nations in Your Womb*, 190–204; and Robert Stacey, "'Adam of Bristol' and the Tales of Ritual Crucifixion in Medieval England," in *Thirteenth-Century England XI: Proceedings of the Gregynog Conference, 2005*, ed. Bjorn K. U. Weiler and Janet E. Burton (Woodbridge: Boydell, 2007), 2–15, at 11–13.

79. Yuval, *Two Nations in Your Womb*, 198.

80. Yuval, 195 n. 129 and 200, where he further connects Samuel's spitting three times at the mention of Jesus's name to contemporary Christian understandings of Jewish blasphemy against Christ and Mary. On the Paris "trial" and accompanying accusations of blasphemy against Mary, see William C. Jordan, "Marian Devotion and the Talmud Trial of 1240," in *Religionsgespräche im Mittelalter*, ed. Bernard Lewis and Friedrich Niewöhner (Wiesbaden: Otto Harrassowitz, 1992), 61–76; and *The Trial of the Talmud: Paris, 1240*, trans. John Friedman and Jean Connell Hoff, with introduction by Robert Chazan (Toronto: PIMS, 2012).

81. Quoted and translated in Yuval, *Two Nations in Your Womb*, 194.

82. Sanford Brown Meech and Hope Emily Allen, eds., *The Book of Margery Kempe* (New York: Oxford Univ. Press, 1940), 195.

83. Claudine Fabre-Vassas, *The Singular Beast: Jews, Christians, and the Pig*, trans. Carol Volk (New York: Columbia Univ. Press, 1997), 135.

84. A popular (often illustrated) apocryphal story of Jesus's childhood—circulating in England by the late thirteenth century as *L'Evangile de l'enfaunce de Jesus Christ*—said that the young Jesus, finding his Jewish playmates hiding in an oven, turned them into pigs. See Fabre-Vassas, *Singular Beast*, 5 and 89–94, with Figures 7–9; and Rubin, *Gentile Tales*, 24–25.

85. Samuel had previously called the Virgin Mary, in response to Adam's prayers to her and Jesus, "meretricem pessimam" (base whore) and "ill[am] meretric[em]" (that whore). See Cluse, "'Fabula ineptissima,'" 308, 309, and 311.

86. Robert Stacey, "From Ritual Crucifixion to Host Desecration: Jews and the Body of Christ," *Jewish History* 12, no. 1 (1998): 11–28, at 21.

87. Yuval, *Two Nations in Your Womb*, 197 and 198.

88. Lipton, *Dark Mirror*, 203–4.

89. Irven M. Resnick, *Marks of Distinction: Christian Perceptions of Jews in the High Middle Ages* (Washington, DC: Catholic Univ. of America Press, 2012), 255–56, discusses the larger image's depiction of Samuel in a racialized register that, in opposition to what the text implies, suggests that he cannot pass as Christian. I read this tension, however, in relation to the narrative's focus on Jewish women's *superior* ability to pass and/or orchestrate passing, and I disagree with Resnick (at 255) that the historiated initial shows "Samuel's wife and son as they are about to accept baptism" and that the son, in this image, wears "a conical hat that identifies him as a Jew" (he does not).

90. Lipton, *Dark Mirror*, 219, and "Where Are the Gothic Jewish Women? On the Non-iconography of the Jewess in the *Cantigas de Santa Maria*," *Jewish History* 22 (2008): 139–77, at 158.

CHAPTER 5

1. Amy-Jill Levine, "A Jewess, More and/or Less," in *Judaism Since Gender*, ed. Miriam Peskowitz and Laura Levitt (New York: Routledge, 1997) 149–57, at 150 and 151.

2. Sander L. Gilman, "Salome, Syphilis, Sarah Bernhardt, and the 'Modern Jewess,'" *German Quarterly* 66, no. 2 (1993): 195–211, at 195 and 210.

3. Cynthia Baker, "The Essentially Ambiguous Jewess: An Ancient Trope in Modern Europe," filmed 23 May 2011 at the *Women, Jews, Venetians* conference, University of California–Santa Cruz. Video available at https://vimeo.com/77806116.

4. Cynthia Baker, *Jew* (New Brunswick, NJ: Rutgers Univ. Press, 2017), 32.

5. Levine, "Jewess," 155.

6. The most influential modern study of the historical case is Gavin Langmuir, "The Knight's Tale of Young Hugh of Lincoln," *Speculum* 47, no. 3 (1972): 459–82. Roger Dahood has discussed the Anglo-French ballad and its connection to Chaucer's "Prioress's Tale" most thoroughly: see his "Alleged Jewish Cannibalism in the Thirteenth-Century Anglo-Norman 'Hugo de Lincolnia,' with Notice of the Allegation in Twelfth-Century England," in *Language in Medieval Britain: Networks and Exchanges: Proceedings of the 2013 Harlaxton Symposium*, ed. Mary Carruthers (Donington, UK: Shaun Tyas, 2015), 229–41; "English Historical Narratives of Jewish Child-Murder, Chaucer's Prioress's Tale, and the Date of Chaucer's Unknown Source," *Studies in the Age of Chaucer* 31 (2009): 125–40; and "The Punishment of the Jews, Hugh of Lincoln, and the Question of Satire in Chaucer's Prioress's Tale," *Viator* 36 (2005): 465–91. Dahood has also produced a new edition and translation of the French ballad as "The Anglo-Norman 'Hugo de Lincolnia': A Critical Edition and Translation from the Unique Text in Paris, Bibliotèque national de France MS fr. 902," *Chaucer Review* 49, no. 1 (2014): 1–38. My thanks to Roger for generously discussing the ballad with me via e-mail and providing me with a pre-publication copy of "Alleged Jewish Cannibalism."

7. All citations of "Hugo de Lincolnia" follow Dahood, "Anglo-Norman 'Hugo de Lincolnia,'" hereafter cited parenthetically in text by line number. Translations are also Dahood's, though I make occasional minor emendations.

8. On Christian wet nurses in thirteenth-century Anglo-Jewish homes, see above, at 126–30, and note 92 below. Modern scholars have indeed understood this context to be significant to the poem: Dahood, "Anglo-Norman 'Hugo de Lincolnia,'" 31 n. 56, cites laws prohibiting the practice to explain the presence of the *noris*; and Geraldine Heng, "England's Dead Boys: Telling Tales of Christian-Jewish Relations Before and After the First European Expulsion of the Jews," *MLN* 127, no. 5, supp. (2012): 54–85, at 63, assumes that the *noris* is "the Christian former nurse of a Jew" because of such laws.

9. See Dahood, "Anglo-Norman 'Hugo de Lincolnia,'" 31 n. 56; and *AND*, s.v. "privé."

10. See above, at 128.

11. Citations of the *Passion of Adam of Bristol* follow Christoph Cluse, ed., "'Fabula ineptissima': Die Ritualmordlegende um Adam von Bristol nach der Handschrift London, British Library, Harley 957," *Ashkenas* 5 (1995): 293–330, hereafter cited parenthetically in text.

12. Latin citations of Thomas of Monmouth's text follow Augustus Jessop and M. R. James, eds. and trans., *The Life and Miracles of St William of Norwich by Thomas of Monmouth* (Cambridge: Cambridge Univ. Press, 1896), here 89–90. English translations follow Miri Rubin, ed. and trans., *The Life and Passion of William of Norwich by Thomas of Monmouth* (London: Penguin, 2014), here 59.

13. Jessop and James, *Life and Miracles*, 19; Rubin, *Life and Passion*, 14.

14. Jessop and James, 19; Rubin, 16.

15. Jessop and James, 18–19; Rubin, 15.

16. *CJB*, 16.

17. See Anthony Bale, "'House Devil, Town Saint': Anti-Semitism and Hagiography in Medieval Suffolk," in *Chaucer and the Jews: Sources, Contexts, Meanings*, ed. Sheila Delany (New York: Routledge, 2002), 185–210, and his *The Jew in the Medieval Book: English Antisemitisms, 1350–1500* (Cambridge: Cambridge Univ. Press, 2006), 105–144.

18. Citations of Lydgate's "Praier to St Robert" follow Bale's edition in *Jew in the Medieval Book*, 173–74, hereafter cited parenthetically in text by line number.

19. See *DMLBS*, s.v. "anus" 2b; and Charlton T. Lewis and Charles Short, *A New Latin Dictionary* (Oxford: Clarendon, 1897), s.v. "anus" 3.

20. Bale, *Jew in the Medieval Book*, 114.

21. Quoted and translated in Bale, *Jew in the Medieval Book*, 121, this poem occupies fol. 43v in Los Angeles, Getty MS 101, where it faces the miniatures related to Robert of Bury.

22. Bale, *Jew in the Medieval Book*, 123.

23. E. M. Rose, *The Murder of William of Norwich: The Origins of the Blood Libel in Medieval Europe* (Oxford: Oxford Univ. Press, 2015), 193 (emphasis mine).

24. Rose, *Murder of William of Norwich*, 194.

25. Bale, *Jew in the Medieval Book*, 124.

26. Bale, 137–38.

27. Heng, "England's Dead Boys," 80.

28. *DMAJH*, s.v. "Huntingdon," 176.

29. Latin citations of the *Life of Christina of Markyate* follow C. H. Talbot, ed. and trans., *The Life of Christina of Markyate: A Twelfth-Century Recluse* (1959; repr., Toronto: Univ. of Toronto Press, 1998), here 72 and 74. I have made slight adjustments to Talbot's punctuation of the Latin and have checked all quoted passages against the unique manuscript copy in BL MS Cotton Tiberius E I (part 2), fols. 145–68. My English translations engage Talbot's but do not follow him slavishly.

30. Talbot, *Life of Christina of Markyate*, 74.

31. The name of Christina's father (Autti) was common in the Danelaw, and the *vita*, along with evidence from surviving legal documents, indicates strong familial roots in pre-Conquest England. See Talbot's introduction to *Life of Christina of Markyate*, 10–13. The anonymous author also notes that Christina's first spiritual mentor—Roger, an anchorite who had a cell at Markyate—spoke English to Christina, calling her "myn sunendaege dohter" (106). For more recent work on Christina's biography, see Christopher Holdsworth, "Christina of Markyate," in *Medieval Women*, ed. Derek Baker and Rosalind M. T. Hill (Oxford: Blackwell, 1978), 185–204; Rachel M. Koopmans, "The Conclusion of Christina of Markyate's *Vita*," *Journal of Ecclesiastical History* 51, no. 4 (2000): 663–98; Samuel Fanous and Henrietta Leyser, eds., *Christina of Markyate: A Twelfth-Century Holy Woman* (London: Routledge, 2005); and Katie Ann-Marie Bugyis, "The Author of the *Life of Christina of Markyate*: The Case for Robert of Gorron (d. 1066)," *Journal of Ecclesiastical History* 68, no. 4 (2017): 719–46.

32. The manuscript—BL MS Cotton Tiberius E I (now in two parts)—was damaged in the 1731 Ashburnham House fire. The passage about the Huntingdon Jewess's intentions (at the top of fol. 150vb) is in a location that, despite conservation efforts, suffered significant fire damage and associated text loss, distortion, and show-through. Talbot, *Life of Christina of Markyate*, 74, sees "ledere" (i.e., *laedere*, to injure or harm), but the word is hardly legible in situ. While "iudea prestigiis" (a Jewess with tricks) is visible, and all of Talbot's readings are plausible, several words in the passage that introduces the Jewess (as quoted in text above) should be approached with caution. It is far from certain that the author characterizes the Jewess as a "wicked Jewish 'witch,'" as Matthew Mesley has described her in "De Judaea, Muta, et Surda: Jewish Conversion in Gerald of Wale's *Life of Saint Remigius*," in *Christians and Jews in Angevin England: The York Massacre of 1190, Narratives and Contexts*, ed. Sarah Rees Jones and Sethina Watson (Woodbridge: York Medieval Press, 2013), 238–49, at 239.

33. Talbot, *Life of Christina of Markyate*, 156.

34. Christina's mature vision of the Trinity may be illustrated in the litany of the St Albans Psalter (Dombibliothek Hildesheim Hs. St. God.1, fol. 403r), a book made for and used by Christina or the nuns of Markyate. See Dombibliotheck Hildesheim, *The Albani Psalter*, with commentary by Jochen Bepler, Peter Kidd, and Jane Geddes (Simbach am Inn: Müller and Schindler, 2008), 108, 183, 213–14, and 217.

35. Talbot, *Life of Christina of Markyate*, 74.

36. Talbot, 56.

37. Talbot, 74.

38. Talbot, 76.

39. Ælfric, for instance, explained in a sermon directed to nuns that Judith was "eadmod 7 clæne" (humble and pure) and thus signified Christ's "an clene bryd þe mid cenum geleafan þam ealdum devil of forcerf þæt heafod" (one pure bride who with sharp belief cuts the head from the old devil); and the author of the *Ancrene Wisse* saw Judith as a type of the anchoress, using Judith 8:5–6 to explain how her isolated mourning in widowhood "bitacneth bitund ancre" (signifies the enclosed anchoress). See *Ælfric's Homilies on Judith, Esther, and Maccabees*, ed. S. D. Lee (Oxford, 1999), at http://users.ox.ac.uk/~stuart/kings/main.htm, lines 344 and 348–50; and *Ancrene Wisse*, ed. Robert Hasenfratz (Kalamazoo: Medieval Institute, 2000), 3.104–8, at 107.

40. I follow the lineation set by Irina Dumitrescu, "Debt and Sin in the Middle English 'Judas,'" *Anglia* 131, no. 4 (2013): 509–37, where she edits and translates the text as an appendix at 531–33. However, I amend text, punctuation, and translation (in minor ways) based on my own examination of the manuscript (Cambridge, Trinity College MS B.14.39, fol. 34r).

41. Dumitrescu, "Debt and Sin."

42. See *MED*, s.v. "swikel."

43. See Greti Dinkova-Bruun, "Biblical Thematics: The Story of Samson in Medieval Literary Discourse," in *The Oxford Handbook of Medieval Latin Literature*, ed. Ralph Hexter and David Townsend (New York: Oxford Univ. Press, 2012), 356–75.

44. Anthony Bale, *Feeling Persecuted: Christians, Jews, and Images of Violence in the Middle Ages* (London: Reaktion, 2010), 83.

45. See Martha Bayless, *Parody in the Middle Ages: The Latin Tradition* (Ann Arbor: Univ. of Michigan Press, 1996), 367. For an early fourteenth-century nonsense-cento that uses this formula as a colophon to a Latin collection of Miracles of the Virgin (to similar ends as argued here), see Adrienne Williams Boyarin, "Anti-Jewish Parody Around Miracles of Virgin? Thoughts on an Early Nonsense-Cento in Berkeley, Bancroft Library, MS UCB 92," *Notes & Queries* 54, no. 4 (2007): 379–85.

46. Bayless, *Parody in the Middle Ages*, 3.

47. Bayless, 197.

48. Bayless, 198.

49. Sara Lipton, *Dark Mirror: The Medieval Origins of Anti-Jewish Iconography* (New York: Metropolitan, 2014), 206.

50. Anthony Bale, "The Female 'Jewish' Libido in Medieval Culture," in *The Erotic in the Literature of Medieval Britain*, ed. Amanda Hopkins and Cory James Rushton (Cambridge: D. S. Brewer, 2007), 94–104, at 102.

51. Efraim Sicher, *The Jew's Daughter: A Cultural History of a Conversion Narrative* (Lanham, MD: Lexington Books, 2017), 45.

52. Mesley, "De Judaea, Muta, et Surda," 238.

53. Dahood, "Anglo-Norman 'Hugo de Lincolnia,'" 31 n. 56.

54. *CT* VII.684–86.

55. See Dahood, "Punishment of the Jews"; Adrienne Williams Boyarin, *Miracles of the Virgin in Medieval England: Law and Jewishness in Marian Legends* (Cambridge: D.S. Brewer, 2010), 149–63; Sicher, *Jew's Daughter*, 30–31; and Langmuir, "Knight's Tale."

56. This paragraph's outline of how "The Prioress's Tale" engages its genre and place of composition summarizes my more extended arguments in *Miracles of the Virgin in Medieval England*, 149–63.

57. See Dahood, "Punishment of the Jews," 471–86, further discussed in Williams Boyarin, *Miracles of the Virgin in Medieval England*, 153–55.

58. Sicher, *Jew's Daughter*, 30.

59. *CT* VII.488.

60. D'Blossiers Tovey, *Anglia Judaica, or the History and Antiquities of the Jews in England* (Oxford: James Fletcher, 1738), 136–46.

61. Thomas Percy, ed., *Reliques of Ancient English Poetry: Consisting of Old Heroic Ballads, Songs, and Other Pieces of Our Earlier Poets (Chiefly of the Lyric Kind), Together with Some Few of Later Date* (London: J. Dodsley, 1765), 1:32.

62. Percy, *Reliques*, 1:33–34 (lines 5–28).

63. This is my transcription from BL MS Additional 22311 (part 2), fol. 108r–v. "Sir Hugh" was not printed in the first edition of Herd's *The Ancient and Modern Scots Songs, Heroic Ballads, Etc. Now First Collected into One Body, from the Various Miscellanies wherein they Formerly Lay Dispersed* (Edinburgh: Martin and Wotherspoon, 1769), but it did appear in the second two-volume edition: David Herd, ed., *Ancient and Modern Scottish Songs, Heroic Ballads, Etc.* (Edinburgh: John Wotherspoon, 1776), 1:96–98.

64. Lipton, *Dark Mirror*, 206.

65. Lipton, 342 n. 9.

66. The surviving Anglo-French "Hugo de Lincolnia," on both internal and paleographical evidence, dates between 1255 (when Hugh died) and Henry III's death (1272). See Dahood, "Anglo-Norman 'Hugo de Lincolnia,'" 4.

67. For a thorough investigation of Chaucer's possible sources, including the relationship of "The Prioress's Tale" to Hugh of Lincoln materials, see Dahood, "English Historical Narratives of Child-Murder," especially 136–40. Dahood convincingly sets the *terminus a quo* for any source of "The Prioress's Tale" to between 1290 and 1307, with the Anglo-French ballad among many possible (but distant and indirect) English influences.

68. Sicher, *Jew's Daughter*, 25 and 26.

69. Sicher, 26–31, at 31.

70. Bale, "Female 'Jewish' Libido," 100–101.

71. Percy, *Reliques*, 1:32.

72. See Francis James Child, ed., *English and Scottish Ballads* (Boston: Little Brown, 1857), 3:136–46 and 331–37, at 137; and Francis James Child, ed., *The English and Scottish Popular Ballads* (Boston: Houghton Mifflin, 1882), 3:233–54. In the later work, Child was more explicit about the lack of connection between the early ballad, contemporary chronicle accounts, Chaucer's "Prioress's Tale," and the later variants of "Sir Hugh" or the "Jew's Daughter" that he catalogued: "The English ballads, the oldest of which were recovered about the middle of last century [i.e., in the middle of the 1700s], must, in the course of five hundred years of tradition, have departed considerably from the early form. . . . And these pretended child-murders, with their horrible consequences, are only part of a persecution which, with all moderation, may be rubricated as the most disgraceful chapter in the history of the human race" (239, 240–41).

73. Child, *English and Scottish Ballads*, 3:137.

74. See Child, *English and Scottish Popular Ballads*, 3:233–54, where the five variants recorded in his earlier *English and Scottish Ballads* become Ballad no. 155A–B and D–F within a larger A–R range.

75. Francisque Michel, "Ballade anglo-normande sur le meurtre commis par les juifs sur un enfant de Lincoln," *Mémoires de la Société des antiquaires de France* 10 (1834): 358–92; and Michel's contribution to *Hugues de Lincoln: Recueil de ballades anglo-normande et écossaises relatives au meurtre de cet enfant commis par les juifs en MCCLV* (Paris: Silvestre and Pickering, 1834), 3–16 and 60–63. Most recently, Maureen B. M. Boulton repeats the claim of cannibalism in the introductory summary that prefaces her translation of the ballad in *Piety and Persecution in the French Texts of England* (Tempe: Arizona Center for Medieval and Renaissance Studies, 2013), 28: "In a burlesque form of the Eucharist, the assembled Jews eat the dead child's heart before trying to hide the corpse." For the most thorough account of the scholarly history of this incorrect claim, see Dahood, "Alleged Jewish Cannibalism."

76. Dahood, "Alleged Jewish Cannibalism," 237.

77. Dahood, 238–39.

78. Betrand Harris Bronson, *The Singing Tradition of Child's Popular Ballads* (Princeton: Princeton Univ. Press, 1976), 294.

79. For my extended discussion of the Jewish wife in the *Passion of Adam of Bristol* and its cannibalistic tropes, see above, at 172–83.

80. Robert Jamieson, ed., *Popular Ballads and Songs from Tradition, Manuscripts, and Scarce Editions* (Edinburgh: Archibald Constable and Co., 1806), 151–56, at 154 (emphasis mine).

81. Henry Richards Luard, ed., *Matthæi Parisiensis monachi Sancti Albani, Chronica majora* (London: Longmans and Trübner, 1880), 5:517.

82. See Bale, "Female 'Jewish' Libido"; Lipton, *Dark Mirror*, 206, 218–21, and 342 n. 9; and Sicher, *Jew's Daughter*, 34–35.

83. *Caesarii Heisterbacensis monachi ordinis Cisterciensis Dialogus miraculorum*, ed. Joseph Strange (Cologne: Heberle and Lempertz, 1851), 1:92–94; Caesarius of Heisterbach, *The Dialogue on Miracles*, trans. H. von E. Scott and C. C. Swinton Bland (London: George Routledge and Sons, 1929), 1:102–03; and Arthur Brandeis, ed. *Jacob's Well: An English Treatise on the Cleansing of Man's Conscience* (London: Kegan Paul, 1900), 175–77.

84. Mary Macleod Banks, ed., *An Alphabet of Tales* (London: Kegan Paul, Trench, Trübner, 1904), 1:144.

85. Banks, *Alphabet of Tales*, 2:278.

86. Strange, *Dialogus Miraculorum*, 95.

87. Bale, "Female 'Jewish' Libido," 96–97.

88. Bale, "Female 'Jewish' Libido," 98.

89. Strange, *Dialogus Miraculorum*, 94: "Numquid non audisti quid nobis locuta sit vox coelica? Respondit mulier: Non."; Banks, *Alphabet of Tales*, 2:277: "þe man was estonyd & askid his wife if sho hard þis voyce, and she said nay."

90. Bale, "Female 'Jewish' Libido," 97.

91. A. V. C. Schmidt, ed., *The Vision of Piers Plowman: The B-Text* (New York: Everyman, 1987), XI.246.

92. The Provincial Council of Canterbury, held at Oxford in April 1222, did issue statutes that implicated Jewish women, but all were in direct accordance with the provisions of Lateran IV (1215): they forbid marriage between Christians and Jews, forbid Christian wet nurses or servants in Jewish homes, and required identifying badges for Jews. Each of these statutes nonethe-

less required frequent reissuance from many different authorities, and none of them seem to have been regularly obeyed. For the civil statutes that repeated the mandates of Lateran IV and the 1222 Provincial Council, see *DMAJH*, s.vv. "1253, Statute Concerning the Jews," 29, and "1275, Statute of the Jewry," 32–33. On the question of whether such statutes ever succeeded in practice, see above, at 126–30. For an account of the influence of the 1222 Council more broadly, see *DMAJH*, s.v. "Oxford," 297–98.

93. In 1931, this conflation was enshrined in a plaque that was installed at Osney Abbey to commemorate the site where "Robert of Reading, otherwise Haggai of Oxford, suffered for his faith on Sunday 17 April 1222 A.D. corresponding to 4 Iyyar 4982 A.M." Robert/Haggai of Reading, however, is the name of the Dominican preacher who converted to Judaism in 1275. See "The Robert of Reading Plaque," Oxford Jewish Heritage, Oxford Jewish Heritage Committee, May 2012, https://www.oxfordjewishheritage.co.uk/projects/osney-abbey-first-public-burning-in-england/137-the-robert-of-reading-plaque.

94. F. W. Maitland, "The Deacon and the Jewess," in *Roman Canon Law in the Church of England: Six Essays by F. W. Maitland* (London: Methuen, 1898), 158–79. This essay has been reprinted in many volumes since Maitland's death in 1906.

95. *The Chronicle of Bury St Edmunds, 1212–1301*, ed. and trans. Antonia Gransden (London: Thomas Nelson and Sons, 1964), 58. This passage appears verbatim in *Florentii Wigorniensis monachi Chronicon ex chronicis*, ed. Benjamnin Thorpe (London: Sumptibus Societatis, 1849), 2:214 (second continuation), and in the *Chronica Johannis de Oxenedes*, ed. Henry Ellis (London: Longman, Brown, Green, Longmans, and Roberts, 1859), 247.

96. On Sampson son of Samuel of Northampton, see above, at 15–20 and 31–33.

97. Robert Stacey, "'Adam of Bristol' and Tales of Ritual Crucifixion in Medieval England," in *Thirteenth Century England XI: Proceedings of the Gregynog Conference, 2005*, ed. Björn K. U. Weiler et al. (Woodbridge: Boydell and Brewer, 2007), 1–15, at 12. For further information and citations related to Haggai's case and its confusion with the nameless 1222 deacon's, see also Irven M. Resnick, *Marks of Distinction: Christian Perceptions of Jews in the High Middle Ages* (Washington, DC: Catholic Univ. of America Press, 2012), 83–85.

98. Sara Lipton, "Isaac and the Antichrist in the Archives," *Past & Present* 232 (2016): 3–44, at 22 (with n. 33).

99. For this summary of the comparative accounts, I rely on Maitland, "Deacon and the Jewess."

100. *Matthæi Parisiensis monachi Sancti Albani Historia Anglorum sive, ut vulgo dicitur, Historia minor*, ed. Frederic Madden (London: Longmans, Green, Reader, and Dyer, 1866), 2:254–55. As Madden notes at 245 n. 1, this episode is written only in the lower margin of the relevant folio in Cambridge, Corpus Christi College MS 26, while in the two other manuscripts he consulted (Cambridge, Corpus Christi College MS 16 and BL MS Cotton Nero D V, part 2) "the story is only briefly alluded to, under the year 1222."

101. See Maitland, "Deacon and the Jewess," 173–75.

102. On Oxford Jewish women and their involvement in the book trade and property transfers, see above, at 120 and 122–23.

103. Quoted in F. Donald Logan, "Thirteen London Jews and Conversion to Christianity: Problems of Apostasy in the 1280s," *Bulletin of the Institute of Historical Research* 45 (1272): 214–29, at 219.

104. The text and translation of "The Jewess and the Priest" miracle is my own and follows Appendix 4 below, where the full text and further information on the manuscript may be found.

105. Resnick, *Marks of Distinction*, 297.

106. Resnick, 299.

107. Gerald of Wales's story (in his *Life of St Remigius*) of a demon-possessed deaf and mute Jewess who enters a church and ends up cured and baptized provides an interesting comparison to this exemplum. Gerald's Jewess is at first marked as dangerous but is unmarked upon entering Christian space. For a thorough discussion, see Mesley, "De Judaea, Muta, et Surda," especially 248–49.

108. John-Paul Sartre, *Anti-Semite and Jew* (1944), trans. George J. Becker (New York: Schocken, 1976), 34.

109. Levine, "Jewess," 154–55, at 155.

110. Lipton, *Dark Mirror*, 221.

111. Miri Rubin, *Gentile Tales: The Narrative Assault on Late-Medieval Jews* (New Haven: Yale Univ. Press, 1999), 27.

112. Lipton, *Dark Mirror*, 220.

113. Levine, "Jewess," 149, 151, and 150.

114. Levine, 151.

CONCLUSION

1. Aguilar's "History of the Jews in England" was one of the last pieces published, in *Chambers Miscellany of Useful and Entertaining Tracts* 18 (1847): 1–37, before her death. A speculative history of Jewish presence in early medieval Britain and an overview of medieval Jewish presence through to expulsion—based on archival research and reading of medieval literatures—occupies the first ten pages. The work also appears in Michael Galchinsky, ed., *Grace Aguilar: Selected Writings* (Toronto: Broadview, 2003), 313–53. For an assessment of Aguilar's work in relationship to historiography of the Jews of England, see also Pinchas Roth, "Medieval English Rabbis: Image and Self-Image," *Early Middle English* 1, no. 1 (2019): 17–33, at 27–28.

2. Rae Greiner, *Sympathetic Realism in Nineteenth-Century British Fiction* (Baltimore: Johns Hopkins Univ. Press, 2012), 158.

3. Greiner, *Sympathetic Realism*, 159.

4. Audre Lorde, "Audre Lorde: Claudia Tate/1982," in *Conversations with Audre Lorde*, ed. Joan Wylie Hall (Jackson: Univ. Press of Mississippi, 2004), 85–100, at 86. Hall's volume reprints Lorde's interview with Tate as it first appeared in *Black Women Writers at Work*, ed. Claudia Tate (New York: Continuum, 1983), 100–116.

5. "The Storie of Asneth," in *Heroic Women from the Old Testament in Middle English Verse*, ed. Russell A. Peck (Kalamazoo: Medieval Institute, 1991), lines 54–55.

6. See Greti Dinkova-Bruun, "Biblical Thematics: The Story of Samson in Medieval Literary Discourse," in *The Oxford Handbook of Medieval Latin Literature*, ed. Ralph Hexter and David Townsend (New York: Oxford Univ. Press, 2012), 356–75, especially 360–61. The Delilah type is also discussed by Irven M. Resnick, *Marks of Distinction: Christian Perceptions of Jews in the Middle Ages* (Washington, DC: Catholic Univ. of America Press, 2012), 37; and see above, at 83–85 and 200–201.

7. Alex Johnson, "Pence Sets Off Firestorm with Campaign Prayer by 'Christian Rabbi,'" *NBC News* (online), 30 October 2018, https://www.nbcnews.com/politics/white-house/pence-sets-firestorm-campaign-prayer-christian-rabbi-n926016 (with video, 1:58).

8. Mike Huckabee, "I will be on with @HARRISFAULKNER on @OutnumberedOT from Jerusalem @FoxNews at 1pm et/12ct and I will begin show by blowing a Shofar and

speaking Hebrew," Twitter, 14 May 2018, https://twitter.com/govmikehuckabee/status/996055352650158082. Huckabee was announcing his appearance from Israel on the Fox News show *Outnumbered: Overtime with Harris Faulkner*. He repeated the performance later in the summer on the morning show *Fox and Friends* and similarly announced via Twitter: "Since I just got back from Israel, I'll be speaking in Hebrew and blowing a Shofar during the segment." Huckabee, Twitter, 5 August 2018, https://twitter.com/GovMikeHuckabee/status/1026067116443742208.

9. Eric Cortellessa, "Why Did a Christian Bishop Give Donald Trump a Jewish Prayer Shawl?," *Times of Israel*, 9 September 2016, https://www.timesofisrael.com/why-did-a-christian-bishop-give-donald-trump-a-jewish-prayer-shawl. See also Adam Eliyahu Berkowitz, "The Surprising Story Behind Trump's Jewish Prayer Shawl," *BreakingIsraelNews*, 13 September 2016, https://www.breakingisraelnews.com/75568/surprising-story-behind-trumps-jewish-prayer-shawl.

10. Lorde, "Audre Lorde: Claudia Tate/1982," 86.

11. Lorde, 86–87 and 99.

12. Homi K. Bhabha, "Of Mimicry and Man: The Ambivalence of Colonial Discourse," *October* 28 (1984): 125–33, at 130–31.

APPENDIX 1

1. *PREJ* 6:49. Paul Brand's introduction to this volume provides thorough information on the administration and records of the Exchequer of the Jews.

2. In the left margin, this place-name indicates jurisdiction not session location. The Exchequer of the Jews held its sessions at Westminster (though sessions for Michaelmas term 1277, when the Northampton sheriff is ultimately ordered to return, were held at Shrewsbury Castle). See *PREJ* 6:3–5.

3. Gilbert de Kirkeby, sheriff of Northampton from 15 October 1274 to 25 October 1278. As discussed above, at 20 and 33, in his dealings with the Exchequer of the Jews, Gilbert seems to have established himself as a difficult (or incompetent) local authority. Nonetheless, his career in the courts continued successfully: in 1293 Edward I made him one of eight justices of assize. See Edward Foss, ed., *Biographia Juridica: A Biographical Dictionary of the Judges of England from the Conquest to the Present Time, 1066–1870* (London: John Murray, 1870), 388, s.v. "Kirkeby, Gilbert de"; and John Rickard, *The Castle Community: English and Welsh Castle Personnel, 1272–1422* (Woodbridge: Boydell Press, 2002), 339.

4. Robert Kilwardby (d. 11 September 1279), archbishop of Canterbury from 11 October 1272 (consecrated 26 February 1273) until his death. See *ODNB*, s.v. "Kilwardby, Robert (c. 1215–1279)."

5. Since the abbreviated form written here is Cant', the city could be Canterbury (*Cantuaria*) or Cambridge (*Cantabrigia*). Cambridge may make more sense within the itinerary described, but the scribe elsewhere uses the same form for the archbishop of Canterbury (i.e., *Archiep's Cant'*).

6. In 1277, the feast of St James fell on a Sunday (25 July), and a return-day on the "morrow of St James" thus indicates the Monday (26 July). The sheriff's claim is that he did not receive the order to appear until that same Monday. That he sent word "ad quem diem," then, probably indicates that his response arrived during the week's session or shortly after. As Brand explains in *PREJ* 6:4, "What is recorded as taking place on a particular 'day'

might, in reality, have occurred at any time within the succeeding week (and sometimes even later than that)."

1. These six accused men, absent from the inquest, are Senioret son of Josce, Deudone (likely the son of Senioret), Joppe son of Elias, Moses son of Solomon, Benedict son of Avigail, and Isaac Parvus (elsewhere known as Isaac son of Solomon or Isaac le Petit). In February 1231, Senioret (likely the father of the appealed Jacob) had been banished from Norwich and his property given to the boy's father by order of the king. See *Calendar of Inquisitions Miscellaneous (Chancery) Preserved in the Public Record Office* (London: HMSO, 1916), 1:171 (item no. 522). The other five are almost certainly those noted on the dorse, imprisoned in the Tower of London at the time of proceedings: in August 1234, the constable of the Tower was ordered to deliver Isaac Parvus ("Isaac filium Salomonis") to the constable of Norwich Castle. See *CCR 1231–35*, 502.

2. Matthew Paris says that four men were dragged behind horses and hanged for the alleged crime, which he characterized as a failed ritual murder attempt. See Henry Richard Luard, ed., *Matthæi Parisiensis monachi Sancti Albani, Chronica majora* (London: Longman, 1877), 4:30–31. Corroborating documents (cited in note 3 below) show that Isaac Parvus, Moses son of Abraham (known elsewhere as Mosse Mokke), Simon Cok son of Sarah (sometimes called "Simecok"), and Diaie le Chat (known elsewhere as Diaie le Français, Diaie father of Jurnin, and, in Anglo-Hebrew documents, Azriel the Martyr) had been executed by 1241.

3. Most related documents are discussed or printed in V. D. Lipman, *Jews of Medieval Norwich* (London: JHSE, 1967), 60–62 and 260–64, though some of Lipman's citations are outdated or incorrect. See *Calendar of Inquisitions*, 1:171 (item no. 522), concerning the grant of Senioret's house to the boy's father (26 Feburary 1231); *CCR 1231–34*, 502 (17 August 1234), concerning the order to deliver Isaac Parvus; *CFR 1234–35*, no. 38 (22 November 1234), concerning the imprisonment of the accused Jews and order for a record of the inquest; *CFR 1235–36*, no. 4 (3 November 1235), concerning fines and bail paid by the accused, specifying Mosse Mokke (Moses son of Abraham), Sampson Blundell (Sampson son of Ursel), Elias son of Vives, Diaie son of Sampson (Diaie le Chat), Leo (son of Margaret), Simon (Cok son of Sarah), Isaac Parvus, Senioret (son of Josce), and two Jacobs (one son of Vives, possibly the same as "Joppe son of Chera" in TNA KB 26/115B, and the other the son of Senioret); *CCR 1237–42*, 168 (18 January 1240), granting a trial by mixed jury to Mosse Mokke, an Aaron Henn, and others imprisoned for the crime; *CCR 1237–42*, 175 (21 February 1240), rescinding the mixed-jury trial and ordering that the Jews be brought to justice; *CCR 1237–42*, 247 (3 November 1240), granting the house of a hanged Jew to the boy's father; *CCR 1237–42*, 314 (6 July 1241), granting Isaac Parvus's property to the Keeper of the Wardrobe; London, Westminster Abbey Muniments 9061 and 6695 (ca. March 1241), comprising, respectively, an order that the Norwich chirographers deposit debts owed to fugitive or executed Norwich Jews (and now owed to the king) and the debt roll itself, which lists the debts of Mosse Mokke and Isaac Parvus (both "dampnati"), Diaie father of Jurnin (le Chat, "suspensi"), Simon (Cok) son of Sarah ("rectati et defuncti"), and others involved in the circumcision case as "fugitivi"; *Calendar of the Charter Rolls Preserved in the Public Record Office: Henry III, 1226–1257* (London: HMSO, 1908), 1:266 (2 November 1241), noting that the gift of Isaac Parvus's houses to the Keeper of the Wardrobe arises because Isaac has been hanged for the circumcision; *Calendar of the Patent Rolls Preserved in the Public Record Office: Henry III, 1232–1247* (London: HMSO, 1906), 274 (5 March 1242), granting the property of Mosse Mokke to the

king's sergeant because Mosse has been hanged; Francisque Michel, ed., *Rôles Gascons, 1242–1254* (Paris: Imprimerie nationale, 1885), 1:259 and 260 (item nos. 2037 and 2044, both dated 15 October 1243), concerning debts to Mosse Mokke and Isaac Parvus quitclaimed by the king after their hanging; and Matthew Paris's short polemical account (ca. 1240–1245) in Luard, *Chronica majora*, 4:30–31. Three Anglo-Hebrew documents concerning the heirs and properties of Diaie le Chat (known in Hebrew as Azriel ha-Qadosh, i.e., the Martyr) also survive. See Judith Olszowy-Schlanger, *Hebrew and Hebrew-Latin Documents from Medieval England: A Diplomatic and Palaeographical Study* (Turnhout: Brepols, 2015), 1:281–82 (item no. 59, 16 January 1253), 458–60 (item no. 131, 24 December 1249), and 479–81 (item no. 141, 24 December 1249).

4. This edition also includes a critical introduction, written by C. A. F. Meekings, that thoroughly describes the origin, provenance, contexts, and damage of TNA KB 26/115B. See *CRR 1233–37*, v–lxiv, at ix–xii.

5. The dorse is blank except for these words at the top right. A small slit cut into the bottom center of the rotulus indicates that it likely traveled on its own (rolled and tied) at some point.

6. Previous editors have printed "Joppe filium Th . . ." instead of "Joppe filium Chere" (the genitive form of Chera, a very common Anglo-Jewish woman's name, while Joppe is a diminutive form of Joseph or Jacob). Lipman, *Jews of Medieval Norwich*, 61, tentatively connected this Joppe to the seized property of a Jew hanged for the alleged crime, oddly called "Theor" in *CCR 1237–42*, 247—and the relevant roll (TNA C 54/51, m. 19) does indeed read "Theor"—and he suggested that "Theor" might be a corruption of "Diaia" (Diaie le Chat). However, the later Anglo-Hebrew documents (see note 3 above) show that Diaie le Chat's wife and sons inherited his property after his death. The suspect word here is at the damaged left edge of the rotulus; the first two letters are visible, and the rest (with the possible exception of the final "e") are visible under ultraviolet light. I am confident that the name reads "Chere." Matrilineal identification is not uncommon for Anglo-Jews, and several Cheras of Norwich are named in documents from this time: the 1241 roll that lists debts of condemned and fugitive Norwich Jews, for instance (London, Westminster Abbey Muniments 6695), even identifies the daughter of Isaac Parvus as Chera (see Lipman, *Jews of Medieval Norwich*, 262).

7. This list of those absent corresponds to crosses placed above the same names in the list just preceding. Senioret son of Josce also has a cross above his name, but see note 1 above.

8. Previous editors print "circa meridiem," though the letters after the "m" at the damaged edges of the rotulus are not legible.

9. As other editors have suggested, this should probably read "vocaverunt predictum puerum Iudeum suum" (that is, "they called the aforesaid boy their Jew" instead of "they called the aforesaid Jew their boy"). The scribal confusion, however, is well suited to the problems that this text presents, as described above, at 20–27 and 30–31.

10. Unduly influenced by Prynne, previous editors have printed "dixit propter timorem *Iudeorum* vocabatur Iurnepin" rather than "dixit propter timorem *Iudeus* vocabatur Jurnepin," though only the "Iu" is visible, and, even with damage considered, there is not enough room for the scribe's usual abbreviation of *Iudeorum*. My reading allows that Odard first claims to be a Jew named Jurnepin (just as he had done with Matilda and her daughter) and claims that he is Odard only after he realizes he is speaking to his father.

11. According to *CRR 1233–37*, 334 note 2, the Norwich sessions of the Norfolk eyre took place between 15 September and 19 October 1234.

12. According to *CRR 1233–37*, 334 note 3, the Cattishall sessions of the Suffolk eyre took place between 24 November and 14 December 1234, and also on or about 14 January 1235. This establishes the date by which the case was referred to the ecclesiastical courts.

APPENDIX 3

1. The page of the archival binder in which this letter is now bound (that is, in SC 1/24) reads 202, but the Public Record Office (PRO) stamp on the dorse reads 201.

2. The lower portion of this leaf is damaged by water as well as minor tearing and trimming. Ultraviolet light was used to read damaged portions. Only the ascender of the letter indicating the regnal year is visible, and an earlier date is possible.

APPENDIX 4

1. "Liber Wilelmi de clara quem portauit ad sanctum augustinum" (fol. iv). Malcolm Parkes notes this manuscript among William's collection, as an example of the thirteenth-century contributions of scholar-monks to monastic libraries, in *Their Hands Before Our Eyes: A Closer Look at Scribes* (Aldershot: Ashgate, 2008), 18. Sophie Page identifies William as a significant donor of occult texts to the abbey's library too, his books revealing the "personal collection . . . of a working scholar." See her *Magic in the Cloister: Pious Motives, Illicit Interests, and Occult Approaches to the Medieval Universe* (University Park: Pennsylvania State Univ. Press, 2013), 11–12.

2. While some of the texts in MS Royal 8 A VI are known from other manuscripts and thus do appear, for instance, in the *Patrologia Latina*, none of the items in this manuscript has been edited or printed. The single exception is a sixteenth-century English poem added in the margins on fol. 52r, printed in James Orchard Halliwell, *The Nursery Rhymes of England* (London: Percy Society, 1842), 15.

BIBLIOGRAPHY

MANUSCRIPTS

Berkeley, Bancroft Library MS UCB 92
Cambridge, Corpus Christi College MS 16
Cambridge, Magdalene College MS
   26
   Pepys 37
   Pepys 2014
Cambridge, Trinity College MS B.14.39 (bound with B.14.40)
Cambridge, University Library MS Additional 3037
Coventry, City Record Office MS 325/1
Hildesheim, Dombibliothek Hildesheim Hs. St. God. 1
Laon, Bibliothèque municipale MS 81
London, British Library MSS
   Additional 10036
   Additional 22311
   Additional 25719
   Additional 27879
   Additional 36523
   Additional 36983
   Additional 39996
   Additional 39999
   Additional 48985
   Arundel 157
   Cotton Nero C IV
   Cotton Nero D V, part 2
   Cotton Tiberius E I, part 2
   Cotton Vitellius D XV
   Egerton 2781
   Harley 79
   Harley 957
   Harley 1005
   Harley 2253
   Harley 4733
   Royal 6 E VI
   Royal 6 E VII

    Royal 8 A VI
London, College of Arms MS Arundel 30
London, Westminster Abbey, Westminster Abbey Muniments
    6695
    6797
    9061
Los Angeles, Getty Museum MS 101 (*olim* Dyson Perrins MS 1)
New Haven, Beinecke Library MS Osborn A 11
New York, Pierpont Morgan Library MS M 898
Oxford, Bodleian Library MSS
    Bodley 343
    Bodley 692
    Digby 230
    Douce 78
    Douce 126
    Eng. poet. a. 1
    Junius 1
    Laud 683
    Laud misc. 622
Oxford, Jesus College MS 29
Oxford, Magdalen College, Muniments Room, St Aldates 34
Paris, Bibliothèque nationale de France MS fr. 902
Richmond (Kew), The National Archives of the UK
    C 54/45
    C 54/51
    C 54/96
    C 60/9
    C 60/15
    C 60/52
    C 85/3/71
    C 85/99/33
    C 255/18/5B
    DL 25/3546
    E 9/1
    E 9/4
    E 9/8
    E 9/11
    E 9/21
    E 9/22
    E 9/24
    E 9/27
    E 9/49
    E 101/249/1
    E 101/249/22
    E 101/251/11
    E 372/43

E 401/1565
KB 26/115B
SC 1/16/63
SC 1/24/201
SC 8/4/154
SC 8/103/5120
San Marino, Huntington Library MS Ellesmere 25.A.13

PUBLISHED PRIMARY SOURCES

Aguilar, Grace. "History of the Jews in England." *Chambers Miscellany of Useful and Entertaining Tracts* 18 (1847): 1–37.

Alfonsi, Petrus. *Dialogue Against the Jews.* Translated and edited by Irven M. Resnick. Fathers of the Church: Medieval Continuation. Washington, DC: Catholic University of America Press, 2007.

Alter, Robert, ed. and trans. *Strong as Death Is Love: The Song of Songs, Ruth, Esther, Jonah, and Daniel; A Translation with Commentary.* New York: Norton, 2015.

Ault, Warren Ortman, ed. *Court Rolls of the Abbey of Ramsey and the Honor of Clare.* New Haven: Yale University Press, 1928.

Baigent, Francis Joseph, ed. *A Collection of Records and Documents Relating to the Hundred and Manor of Crondal in Southampton.* Vol. 1. London: Simpkin, 1891.

Banks, Mary Macleod, ed. *An Alphabet of Tales.* 2 vols. EETS o.s. 126–127. London: Kegan Paul, Trench, Trübner, 1904–5.

Belfour, A. O., ed. *Twelfth-Century Homilies in MS. Bodley 343.* EETS o.s. 137. London: Kegan Paul, 1909.

Benson, Larry D., ed. *The Riverside Chaucer.* 3rd ed. Boston: Houghton Mifflin, 1987.

Bergen, Henry, ed. *Lydgate's Fall of Princes: Part III.* EETS e.s. 123. London: Oxford University Press, 1924.

Brandeis, Arthur, ed. *Jacob's Well: An Englisht Treatise on the Cleansing of Man's Conscience.* EETS o.s. 115. London: Kegan Paul, 1900.

Butler, H. E., ed. and trans. *The Chronicle of Jocelin of Brakelond Concerning the Acts of Samson, Abbot of the Monastery of St Edmund.* Oxford: Oxford University Press, 1949.

Caesarius of Heisterbach. *Caesarii Heisterbacensis monachi ordinis Cisterciensis Dialogus miraculorum.* Edited by Joseph Strange. Vol. 1. Cologne: Heberle and Lempertz, 1851.

———. *The Dialogue on Miracles.* Translated by H. von E. Scott and C. C. Swinton Bland. Vol. 1. London: George Routledge and Sons, 1929.

Calendar of the Charter Rolls Preserved in the Public Record Office: Henry III, 1226–1257. Vol. 1. London: HMSO, 1908.

Calendar of Inquisitions Miscellaneous (Chancery) Preserved in the Public Record Office. Vol. 1. London: HMSO, 1916.

Calendar of the Patent Rolls Preserved in the Public Record Office: Henry III, 1232–1247. London: HMSO, 1906.

Carlyle, Thomas. *Past and Present.* 1843. Edited by Richard Altick as *Past and Present by Thomas Carlyle.* New York: New York University Press, 1965.

Child, Francis James. *English and Scottish Ballads.* Vol. 3. Boston: Little Brown, 1857.

———. *The English and Scottish Popular Ballads*. Vol. 3. Boston: Houghton Mifflin, 1882.

Clark, Cecily, ed. *The Peterborough Chronicle, 1070–1154*. 2nd ed. Oxford: Oxford University Press, 1970.

Cluse, Christoph, ed. "'Fabula ineptissima': Die Ritualmordlegende um Adam von Bristol nach der Handschrift London, British Library, Harley 957." *Ashkenas* 5 (1995): 293–330.

Cohen, Leonard. "Not a Jew." In *Book of Longing*, 158. Toronto: McLelland and Stewart, 2006.

———. "Not a Jew." *The Leonard Cohen Files*, edited by Eija Arjatsalo and Jarkko Arjatsalo, 2008. https://www.leonardcohenfiles.com/jew.html.

Cornfeld, Gaalya, ed. and trans. *Josephus: The Jewish War*. Grand Rapids, MI: Zondervan, 1982.

Crawford, Anne, ed. *Letters of the Queens of England, 1100–1547*. Thrupp: Sutton, 1994.

Dahood, Roger. "The Anglo-Norman 'Hugo de Lincolnia': A Critical Edition and Translation from the Unique Text in Paris, Bibliothèque nationale de France MS fr. 902." *Chaucer Review* 49, no. 1 (2014): 1–38.

Davis, M. D., ed. *Hebrew Deeds of English Jews Before 1290*. Publications of the Anglo-Jewish Historical Exhibition 2. London: Jewish Chronicle, 1888.

D'Evelyn, Charlotte, and Anna J. Mill, eds. *The South English Legendary*. Vol. 2. EETS o.s. 236. London: Oxford University Press, 1956.

Ellis, Henry, ed. *Chronica Johannis de Oxenedes*. Rolls. London: Longman, Brown, Green, Longmans, and Roberts, 1859.

Fein, Susanna, David Raybin, and Jan Ziolkowski, ed. and trans. *The Complete Harley 2253 Manuscript*. 3 vols. TEAMS Middle English Texts Series. Kalamazoo: Medieval Institute Publications, 2015.

Fischer, Rudolf. "Vindicta Salvatoris Mittlenglisches Gedicht des 13. Jahrhunderts, zum erstenmal herausgegeben." Pts. 1 and 2. *Archiv für das Studium der neuren Sprachen und Literaturen* 111, no. 11 (1903): 285–98; 112, no. 12 (1904): 24–45.

Florence of Worcester. *Chronicon ex Chronicis, Florentii Wigorniensis Monachi Chronicon ex Chronicis*. Edited by Benjamin Thorpe. Vol. 2. London: English Historical Society, 1848.

Friedman, John, and Jean Connell Hoff, trans. *The Trial of the Talmud: Paris, 1240*. With introduction by Robert Chazan. Medieval Sources in Translation 53. Toronto: PIMS, 2012.

Galchinsky, Michael, ed., *Grace Aguilar: Selected Writings*. Toronto: Broadview, 2003.

Gransden, Antonia, ed. and trans. *The Chronicle of Bury St Edmunds, 1212–1301*. London: Thomas Nelson and Sons, 1964.

Habermann, A. M., ed. *Sefer Gezerot Ashkenaz ve-Zorfat*. Jerusalem: Tarshish, 1945.

Halliwell, James Orchard, ed. *The Nursery Rhymes of England*. London: Percy Society, 1842.

Hanna, Ralph, and David Lawton, ed. *The Siege of Jerusalem*. EETS o.s. 320. Oxford: Oxford University Press, 2003.

Hasenfratz, Robert, ed. *Ancrene Wisse*. TEAMS Middle English Texts Series. Kalamazoo: Medieval Institute Publications, 2000.

HeHasid, Judah. *Sefer Hasidim*. With Hebrew introduction by Jacob Freimann. Edited by Jehudah Wistinetzky. 2nd ed. Frankfurt: Wahrmann, 1924.

Henry III Fine Rolls Project. TNA and King's College London, 2009. https://finerollshenry3.org.uk.

Herbert, J. A., ed. *Titus and Vespasian, or The Destruction of Jerusalem in Rhymed Couplets*. London: Roxburghe Club, 1905.

Herd, David, ed. *The Ancient and Modern Scots Songs, Heroic Ballads, Etc. Now First Collected into One Body, from the Various Miscellanies wherein they Formerly Lay Dispersed*. Edinburgh: Martin and Wotherspoon, 1769.

————, ed. *Ancient and Modern Scottish Songs, Heroic Ballads, Etc.* 2 vols. Edinburgh: John Wotherspoon for James Dickson and Charles Elliot, 1776.

Holt, Robert, ed. *The Ormulum with the Notes and Glossary of Dr. R. M. White.* 2 vols. Oxford: Clarendon, 1878.

Huckabee, Mike. "I will be on with @HARRISFAULKNER on @OutnumberedOT from Jerusalem @FoxNews at 1pm ET/12CT and I will begin show by blowing a Shofar and speaking Hebrew." Twitter, 14 May 2018. https://twitter.com/govmikehuckabee/status /996055352650158082.

————. "Will be on @foxandfriends today at 8amET/7amCT and since I just got back from Israel, I'll be speaking in Hebrew and blowing a Shofar during the segment. Watch and have a great Sunday!" Twitter, 5 August 2018. https://twitter.com/GovMikeHuckabee /status/1026067116443742208.

Irvine, Susan, ed. *Old English Homilies from MS Bodley 343.* EETS o.s. 302. Oxford: Oxford University Press, 1993.

Jamieson, Robert, ed. *Popular Ballads and Songs from Tradition, Manuscripts, and Scarce Editions.* Edinburgh: Archibald Constable and Co., 1806.

Jessop, Augustus, and M. R. James, eds. and trans. *The Life and Miracles of St William of Norwich by Thomas of Monmouth.* Cambridge: Cambridge University Press, 1896.

Larson, Nella. *Passing.* Edited by Carla Kaplan. 2nd ed. Norton Critical Editions. New York: Norton, 2007.

Lee, Stuart D., ed. *Ælfric's Homilies on Judith, Esther, and Maccabees.* Oxford: Arts and Humanities Community Resource, 1999. http://users.ox.ac.uk/~stuart/kings/main.htm.

Livingston, Michael, ed. *Siege of Jerusalem.* TEAMS Middle English Texts Series. Kalamazoo: Medieval Institute Publications, 2004.

Luard, Henry Richards, ed. *Bartholomaei de Cotton monachi Norwicensis, Historia anglicana.* Rolls. London: Longman, Green, Longman, and Roberts, 1859.

————, ed. *Matthæi Parisiensis monachi Sancti Albani, Chronica majora.* 7 vols. Rolls. London: Longman and Trübner, 1872–83.

Madden, Frederic, ed. *Matthæi Parisiensis monachi Sancti Albani Historia Anglorum sive, ut vulgo dicitur, Historia minor.* Vol. 2. Rolls. London: Longmans, Green, Reader, and Dyer, 1866.

Meech, Sanford Brown, and Hope Emily Allen, eds. *The Book of Margery Kempe.* EETS o.s. 212. New York: Oxford University Press, 1940.

Michel, Francisque. "Ballade anglo-normande sur le meurtre commis par les juifs sur un enfant de Lincoln." *Memoires de la Société des antiquaires de France* 10 (1834): 358–92.

————. "Hugo de Lincolnia." In *Hugues de Lincoln: Recueil de ballades anglo-normande et écossaises relatives au meurtre de cet enfant commis par les juifs en MCCLV,* with introduction and notes by Francisque Michel, 1–16. Paris: Silvestre and Pickering, 1834.

————, ed. *Rôles gascons, 1242–1254.* Vol. 1. Paris: Imprimerie nationale, 1885.

Millett, Bella, and Jocelyn Wogan-Browne, eds. *Medieval English Prose for Women: Selections from the Katherine Group and "Ancrene Wisse."* Oxford: Clarendon, 1993.

Morris, Richard, ed. *An Old English Miscellany.* EETS o.s. 49. London: N. Trübner, 1872.

Peck, Russell A., ed. "The Storie of Asneth." In *Heroic Women from the Old Testament in Middle English Verse,* edited by Russell A. Peck, 1–23. TEAMS Middle English Texts Series. Kalamazoo: Medieval Institute Publications, 1991.

Percy, Thomas, ed. *Reliques of Ancient English Poetry: Consisting of Old Heroic Ballads, Songs, and Other Pieces of Our Earlier Poets (Chiefly of the Lyric Kind), Together with Some Few of Later Date.* Vol. 1. London: J. Dodsley, 1765.

Prou, Maurice, ed. *Registres d'Honorius IV.* Paris: Ernst Thorin, 1886.

Prynne, William. *Short Demurrer to the Jews Long Discontinued Barred Remitter into England.* London: Edward Thomas,1656; Ann Arbor: Text Creation Partnership, 2007. http://name .umdl.umich.edu/A56206.0001.001.

Resnick, Irven M., trans. *Petrus Alfonsi: Dialogue Against the Jews.* Fathers of the Church Medieval Continuation 8. Washington, DC: Catholic University of America Press, 2006.

"The Robert of Reading Plaque." Oxford Jewish Heritage. Oxford Jewish Heritage Committee. May 2012. https://www.oxfordjewishheritage.co.uk/projects/osney-abbey-first-public -burning-in-england/137-the-robert-of-reading-plaque.

Rubin, Miri, ed. and trans. *The Life and Passion of William of Norwich by Thomas of Monmouth.* London: Penguin, 2014.

Rye, Walter, ed. *The Norfolk Antiquarian Miscellany.* Vol. 1, no. 2. Norwich: Samuel Miller, 1877.

Schmidt, A. V. C., ed. *The Vision of Piers Plowman: The B-Text.* Rev. ed. New York: Everyman, 1987.

Schroeder, H. J., ed. and trans. *Disciplinary Decrees of the General Councils: Text, Translation, and Commentary.* St. Louis: B. Herder, 1937.

Staley, Lynne, ed. *The Book of Margery Kempe.* TEAMS Middle English Texts Series. Kalamazoo: Medieval Institute Publications, 1996.

Sweet, Henry. *First Middle English Primer: Extracts from the "Ancren Riwle" and "Ormulum" with Grammar and Glossary.* Oxford: Clarendon, 1884.

Talbot, C. H., ed. and trans. *The Life of Christina of Markyate: A Twelfth-Century Recluse.* Medieval Academy Reprints for Teaching. Toronto: University of Toronto Press, 1998. First published by Clarendon (Oxford), 1959.

Tanquerey, F. J., ed. *Recueil de lettres anglo-françaises (1265–1399).* Paris: Édouard Champion, 1916.

Thorpe, Benjamin, ed. *Florentii Wigorniensis monachi Chronicon ex chronicis.* Vol. 2. London: Sumptibus Societatis, 1849.

Tovey, D'Blossiers. *Anglia Judaica, or the History and Antiquities of the Jews in England.* Oxford: James Fletcher, 1738.

Treharne, Elaine, ed. *Old and Middle English, c. 890–1450: An Anthology.* 3rd ed. Malden, MA: Wiley-Blackwell, 2010.

Whiston, William, trans. *The Complete Works of Flavius Josephus.* London: Nelson, 1860.

White, R. M., ed. *The Ormulum, Now First Edited from the Original Manuscript in the Bodleian with Notes and Glossary.* Oxford: Oxford University Press, 1852.

———. "Preface." In *The Ormulum with the Notes and Glossary of Dr. R. M. White,* edited by Robert Holt, 1:vii–lxxv. Oxford: Clarendon, 1878.

Williams Boyarin, Adrienne, ed. and trans. *Miracles of the Virgin in Middle English.* Broadview Anthology of British Literatures Edition. Toronto: Broadview, 2015.

———, ed. and trans. *The Siege of Jerusalem.* Broadview Anthology of British Literatures Edition. Toronto: Broadview, 2014.

Yalkut Shim'oni: Midrash 'al Torah, Neviim u-Khetuvim. [In Hebrew.] 5 vols. Jerusalem: Yerid Ha-seferim, 2006.

SECONDARY SOURCES

Abad, Anna Rich. "Able and Available: Jewish Women in Medieval Barcelona and Their Economic Activities." *Journal of Medieval Iberian Studies* 6, no. 1 (2014): 71–86.

Adelman, Janet. *Blood Relations: Christian and Jew in "The Merchant of Venice."* Chicago: University of Chicago Press, 2008.

Adler, Michael. *Jews of Medieval England.* London: JHSE, 1939.

Akbari, Suzanne. "Erasing the Body: History and Memory in Medieval Siege Poetry." In *Remembering the Crusades: Myth, Image, and Identity,* edited by Nicholas Paul and Suzanne Yeager, 146–73. Baltimore: Johns Hopkins University Press, 2012.

Anderson, George K. *The Legend of the Wandering Jew.* Providence: Brown University Press, 1965.

Ashe, Laura. "The Originality of the *Orrmulum.*" *Early Middle English* 1, no. 1 (2019): 35–54.

Auerbach, Erich. "Figura." Translated by Ralph Manheim. In *Scenes from the Drama of European Literature,* 11–76. Theory and History of Literature 9. Minneapolis: University of Minnesota Press, 1984.

Baker, Cynthia. "The Essentially Ambiguous Jewess: An Ancient Trope in Modern Europe." Filmed 23 May 2011 at the *Women, Jews, Venetians* conference, University of California–Santa Cruz. Video, 57:57. https://vimeo.com/77806116.

———. *Jew.* Key Words in Jewish Studies. New Brunswick, NJ: Rutgers University Press, 2017.

———. "One Final Word on *Jew*: A Response." In Reed and Magid, "Forum."

Bale, Anthony. *Feeling Persecuted: Christians, Jews, and Images of Violence in the Middle Ages.* London: Reaktion, 2010.

———. "The Female 'Jewish' Libido in Medieval Culture." In *The Erotic in the Literature of Medieval Britain,* edited by Amanda Hopkins and Cory James Rushton, 94–104. Cambridge: D. S. Brewer, 2007.

———. "Fictions of Judaism in England Before 1290." In *Jews in Medieval Britain: Historical, Literary, Archaeological Perspectives,* edited by Patricia Skinner, 129–44. Woodbridge: Boydell, 2003.

———. "'House Devil, Town Saint': Anti-Semitism and Hagiography in Medieval Suffolk." In *Chaucer and the Jews: Sources, Contexts, Meanings,* edited by Sheila Delany, 185–210. New York: Routledge, 2002.

———. *The Jew in the Medieval Book: English Antisemitisms, 1350–1500.* Cambridge Studies in Medieval Literature 60. Cambridge: Cambridge University Press, 2006.

———. "Richard of Devizes and Fictions of Judaism." *Jewish Culture and History* 3, no. 2 (2000): 55–72.

Barber, Tamsin. "The Plasticity of Diasporic Identities in Super-Diverse Cities." In *The Routledge Handbook of Diaspora Studies,* edited by Robin Cohen and Carolin Fischer, 268–75. New York: Routledge, 2018.

Bartlet, Suzanne. *Licoricia of Winchester: Marriage, Motherhood, and Murder in the Medieval Anglo-Jewish Community.* Edited by Patricia Skinner. London: Vallentine-Mitchell, 2009.

———. "Three Jewish Businesswomen in Thirteenth-Century Winchester." *Jewish Culture and History* 3, no. 2 (2003): 31–54.

———. "Women in the Medieval Anglo-Jewish Community." In *The Jews of Medieval Britain: Historical, Literary, and Archaeological Perspectives,* edited by Patricia Skinner, 113–27. Woodbridge: Boydell, 2003.

Bartlett, Robert. "Illustrating Ethnicity in the Middle Ages." In *The Origins of Racism in the West,* edited by Miriam Eliav-Feldon, Benjamin Isaac, and Joseph Ziegler, 132–56. Cambridge: Cambridge University Press, 2009.

Bauman, Zygmunt. "Allosemitism: Premodern, Modern, Postmodern." In *Modernity, Culture, and "The Jew,"* edited by Bryan Cheyette and Laura Marcus, 143–56. Stanford: Stanford University Press, 1998.

Baumgarten, Elisheva. *Mothers and Children: Jewish Family Life in Medieval Europe*. Princeton: Princeton University Press, 2004.

———. *Practicing Piety in Medieval Ashkenaz: Men, Women, and Everyday Religious Observance*. Jewish Culture and Contexts. Philadelphia: University of Pennsylvania Press, 2014.

Bayless, Martha. *Parody in the Middle Ages: The Latin Tradition*. Ann Arbor: University of Michigan Press, 1996.

Bennett, J. A. W. *Middle English Literature*. Oxford: Clarendon, 1986.

Bennett, J. A. W., and G. V. Smithers, eds. *Early Middle English Verse and Prose*. Oxford: Clarendon, 1968.

Berkowitz, Adam Eliyahu. "The Surprising Story Behind Trump's Jewish Prayer Shawl." *BreakingIsraelNews*, 13 September 2016. https://www.breakingisraelnews.com/75568/surprising-story-behind-trumps-jewish-prayer- shawl/.

Bhabha, Homi K. *Location of Culture*. London: Routledge, 1994.

———. "Of Mimicry and Man: The Ambivalence of Colonial Discourse." *October* 28 (1984): 125–33.

Biddick, Kathleen. *The Typological Imaginary: Circumcision, Technology, History*. Philadelphia: University of Pennsylvania Press, 2003.

Birenbaum, Maija. "Affective Vengeance in *Titus and Vespasian*." *Chaucer Review* 43, no. 3 (2009): 330–44.

Blurton, Heather. "Richard of Devizes's *Cronicon*, Menippean Satire, and the Jews of Winchester." *Exemplaria* 22, no. 4 (2010): 265–84.

Boulton, Maureen B. M. *Piety and Persecution in the French Texts of England*. French of England Translation Series 6. Tempe: Arizona Center for Medieval and Renaissance Studies, 2013.

Boyarin, Daniel. "Yeah, Jew!" In Reed and Magid, "Forum."

Breen, Katharine. *Imagining an English Reading Public, 1150–1400*. Cambridge Studies in Medieval Literature 79. Cambridge: Cambridge University Press, 2010.

Bronson, Betrand Harris. *The Singing Tradition of Child's Popular Ballads*. Princeton: Princeton University Press, 1976.

Bugyis, Katie Ann-Marie. "The Author of the *Life of Christina of Markyate*: The Case for Robert of Gorron (d. 1066)." *Journal of Ecclesiastical History* 68, no. 4 (2017): 719–46.

Bynum, Caroline Walker. *Holy Feast and Holy Fast: The Religious Significance of Food to Medieval Women*. Berkeley: University of California Press, 1987.

Cannon, Christopher. *The Grounds of English Literature*. Oxford: Oxford University Press, 2004.

———. "Spelling Practice: The *Ormulum* and the Word." *Forum for Modern Language Studies* 33, no. 3 (1997): 229–44.

Cardwell, Samuel. "Wurrþlike shridd: *Cossmós, Mycrocossmós*, and the Use of Greek in Orrm's Exegesis of John 3:16." *Early Middle English* 1, no. 2 (2019): 1–12.

A Catalogue of the Harleian Manuscripts in the British Museum. Vol. 1. London: British Museum, 1808.

Cheyette, Brian. *Constructions of "The Jew" in English Literature and Society: Racial Representations, 1875–1945*. Cambridge: Cambridge University Press, 1993.

Cixous, Hélène. *Portrait of Jacques Derrida as a Young Jewish Saint*. Translated by Beverley Bie Brahic. New York: Columbia University Press, 2004.

Clanchy, Michael. *From Memory to Written Record: England 1066–1307*. 2nd ed. Oxford: Blackwell, 1993.

Classen, Albrecht, ed. *Childhood in the Middle Ages and Renaissance*. Berlin: Walter de Gruyter, 2005.

Cluse, Christoph. "Stories of Breaking and Taking the Cross: A Possible Context for the Oxford Incident of 1268." *Revue d'histoire ecclésiastique* 90, no. 3 (1995): 396–442.

Cohen, Jeffrey Jerome. *Hybridity, Identity, and Monstrosity in Medieval Britain: On Difficult Middles*. The New Middle Ages. New York: Palgrave Macmillan, 2006.

———. "Stories of Blood 2: The Blood of Race." *In the Middle* (blog), 17 April 2017. http://www .inthemedievalmiddle.com/2017/04/stories-of-blood-2-blood-of-race.html.

Cohen, Jeremy. *The Friars and the Jews: The Evolution of Medieval Anti-Judaism*. Ithaca: Cornell University Press, 1982.

———. *Living Letters of the Law: Ideas of the Jew in Medieval Christianity*. S. Mark Taper Foundation Imprint in Jewish Studies. Berkeley: University of California Press, 1999.

———. *Sanctifying the Name of God: Jewish Martyrs and Jewish Memories of the First Crusade*. Jewish Culture and Contexts. Philadelphia: University of Pennsylvania Press, 2006.

Colish, Marcia L. "Another Look at the School of Laon." *Archives d'histoire doctrinale et littéraire du moyen âge* 53 (1986): 7–22.

———. *Studies in Scholasticism*. Variorum Collected Studies. Aldershot: Variorum, 2006.

Cortellessa, Eric. "Why Did a Christian Bishop Give Donald Trump a Jewish Prayer Shawl?" *Times of Israel*, 9 September 2016. http://www.timesofisrael.com/why-did-a-christian -bishop-give-donald-trump-a-jewish-prayer- shawl/.

Curry, Walter Clyde. *Chaucer and the Mediaeval Sciences*. Oxford: Clarendon, 1926.

———. "Chaucer's Reeve and Miller." *PMLA* 35 (1920): 189–209.

Dahood, Roger. "Alleged Jewish Cannibalism in the Thirteenth-Century Anglo-Norman 'Hugo de Lincolnia,' with Notice of the Allegation in Twelfth-Century England." In *Language in Medieval Britain: Networks and Exchanges; Proceedings of the 2013 Harlaxton Symposium*, edited by Mary Carruthers, 229–41. Donington, UK: Shaun Tyas, 2015.

———. "English Historical Narratives of Jewish Child-Murder, Chaucer's Prioress's Tale, and the Date of Chaucer's Unknown Source." *Studies in the Age of Chaucer* 31 (2009): 125–40.

———. "The Punishment of the Jews, Hugh of Lincoln, and the Question of Satire in Chaucer's Prioress's Tale." *Viator* 36 (2005): 465–91.

Deleuze, Gilles, and Félix Guattari. *A Thousand Plateaus: Capitalism and Schizophrenia*. Translated by Brian Massumi. London: Continuum, 1987.

Despres, Denise. "Adolescence and Sanctity: *The Life and Passion of Saint William of Norwich*." *Journal of Religion* 90, no. 1 (2010): 33–62.

———. "Immaculate Flesh and the Social Body: Mary and the Jews." *Jewish History* 12, no. 1 (1998): 47–69.

———. "Mary of the Eucharist: Cultic Anti-Judaism in Some Fourteenth-Century English Devotional Manuscripts." In *From Witness to Witchcraft: Jews and Judaism in Christian Thought*, edited by Jeremy Cohen, 375–401. Wolfenbüttler Mittelalter Studien 11. Wiesbaden: Harrassowitz, 1996.

———. "The Protean Jew in the Vernon Manuscript." In *Chaucer and the Jews: Sources, Contexts, Meanings*, edited Shiela Delany, 145–64. New York: Routledge, 2002.

Dinkova-Bruun, Greti. "Biblical Thematics: The Story of Samson in Medieval Literary Discourse." In *The Oxford Handbook of Medieval Latin Literature*, edited by Ralph Hexter and David Townsend, 356–75. New York: Oxford University Press, 2012.

Dinshaw, Carolyn. "Pale Faces: Race, Religion, and Affect in Chaucer's Texts and Their Readers." *Studies in the Age of Chaucer* 23 (2001): 19–41.

Dobson, E. J. *The Origins of "Ancrene Wisse."* Oxford: Clarendon, 1976.

Dobson, R. Barrie. "The Jews of Medieval Cambridge." In *The Jewish Communities of Medieval England: The Collected Essays of R. B. Dobson*, edited by Helen Birkett, 101–26. Borthwick Texts and Studies 39. York: The Borthwick Institute, University of York, 2010.

———. "The Medieval York Jewry Reconsidered." In *The Jews of Medieval Britian: Historical, Literary, and Archaeological Perspectives*, edited by Patricia Skinner, 145–56. Woodbridge: Boydell, 2003.

———. "A Minority Within a Minority: The Jewesses of Thirteenth-Century England." In *The Jewish Communities of Medieval England: The Collected Essays of R. B. Dobson*, edited by Helen Birkett, 149–66. Borthwick Texts and Studies 39. York: The Borthwick Institute, University of York, 2010.

———. "The Role of Jewish Women in Medieval England (Presidential Address)." *Studies in Church History* 29 (1992): 145–68.

Dombibliotheck Hildesheim. *The Albani Psalter*. With commentary by Jochen Bepler, Peter Kidd, and Jane Geddes. Simbach am Inn: Müller and Schindler, 2008.

Donovan, Claire. *The de Brailes Hours*. Toronto: University of Toronto Press, 1991.

Dumitrescu, Irina. "Debt and Sin in the Middle English 'Judas'." *Anglia* 131, no. 4 (2013): 509–37.

Edelman, Lee. *No Future: Queer Theory and the Death Drive*. Durham: Duke University Press, 2004.

Ephraim, Michelle. *Reading Jewish Women on the Elizabethan Stage*. Women and Gender in the Early Modern World. Aldershot: Ashgate, 2008.

Fabre-Vassas, Claudine. *The Singular Beast: Jews, Christians, and the Pig*. Translated by Carol Volk. European Perspectives. New York: Columbia University Press, 1997.

Fanous, Samuel, and Henrietta Leyser, eds. *Christina of Markyate: A Twelfth-Century Holy Woman*. London: Routledge, 2005.

Feldman, Louis H., and Gohei Hata, eds. *Josephus, Judaism, and Christianity*. Detroit: Wayne State University Press, 1987.

Finlayson, John. "The Contexts of the Crusading Romances in the London Thornton Manuscript." *Anglia* 130, no. 2 (2012): 240–63.

Ford, Alvin A., ed. *La Vengeance de Nostre-Seigneur: The Old and Middle French Prose Versions*. 2 vols. Toronto: PIMS, 1984–93.

Foss, Edward, ed. *Biographia juridica: A Biographical Dictionary of the Judges of England from the Conquest to the Present Time, 1066–1870*. London: John Murray, 1870.

Friedenberg, Daniel M. *Medieval Jewish Seals from Europe*. Detroit: Wayne State University Press, 1987.

Fulk, R. D. *An Introduction to Middle English*. Peterborough, ON: Broadview, 2012.

Gabriele, Matthew. "The Chosen Peoples of the Eleventh and Twenty-First Centuries." *Relegere: Studies in Religion and Reception* 2, no. 2 (2012): 281–90.

Galloway, Andrew. "Alliterative Poetry in Old Jerusalem: The Siege of Jerusalem and Its Sources." In *Medieval Alliterative Poetry: Essays in Honour of Thorlac Turville-Petre*, edited by John A. Burrow and Hoyt N. Duggan, 96–106. Dublin: Four Courts Press, 2010.

Gerrard, Daniel. "Jocelin of Brakelond and the Power of Abbot Samson." *Journal of Medieval History* 40, no. 1 (2014): 1–23.

Gilman, Sander L. "Salome, Syphilis, Sarah Bernhardt, and the 'Modern Jewess'." *German Quarterly* 66, no. 2 (1993): 195–211.

Goldy, Charlotte Newman. "Muriel, a Jew of Oxford: Using the Dramatic to Understand the Mundane in Anglo-Norman Towns." In *Writing Medieval Women's Lives*, edited by

Charlotte Newman Goldy and Amy Livingstone, 227–45. The New Middle Ages. New York: Palgrave, 2012.

Gransden, Antonia. "Realistic Observation in Twelfth-Century England." *Speculum* 47, no. 1 (1972): 29–51.

Greatrex, Joan. "Monastic Charity for Jewish Converts: The Requisition of Corrodies by Henry III." *Studies in Church History* 29 (1992): 133–43.

Green, Monica. "Conversing with the Minority: Relations Among Christian, Jewish, and Muslim Women in the High Middle Ages." *Journal of Medieval History* 34, no. 2 (2008): 105–18.

Gregg, Joan Young. *Devils, Women, and Jews: Reflections on the Other in Medieval Sermon Stories*. SUNY Series in Medieval Studies. Albany: State University of New York Press, 1997.

Greiner, Rae. *Sympathetic Realism in Nineteenth-Century British Fiction*. Baltimore: Johns Hopkins University Press, 2012.

Guibbory, Achsah. *Christian Identity, Jews, and Israel in Seventeenth-Century England*. Oxford: Oxford University Press, 2010.

Hall, J. R. Clark. *A Concise Anglo-Saxon Dictionary*. Cambridge: Cambridge University Press, 1960.

Hamel, Mary. "*The Siege of Jerusalem* as a Crusading Poem." In *Journey Toward God: Pilgrimage and Crusade*, edited by Barbara N. Sargent-Baur, 177–94. Studies in Medieval Culture 30. Kalamazoo: Medieval Institute Publications, 1992.

Hames, Harvey J. "The Limits of Conversion: Ritual Murder and the Virgin Mary in the Account of Adam of Bristol." *Journal of Medieval History* 33 (2007): 43–59.

Hanska, Jussi. "Sermons on the Tenth Sunday After Holy Trinity: Another Occasion for Anti-Jewish Preaching." In *The Jewish-Christian Encounter in Medieval Preaching*, edited by Jonathan Adams and Jussi Hanska, 195–212. New York: Routledge, 2014.

Hassan-Rokem, Galit, and Alan Dundes, eds. *The Wandering Jew: Essays in the Interpretation of a Christian Legend*. Bloomington: Indiana University Press, 1986.

Heng, Geraldine. *England and the Jews: How Religion and Violence Created the First Racial State in the West*. Cambridge Elements in Religious and Violence. Cambridge: Cambridge University Press, 2018.

———. "England's Dead Boys: Telling Tales of Christian-Jewish Relations Before and After the First European Expulsion of the Jews." *MLN* 127, no. 5, supp. (2012): 54–85.

———. *The Invention of Race in the European Middle Ages*. Cambridge: Cambridge University Press, 2018.

Hillaby, Joe. "Hereford Gold: Irish, Welsh, and English Land—The Jewish Community at Hereford and Its Clients, 1179–1253: Four Case Studies, Part 2." *Transactions of the Woolhope Naturalists Field Club* 45, no. 1 (1985): 193–270.

———. "A Magnate Among the Marchers: Hamo of Hereford, His Family and Clients, 1218–1253." *Jewish Historical Studies* 31 (1990): 23–82.

———. "The Worcester Jewry, 1158–1290: Portrait of a Lost Community." *Transactions of the Worcestershire Archaeological Society*, 3rd ser., 12 (1990): 73–122.

Holdsworth, Christopher. "Christina of Markyate." In *Medieval Women*, edited by Derek Baker and Rosalind M. T. Hill, 185–204. Oxford: Blackwell, 1978.

Horowitz, Elliott. "Between Masters and Maidservants: The Jewish Society of Europe in Late Medieval and Early Modern Times." [In Hebrew.] In *Sexuality and the Family in History*, edited by Isaiah Gafni and Israel Bartal, 193–211. Jerusalem: Zalman Shatar Center, 1998.

Howe, Nicholas. *Migration and Mythmaking in Anglo-Saxon England*. New Haven: Yale University Press, 1989.

Hoyle, Victoria. "The Bonds That Bind: Money Lending Between Anglo-Jewish and Christian Women in the Plea Rolls of the Exchequer of the Jews, 1218–1280." *Journal of Medieval History* 34, no. 2 (2008): 119–29.

Jacobs, Andrew S. *Christ Circumcised: A Study in Early Christian History and Difference*. Divinations: Rereading Late Ancient Religion. Philadelphia: University of Pennsylvania Press, 2012.

James, M. R. *On the Abbey of S. Edmund at Bury*. Henry Bradshaw Society. Cambridge: Cambridge University Press, 1895.

———. *The Western Manuscripts in the Library of Trinity College, Cambridge: A Descriptive Catalogue*. 4 vols. Cambridge: Cambridge University Press, 1902.

Johannesson, Nils-Lennart. "Bread Crumbs and Related Matters in the *Ormulum*." In *Selected Proceedings of the 2005 Symposium on New Approaches in English Historical Lexis (HEL-LEX)*, edited by R. W. McConchie et al., 69–82. Somerville, MA: Cascadilla, 2006.

———. "The Four-Wheeled Quadriga and the Seven Sacraments: On the Sources of the 'Dedication' of the *Ormulum*." In *Bells Chiming from the Past: Cultural and Linguistic Studies on Early English*, edited by Isabel Moskowich-Spiegel and Begoña Crespo-García, 227–45. Amsterdam: Rodopi, 2007.

———. "'Icc Hafe Don Swa Summ Þu Badd': An Anatomy of the Preface of the *Ormulum*." *SELIM* 14 (2007): 107–40.

———. "Orm's Relationship to His Latin Sources." In *Studies in Middle English Forms and Meanings*, edited by Gabriella Mazzon, 133–43. Frankfurt: Peter Lang, 2007.

———. "'Þurrh beȝȝske 7 sallte tæress': Orm's Use of Metaphor and Simile in Exegesis of John 1:51." In *Selected Papers from the 2006 and 2007 Stockholm Metaphor Festivals*, edited by Nils-Lennart Johannesson and D. C. Minugh, 85–96. Stockholm: University of Stockholm, 2008.

Johnson, Alex. "Pence Sets Off Firestorm with Campaign Prayer by 'Christian Rabbi'." *NBC News* (online), 30 October 2018. Video, 1:58. https://www.nbcnews.com/politics/white -house/pence-sets-firestorm-campaign-prayer-christian-rabbi-n926016.

Johnson, Willis. "Textual Sources for the Study of Jewish Currency Crimes in Thirteenth-Century England." *British Numismatic Journal* 66 (1996): 21–32.

Jordan, William Chester. "Jews on Top: Women and the Availability of Consumption Loans in Northern France in the Mid-Thirteenth Century." *Journal of Jewish Studies* 29 (1978): 39–56.

———. "Marian Devotion and the Talmud Trial of 1240." In *Religionsgespräche im Mittelalter*, edited by Bernard Lewis and Friedrich Niewöhner, 61–76. Wolfenbütteler Mittelalter-Studien 4. Wiesbaden: Otto Harrassowitz, 1992.

Kaplan, M. Lindsay. "Jessica's Mother: Medieval Constructions of Jewish Race and Gender in *The Merchant of Venice*." *Shakespeare Quarterly* 58, no. 1 (2007): 1–30.

Kerby-Fulton, Kathryn. "Afterword: Social History of the Book and Beyond; *Originalia*, Medieval Literary Theory, and the Aesthetics of Paleography." In *The Medieval Manuscript Book: Cultural Approaches*, edited by Michael Johnston and Michael Van Dussen, 243–54. Cambridge Studies in Medieval Literature 94. Cambridge: Cambridge University Press, 2015.

———. "Competing Archives, Competing Languages: Office Vernaculars, Civil Servant Raconteurs, and the Porous Nature of French During Ireland's Rise of English." *Speculum* 90, no. 3 (2015): 674–700.

Klawans, Jonathan. "An Invented Revolution." In Law and Halton, "Jew and Judean."

Kletter, Karen. "The Uses of Josephus: Jewish History in the Medieval Christian Tradition." PhD diss., University of North Carolina, Chapel Hill, 2005.

Koopmans, Rachel M. "The Conclusion of Christina of Markyate's *Vita*." *Journal of Ecclesiastical History* 51, no. 4 (2000): 663–98.

Kruger, Steven F. "Conversion and Medieval Sexual, Religious, and Racial Categories." In *Constructing Medieval Sexuality*, edited by Karma Lochrie, Peggy McCracken, and James A. Shultz, 158–79. Minneapolis: University of Minnesota Press, 1997.

———. *Dreaming in the Middle Ages*. Cambridge: Cambridge University Press, 1992.

———. *The Spectral Jew: Conversion and Embodiment in Medieval Europe*. Medieval Cultures. Minneapolis: University of Minnesota Press, 2005.

———. "The Times of Conversion." *Philological Quarterly* 92, no. 1 (2013): 19–39.

Krummel, Miriamne Ara. *Crafting Jewishness in Medieval England: Legally Absent, Virtually Present*. The New Middle Ages. New York: Palgrave Macmillan, 2011.

Kwakkel, Erik. "Discarded Parchment as Writing Support in English Manuscript Culture." In *English Manuscripts Studies, 1100–1700*, vol. 17, *English Manuscripts Before 1400*, edited by A. S. G. Edwards and Orietta Da Rold, 238–64. London: British Library, 2012.

Lagerlund, Henrik, and Paul Thom, eds. *A Companion to the Philosophy of Robert Kilwardby*. Brill's Companions to the Christian Tradition 37. Leiden: Brill, 2012.

Lampert-Weissig, Lisa. "Chaucer's Pardoner and the Jews." *Exemplaria* 28, no. 4 (2016): 337–60.

———. *Gender and Jewish Difference from Paul to Shakespeare*. The Middle Ages Series. Philadelphia: University of Pennsylvania Press, 2004.

———. "The Once and Future Jew: Little Robert of Bury, Historical Memory, and the Croxton Play of the Sacrament." *Jewish History* 15, no. 3 (2001): 235–55.

———. "The Wandering Jew as Relic." *English Language Notes* 53, no. 2 (2015): 83–96.

Langmuir, Gavin. "The Knight's Tale of Young Hugh of Lincoln." *Speculum* 47, no. 3 (1972): 459–82.

Lavezzo, Kathy. *The Accommodated Jew: English Antisemitism from Bede to Milton*. Ithaca: Cornell University Press, 2016.

Law, Timothy Michael, and Charles Halton, eds. "Jew and Judean: A *Marginalia* Forum on Politics and Historiography in the Translation of Ancient Texts." *Marginalia Review of Books,* 26 August 2014. http://marginalia.lareviewofbooks.org/jew-judean-forum/.

Lawton, David. "Englishing the Bible, 1066–1549." In *Cambridge History of Medieval English Literature*, edited by David Wallace, 454–82. Cambridge: Cambridge University Press, 1999.

Levine, Amy-Jill. "A Jewess, More and/or Less." In *Judaism Since Gender*, edited by Miriam Peskowitz and Laura Levitt, 149–57. New York: Routledge, 1997.

Lewis, Charlton T., and Charles Short. *A New Latin Dictionary*. Oxford: Clarendon, 1897.

Lewis, Suzanne. *The Art of Matthew Paris in the "Chronica Majora."* California Studies in the History of Art. Berkeley: University of California Press in association with Corpus Christi College, Cambridge, 1987.

Librett, Jeffrey. *The Rhetoric of Cultural Dialogue: Jews and Germans from Moses Mendelssohn to Richard Wagner and Beyond*. Stanford: Stanford University Press, 2000.

Lipman, Vivian D. *The Jews of Medieval Norwich*. London: JHSE, 1967.

Lipton, Sara. *Dark Mirror: The Medieval Origins of Anti-Jewish Iconography*. New York: Metropolitan, 2014.

———. "Isaac and the Antichrist in the Archives." *Past & Present* 232, no. 1 (2016): 3–44.

———. "Where Are the Gothic Jewish Women? On the Non-iconography of the Jewess in the *Cantigas de Santa Maria*." *Jewish History* 22 (2008): 139–77.

Logan, F. Donald. "Thirteen London Jews and Conversion to Christianity: Problems of Apostasy in the 1280s." *Bulletin of the Institute of Historical Research* 45, no. 112 (1972): 214–29.

Lorde, Audre. "Audre Lorde: Claudia Tate/1982." In *Conversations with Audre Lorde*, edited by Joan Wylie Hall, 85–100. Jackson: University Press of Mississippi, 2004.

Madicott, J. R. *Simon de Montfort*. Cambridge: Cambridge University Press, 1996.

Maitland, F. W. "The Deacon and the Jewess." In *Roman Canon Law in the Church of England: Six Essays by F. W. Maitland*, 158–79. London: Methuen, 1898.

Mancho, Guzmán. "Considering *Orrmulum*'s Exegetical Discourse: Canon Orrmin's Preaching and His Audience." *English Studies* 6 (2004): 508–19.

———. "Is the *Orrmulum*'s Introduction an Instance of Aristotelian Prologue?" *Neophilologus* 88 (2004): 477–92.

Mann, Jill. *Chaucer and Medieval Estates Satire*. Cambridge: Cambridge University Press, 1973.

Marcus, Ivan G. "A Jewish-Christian Symbiosis: The Culture of Early Ashkenaz." In *The Cultures of the Jews: A New History*, edited by David Biale, 2:449–516. New York: Schocken, 2002.

———. *Rituals of Childhood: Jewish Acculturation in Medieval Europe*. New Haven: Yale University Press, 1996.

McCulloh, John M. "Jewish Ritual Murder: William of Norwich, Thomas of Monmouth, and the Early Dissemination of the Myth." *Speculum* 72, no. 3 (1997): 698–740.

Meale, Carol M. "The Miracles of Our Lady: Context and Interpretation." In *Studies in the Vernon Manuscript*, edited by Derek Pearsall, 115–36. Cambridge: D. S. Brewer, 1990.

Mell, Julie L. *The Myth of the Medieval Jewish Moneylender*. Vol. 1. New York: Palgrave Macmillan, 2017.

Mellinkoff, Ruth. "Judas's Red Hair and the Jews." *Journal of Jewish Art* 9 (1982): 31–46.

Mesley, Matthew. "De Judaea, Muta, et Surda: Jewish Conversion in Gerald of Wale's *Life of Saint Remigius*." In *Christians and Jews in Angevin England: The York Massacre of 1190, Narratives and Contexts*, edited by Sarah Rees Jones and Sethina Watson, 238–49. Woodbridge: York Medieval Press, 2013.

Meyer, Hannah. "Female Moneylending and Wet-Nursing in Jewish-Christian Relations in Thirteenth-Century England." PhD diss., University of Cambridge, 2009.

Millar, Bonnie. *The Siege of Jerusalem in Its Physical, Literary, and Historical Contexts*. Dublin: Four Courts Press, 2000.

Millett, Bella. "Change and Continuity: The English Sermon Before 1250." In *The Oxford Handbook of Medieval Literature in English*, edited by Elaine Treharne and Greg Walker, 221–39. Oxford: Oxford University Press, 2010.

Mitchell, J. Allan. *Becoming Human: The Matter of the Medieval Child*. Minneapolis: Minnesota University Press, 2014.

Moore, R. I. *The Formation of Persecuting Society: Power and Deviance in Western Europe*. Oxford: Oxford University Press, 1987.

Morey, James. *Book and Verse: A Guide to Middle English Biblical Literature*. Urbana: University of Illinois Press, 2000.

Morrison, Stephen. "New Sources for the *Ormulum*." *Neophilologus* 68 (1984): 444–50.

———. "Orm's English Sources." *Archiv* 221 (1984): 54–63.

———. "Sources for the *Ormulum*: A Re-examination." *Neuphilologische Mitteilungen* 84, no. 4 (1983): 419–36.

Mundill, Robin R. *England's Jewish Solution: Experiment and Expulsion, 1262–1290*. Cambridge Studies in Medieval Life and Thought. Cambridge: Cambridge University Press, 1998.

————. *The King's Jews: Money, Massacre, and Exodus in Medieval England*. London: Continuum, 2010.

Murphy, Sean Eisen. "Concern About Judaizing in Academic Treatises on the Law, c. 1130–c. 1230." *Speculum* 82, no. 3 (2007): 560–94.

"A Medieval Mystery" (web page). The National Archives: Classroom Resources. Accessed 24 September 2019. http://www.nationalarchives.gov.uk/education/resources/medieval-mystery.

Newman, Barbara. *Medieval Crossover: Reading the Secular Against the Sacred*. Notre Dame: Notre Dame University Press, 2013.

————. "The Passion of the Jews of Prague: The Pogrom of 1389 and the Lessons of a Medieval Parody." *Church History* 81, no. 1 (2012): 1–26.

————. Response to "Barbara Newman's *Medieval Crossover*." Session presented at the Convention of the Modern Language Association, Vancouver, British Columbia, 9 January 2015.

Nirenberg, David. *Anti-Judaism: The Western Tradition*. New York: Norton, 2013.

Nisse, Ruth. *Jacob's Shipwreck: Diaspora, Translation, and Jewish-Christian Relations in Medieval England*. Ithaca: Cornell University Press, 2017.

Olszewska, E. S. "Alliterative Phrases in the *Ormulum*: Some Norse Parallels." In *English and Medieval Studies: Presented to J. R. R. Tolkien on the Occasion of His Seventieth Birthday*, edited by Norman Davis and C. L. Wrenn, 112–27. London: George Allen and Unwin, 1962.

Olszowy-Schlanger, Judith. "Christian Hebraism in Thirteenth-Century England: The Evidence of Hebrew-Latin Manuscripts." In *Crossing Borders: Hebrew Manuscripts as a Meeting-Place of Cultures*, edited by Piet van Boxel and Sabine Arndt, 115–22. Oxford: Bodleian Library, 2009.

————. "Hebrew Documents in Medieval England: A Lecture at the Official Opening of the Relocated Hebrew and Jewish Studies Centre of the University of Oxford." Oxford Jewish Heritage. Oxford Jewish Heritage Committee. 8 December 2014. https://www.oxfordjewishheritage.co.uk/news-a-events/lectures-and-special-events/251-hebrew-documents-from-medieval-england.

————. *Hebrew and Hebrew-Latin Documents from Medieval England: A Diplomatic and Palaeographical Study*. 2 vols. Monumenta Palaeographica Medii Aevi: Series Hebraica. Turnhout: Brepols, 2015.

————. *Les manuscrits hébreux dans l'Angleterre médiévale: Étude historique et paléographique*. Collection de la Revue des études juives 29. Paris: Peeters, 2003.

————. "Robert Wakefield and His Hebrew Manuscripts." *Zutot* 6, no. 1 (2009): 25–33.

————. "A School of Christian Hebraists in Thirteenth-Century England: A Unique Hebrew-Latin-French and English Dictionary and Its Sources." *European Journal of Jewish Studies* 1, no. 2 (2007): 249–77.

Olszowy-Schlanger, Judith, and Patricia Stirnemann. "The Twelfth-Century Trilingual Psalter in Leiden." *Scripta* 1 (2008): 103–12.

Page, Sophie. *Magic in the Cloister: Pious Motives, Illicit Interests, and Occult Approaches to the Medieval Universe*. Magic in History. University Park: Pennsylvania State University Press, 2013.

Parkes, Malcolm. "On the Presumed Date and Possible Origin of the Manuscript of the 'Orrmulum': Oxford, Bodleian Library, MS Junius 1." In *Five Hundred Years of Words and Sounds*, edited by E. G. Stanley and Douglas Gray, 115–27. Cambridge: D. S. Brewer, 1983.

———. "The Provision of Books." In *The History of the University of Oxford*, vol. 2, *Late Medieval Oxford*, edited by J. I. Catto and T. A. R. Evans, 407–83. Oxford: Clarendon, 1992.

———. *Their Hands Before Our Eyes: A Closer Look at Scribes; The Lyell Lectures Delivered in the University of Oxford 1999*. Aldershot: Ashgate, 2008.

Peck, Russell, ed. *Heroic Women from the Old Testament in Middle English Verse*. TEAMS Middle English Texts Series. Kalamazoo: Medieval Institute Publications, 1991.

Price, Merrall Llewelyn. "Imperial Violence and the Monstrous Mother: Cannibalism at the Siege of Jerusalem." In *Domestic Violence in Medieval Texts*, edited by Eve Salisbury, Georgiana Donavin, and Merrall Llewelyn Price, 272–98. Gainesville: University Press of Florida, 2002.

Reed, Annette Yoshiko, and Shaul Magid, eds. "A Forum on Cynthia Baker's *Jew*." *Marginalia Review of Books*, 6 May–4 July 2017. http://marginalia.lareviewofbooks.org/introduction-forum-on-cynthia-baker-jew/.

Reichardt, Jasia. *Robots: Fact, Fiction, and Prediction*. New York: Viking Penguin, 1978.

Reid, Heather A. "Female Initiation Rites and Women Visionaries: Mystical Marriage in the Middle English Translation of *The Storie of Asneth*." In *Women and the Divine in Literature Before 1700: Essays in Memory of Margot Louis*, edited by Kathryn Kerby-Fulton, 137–52. Victoria, BC: ELS Editions, 2009.

Reinhartz, Adele. "The Vanishing Jews of Antiquity." *Marginalia Review of Books*, 24 June 2014. http://marginalia.lareviewofbooks.org/vanishing-jews-antiquity-adele-reinhartz/.

Resnick, Irven M. *Marks of Distinction: Christian Perceptions of Jews in the High Middle Ages*. Washington, DC: Catholic University of America Press, 2012.

Richardson, Malcolm. *Middle-Class Writing in Late Medieval London*. The History of the Book 7. London: Pickering and Chatto, 2011.

Richmond, Colin. "Englishness and Medieval Anglo-Jewry." In *Chaucer and the Jews: Sources, Contexts, Meanings*, edited by Sheila Delany, 213–27. New York: Routledge, 2002.

Rickard, John. *The Castle Community: English and Welsh Castle Personnel, 1272–1422*. Woodbridge: Boydell Press, 2002.

Rokéah, Zefira Entin. "Money and the Hangman in Late Thirteenth-Century England: Jews, Christians, and Coinage Offences Alleged and Real (Part I)." *Jewish Historical Studies* 31 (1990): 83–109.

———. "Money and the Hangman in Late Thirteenth-Century England: Jews, Christians, and Coinage Offences Alleged and Real (Part II)." *Jewish Historical Studies* 32 (1992): 159–218.

Rose, E. M. *The Murder of William of Norwich: The Origins of the Blood Libel in Medieval Europe*. Oxford: Oxford University Press, 2015.

Roth, Pinchas. "Jewish Courts in Medieval England." *Jewish History* 21, nos. 1–2 (2017): 67–82.

———. "Medieval English Rabbis: Image and Self-Image." *Early Middle English* 1, no. 1 (2019): 17–33.

———. "New Responsa by Isaac ben Peretz of Northampton." *Jewish Historical Studies* 46 (2014): 1–17.

———. "Who Speaks for the Jews? Latin and Hebrew Sources." In "The Myth of the Medieval Jewish Moneylender: A Forum," edited by Nina Caputo. *Marginalia Review of Books*, 8 May 2020. https://marginalia.lareviewofbooks.org/who-speaks-for-the-jews-latin-and-hebrew-sources/.

Roth, Pinchas, and Ethan Zadoff. "The Talmudic Community of Thirteenth-Century England." In *Christians and Jews in Angevin England: The York Massacre of 1190, Narratives and Contexts*, edited by Sarah Rees Jones and Sethina Watson, 184–203. Woodbridge: Boydell and Brewer, 2013.

Rowe, Nina. *The Jew, the Cathedral, and the Medieval City: Synagoga and Ecclesia in the Thirteenth Century*. Cambridge: Cambridge University Press, 2011.

Rubin, Miri. *Gentile Tales: The Narrative Assault on Late Medieval Jews*. The Middle Ages Series. Philadelphia: University of Pennsylvania Press, 2004.

Salter, Elizabeth. *English and International: Studies in the Literature, Art, and Patronage of Medieval England*. Cambridge: Cambridge University Press, 1988.

Sartre, John-Paul. *Anti-Semite and Jew*. 1944. Translated by George J. Becker. New York: Schocken, 1976.

Scheil, Andrew. *The Footsteps of Israel: Understanding Jews in Anglo-Saxon England*. Ann Arbor: University of Michigan Press, 2004.

Scheller, Robert. *Exemplum: Model-Book Drawings and the Practice of Artistic Transmission in the Middle Ages, ca. 900–1450*. Translated by Michael Hoyle. Amsterdam: Amsterdam University Press, 1995.

Seror, Simon. "Les noms des femmes juives en Angleterre au moyen âge." *Revue des études juives* 154, nos. 3–4 (1995): 295–325.

Sharpe, R. et al., eds. *English Benedictine Libraries: The Shorter Catalogues*. Corpus of British Medieval Library Catalogues 4. London: British Academy, 1996.

Shatzmiller, Joseph. *Cultural Exchange: Jews, Christians, and Art in the Medieval Marketplace*. Princeton: Princeton University Press, 2013.

Shoulson, Jeffrey. *Fictions of Conversion: Jews, Christians, and Cultures of Change in Early Modern England*. Philadelphia: University of Pennsylvania Press, 2013.

Sicher, Efraim. *The Jew's Daughter: A Cultural History of a Conversion Narrative*. Lanham, MD: Lexington Books, 2017.

Sirat, Collette. "Looking at Latin Books, Understanding Latin Texts: Different Attitudes in Different Jewish Communities." In *Hebrew to Latin, Latin to Hebrew: The Mirroring of Two Cultures in the Age of Humanism*, edited by Giulio Busi, 7–22. Berlin Studies in Judaism. Berlin: Institut für Judaistik, Freie Universität Berlin, 2004.

Smith, Kathryn A. *Art, Identity, and Devotion in Fourteenth-Century England: Three Women and Their Books of Hours*. British Library Studies in Medieval Culture. London and Toronto: The British Library and University of Toronto Press, 2003.

Smith, Lesley. *The "Glossa Ordinaria": The Making of a Medieval Bible Commentary*. Commentaria 3. Leiden: Brill, 2009.

Sommer-Seckendorff, Ellen M. F. *Studies in the Life of Robert Kilwardby O.P.* Dissertationes historicae 8. Rome: Istituto Storico Domenicano, 1937.

Stacey, Robert C. "'Adam of Bristol' and the Tales of Ritual Crucifixion in Medieval England." In *Thirteenth-Century England XI: Proceedings of the Gregynog Conference, 2005*, edited by Bjorn K. U. Weiler and Janet E. Burton, 1–15. Woodbridge: Boydell, 2007.

———. "The Conversion of Jews to Christianity in Thirteenth-Century England." *Speculum* 67 (1992): 263–83.

———. "From Ritual Crucifixion to Host Desecration: Jews and the Body of Christ." *Jewish History* 12, no. 1 (1998): 11–28.

———. "Jews and Christians in Twelfth-Century England: Some Dynamics of a Changing Relationship." In *Jews and Christians in Twelfth-Century Europe*, edited by Michael A. Signer and John Van Engen, 340–54. Notre Dame Conferences in Medieval Studies 10. Notre Dame: University of Notre Dame Press, 2001.

———. Review of *The Palgrave Dictionary of Medieval Anglo-Jewish History*, by Joe Hillaby and Caroline Hillaby. *Jewish Historical Studies* 48 (2016): 257.

Tate, Claudia, ed. *Black Women Writers at Work*. New York: Continuum, 1983.

Thomson, R. M. *The Archives of the Abbey of Bury St Edmunds*. Woodbridge: Boydell and Brewer, 1980.

Tinkle, Theresa. "Jews in the Fleury Playbook." *Comparative Drama* 38, no. 1 (2004): 1–38.

Tomasch, Sylvia. "Post-Colonial Chaucer and the Virtual Jew." In *Chaucer and the Jews: Sources, Contexts, Meanings*, edited by Shiela Delany, 69–85. New York: Routledge, 2002.

Tryon, Ruth Wilson. "Miracles of Our Lady in Middle English Verse." *PMLA* 38, no. 2 (1923): 308–88.

van Court, Elisa Narin. "*The Siege of Jerusalem* and Augustinian Historians: Writing About Jews in Fourteenth-Century England." In *Chaucer and the Jews: Sources, Contexts, Meanings*, edited by Shiela Delany, 165–84. New York: Routledge, 2002.

Widner, Michael. "Samson's Touch and a Thin Red Line: Reading the Bodies of Saints and Jews in Bury St Edmunds." *JEGP* 111, no. 3 (2012): 339–59.

Williams Boyarin, Adrienne. "Anglo-Jewish Women at Court." In *Women Intellectuals and Leaders in the Middle Ages*, edited by Kathryn Kerby-Fulton, Katie Ann-Marie Bugyis, and John Van Engen, 55–70. Cambridge: D. S. Brewer, 2020.

———. "Anti-Jewish Parody Around Miracles of Virgin? Thoughts on an Early Nonsense-Cento in Berkeley, Bancroft Library, MS UCB 92." *Notes & Queries* 54, no. 4 (2007): 379–85.

———. "Desire for Religion: Mary, a Murder Libel, a Jewish Friar, and Me." *Religion and Literature* 41, nos. 1–2 (2010): 23–48.

———. "Difficult Sameness and Weird Time: Starting with *The Siege of Jerusalem*." In *Jews in Medieval England: Teaching Representations of the Other*, edited by Tison Pugh and Miriamne Ara Krummel, 311–28. The New Middle Ages. New York: Palgrave Macmillan, 2017.

———. "Inscribed Bodies: The Virgin Mary, Jewish Women, and Medieval Feminine Legal Authority." In *Law and Sovereignty in the Middle Ages and Renaissance*, edited by Robert S. Sturges, 229–51. Arizona Studies in the Middle Ages and Renaissance 28. Turnhout: Brepols, 2011.

———. *Miracles of the Virgin in Medieval England: Law and Jewishness in Marian Legends*. Cambridge: D. S. Brewer, 2010.

———. Review of *Crafting Jewishness in Medieval England*, by Miriamne Ara Krummel. *JEGP* 112, no. 3 (2013): 382–85.

Wirth, Karl-August, ed. *Pictor in Carmine: Ein Handbuch der Typologie aus der Zeit um 1200 nach MS 300 des Corpus Christi College in Cambridge*. Berlin: Gebr. Mann, 2006.

Worley, Meg. "Using the *Ormulum* to Redefine Vernacularity." In *The Vulgar Tongue: Medieval and Postmedieval Vernacularity*, edited by Fiona Somerset and Nicholas Watson, 19–30. University Park: Penn State University Press, 2003.

Wright, Steven K. *The Vengeance of Our Lord: Medieval Dramatizations of the Destruction of Jerusalem*. Toronto: PIMS, 1989.

Yeager, Suzanne. *Jerusalem in Medieval Narrative*. Cambridge: Cambridge University Press, 2008.

Yuval, Israel Jacob. "Jewish Messianic Expectations Towards 1240 and Christian Reactions." In *Toward the Millenium: Messianic Expectations from the Bible to Waco*, edited by Peter Schäfer and Mark Cohen, 105–21. Leiden: Brill, 1998.

———. *Two Nations in Your Womb: Perceptions of Jews and Christians in Late Antiquity and the Middle Ages*. Translated by Barbara Harshaw and Jonathan Chipman. Berkeley: University of California Press, 2006.

Zacher, Samantha, ed. *Imagining the Jew in Anglo-Saxon Literature and Culture*. Toronto Anglo-Saxon Series. Toronto: University of Toronto Press, 2016.

INDEX

Page numbers in italics indicate illustrations.

ACKNOWLEDGMENTS

This book was funded by the Social Sciences and Humanities Research Council of Canada (SSHRC), the Jewish Historical Society of England (JHSE), and the University of Victoria (UVic) Faculty of Humanities. I am grateful for the support of these institutions at a time when humanities research is often woefully undervalued. The National Archives of the UK, the British Library, the Bodleian Libraries at the University of Oxford, and the President and Fellows of Magdalen College Oxford provided and gave permissions for reproduction of illustrations, and the Getty Museum in Los Angeles provided an image through their progressive Open Content Program. Every librarian, archivist, or staff member with whom I worked or corresponded at these institutions was efficient, helpful, and kind. I could not do my work without theirs. An earlier version of part of Chapter 2 appeared as "'Venit iudeus portans literas': Jewish Types in the *Chronicle of Jocelin of Brakelond*" in *Medieval Chronicle* 12, edited by Erik Kooper and Sjoerd Levelt (Leiden: Brill, 2019), 192–211; sections of Part I's *Historiae* and Chapter 4 appeared in "Desire for Religion: Mary, a Murder Libel, a Jewish Friar, and Me," in *Religion and Literature* 42, nos. 1–2 (2010): 23–48; and sections of Part II's *Historiae* and Chapter 3, as well as the texts and translations in Appendix 3, appeared in "Anglo-Jewish Women at Court," in *Women Intellectuals and Leaders in the Middle Ages*, edited by Kathryn Kerby-Fulton, Katie Ann-Marie Bugyis, and John Van Engen (Cambridge: D.S. Brewer, 2020), 55–70. I thank Kate Hammond at Brill, the managing editors of *Religion and Literature* at the University of Notre Dame, and Caroline Palmer and Rachel Reeder at Boydell and Brewer for their permission to reuse, expand, and reframe these articles here. I also acknowledge that this book was written on the traditional territory of the Lekwungen peoples, where UVic stands. I am thankful to live and work as a visitor among the Songhees, Esquimalt, and WSÁNEĆ peoples, whose historical relationships with the land continue to this day.

Writing an academic book is never an isolated or quick production, and I have profound gratitude for those who have collaborated with me and bolstered my progress over the years. My colleagues at UVic—especially Margaret Cameron, Alexandra D'Arcy, Heather Dean, Christopher Douglas, Iain Macleod Higgins, Janelle Jenstad, Erin Kelly, Patricia Ormond, Dailyn Ramirez, Stephen Ross, Lisa Surridge, and Lara Wilson—have provided mentorship, practical assistance, and friendship. I want to recognize, too, the scholars whose published works have guided me most significantly: while much excellent scholarship has, of course, provided background and context for this book, I thank in particular Anthony Bale, Christopher Cannon, Michael Clanchy, Jeremy Cohen, Sara Lipton, and Ruth Nisse, all of whose words and ideas have immeasurably influenced my own. I honor their labor, and I enjoy my conversations with them— quiet as it is alone in my office—so very much.

Several scholars, further, have generously provided feedback on this work: Kathy Lavezzo, Lisa Lampert-Weissig, Heather Blurton, and Hannah Johnson saw an early iteration of the first *Historiae* and Chapter 1, and they responded in ways that changed the trajectory of the project for the better; Christopher Cannon read later drafts of Chapters 1 and 2 and provided encouragement as well as incisive notes for improvement; Pinchas Roth read and offered enthusiasm and citations for my work on Anglo-Jewish women in Chapter 3; Stephanie J. Lahey not only copyedited but also commented usefully on every chapter and constructed the first draft of the bibliography; Janice Niemann proofread chapters and offered a great deal of moral support along the way; and Iain Macleod Higgins read a late version of the Introduction and gave me a good pep talk just at the right (final) moment. Iain is one of those medievalists—in addition to Kathryn Kerby-Fulton, Erik Kwakkel, and Dorothy Kim—who have given me so much of themselves, in both friendship and scholarship, in recent years. I will pay their gifts back and forward.

The anonymous readers for University of Pennsylvania Press—who read my prose to bits and wrote up unusually extensive and encouraging feedback for revisions—also allowed me to make this book what it is, as did Jerry Singerman, Ruth Mazo Karras, and Lily Palladino in their editorial roles. The index was done by David Luljak, who worked very quickly, caught several minor errors that I had missed, and understood the book's terms and stakes utterly. Several arguments and readings, in addition, benefited from the responses of conference participants who listened to in-progress versions, particularly at the Women Leaders and Intellectuals of the Medieval World conference at the University of Notre Dame in 2015, the SSHRC-funded Making Early Middle English conference at the University of Victoria in 2016, the International Medieval Congress at the University of Leeds in 2017 and 2018, and the Reimagining Records conference at the National Archives of the UK in 2018. Additionally, Marjorie Harrington and Paul Dryburgh spent hours reviewing transcriptions and Latin translations with me in the final revision stages, and I am grateful for their warmth and expertise. All remaining errors are, naturally, my own.

Finally, I thank my family for their unflinching support over the last decade, which witnessed the death of my mother, the birth of my daughter, my two sons' bar mitzvahs, and the entire life of this book, from funding applications to marketing guidelines. To my husband, Shamma, and my sons, Gabriel and Ephraim, I owe my humanity and my sanity. I dedicate this book to my late mother, Suzanne Neta ז״ל, and my daughter, Eleni Neta, who carries my mother's and my great-grandmother's name. Mum and Leni crossed paths only very briefly in this world, but their paths shape mine—and, indelibly, have shaped this book. I hope it is a fitting memorial to both the pasts and futures of ordinary women, to those who are not noble, visible, or even named but, still, have a history.